Anonymous

New jubliee harp: Christian hymns and songs

A new collection of hymns and tunes for public and social worship

Anonymous

New jubliee harp: Christian hymns and songs
A new collection of hymns and tunes for public and social worship

ISBN/EAN: 9783337266363

Printed in Europe, USA, Canada, Australia, Japan

Cover: Foto ©Thomas Meinert / pixelio.de

More available books at **www.hansebooks.com**

THE

NEW JUBILEE HARP,

OR

CHRISTIAN HYMNS AND SONGS.

A NEW COLLECTION OF HYMNS AND TUNES FOR
PUBLIC AND SOCIAL WORSHIP.

"O, come, let us sing unto the Lord; let us make a joyful noise to the
Rock of our Salvation."—Ps. xcv.

BOSTON:
ADVENT CHRISTIAN PUBLICATION SOCIETY,
144 HANOVER STREET,
1888.

PREFACE.

——o——

The anticipated sounding of the Jubilee Trumpet, in the year of release, produced joy in the hearts of God's ancient people, and with gladness they sang of their approaching earthly redemption. We have not that Jubilee to look forward to, but we have a greater one, the antitype of that which was appointed for that people. With hearts now joyful in the prospect of a heavenly redemption, we sing in anticipation of the Great Jubilee of the Church of all ages.

This book is prepared as an aid in the praise of God, and in expressing the joy we have in view of the approaching day of redemption, with the hope also that it may be a blessing to all into whose hands it may come.

We here wish to acknowledge our great obligations to many authors and publishers of music, for permission to use their choice copyrighted tunes and hymns, found on these pages. Among these are: Messrs. Biglow & Main, Philip Phillips, L. Hartsough, Asa Hull, T. C. O'Kane, Wm. G. Fiscner, Prof. C. S. Harrington, Brainard's Sons, I. Baltzell, Jno. R. Sweeney, E. S. Lorenz, W. W. Bentley, G. F. Root, John J. Hood, S. Hillman, Prof. W. H. McNeal, E. A. Hoffman, S. J. Graham, E. M. Bruce & Co., J. H. Kurzenknabe and Son, W. J. Kirkpatrick, J. H. Tenney, F. H. Revell, D. F. Hodges, C. C. Barker, F. A. Blackmer, A. T. Gorham, E. Hall, F. O. Wellcome, F. A. Pelton. F. A. North & Co., Dr. W. C. Palmer, A. Ross, Wm. A. Pond & Co., O. Ditson & Co., David C. Cook, C. E. Pond, J. C. Stoddard, H. R. Palmer, L. O. Emerson, T. E. Perkins, S. J. Vail, T. J. Cook, J. G. Clark, F. M. Davis, J. Maxim. R. Torrey, Jr., F. H. Thomson, Amanda Bailey, Mrs. J. H. Stockton, Heirs of Geo. E. Lee, and others.

A careful Selection of old tunes and hymns is also here presented for the use of churches and congregations in each department of Christian worship. With this statement and acknowledgment, the Book is commended to all who would engage in the praise and worship of God.

S. G. MATHEWSON.   H. C. FREEMAN.
    F. BURR.   L. T. CUNNINGHAM.
      OZIAS GOODRICH.   L. G. KIMBALL.
        M. GRANT.   I. I. LESLIE.
          L. BOUTELL.   H. A. KING.
            R. H. BATEMAN.

1   There is a Fountain.

1. There is a fountain fill'd with blood, Drawn from Immanuel's veins; And sinners plung'd be- neath that flood, Lose all their guilt-y stains. Lose all their guilty stains, ... Lose all their guilty stains. And sinners plung'd beneath that flood, Lose all their guilty stains.

2 The dying thief rejoiced to see
   That fountain in his day;
And there may I, though vile as he,
   Wash all my sins away.

3 Dear dying Lamb, thy precious blood
   Shall never lose its power,
Till all the ransomed church of God
   Be saved, to sin no more.

4 E'er since, by faith, I saw the stream
   Thy flowing wounds supply,
Redeeming love has been my theme,
   And shall be till I die.

5 Then in a nobler, sweeter song,
   I'll sing thy power to save, [tongue
When this poor lisping, stammering
   Is ransomed from the grave.

——0——

2

1 O, what hath Jesus bought for me!
   Before my ravished eyes
Rivers of life divine I see,
   And trees of Paradise.

2 In hope of that immortal crown,
   I now the cross sustain;
And gladly wander up and down,
   And smile at toil and pain.

3 O, what are all my suff'rings here,
   If, Lord, thou count me meet
With that enraptured host t'appear,
   And worship at thy feet?

4 Give joy or grief, give ease or pain,
   Take life or friends away;
But let me find them all again
   In that eventful day.

——0——

3

1 Come, let us join our cheerful songs
   With angels round the throne;
Ten thousand thousand are their tongues,
   But all their joys are one.

2 "Worthy the Lamb that died," they cry,
   "To be exalted thus!"
"Worthy the Lamb." our lips reply,
   "For he was slain for us!"

3 Jesus is worthy to receive
   Honor and power divine;
And blessings, more than we can give,
   Be, Lord, forever thine.

4 Let all that dwell above the sky,
   And air, and earth, and seas,
Conspire to lift thy glories high,
   And speak thine endless praise.

4   Jesus Paid It All.

Words by Mrs. E. M. Hall.   Music by J. T. Grape.

1. I hear the Saviour say, Thy strength in-deed is small;

Child of weak-ness, watch and pray, Find in me thy all in all.

CHORUS.

Je - sus paid it all, All to him I owe;

Sin had left a crim-son stain, He wash'd it white as snow.

2
Lord, now indeed I find
   Thy pow'r, and thine alone
Can change the leper's spots,
   And melt the heart of stone.
     Jesus paid it all, &c.

3
For nothing good have I,
   Whereby Thy grace to claim,—
I'll wash my garments white
   In the blood of Calvary's Lamb.
     Jesus paid it all, &c.

4
Then down beneath the cross
   I'll lay my sin-sick soul;
For naught have I to bring,—
   Thy grace must make me whole.
     Jesus paid it all, &c.

5
And when before the throne
   I stand, in Him complete,
I'll lay my trophies down,—
   All down at Jesus' feet.
     Jesus paid it all, &c.

Hebron. L M.

L. MASON.

1. Thus far the Lord has led me on; Thus far his pow'r pro-longs my days;

2. Much of my time has run to waste, And I, perhaps, am near my home;

And ev-'ry evening shall make known Some fresh memorial of his grace.

But he for-gives my fol-lies past, He gives me strength for days to come.

3
Weary, I lay me down to sleep;
Peace is the pillow for my head;
While well-appointed angels keep
Their watchful stations round my bed.

4
Thus, when the night of death shall come,
My flesh shall rest beneath the ground,
And wait thy voice to rouse my tomb,
With sweet salvation in the sound.

—o—

6

1
Go forth, ye heralds, in my name;
Sweetly the Gospel trumpet sound;
The glorious jubilee proclaim
Where'er the human race is found.

2
The joyful news to all impart,
And teach them where salvation lies;
With care bind up the broken heart,
And wipe the tears from weeping eyes.

3
Be wise as serpents, where you go,
But harmless as the peaceful dove;
And let your heav'n-taught conduct show
That you're commissioned from above,

4
Freely from me ye have received,
Freely, in love, to others give;
Thus shall your doctrines be believed,
And, by your labors, sinners live.

—o—

7

1
With all my pow'rs of heart and tongue,
I'll praise my Maker in my song;
Angels shall hear the notes I raise,
Approve the song, and join the praise.

2
To God I cried, when troubles rose;
He heard me, and subdued my foes;
He did my rising fears control,
And strength diffused thro' all my soul.

3
Amidst a thousand snares I stand,
Upheld and guarded by thy hand;
Thy words my fainting soul revive,
And keep my dying faith alive.

4
Grace will complete what grace begins,
'To save from sorrow or from sins;
The work that wisdom undertakes,
Eternal mercy ne'er forsakes.

1. A-rise, my soul, a-rise; Shake off thy guilty fears: The bleeding sac-ri-fice

In my be-half ap-pears. Be-fore the throne my Sure-ty stands,

My name is written on his hands, My name is writ-ten on his hands.

2 He ever lives above,
  For me to intercede;
His all-redeeming love,
  His precious blood to plead;
His blood atoned for all our race,
And sprinkles now the throne of grace.

3 Five bleeding wounds he bears,
  Received on Calvary;
They pour effectual prayers,
  They strongly speak for me:
"Forgive him, O forgive," they cry,
"Nor let that ransomed sinner die."

4 The Father hears him pray,
  His dear anointed One;
He cannot turn away
  The presence of his Son;
His spirit answers to the blood,
And tells me I'm a child of God.

5 To God I'm reconciled;
  His pardoning voice I hear;
He owns me for his child;
  I can no longer fear;
With confidence I now draw nigh,
And Father, Abba, Father, cry.

——0——

9

1 Blow ye the trumpet, blow
  The gladly solemn sound;
Let all the nations know,
  To earth's remotest bound:
The year of Jubilee is come;
Return, ye ransomed sinners, home.

2 Jesus, our great High Priest,
  Hath full atonement made:
Ye weary spirits, rest;
  Ye mournful souls, be glad.
The year of Jubilee is come;
Return, ye ransomed sinners, home.

3 Ye slaves of sin and hell,
  Your liberty receive,
And safe in Jesus dwell,
  And blest in Jesus live.
The year of Jubilee is come;
Return, ye ransomed sinners, home.

4 The gospel trumpet hear,
  The news of heavenly grace;
And, saved from earth, appear
  Before your Saviour's face.
The year of Jubilee is come;
Return, ye ransomed sinners, home.

Take my Heart. 8s & 7s.

Spanish Melody. From "MARECHIO."

1. Take my heart, O Fath-er, take it, Make and keep it all thine own;

Let thy Spir - it come and break it, Turn to flesh this heart of stone.

Heav'nly Fath-er, deign to mould it In o - bedience to thy will:

And, as pass - ing years un - fold it, Keep it meek and child-like still.

2 Father, make it pure and lowly,
   Peaceful, kind, and free from strife,
Turning from the paths unholy,
   Of this vain and sinful life.
May the blood of Jesus heal it,
   From its sins give full release;
Holy Spirit, take and seal it,
   Guide it in the path of peace.

11

1 Saviour, breathe an evening blessing,
   Ere repose our spirits seal;
Sin and want we come confessing;
   Thou canst save and thou canst heal.

2 Though destruction walk around us,
   Though the arrows past us fly;
Angel guards from thee surround us;
   We are safe, if they are nigh.

3 Though the night be dark and dreary,
   Darkness cannot hide from thee;
Thou art he who, never weary,
   Watchest where thy people be.

4 Should swift death this night o'ertake us,
   And command us to the tomb,
May that morning's dawn awake us,
   Clad in bright, immortal bloom.

1. In ex - pec - ta - tion sweet, We'll wait, and sing, and pray,

Till Christ's tri - umph - al car we meet, And see an end - less day.

2
He comes, the Conq'ror comes!
  Death falls beneath his sword;
The joyful pris'ners burst the tombs,
  And rise to meet their Lord!

3
The trumpet sounds!—"Awake,
  Ye dead! to judgment come!"
The pillars of creation shake,
  While man receives his doom.

4
Thrice happy morn for those
  Who love the ways of peace!
No night of sorrow e'er shall close,
  Or shade their perfect bliss.

5
Great God, in whom we live,
  Prepare us for that day;
Help us in Jesus to believe,
  To watch, and wait, and pray.

— —0—

13

1
How gentle God's commands!
  How kind his precepts are!
"Come, cast your burdens on the Lord,
  And trust his constant care."

2
While Providence supports,
  Let saints securely dwell;
That hand which bears all nature up,
  Shall guide his children well.

3
Why should this anxious load
  Press down your weary mind?
Haste to your heav'nly Father's throne,
  And sweet refreshment find.

4
His goodness stands approved,
  Down to the present day;
I'll drop my burden at his feet,
  And bear a song away.

—0—

14

1
With Jesus in our midst,
  We gather round the board;
Though many, we are one in Christ,
  One body in the Lord.

2
Our sins were laid on him,
  When bruised on Calvary:
For us he died and rose again,
  A pledge of victory.

3
Faith eats the bread of life,
  And drinks the living wine;
Thus we, in love together knit,
  On Jesus' breast recline.

4
Soon shall the night be gone,
  And we with Jesus reign;
The marriage supper of the Lamb
  Shall banish every pain.

15   I Love Thee.   P. M.

1. I love thee, I love thee, I love thee, my Lord; I love thee, my
Saviour; I love thee, my God; I love thee, I love thee, and
that thou dost know; And how much I love thee, I ev - er would show.

2 I'm happy, I'm happy, oh, wondrous account!
  My joys are immortal, I stand on the mount;
  I gaze on my treasure, and long to be there,
  With Jesus and angels, my kindred so dear.

3 O Jesus my Saviour, with thee I am blest!
  My life and salvation, my joy and my rest!
  Thy name be my theme, and thy love be my song:
  Thy grace shall inspire both my heart and my tongue.

4 Oh! who's like my Saviour? He's Salem's bright King;
  He smiles, and he love's me, and helps me to sing:
  I'll praise him, I'll praise him, with notes loud and shrill,
  While rivers of pleasure my spirit do fill.

16
—o—

1 Delay not, delay not, O sinner, draw near,
  The waters of life are now flowing for thee;
  No price is demanded, the Saviour is here,
  Redemption is purchased, salvation is free.

2 Delay not, delay not, why longer abuse
  The love and compassion of Jesus, thy God?
  A fountain is open, how canst thou refuse
  To wash and be cleansed in his pardoning blood?

3 Delay not, delay not, the Spirit of grace
  Long grieved and resisted, may take his sad flight,
  And leave thee in darkness to finish thy race,
  To sink in the gloom of eternity's night.

4 Delay not, delay not, the hour is at hand,
  The earth shall dissolve, and the heavens shall fade,
  The dead, small and great, in the judgment shall stand;
  What power then, O sinner, will lend thee its aid?

THOMAS HASTINGS.

Coronation. C. M.

O. HOLDEN.

1. All hail the pow'r of Je-sus' name! Let an-gels pros-trate fall;

Bring forth the roy-al di-a-dem, And crown him Lord of all;

Bring forth the roy-al di-a-dem, And crown him Lord of all.

2
Let every kindred, every tribe,
On this terrestrial ball,
To him all majesty ascribe,
And crown him Lord of all!

3
Oh that, with yonder sacred throng,
We at his feet may fall!
We'll join the everlasting song,
And crown him Lord of all.

—o—

18

1
Jesus, our strength and righteousness,
Our Saviour and our King,
Triumphantly thy name we bless,
Thy conquering name we sing.

2
Thou, Lord, hast magnified thy name,
Thou hast maintained thy cause;
We triumph in reproach and shame,
And sufferings of the cross.

3
Superior to our foes we've stood
Above their smile or frown;
On all the strangers to thy blood
With pitying love looked down.

4
O let us have thy presence still;
Set as a flint our face,
To show the counsel of thy will,
Which saves a world by grace!

—o—

19

1
Jesus, our hope, our life, our heaven,
The lingering years have flown;
To thee the kingdom now is given;
Return and claim thine own.

2
And, as we wait, along the skies
Unearthly glory steals,
And our glad spirits seem to rise,
To haste thy chariot wheels.

3
Although they seem to linger, still
Thy retinue on high
Is marshalled, and awaits the will
That bids its myriads fly.

4
Then we will wait, nor deem too long
The closing hours of grace,
But trim our lamps with cheerful song,
Till we shall see his face.

20   Arlington. C. M.

1. God moves in a mys-te-rious way, His won-ders to per-form;

2. Deep in un-fath-om-a-ble mines Of nev-er-fail-ing skill,

He plants his foot-steps in the sea, And rides up-on the storm.

He treasures up his bright de-signs, And works his sov'reign will.

3
Ye fearful saints, fresh courage take;
  The clouds ye so much dread
Are big with mercy, and shall break
  In blessings on your head.

4
Judge not the Lord by feeble sense,
  But trust him for his grace;
Behind a frowning providence
  He hides a smiling face.

5
His purposes will ripen fast,
  Unfolding every hour;
The bud may have a bitter taste,
  But sweet will be the flower.

6
Blind unbelief is sure to err,
  And scan his work in vain;
God is his own interpreter,
  And he will make it plain.

——o——

21

1
Ho! Christian, to the rescue come;
  Speed, speed the gospel sound;
Our arduous toil will not be o'er
  Till we receive the crown.

2
We're marching thro' a world of strife,
  With hearts oft fill'd with grief;
And pray that some strong helping hand
  Will come to our relief.

3
We battle with the hosts of sin,
  Our Leader bids us on;
We storm the fortress of the foe,—
  The victory will be won.

4
And when we reach the heavenly land,
  A joyous strain we'll raise;
Redeeming love, our glorious theme,
  Shall mingle in his praise.

22   I Love to Tell the Story.

Music by W. G. Fischer. By per.

1. I love to tell the sto-ry, Of unseen things a-bove, Of Je-sus and his glo-ry, Of Je-sus and his love. I love to tell the sto-ry, Be- - - cause I know it's true: It sat-isfies my longings, As nothing else would do.

CHORUS.

I love to tell the sto-ry, 'Twill be my theme in glo-ry To tell the old, old sto-ry Of Je-sus and his love.

2 I love to tell the story:
    More wonderful it seems
Than all the golden fancies,
    Of all our golden dreams.
I love to tell the story,
    It did so much for me!
And that is just the reason
    I tell it now to thee.—Cho.

3 I love to tell the story;
    'Tis pleasant to repeat
What seems, each time I tell it,
    More wonderful and sweet.

I love to tell the story;
    For some have never heard
The message of salvation
    From God's own holy word.—Cho.

4 I love to tell the story;
    For those who know it best
Seem hungering and thirsting
    To hear it like the rest.
And when, in scenes of glory,
    I sing the *New, New Song,*
'Twill be—the *Old, Old Story*
    That I have loved so long!—Cho.

14

23   Beulah Land.

Words Arr. by I. I. Leslie.

Jno. R. Sweney.

"Thy land shall be called Beulah."—Isa. lxii: 4.

1. I see the land of corn and wine, And all its joys are to be mine;
2. My Saviour then will walk with me, And sweet communion there will be;
3. A sweet perfume up-on the breeze, Will come from ev-er ver-nal trees,
4. The breezes there will la-den be With sounds of sweet-est mel-o-dy,

There shines undimm'd one blissful day, For earth's dark night is pass'd a-way.
He'll gen-tly lead me by the hand, In that bright-shining Beulah land.
And flow'rs that, never-fa-ding, grow Where streams of life will ev-er flow.
As angels with the ransom'd throng Join in the sweet re-demption-song.

CHORUS.

O, Beulah land! fair Beulah land! Up-on thy heights I long to stand.

And look away, 'neath radiant skies, O'er E-den blest, sweet Par-a-dise,

And view the ev-er-shining shore, To be my home for-ev-er-more.

24 Brewer. L. M.

Bold and Joyous.

1. The Christian warrior, see him stand, In the whole ar - mor of his God;
2. In pan-o-ply of truth complete, Sal-va-tion's hel - met on his head,

The Spir-it's sword is in his hand; His feet are with the gos-pel shod.
With righteousness a breast-plate meet, And faith's broad shield before him spread.

3 With this, Omnipotence he moves,
From this the alien armies flee;
Till more than conqueror he proves,
Through Christ, who gives him victory.

4 Thus strong in his Redeemer's strength,
Sin, death and foes he tramples down;
Fights the good fight, and wins at length
Thro' grace the bright immortal crown

25 Park Street. L. M.

FREDERICK MARC ANTOINE VENUA.

1. Lord, in thy great, thy glor-ous name, I place my hope, my on - ly trust; Save
2. Thou art my Rock—thy name a-lone The fortress where my hopes re-treat; O,

me from sorrow, guilt, and shame, Thou ever gracious, ev - er just. Thou ev-er
make thy pow'r and mercy known; To safety guide my wand'ring feet. To safety

gra - cious, ev - er just.
guide my wand-'ring feet.

3
Bless'd be the Lord—forever bless'd,
Whose mercy bids my fears remove;
The sacred walls which guard my rest,
‖: Are his Almighty power and love. :‖

4
Ye humble souls, who seek his face,
Let sacred courage fill your heart!
Hope in the Lord, and trust his grace,
‖: And he shall heavenly strength impart

26 Cambridge. C. M.

1. Salvation! O the joyful sound! What pleasure to our ears! A sov'reign balm for

ev-'ry wound, A cordial for our fears, A cordial for our fears.

A cordial for our fears, A cor-dial for our fears.

2 Salvation! let the echo fly
  The spacious earth around;
While all the armies of the sky
  |: Conspire to raise the sound! :|
3 Salvation! O thou bleeding Lamb,
  To thee the praise belongs;

Salvation shall inspire our hearts,
  |: And dwell upon our tongues. :|
4 And when we join the heavenly throng,
  Upon that blissful shore;
Salvation then shall be the song,
  |: The song forevermore. :|

——0——

27 Peterboro'. C. M.

SAMUEL WESLEY.   R. HARRISON.

1. What shall I ren-der to .. my God, For all his kindness shown?

My feet shall visit thine a - bode, My songs ad - dress thy throne.

2 Among the saints who fill thy house,
  My offering shall be paid;
There shall my zeal perform the vows
  My soul in anguish made.
3 How happy all thy servants are!
  How great thy grace to me!

My life, which thou hast made thy care,
  Lord, I devote to thee.
4 Now I am thine, forever thine,
  Nor shall my purpose move;
Thy hand hath loosed my bonds of pain,
  And bound me with thy love.

17

28   Ortonville.   C. M.

SAMUEL STENNETT, 1727.   THOMAS HASTINGS.

1. Majestic sweetness sits enthron'd Upon the Saviour's brow; His head with

radiant glories crown'd, His lips with grace o'erflow. His lips with grace o'erflow.

2 No mortal can with him compare,
  Among the sons of men;
Fairer is he than all the fair
|: That fill the heavenly train. :|

3 He saw me plunged in deep distress,
  He flew to my relief;
For me he bore the shameful cross,
|: And carried all my grief. :|

4 Since from his bounty I receive
  Such proofs of love divine,
Had I a thousand hearts to give,
|: Lord, they should all be thine. :|

29

1 I've found the Pearl of greatest price,
  My heart doth sing for joy;

And sing I must, for Christ is mine;
|: Christ shall my song employ. :|

2 My Christ, he is the Lord of lords,
  He is the King of kings;
He is the Sun of righteousness,
|: With healing in his wings. :|

3 Christ is my Saviour, and my Friend,
  My Brother and my love,
My Head, my hope, my Counsellor,
|: My Advocate above. :|

4 He is the all-and-all to me,
  Now and forevermore;
I shall his face and glory see,
|: And ever Him adore. :|

—o—

30   I Shall Meet Thee.

Fine.

1. { I shall meet thee in the morn - ing, When Je - sus calls his own; }
{ In the res - ur - rec - tion morn - ing, When all our work is done. }

D.C. I shall meet thee in the morn - ing, When all the saints a - rise.

D.C.

On the right hand where they gath - er Who are to have the prize;

2 I shall know thee in the morning,
  In immortality;
But though in that bright adorning,
  I shall know it is thee.

And the glory will be shining,
  And in it thou shalt be—
I shall know thee in the morning,
  In immortality.

When the King Comes In.

J. E. LANDOR.

From "Songs of Grace," by per.

E. S. LORENZ.

1. Call'd to the feast by the King are we, Sit-ting, perhaps, where his peo - ple be: How will it fare, friend, with thee and me,

REFRAIN.

When the King comes in? When the King comes in, brother, When the King comes in! How will it fare with thee and me When the King comes in?

2
Crowns on the head where the thorns have been,
Glorified he who once died for men;
Splendid the vision before us then,
    When the King comes in.—*Refrain.*

3
Like lightning's flash will that instant show
Things hidden long from both friend and foe,
Jus. what we are will every one know,
    When the King comes in.—*Refrain.*

4
Joyful his eye shall on each one rest
Who is in white wedding garments dressed—
Ah! well for us if we stand the test,
    When the King comes in.—*Refrain.*

32   Siloam. C. M.

COWPER.   By permission of O. Ditson & Co.   I. B. WOODBURY.

1. O for a clo-ser walk with God, A calm and heav'nly frame;

A light to shine up - on the road That leads me to the Lamb.

2 The dearest idol I have known,
   Whate'er that idol be,
Help me to tear it from thy throne,
   And worship only thee.

3 So shall my walk be close with God,
   Calm and serene my frame;
So purer light shall mark the road
   That leads me to the Lamb.

33

1 O for that tenderness of heart
   That bows before thee, Lord;
That owns how good and just thou art,
   And trembles at thy word!

2 O for those humble, contrite tears,
   Which from repentance flow!
That sense of guilt, which, trembling,
   The long-suspended blow! [fears

3 Saviour, to me in pity give,
   For sin, the deep distress;

The pledge thou wilt at last receive,
   And bid me go in peace.

34

1 Blest is the dear, uniting love,
   That will not let us part;
Our bodies may far off remove;
   We still are one in heart.

2 Joined in one spirit to our Head,
   Where he appoints we go;
We still in Jesus' footsteps tread,
   And still his praise we show.

3 O may we ever walk in him,
   And nothing know beside;
Nothing desire—nothing esteem,
   But Jesus crucified.

4 Then let us hasten to the day
   Which shall our flesh restore;
When death shall all be done away,
   And bodies part no more.
                      C. WESLEY.

—o—

35   The Saviour Calls.   6s & 4s.

1. To - day the Saviour calls! Ye wand'rers come; O, ye be-
2. To - day the Saviour calls! O, listen now; With-in these

- night-ed souls, Why long-er roam?
hallow'd walls, To Je - sus bow.

3 To-day the Saviour calls!
   For refuge fly;
The storm of vengeance falls;
   Ruin is nigh!

4 O hear his call to-day!
   Yield to his power:
O, turn him not away;
   'Tis mercy's hour.

Millennial Dawn. 7s & 6s.

G. J. WEBB.

1. How long, O Lord, our Saviour, Wilt thou remain away? Our hearts are growing weary Of thy so long de-lay; O, when shall come the moment When brighter far than morn, The sunshine of thy glo-ry Shall on thy people dawn?

2 How long, O gracious Master,
  Wilt thou thy household leave?
So long hast thou now tarried,
  Few thy return believe.
Immersed in sloth and folly,
  Thy servants, Lord we see;
And few of us stand ready
  With joy to welcome thee.

3 How long, O heav'nly Bridegroom!
  How long wilt thou delay?
And yet how few are grieving
  That thou dost absent stay!
The very bride her portion
  And calling hath forgot,
And seeks for ease and glory
  Where thou, her Lord, art not.

4 O, wake thy slumb'ring virgins!
  Send forth the solemn cry,
Let all thy saints repeat it,
  "The Bridegroom draweth nigh!"
May all our lamps be burning,
  Our loins well girded be,
Each longing heart preparing
  With joy thy face to see.

37

1 O when shall I see Jesus,
  And in his presence dwell;
Possess that rest eternal,
  Where songs triumphant swell?
When shall I be delivered
  From this vain world of sin,
And, with my blessed Saviour,
  Drink endless pleasures in?

2 Here now I am a soldier;
  My Captain's gone before;
He's given me my orders,
  And bids me not give o'er:
If I continue faithful,
  A righteous crown he'll give,
And all his valiant soldiers
  Eternal life shall have.

3 Our eyes shall then, with rapture,
  His smiling face behold;
Our feet, no more diverted,
  Shall walk the streets of gold;
Our ears shall hear with transport
  The hosts celestial sing;
Our tongues shall chant the glory
  Of our immortal King.

38 I Hear Thy Welcome Voice.

L. HARTSOUGH.

By per. PHILIP PHILLIPS.

1. I hear Thy welcome voice That calls me, Lord, to Thee For cleans-ing in Thy pre-cious blood That flow'd on Cal-va-ry.

CHORUS.

I am com-ing, Lord! Com-ing now to Thee! Wash me, cleanse me, in the blood That flow'd on Cal-va-ry.

2 Though coming weak and vile,
  Thou dost my strength assure;
Thou dost my vileness fully cleanse,
  Till spotless all and pure.

3 'Tis Jesus calls me on
  To perfect faith and love,
To perfect hope, and peace, and trust,
  From Him who reigns above.

4 'Tis Jesus who confirms
  The blessed work within,
By adding grace to welcomed grace,
  Where reigned the power of sin.

5 And He the witness gives
  To loyal hearts and free,
That every promise is fulfilled,
  If faith but brings the plea.

6 All hail, atoning blood!
  All hail, redeeming grace!
All hail, the Gift of Christ, our Lord,
  Our Strength and Righteousness!

Rest Yonder. 8, 7.

E. W. KELLOGG.

1. This is not my place of resting, Mine's a cit-y yet to come;

2. In it all is light and glo-ry, O'er it shines a nightless day;

On-ward to it I am hast'ning, On to my e-ter-nal home.

Ev-'ry trace of sin's sad sto-ry—All the curse hath pass'd a-way.

REFRAIN.

There is rest yonder, There is rest yonder, There is rest in that happy land;

There is rest yonder, There is rest yonder, There is rest in that happy land;

There is rest yonder, There is rest yonder, There is rest in that happy land.

There is rest yonder, There is rest yonder, There is rest in that happy land.

3 Here the Lamb, our Shepherd, leads us
By the streams of life along,
On the freshest pastures feeds us,
Tnrns our sighing into song.
Refrain.—There is rest, &c.

4 Soon we pass this desert dreary,
Soon we bid farewell to pain,
Never more are sad or weary,
Never, never sin again!
Refrain.—There is rest, &c.

St. Martin's. C. M.

TANSUR.

1. O God, our help in a - - ges past, Our hope for years to come;

Our shelter from the storm - y blast, And our e - ter - nal home.

2 Under the shadows of thy throne
Still may we dwell secure;
Sufficient is thine arm alone,
And our defence is sure.

3 Before the hills in order stood,
Or earth received her frame,
From everlasting thou art God,
To endless years the same.

4 A thousand ages, in thy sight,
Are like an evening gone;
Short as the watch that ends the night,
Before the rising sun.

5 Time, like an ever-rolling stream,
Bears all its sons away;
They fly, forgotten, as a dream
Dies at the opening day.

———o———

41 **I Will Believe. C. M.**

1. O God of mer - cy hear my call; My load of guilt re - move;

Cho.—I will be - lieve, I do be - lieve That Je - sus died for me;

Break down this sep - ar - a - ting wall, And let me feel thy love.

And thro' his blood, his precious blood, I shall from sin be free.

2 I nail my passions to the cross,
Where my Redeemer died;
And all things else I count but loss
For Jesus crucified.

3 Give me the presence of thy grace;
Then my rejoicing tongue
Shall speak aloud thy righteousness,
And make thy praise my song.

42 Come to Pisgah's Mountain.

1. Come all ye saints to Pisgah's mountain, Come view your home beyond the tide;

The land we love is just before us, Soon we'll be on the oth-er side.

2d time Chorus.

O! there are the bright crowns of glory, And all that the Saviour will give,

Cho. O! the prospect it is so transporting, Saviour, hasten thy coming, we pray,

D.S.

And they who have lov'd His appearing, With Him shall e-ter-nal-ly live.

Cho. We sigh for the land thou hast promis'd, And the dawn of the bright, endless day.

2 There endless springs of life are flowing
  There are the fields of living green;
Mansions of beauty are before them,
  And the King of the Saints is seen.
Soon our conflicts and toils will be ended,
  We'll be tried and be tempted no **more**;
And the Saints of all ages and nations
  We shall greet on that heavenly shore.
  Cho.—O! the prospect, &c.

3 Faith now beholds the flowing river,
  Coming from underneath the throne;
There, too, the Saviour reigns forever,
  And he'll welcome the faithful home.
Would you walk by the banks of the river,
  With the friends you have lov'd by **your side?**
Would you join in the song of the angels?
  Then be ready to follow your guide.
  Cho.—O! the prospect. &c.

43 **Hallowell. C. M.**

1. O for a faith that will not shrink, Tho' press'd by many a foe;

1. O for a faith that will not shrink, Tho' press'd by many a foe; That

That will not tremble

That will not tremble on the brink Of pov - - - er -

will not trem-ble on the brink, That will not tremble on the brink Of

on the brink Of pov - - er - - ty or woe, Of

- ty...... or woe. That will not tremble on the brink Of pov-er-ty or woe.

pov-er-ty or woe. That will not tremble on the brink Of pov-er-ty or woe.

pov-er-ty or woe. That will not, &c.

2
That will not murmur nor complain
Beneath the chast'ning rod;
But in the hour of grief or pain
Can lean upon its God:

3
A faith that shines more bright and clear
When tempests rage without;
That when in danger knows no fear,
In darkness feels no doubt:

4
A faith that keeps the narrow way,
By truth restrain'd and led,
And with a pure and heav'nly ray
Lights up a dying bed.

5
Lord, give me such a faith as this,
And then, whate'er may come,
I'll taste, e'en here, the hallow'd bliss
Of an eternal home.

The Prodigal's Call.

Words and Music by F. A. BLACKMER, by per.

1. O, prod-i-gal, now re-turn, Thy Fath-er bids thee come;

And all thy sins He'll for-give, And glad-ly re-ceive you home.

CHORUS.

Re-turn,.... re-turn,... Un-to thy Father's house re-turn;

Re-turn, re-turn, re-turn, re-turn,

O, prod-i-gal, now re-turn, The proffer'd grace no long-er spurn.

2
Dear wanderer, now return,
From darkness make your way
To God, who graciously waits
To turn all your night to day.
Cho.—Return, &c.

3
Come, prodigal, to the feast;
On husks no longer feed;

The banquet waiteth for you,
O, hasten with all your need.
Cho.—Return, &c.

4
O, prodigal, now return,
While yet thy Lord doth wait;
For soon, you know not how soon,
Forever 'twill be too late.
Cho.—Return, &c.

1. How cheer - ing is the Christian's hope, While toil - ing here.. be-

- low! It buoys us up while passing thro' This wilderness of woe,............ This wil-der-ness of woe.

It buoys us up, &c.

2
It points us to a land of rest,
  Where saints with Christ will reign;
Where we shall meet the lov'd of earth,
  And never part again.

3
A land where sin can never come,
  Temptations ne'er annoy;
Where happiness will ever dwell,
  And that without alloy.

4
O how unlike the present world
  Will be the one to come!

Here, pain and sorrow, care and fear,
  Attend where'er we roam.

5
In that bright world no tears will flow,
  Death ne'er can enter there—
For all who gain that heav'nly land
  Will be as angels are.

6
Fly, ling'ring moments, fly, O fly!
  Dear Saviour, quickly come!
We long to see thee as thou art,
  And reach that blissful home.

46. Work, for the Night is Coming.

By permission of O. Ditson & Co. L. MASON.

1. Work, for the night is com - ing, Work thro' the morn-ing hours;
2. Work, for the night is com - ing, Work thro' the sun - ny noon;

Work, while the dew is sparkling, Work 'mid spring-ing flow'rs;
Fill bright-est hours with la - bor, Rest comes sure and soon.

cres.

Work when the day grows bright - er, Work in the glow-ing sun;
Give ev - 'ry fly - ing min - ute Something to keep in store;

Work, for the night is com-ing, When man's work is done.
Work, for the night is com-ing, When man works no more.

3
Work, for the night is coming,
  Under the sunset skies;
While their bright tints are glowing,
  Work, for daylight flies.
Work till the last beam fadeth,
  Fadeth to shine no more;
Work, while the night is dark'ning,
  When man's work is o'er.

4
Work, for the night is coming—
  Soon must thy work be done,
Or 'twill be left unfinished,
  All thou hast begun.
Work ere thy strength shall fail thee,
  And thou canst work no more;
Work, for life's day is ending,
  And will soon be o'er.

Loving - Kindness. L. M.

1. A-wake, my soul, in joy-ful lays, And sing thy great Re-
2. He saw me ru-in'd in the fall, Yet lov'd me, not-with-

- deem-er's praise; He just-ly claims a song from me;
- stand-ing all; He sav'd me from my lost es-tate:

His lov-ing-kind-ness, oh, how free! His lov-ing-kind-ness,
His lov-ing-kind-ness, oh, how great! His lov-ing-kind-ness,

lov-ing-kind-ness, His lov-ing-kind-ness, oh, how free!
lov-ing-kind-ness, His lov-ing-kind-ness, oh, how great!

3
Though numerous hosts of mighty foes,
Though earth and hell its way oppose;
He safely leads his church along;
His loving-kindness, O, how strong! &c.

4
When trouble, like a gloomy cloud,
Has gathered thick and thunder'd loud,
He near my soul has always stood;
His loving-kindness, O, how good! &c.

5
Soon shall I pass the gloomy vale,
Soon all my mortal powers must fail;
O, may my last, expiring breath,
His loving-kindness sing in death; &c.

6
And when earth's rightful King shall come,
To take his ransomed people home,
I'll sing upon that blissful shore
His loving-kindness evermore. &c.

Oh, Happy Day.

1. { Oh, happy day, that fix'd my choice On thee, my Sav-iour and my God; }
   { Well may this glowing heart re-joice, And tell its rap-tures all a - broad. }

CHORUS. **FINE.**

Hap-py day, hap-py day, When Je - sus wash'd my sins a - way!

D.S. Hap-py day, hap-py day, When Je - sus wash'd my sins a - way!

D.S.

He taught me how to watch and pray, And live re - joic-ing ev - 'ry day;

2
Oh, happy bond that seals my vows
To him who merits all my love!
: et cheerful anthems fill his house,
While to that sacred shrine I move.

3
'Tis done, the great transaction's done!
I am my Lord's, and he is mine;
He called me, and I followed on,
Charm'd to confess the voice divine.

4
Now rest, my long divided heart!
Fixed on this blissful center, rest;
Here have I found a noble part,
Here heavenly pleasures fill my breast.

5
High heav'n hath heard the solemn vow;
That vow renewed shall daily be;
Till in life's latest hour I bow,
And bless the bond that saveth me.

————0————

49

1
Sweet is the work, my God, my King,
To praise thy name, give thanks, and
    sing;
To show thy love by morning light,
And talk of all thy truth by night.

2
Sweet is the day of sacred rest;
No mortal cares shall seize my breast:
Oh, may my heart in tune be found,
Like David's harp of solemn sound.

3
When grace has purified my heart,
Then I shall share a glorious part;
And fresh supplies of joy be shed,
Like holy oil to cheer my head.

4
Then shall I see, and hear, and know
All I desired or wished below;
And every power find sweet employ
In that eternal world of joy.

Sweet Hour of Prayer.

Rev. W. W. WALFORD, 1846.   WM. B. BRADBURY.

1. Sweet hour   of prayer! Sweet hour of   prayer! That calls me

D.C. And   oft   es - cap'd   the   tempt-er's snare, By   thy   re -

from a world of care, And bids me at my Fa - ther's

- turn, sweet hour of prayer! And oft es - cap'd the tempt - er's

FINE.

throne, Make all   my wants and wish - es known; In sea - sons

snare, By thy   re - turn, sweet hour   of prayer!

D.C.

of dis - tress and grief, My soul   has oft - en found re - lief;

2
Sweet hour of prayer! sweet hour of
prayer!
Thy wings shall my petition bear,
To him whose truth and faithfulness
Engage the waiting soul to bless:
And since he bids me seek his face,
Believe his word, and trust his grace,
|: I'll cast on him my every care,
And wait for thee, sweet hour of prayer. :|

3
Sweet hour of prayer! sweet hour of
prayer!
May I thy consolation share,
Till from Mount Zion's sacred height
I view my home in Eden bright.
With songs that evermore shall rise,
I'll seize the everlasting prize,
|: And shout, amid the glories there,
Farewell, farewell, sweet hour of pray'r. :|

He's Coming.

Arr. by Geo. E. Lee.

1. How sweet are the tidings that greet the pilgrim's ear, As he wanders in ex-ile from home;

Soon, soon will the Saviour in glory ap-pear, And soon will the kingdom come.

Chorus.

He's com-ing, com-ing, coming soon I know! Coming back to this earth a-gain;

And the weary pilgrims will to glo-ry go, When the Saviour comes to reign.

2 The mossy old graves where the pilgrims sleep,
    Shall be opened as wide as before,
And the millions that sleep in the mighty deep,
    Shall live on this earth once more.—*Cho.*

3 There we'll meet ne'er to part in our happy Eden home,
    Sweet songs of redemption we'll sing :
From the North, from the South, all the ransomed shall come,
    And worship our heav'nly King.—*Cho.*

4 Hallelujah, amen ! Hallelujah again !
    Soon, if faithful, we all shall be there ;
O, be watchful, be hopeful, be joyful till then,
    And a crown of bright glory we'll wear.—*Cho.*

52 Submission.

"Thoughts that Cluster."   FRANK O. WELLCOME.

1. Since a Fa-ther's arm sus-tains thee, Peace-ful be;

When a chastening hand re-strains thee, It is He.

Know His love in full com-plete-ness, Feel the measure of thy

weak-ness; If He wound thy spir-it sore, Trust him more.

2 Without murmur, uncomplaining,
   In His hand
Leave whatever things thou canst not
   Understand.
Though the world thy spirit spurneth,
From thy faith in pity turneth,
Peace thy inmost soul shall fill
   Lying still.

3 Fearest sometimes that thy Father
   Hath forgot?
Though the clouds around thee gather,
   Doubt Him not.
Always hath the daylight broken,
Always hath He comfort spoken,
Better hath He been for years
   Than thy fears.

4 Therefore whatsoe'er betideth,
   Night or day,
Know His love for thee provideth
   Good alway.
Crown of sorrows gladly taking,
For His sake all else forsaking,
Sweetly bending to His will,
   Patient—still.

5 To His own the Saviour giveth
   Daily strength;
And to each heart that believeth,
   Joy at length.
For the lambs the Shepherd careth,
In His bosom them He beareth:
While thus folded to His breast,
   They may rest.

53 Rest over There.

Words by M. V. SALTMARSH.

Music by GEO. E. LEE.

1. O Christian, toil on, work, work while 'tis day, And soon a bright crown you will gain.

In the land of the blest the wea-ry shall rest, From la-bor, tempta-tion, and pain.

Chorus.

There is rest o-ver there, blessed rest o-ver there,

There is rest over there, over there, blessed rest, sweet rest over there, over there;

Sweet rest on that heavenly shore; Yes, there's rest o-ver

Rest, sweet rest, o-ver

there, sweet rest o-ver there, Where sorrow will come never-more.

there, over there, sweet rest o-ver there, Where sorrow will come never more.

2 Though often your heart is sad and oppressed,
  And weary of toil you may be,
O, then think of that home, where grief is **unknown**,
  That Jesus has promised to thee.—*Cho.*

3 Yes, think of that home, of that happy home,
  Its glories have never been told;
O, **your** rest will be sweet, your joy be **complete**,
  In yonder bright city of gold.—*Cho.*

1. Un - veil thy bo-som, faithful tomb; Take this new treasure to thy trust,

2. Nor pain, nor grief, nor anxious fear, Invades thy bounds; no mortal woes

And give these sa - cred rel - ics room To slumber in the si - lent dust.

Can reach the peace-ful sleep-er here, While an-gels watch the soft re - pose.

3 So Jesus slept; God's only Son
  Passed thro' the grave and blest its bed;
  Rest here, blest saint, till from his throne
  The morning break and pierce the shade.

4 Break from his throne, illustrious morn!
  Attend, O earth, his sov'reign word!—
  Restore thy trust! a glorious form
  Shall then arise to meet the Lord.

—o—

55

1 I'm not ashamed to own my Lord,
  Who lives by angels now adored;
  That Jesus who once died for me,
  Who bore my sins in agony.

2 I'm not ashamed to own his laws,
  Nor to defend his noble cause;
  The way he's gone is lined with blood;
  O may I tread the steps he trod!

3 I'm not ashamed to bear my cross,
  For which I count all things but dross;
  Whate'er I'm bid to do or say,
  When Christ commands, I will obey.

4 This world's vain honors will I shun,
  The narrow way to life I'll run;
  That this at last my boast may be:
  My Saviour's not ashamed of me.

—o—

56

1 Show pity, Lord, O Lord, forgive;
  Let a repenting rebel live;
  Are not thy mercies large and free?
  May not a sinner trust in thee?

2 My crimes are great, but can't surpass
  The power and glory of thy grace:
  Great God, thy goodness hath no bound;
  So let thy pardoning love be found.

3 O, wash my soul from every sin,
  And make my guilty conscience clean;
  Here on my heart the burden lies,
  And past offences pain my eyes.

4 My lips with shame my sins confess,
  Against thy law, against thy grace;
  Lord, should thy judgment grow severe,
  I am condemned, but thou art clear.

—o—

57

1 Broad is the road that leads to death,
  And thousands walk together there;
  But wisdom shows a narrow path,
  With here and there a traveller.

2 "Deny thyself and take thy cross,"
  Is thy Redeemer's great command;
  Mortals must count their gold but dross,
  If they would gain the heavenly land.

58. The Voice of Free Grace.

R. BURDSALL.   JOHN CLARKE.

1. The voice of free grace cries, "Es - cape to the mountain;

For A - dam's lost race, Christ has o - pen'd a fountain:

For sin and un - cleanness, and ev - 'ry transgression,

D.S. Hal - le - lu - jah to the Lamb, who has pur - chas'd our par - don!

His blood flows most freely, in.. streams of sal - vation."

We'll praise him a - - gain when we pass o - ver Jordan.

His blood flows most freely in.. streams of sal - va - tion.

We'll praise him a - gain when we pass o - ver Jor - dan.

2 Now glory to God in the highest is given;
Now glory to God is re-echoed in heaven;
Around the whole earth let us tell the glad story,
|: And sing of his love, his salvation and glory. :|| Hallelujah, &c.

3 O Jesus, ride on,—thy kingdom is glorious;
O'er sin, death, and hell, thou wilt make us victorious:
Thy name shall be praised in the great congregation,
|: And saints shall ascribe unto thee their salvation. :|| Hallelujah, &c.

4 When on Zion we stand, having gained the blest shore,
With our harps in our hands, we will praise evermore:
We'll range the blest fields on the banks of the river,
|: And sing of redemption forever and ever. :| Hallelujah, &c.

59 There are Angels Hovering Round.

1. There are an-gels hovering round, There are an-gels hovering round,
2. They will car-ry the tidings home, They will car-ry the tidings home,

There are an - - gels, an - - gels hov-'ring round.
They will car - - ry, car - - ry the ti - dings home.

3 To the new Jerusalem,
   To the new Jerusalem,
To the new, the new Jerusalem.

4 Poor sinners are coming home,
   Poor sinners are coming home,
Poor sinners, sinners are coming home.

5 And Jesus bids them come,
   And Jesus bids them come,
And Jesus, Jesus bids them come.

6 There's glory all around,
   There's glory all around,
There's glory, glory all around.

——0——

60 Come, Thou Fount of Every Blessing.

1. { Come, thou Fount of every blessing, Tune my heart to sing thy grace; }
  { Streams of mer-cy, ne-ver ceas-ing, Call for songs of loudest praise; }

D.C. Praise the mount—I'm fix'd up-on it! Mount of thy re-deem-ing love.

Teach me some melodious sonnet, Sung by flaming tongues a-bove;

D.C.

2 Here I raise my Ebenezer,
   Hither by thy help I'm come;
And I hope by thy good pleasure,
   Safely to arrive at home.
Jesus sought me when a stranger,
   Wandering from the fold of God;
He, to rescue me from danger,
   Interposed his precious blood.

3 Oh, to grace how great a debtor,
   Daily I'm constrained to be!
Let thy goodness, like a fetter,
   Bind my wandering heart to thee;
Prone to wander, Lord, I feel it—
   Prone to leave the God I love—
Here's my heart, oh, take and seal it,
   Seal it from thy courts above.

33

61   Emmons. C. M.

By permission of O. DITSON & Co.

1. Thou dear Redeemer, dying Lamb! We love to hear of thee; No music's like thy
2. When we appear in yonder cloud, With all the favor'd throng; Then we will sing more

charming name, Nor half so sweet to me, Nor half so sweet to me.
sweet, more loud, And Christ shall be our song, And Christ shall be our song.

62

1 Let us rejoice in Christ the Lord,
  Who claims us for his own;
The hope that's built upon his word,
|: Can ne'er be overthrown. :|

2 Though many foes beset us round,
  And feeble is our arm,
Our life is hid with Christ in God
|: Beyond the reach of harm. :|

3 Weak as we are, we will not faint,
  Or, fainting, cannot fail;
Jesus, the strength of every saint,
|: Must in the end prevail. :|

4 As surely as he overcame,
  And conquered death and sin,
So surely those that trust his name
|: Will all his triumph win. :|

63   Marlow. C. M.

JOHN CHETHAM.

1. Come, hap-py souls, approach your God, With new, me-lo-dious songs;

Come, ren-der to Al-migh-ty grace The trib-ute of your tongues.

2 So strange, so boundless was the love
  That pitied dying men,
The Father sent his only Son
To give them life again.

3 Thy hands, dear Jesus, were not arm'd
  With a revengeful rod;

No hard commission to perform,
  The vengeance of a God.

4 But all was mercy, all was mild,
  And wrath forsook the throne,
When Christ on the kind errand came,
  And brought salvation down.

Woodland. C. M.

Words by G. L. Tremle.

N. D. Gould.

1. How sweet the Christian's hope to me, While here I'm call'd to roam: It points me to a

2. This hope reminds me of the time When Je - sus will ap-pear: It gives me joy, it

bet - ter land. It points me to a bet - ter land That I may call my home.

gives me peace. It gives me joy, it gives me peace. It drives a - way my fear.

3 When darkness hovers o'er my path,
  And I no light can see,
This hope sustains my drooping heart,
  And bids me joyful be.

4 When friends that once I loved so well,
  Leave me alone to sigh,
This hope bids me rejoice and sing,
  For my redemption's nigh.

5 This hope—it purifies my heart,
  And turns my night to day;
It plants my feet upon the Rock,
  And keeps me in the way.

6 The day is near—O joyful thought,
  When I shall gain the prize;
This hope will then be turned to sight
  Before my wondering eyes.

——o——

65

1 O glorious day of heavenly rest!
  We hail each sign of thee;
With eager hearts and longing eyes
  We wait thy dawn to see.

2 Those gilded rays of glory bright,
  Resplendent as the sun,
Must soon to every eye make known
  The holy, coming One.

3 With cheerful hope and earnest prayer,
  Still trusting in thy word,
We long to see the eastern skies
  Reveal thy advent, Lord.

4 Then would our waiting souls rejoice,
  Could we thy face behold;
In ages of triumphant bliss
  Our joys could ne'er be told.

——o——

66

1 O happy they who know the Lord,
  With whom he deigns to dwell!
He feeds and cheers them with his word,
  His arm supports them well.

2 To them, in each distressing hour,
  His throne of grace is near;
And when they plead his love and power
  He stands engaged to hear.

3 His presence sweetens all our cares,
  And makes our burdens light;
A word from him dispels our fears
  And gilds the gloom of night.

4 Lord, we expect to suffer here,
  Nor would we dare repine,
But give us still to find thee near
  And own us still for thine.

67 Gathering Home.

Rev. I. Baltzell.   Rev. I. Baltzell, by per.

1. We'll all gath-er home in the morning, At the sound of the great ju-bi-lee; We'll all gather home in the morning, What a gath'ring that will be!

CHORUS.

What a gath - 'ring, gath - 'ring, gath'ring that will be!

What a gath'ring that will be, that will be, What a gath'ring that will be, that will be,

What a gath - 'ring, gath - - 'ring,

While the angels sing, we'll all gather home, What a gath'ring that will be!

2
We'll all gather home in the morning,
Our blessed Redeemer to see;
We'll meet with the true and the faithful,
What a gath'ring that will be!—*Cho.*

3
We'll all gather home in the morning,
On the banks of the bright jasper sea,
We'll meet all the pure and redeemed ones;
What a gath'ring that will be!—*Cho.*

4
Oh, hasten thou bright, coming morning,
We're waiting and longing for thee;
Thy glorious light, earth adorning—
What a morning that will be!—*Cho.*

5
We'll all gather home in the morning,
At the sound of the great jubilee;
When the captives all are returning,
What a gath'ring that will be!—*Cho.*

68 We'll Stand the Storm. C. M.

1. { O shout for joy! let songs a - rise, / Will come in glory from the skies, } O shout for joy! let songs a -
Will come in glory from the

songs a-rise,
from the skies,

- rise; O shout for joy! let songs arise, The Lamb that once was slain
skies, Will come in glory from the skies, Upon the earth to reign.

songs a-rise
from the skies.

Chorus.

We will stand the storm, We will
We will stand, stand the storm; It will not be very long; We will

an - chor by and by, by and by, We will stand the
anchor by and by, We will anchor by and by, We will stand, stand the storm; It will

storm, We will an - chor by and by, by and by.
not be ver-y long; We will an - chor by and by.

2 The trumpet sounds! its awful voice
Is heard o'er land and sea:
And saints arising now rejoice,
To live eternally.— *Cho.*
3 Yes, they shall live forevermore,
Secure from toil and pain;

And on that bright and happy shore
With their Redeemer reign.— *Cho.*
4 All hail that bright, eternal day,
When David's rightful heir
Shall take the throne, and hold the sway
In glorious triumph there.— *Cho.*

(musical notation)

1. If   I in thy likeness, O Lord, may awake, And shine a pure image of thee,

Then I shall be sat - is-fied when I shall break The fetters   of flesh, and be free.

I know this stained tablet must first be made white, To let thy bright features be drawn;

I   know I must pass thro' the darkness of night, To witness the coming of dawn.

2 O, I shall be satisfied when I can cast
   The shadows of nature all by;
When this dreary scene from my vision has pass'd,
   And there is an unclouded sky.
I feel that bright morning is now drawing near,
   When earth's fairest objects will fade;
'Tis then in thy likeness, O let me appear,
   In glory and beauty arrayed.

3 To see thee in glory, dear Lord, as thou art,
   When freed from this wearisome clay,
My spirit is longing—and ever my heart,
   It sighs for the dawn of that day.
Then when on thine image in me thou hast smiled,
   Within those blest mansions, and when
The arms of my Father encircle his child,
   O, I shall be satisfied then.

Wholly Thine.

Mrs. Anna S. Hawks.

F. A. Blackmer, by per

1. Thine, most gra - cious Lord,.. O make me whol - ly Thine—

Thine in thought, and word, and deed, For Thou, O Christ, art mine.

REFRAIN.

Whol - ly Thine, whol - ly Thine; Thou hast bought me, I am Thine;

Bless - ed Saviour, Thou art mine; Make me whol - ly Thine.

2
Wholly Thine, my Lord,
To go when Thou dost call;
Thine to yield my very self
In all things, great and small.
Refrain.—Wholly Thine, &c.

3
Wholly Thine, O Lord,
In every passing hour;
Thine in silence, Thine to speak,
As Thou dost grant the power.
Refrain.—Wholly Thine, &c.

4
Wholly Thine, O Lord,
To fashion as Thou wilt,—
Strengthen, bless, and keep the soul
Which Thou hast sav'd from guilt.
Refrain.—Wholly Thine, &c.

5
Thine, Lord, wholly Thine,
Forever one with Thee—
Rooted, grounded in Thy love
Abiding, sure and free.
Refrain.—Wholly Thine, &c.

71 Love and Grace.

Words and Melody by I. I. LESLIE, by per.   Arranged by F. A. BLACKMER.

1. Oh! 'twas love that brought me to Him, And 'tis love that keeps me there;

By His grace it was I knew Him, Now my Saviour dear and fair.

CHORUS.

Love and grace, His love and grace, I will sing in ev - 'ry place,

Till I reach that bliss-ful shore, Where I'll praise Him ev - er - more!

2
Dark it was before I found Him,
  And the way I could not see;
Now the light that shines around Him,
  As I follow, falls on me.
  Cho.—Love and grace, &c.

3
O how blest to walk with Jesus!
  Joy we never knew before;
From our fears His presence frees us,
  While we trust Him more and more.
  Cho.—Love and grace, &c.

4
Now it is by faith I view Him,
  As I walk this narrow way;
But He soon will call me to Him,
  In that bright approaching day.
  Cho.—Love and grace, &c.

5
Then my joy will be forever,
  There no clouds will intervene;
And the darkness comes there never—
  I shall see Him as I'm seen.
  Cho.—Love and grace, &c.

72 A Home by Life's Fountain Tree.

Words by S. S. BREWER. Arranged by F. BURR.

1. Oh! the home we have in that heav'nly land Where the hills with glory glow ; And the
trees so grand, all in or-der stand, And where life's crystal waters flow. I remember yet, and can-not forget The pangs on the blood-y tree; I will
watch and pray all the long, long day, As I think of Mount Cal-va - ry,

As I think of Mount Cal-va - ry.

2 We are pilgrims now in a stranger's
        land,
  And life's sands are sinking fast ;
  Lov'd ones are gone, but God's
        promise stands
  Untouch'd by sin's withering blast.
  Let us pray and sing to our coming
        King,
  That we soon may his glory see,
  Where forever blest in that land of
        rest,   [tree :]
  |: Is our home by life's clear fountain

3 Ah! the years roll on, and we all grow old
  In this land that gave us birth ;
  And many we lov'd, in the grave-yard cold
  Find rest from the ills of earth.
  Now our heart-strings groan, and we sigh,
        Lord come !
  Oh! that home we long to see,
  With its sweet fragrant shade, all in
        beauty arrayed,   [tree. :]
  |: With a home by life's clear fountain

4 Many friends we lov'd from their homes
        are gone ;   [pass'd ;
  Through earth's fitful scenes they've
  And the warm heart chilled, and the
        kind voice stilled
  By death with his icy blast. [awake,
  Soon the day will break and they'll all
  And forever united be: [white !
  Oh! what holy delight when arrayed in
  We all meet by life's clear fountain tree

46

73 I am Bound for the Land of Canaan.

1. To-geth-er let us sweetly live; I am bound for the land of Ca-naan;

2. To-geth-er let us watch and pray; I am bound for the land of Ca-naan;

To-geth-er let us sweetly die, I am bound for the land of Canaan;

And wait redemption's joy-ous day; I am bound for the land of Canaan;

O Canaan, bright Canaan, I am bound for the land of Canaan; O

O Canaan, bright Canaan, I am bound for the land of Canaan; O

Canaan, it is my hap-py home; I am bound for the land of Canaan.

Canaan, it is my hap-py home; I am bound for the land ot Canaan.

3 Our songs of praise shall fill the skies;
I am bound for the land of Canaan;
While higher still our joys shall rise;
I am bound for the land of Canaan.
O Canaan, bright Canaan, &c.

4 Then come with me, beloved friend;
I am bound for the land of Canaan;
The joys to come shall never end;
I am bound for the land of Canaan.
O Canaan, bright Canaan, &c.

74 O, I must be a Lover of the Lord.

1. { Am I a sol-dier of the cross, A fol-low'r of the Lamb,
And shall I fear to own his cause, Or blush to speak his name? }

2. { Must I be borne to Par-a-dise On flow'ry beds of ease,
While others fought to win the prize, And sail'd thro' bloody seas? }

CHORUS.

O, I must be a lov-er of the Lord, O, I must be a lov-er of the

O, I must be a lov-er of the Lord, O, I must be a lov-er of the

FINE.

Lord,.... If I want to reign with Je-sus when he comes.

Lord, of the Lord, If I want to reign with Je-sus when he comes.

3 Are there no foes for me to face?
Must I not stem the flood?
Is this vile world a friend to grace,
To help me on to God?

4 Sure I must fight, if I would reign;
Increase my courage, Lord;
I'll bear the toil, endure the pain,
Supported by thy word.

5 Thy saints, in all this glorious war,
Shall conquer, though they die;
They see the triumph from afar,
And seize it with their eye.

6 When that illustrious day shall rise,
And all thy armies shine
In robes of vict'ry through the skies,
The glory shall be thine.

75

1 When I can read my title clear
To promised mansions fair,
I'll bid farewell to every fear,
And banish every care.

2 Should earth against my soul engage,
And fiery darts be hurled:
Then I can smile at Satan's rage,
And face a frowning world.

3 Let cares, like a wild deluge, come,
And storms of sorrow fall;
So I but safely reach my home,
My God, my heaven, my all;—

4 There shall I bathe my weary soul
In seas of heavenly rest;
And not a wave of trouble roll
Across my peaceful breast.

76 Lo, What a Glorious Sight.

I. WATTS.

1. { Lo, what a glorious sight ap-pears, To our be-liev-ing eyes; }
   { The earth and seas are pass'd a - way, And the old roll-ing skies! } And When we

the old rolling skies! And the old rolling skies! The earth and seas are
meet to part no more, On Canaan's happy shore; 'Tis there we'll meet at

CHORUS.

Fine.

pass'd a-way, And the old roll - ing skies! — O that will be joy-ful,
Je - sus' feet, When we meet to part no more.—

joy-ful, joy-ful, O that will be joy-ful, When we meet to part no more.

2 From the third heaven, where God re-
        sides,
    That holy, happy place,
The New Jerusalem comes down,
    Adorned with shining grace.—*Cho.*

3 Attending angels shout for joy,
    And the bright armies sing,
"Mortals, behold the sacred seat
    Of your descending King!—*Cho.*

4 "The God of glory down to men
    Removes his blest abode;

Men are the objects of his love,
    And he their gracious God.—*Cho.*

5 " His own soft hand shall wipe the tears
        From every weeping eye;
And pains, and groans, and griefs, and
        fears,
    And death itself, shall die. —*Cho.*

6 How bright the vision! O, how long
    Shall this glad hour delay?
Fly swifter round, ye wheels of time,
    And bring the welcome day!—*Cho.*

77   Life's Harvest. 7s & 6s.

By permission of O. Ditson & Co.

1. Ho, reap-ers of Life's Harvest, Why stand with rusted blade,

2. Thrust in your sharpened sickle, And gather in the grain:

Un - til the night draws round thee, And day begins to fade?
D.S. The golden morn is passing, Why sit ye i - dle, dumb?

The night is fast ap - proaching, And soon will come a - gain.
D.S. Shall sheaves lie there un - gathered, And waste up - on the plain?

Why stand ye i - dle, waiting For reapers more to come?

Thy Mas - ter calls for reapers, And shall he call in vain?

3 Come down from hill and mountain,
  In morning's ruddy glow.
Nor wait until the dial
  Points to the noon below;
And come with the strong sinew,
  Nor faint in heat or cold :
And pause not till the evening
  Draws round its wealth of gold.

4 Mount up the heights of Wisdom,
  And crush each error low ;
Keep back no words of knowledge
  That human hearts should know.
Be faithful to thy mission,
  In service of thy Lord ;
And then a golden chaplet
  Shall be thy just reward.

78 Let Her Rest.*

A. T. GORHAM. "CARL CLEVELAND."

Tenderly.

1. We have laid her to rest 'mong the jew-els of His, Folded close in death's

i - cy em-brace; We have press'd the last kiss, we have dropp'd the last tear

D.S. For we know there is One who her ash - es will keep,

REFRAIN.

p

On the dead and the beau-ti-ful face. Let her rest—let her

And re-deem her fair form from the grave.

sleep where the lone wil-lows weep, And the blossoms of sweet summer wave,

D. S.

2
O, soft be her slumber—the young and the fair,
Whose life-sands so gently have run;
Though the night-dews now cling to her bright, flowing hair,
There's a morn for our beautiful one.

3
Fare you well for a while, faded star of our home;
Sweetly rest from all sorrow and pain
Till the Prince of the angels in triumph shall come,
And restore your lost glory again.

For the Closing of Funeral Service.

79 The Gospel Ship.

I. I. Leslie, 1845.   F. A. Blackmer, by per.

1. On time's tempestuous o-cean wide, A gal-lant ship set sail;
2. Long was to be her pas-sage o'er The boist'rous sea of time,
3. Oft tem-pests have as-sail'd her fierce, The stormy winds rose high;

And out in-to the ra-ging tide She stood be-fore the gale;
Ere she would reach the heav'nly shore, In that far dis-tant clime;
And dark have been the mountain waves That toss'd her near the sky;

Well fit-ted to a-bide the storm, And an-gry wa-ters' foam,
Yet with her sails spread high and wide, On, on, she swift-ly flew,
But o'er them all, with stead-y helm, She on-ward press'd her way;

And bring the cap-tives that she bore, Un-to their ha-ven home.
Bear-ing in ar-dent hope and love, Her pas-sen-gers and crew.
Her com-pass true un-to the pole, Guides her to end-less day.

CHORUS.

Sail on, proud ship! tho' thy white sails dip, And the tempests loudly roar;

With Pi - lot true, thou wilt land thy crew, Safe on the e - ter - nal shore.

4 Long, long she has been out, and now
  She nears her haven home;
  A beacon light streams o'er her bow,
  And bids her hither come;
  And voices joyful oft are heard,
  And music swelling high;
  "The land! the land! the land ahead!"
  With rapture now they cry.

5 Now soon will she be safely moored,
  Fast anchored in the bay;
  And all her gallant crew on shore,
  Will keep a festal day;
  And long their songs of joy will rise,
  Beneath high heaven's dome—
  They've passed the stormy sea of time,
  They've reached their haven home.

80   Come and Reign.

1. Come and reign; come and reign, Jesus, quickly come; For now it fills my heart with

Chorus.—Come and reign, &c.

Fine.

joy   To know I'm al-most home.   Here I see the fall-ing tear, As
2. Here I grieve the friends I love, And

D.C.

pilgrim now I roam An exile from my Father's house; But soon he'll call me home.
they in turn grieve me; But, O my Saviour grant me grace, That I may not grieve thee.

3 Here disease invades our frame,
  We sicken, droop and die;
  But there eternal youth shall bloom,
  And bright shall beam each eye.
  Come, and reign, &c.

4 Here we meet and part again,
  As far and near we roam;
  But there we'll meet to part no more,
  And sweetly rest at home.
  Come, and reign, &c.

81 Going Home By-and-by.

A. T. G.

ADRIAN T. GORHAM.

1. We have heard the glad tidings of joy, And our voices we lift up-on high;

Here's a - dieu to each vain earthly toy— We are all go-ing home by-and-by.

REFRAIN.

Go - ing home by - and-by, go - ing home by - and-by

Where the shad-ows shall come nev - er - more; Go - ing home by - and-

- by, go-ing home by-and-by, To our rest on that beau-ti - ful shore.

2 Long and weary the journey has been;
  In our path has been many a sigh;
From this dark land of sorrow and sin
  We are all going home by-and-by.

3 With the lost ones of earth we shall meet
  When the trumpet of God rends the
    sky;

Clad in garments of beauty complete,
  They are all going home by-and-by.

4 Hasten, Saviour, Thy coming we pray,
  Bid Thy saints upward mount to the
    sky;
Usher in glad eternity's day,
  Come and gather us home by-and-by.

82 Precious Fountain.

F. A. BLACKMER.

1. There is a fountain fill'd with blood, Drawn from Immanuel's veins,
There is a fountain fill'd with blood,

And sinners plung'd beneath that flood, Lose all their guilt-y stains.
And sin - ners plung'd beneath that flood,

CHORUS.

Oh pre - cious fountain, cleansing stream, Where
Oh pre - - cious fountain, cleansing stream,

all may plunge and be made clean; All glo - ry to my Saviour
be made clean, All glo - ry

be, Who shed His blood to ran-som me, to ransom me.
to my Saviour be, *rit.*

2 Thou dying Lamb! thy precious blood
Shall never lose its power,
Till all the ransomed Church of God
Are saved, to sin no more.

3 E'er since, by faith, I saw the stream
Thy flowing wounds supp'y,

Redeeming love has been my theme,
And shall be till I die.

4 Then in a nobler, sweeter song,
I'll sing thy power to save, [tongue
When this poor, lisping, stammering
Is ransomed from the grave.

The Tree of Life.

Words by R. TORREY, JR.　　Copyright, 1874, by ASA HULL.　　Music by ASA HULL.

1. { There's a tree that's ev-er growing, growing, Growing on the heav'nly shore;
   { Where the stream of Life is flow-ing, flow-ing, Flowing on for-ev-er-more! }

CHORUS.

cres.

O, how bright, O, how bright, O, how bright.... the flowers
O, how bright, O, how bright, O, how bright

p　　cres.

grow,.. O, how soft, O, how soft, O, how soft......
O, how soft, O, how soft, O, how

.... the waters flow On that heav'nly shore, On that heav'nly shore.

soft

2
Its bright flowers are ever flinging,
　flinging,
Flinging perfume on the air,
While angelic harps are ringing, ring-
　ing,
Ringing heav'nly music there!
O, how sweet the angels sing,
O, how loud their glad harps ring,
　In those regions fair!

3
Its green leaves are for the healing,
　healing,
Healing of the nations all;
Send the glorious tidings pealing, peal-
　ing,
Pealing like the trumpet's call!
Tell all men this wondrous tree
From all pain shall set them free,
　If on Christ they call!

84 The Voice of The Spirit.

Edwin H. Nevin.   Frank H. Thomson.

1. O, fly to the arms of the Saviour, The arms that are o-pen for thee; O,

bathe in the fountain of mer-cy, The fountain so rich and so free.

CHORUS.

O, turn to the light that is shin - - - ing, Is
O, turn to the light, to the light that is shining, The

shining so bright and so clear;..... O, list to the voice that is
light that is shining so bright and so clear; O, list to the voice, to the

speak - - ing, Is speaking in ac-cents so dear......

voice that is speaking, The voice that is speaking in accents so dear.

Is speaking in ac-cents so dear......

2 O, seek for the hope of the Christian,   O, strive to inherit the treasure,
   The hope that will never betray;   The treasure whose wealth is untold.
O, ever be faithful to duty
   And angels will guard all thy way.   4 O, seek for the crown that is promis'd,
                                                 The crown that the conquerors win;
3 O, aim to inhabit the city,   The robe and the harp that are given
   The city of crystal and gold;   To those that shall enter therein.

57

Triumph. 10s & 5s.

D. T. TAYLOR.   S. C. HANCOCK.

1. Lift your glad voi-ces in tri-umph on high; Shout, for the day of re-
- demption is nigh; Sing, for the Lord will ap-pear in his glo-ry,
Mountains and val-leys re - peat the glad sto-ry; Tune ev-'ry lyre,
Lift the strain high-er, Far o'er the o - cean the ti-dings shall fly.

2
Lift your glad voices ye nations and sing;
Let the high anthem re-echo and ring,
Sing, for the bright one that slept in the
    manger
Comes; and the earth that once pillow'd
    the stranger,
        In rich adorning,
        Hails the glad morning
Blossoms like Eden, and welcomes her
    King.

3
Lift your glad voices, he conquered the
    grave,
Jesus, Immanuel, Almighty to save;
Shout to the tyrant "Thy chains are
    all broken!

Sing, for the voice of Jehovah hath
    spoken.
        "Open the portal,
        Make them immortal;
Life shall endure with Eternity's wave.'

4
Lift your glad voices, he cometh again,
Sound out the tidings o'er earth and o'er
    main!
Sing, for the dark days of evil are ending:
Shout to the Bridegroom with angels
    descending,
        Bride of Jehovah,
        Welcome thy lover.
Sing, for He cometh, He cometh to reign!

86 The Home Over There.

Words by Mrs. E. R. Wells.　　　　　Music by J. Wells.

1. In that beau - ti - ful home o - ver there, By the side of the
Where the flow - ers are fade - less and fair, Is no sor - row, nor

riv - er of life,
sighing, nor strife. Where the flowers are fadeless and fair, ev - er fair,

Is no sor - row, nor sigh - ing, nor strife. 'Tis a beau - ti - ful

land o - ver there, O - ver there, o - ver there, o - ver there, o - ver there.

2 All the glorified saints will be there,
　Who have suffer'd and toil'd here below;
　In the triumph of Christ they will share, they will share,
　And the victory shout o'er the foe. *Cho.*—'Tis a beautiful land, &c.

3 They will shine in that home over there,
　In the city, so glorious and bright;
　And the crown of the victor they'll wear, they will wear,
　Where their God and the Lamb are the light.—*Cho.*

4 To that heavenly land over there,
　All the prophets and martyrs will come;
　And the ransomed of God everywhere, everywhere,
　Will at length reach that beautiful home.—*Cho.*

5 Oh! that beautiful home over there!
　How I long to behold it, and be
　With the One who that home shall prepare, shall prepare
　For His loved ones—for you and for me.—*Cho.*

87 Oh, to be Over Yonder!

FLORENCE C. ARMSTRONG.

F. A. BLACKMER.

1. Oh! to be o - ver yon - der! In that land of won - der,
2. Oh! to be o - ver yon - der! My yearn - ing heart grows fon - der,

Where the an - gel voi - ces min - gle, And the harps of ser - aphs ring;
Of look - ing, look - ing east - ward, To see the day - star bring

To be free from pain and sor - row, And the dread of dark to - mor - row,
Some tid - ings of the wak - ing, The cloud - less, pure day - breaking;

To rest in light and sun - shine, In the pres - ence of the King.
My heart is long - ing, long - ing For the com - ing of the King.

To rest in light and sun - shine, In the presence of the King.
My heart is long - ing, long - ing For the com - ing of the King.

cres.   dim. e rit.

3 Oh! to be over yonder!
Alas! I sigh and wonder
Why clings my poor heart ever
To any earthly thing;
Each tie of earth must sever,
And pass away forever,
But there's no fading, dying
In the presence of the King

4 When shall I be o'er yonder?
My longing groweth stronger
To join in all the praises
The ransomed ones will sing—
Where the pearly gates are gleaming
And the endless light is streaming;
Oh! when shall I be yonder
In the presence of the King?

The Pearl and Crown.

Andantino.

1. The pearl that worldlings cov-et, Is not the pearl for me, Its beauty fades as

2. The crown that decks the monarch, Is not the crown for me, It dazzles but a

quick-ly As sunshine on the sea; But there's a pearl sought by the wise, 'Tis

moment, Its brightness soon will flee; But there's a crown prepared above, For

call'd "the pearl of greatest price;" Tho' few its value see,—O, that's the pearl for me.

all who walk in humble love, For-ev-er bright 'twill be, O, that's the crown for me,

O, that's the pearl for me, O, that's the pearl for me.

O, that's the. crown for me, O, that's the crown for me.

3 The road that many travel,
  Is not the road for me;
  It leads to death and sorrow;
  In it I would not be.
But there's a path that leads to God;
Tis mark'd by Christ's most precious blood;
  The way for all is free;
  c: O, that's the path for me!:t

4 The hope that sinners cherish,
  Is not the hope for me,
  Most surely will they perish,
  Unless from sin made free.
But there's a hope which rests in God,
And leads the soul to keep his word,
  And sinful pleasures flee;
  t: O, that's the hope for me! t

1. Hark, my soul, it is the Lord! 'Tis thy Sav-iour, hear his word!

2. I de - liv - er'd thee, when bound, And when bleeding, heal'd thy wound;

Je - sus speaks, he speaks to thee,— Say, poor sin - ner, lov'st thou me?

Sought thee wand'ring, set thee right, Turn'd thy dark-ness in - to light.

3
Mine is an unchanging love,
Higher than the heights above,
Deeper than the depths beneath,
Free and faithful, strong as death.

4
Thou shalt see my glory soon,
When the work of faith is done,
Partner of my throne shalt be,—
Say, poor sinner, lov'st thou me?

———0———

90

1
Lord, accept our feeble song!
Power and praise to thee belong!
We would all thy grace record,
Holy, holy, holy Lord!

2
Rich in glory, thou didst stoop:
Thence is all thy people's hope;
Thou wast poor, that we might be
Rich in glory, Lord, with thee.

3
When we think of love like this,
Joy and shame our hearts possess;
Joy, that thou couldst pity thus,
Shame, for such returns from us.

4
Yet we hope the day to see,
When we shall from sin be free;
When to thee in glory brought,
We shall serve thee as we ought.

———0———

91

1
Come, my soul, thy suit prepare;
Jesus loves to answer prayer;
He himself has bid thee pray;
Therefore will not say thee nay.

2
Thou art coming to a King;
Large petitions with thee bring;
For his grace and power are such,
None can ever ask too much.

3
With my burden I begin:
Lord, remove this load of sin;
Let thy blood, for sinners spilt,
Set my conscience free from guilt.

4
Lord, I come to thee for rest;
Take possession of my breast;
There thy blood-bought right maintain,
And without a rival reign.

92   Will You Go?

Words by I. I. L.

1. {
We're trav'ling home to mansions bright; Will you go? Will you go?
'Tis Je - sus who doth us invite; Will you go? Will you go?
} Tha'

D.C. 'Tis there with Je - sus we shall be; Will you go? Will you go?

Cit - y fair we soon shall see, And be from death and sorrow free—

D.C.

2 We're going to walk the streets of gold;
    Will you go? will you go?
And all the glory there behold;
    Will you go? will you go?
The tree of life, the river clear,
The pearly gates that open there,
We soon shall see—forever fair;
    Will you go? will you go?

3 The way to life is free for all;
    Will you go? will you go?
O listen to the Saviour's call;
    Will you go? will you go?

He now invites you all to come,
And share with Him that blissful home,
Where nevermore your feet shall roam;
    Will you go? will you go?

4 O could I hear some wand'rer say,
    "I will go, I will go,"
"I now will leave destruction's way—
    I will go, I will go."
Yes, come dear sinner, wand'rer come,
In those bright mansions there is room
And you with Christ may have a home;
    Wand'rer come—wand'rer come.

——o——

93   Come to Jesus Just Now.

1. Come to Jesus, Come to Jesus, Come to Jesus just now, Just now come to Jesus, Come to Jesus just now.

2 |: He will save you, :||
    He will save you just now;
Just now He will save you,
    He will save you just now.

3 |: He is able, :||
    He is able just now;
Just now He is able,
    He is able just now.

4 |: He is willing :||
    He is willing just now;
Just now He is willing,
    He is willing just now.

5 |: He is waiting, :||
    He is waiting just now;
Just now He is waiting,
    He is waiting just now.

6 |: O believe Him, :||
    O believe Him just now;
Just now O believe Him,
    O believe Him just now.

7 |: He will bless you, :||
    He will bless you just now;
Just now He will bless you,
    He will bless you just now.

94   Rest for the Weary.   8s & 7s.

1. In the Christian's home in glo-ry, There re-mains a land of rest;

There my Saviour's gone be-fore me, To ful-fil my soul's re-quest:

CHORUS.

There is rest for the weary, There is rest for the weary, There is rest for the

weary, There is rest for you—On the other side of Jordan, In the

sweet fields of E-den, Where the tree of life is blooming, There is rest for you.

2 He is fitting up my mansion,
    Which eternally shall stand;
For my stay shall not be transient
    In that holy, happy land.

3 Pain nor sickness ne'er shall enter,
    Grief nor woe my lot shall share;
But in that celestial centre,
    I a crown of life shall wear.

4 Death itself shall then be vanquish'd
    And his sting shall be withdrawn
Shout for gladness, O ye ransomed!
    Hail with joy the rising morn.

5 Sing, O sing, ye heirs of glory;
    Shout your triumph as you go,
Zion's gates will open for you,
    You shall find an entrance through

94

95 Rockingham. L. M.

LOWELL MASON.

1. O ren-der thanks to God a-bove, The fountain of e-ter-nal love;
2. Who can his mighty deeds ex-press, Not on-ly vast—but numberless?

Whose mer-cy firm, through a-ges past, Hath stood, and shall for-ev-er last.
What mor-tal el-o-quence can raise His trib-ute of im-mortal praise?

1 Extend to me that favor, Lord,
Thou to thy chosen dost afford;
When thou return'st to set them free,
Let thy salvation visit me.

2 The Lord, in righteousness arrayed,
Surveys the world his hands have made;
Pierces the heart, and tries the reins,
And judgment from on high ordains.

96

1 The Lord is Judge: before his throne
All nations shall his justice own:
O, may my soul be found sincere,
And stand, approved, with courage there!

3 My God, my Shield! around me place
The shelter of thy sov'reign grace;
That when thine arm the just shall save,
I then may triumph o'er the grave.

—o—

97 Olives' Brow. L. M.

WM. B. TAPPAN.   WM. B. BRADBURY.

1. 'Tis midnight; and on Ol-ive's brow The star is dimm'd that lately shone:
2. 'Tis midnight; and, from all removed, The Saviour wrestles lone, with fears;

'Tis midnight; in the gar-den, now, The suffering Saviour prays a-lone.
E'en that dis-ci-ple whom he lov'd Heeds not his Master's grief and tears.

3 'Tis midnight; and for others' guilt
The Man of sorrows weeps in blood;
Yet he that hath in anguish knelt
Is not forsaken by his God.

4 'Tis midnight; and from ether plains
Is borne the song that angels know;
Unheard by mortals are the strains
That sweetly soothe the Saviour's woe.

COUNTESS OF HUNTINGDON.

LOWELL MASON.

1. When thou, my righteous Judge, shalt come To call thy ransom'd people home,

Shall I a - mong them stand! Shall such a worthless worm as I,

Who sometimes am a-fraid to die, Be found at thy right hand?

2 I love to meet among them now,
Before thy gracious throne to bow,
    Though weakest of them all;
But can I bear the piercing thought,
To have my worthless name left out,
    When thou for them shalt call?

3 Prevent, prevent it, by thy grace!
Be thou, dear Lord, my hiding-place,
    In that expected day:
Thy pard'ning voice, O let me hear,
To still each unbelieving fear,
    Nor let me fall, I pray!

4 Among thy saints let me be found,
Whene'er the archangel's trump shall
    To see thy smiling face;   [sound,
Then loudest of the throng I'll sing,
While heaven's resounding mansions ring
    With shouts of sovereign grace.

99

1 How happy are the little flock,
Who, safe beneath their guardian Rock,
    In all commotions rest!
When war's and tumult's waves run high,
Unmoved above the storm they lie,
    And lodge in Jesus' breast.

2 Such happiness, O Lord, have we,
By mercy gathered into thee
    Before the floods descend;   [down,
And while the bursting cloud comes
We mark the vengeful day begun,
    And calmly wait the end.

3 The plague, the dearth, and din of war,
Our Saviour's swift approach declare,
    And bid our hearts arise;
Earth's basis shook, confirms our hope,
Its cities' fall but lifts us up
    To meet thee in the skies.

100

1 That warning voice, O sinner, hear!
And, while salvation lingers near,
    The heav'nly call obey:
Flee from destruction's downward path,
Flee from the threat'ning storm of wrath,
    That rises o'er thy way.

2 That warning voice, O, sinner, hear!
Whose accents linger on thine ear;
    Thy footsteps now retrace;
Renounce thy sins, and be forgiven;
Believe, become an heir of heaven,
    And sing redeeming grace.

101   Rock of Ages.   7s.

A. M. TOPLADY.

DR. T. HASTINGS.

Fine

1. Rock of A-ges, cleft for me, Let me hide my-self in thee;

D.C. Be of sin the dou-ble cure, Save from wrath and make me pure.

D.C.

Let the wa-ter and the blood, From thy wounded side which flow'd,

2 Could my tears forever flow,
Could my zeal no languor know,
These for sin could not atone,
Thou must save, and thou alone:
In my hand no price I bring,
Simply to thy cross I cling.

3 While I draw this fleeting breath,
When my eyes shall close in death,
When I with the throng unknown,
See thee on thy judgment throne—
Rock of Ages, cleft for me,
Let me hide myself in thee.

——o——

102   Greenville.   8s & 7s.

R. ROBINSON.

JEAN JACQUES ROUSSEAU.

Fine.

1. { Come, thou Fount of every blessing, Tune my heart to sing thy grace;
{ Streams of mer-cy never ceasing, Call for songs of loud-est praise.

D.C. Praise the mount, O, fix me on it! Mount of God's un-changing love

D.C.

Teach me some me-lodious son-net, Sung by flaming tongues a-bove;

2 Here I raise my Ebenezer;
Hither by Thy help I'm come;
And I hope, by Thy good pleasure,
Safely to arrive at home.
Jesus sought me when a stranger,
Wand'ring from the fold of God;
He, to save my soul from danger,
Interposed his precious blood.

3 O, to grace how great a debtor
Daily I'm constrain'd to be!
Let that grace, Lord, like a fetter,
Bind my wand'ring heart to thee:
Prone to wander, Lord, I feel it,
Prone to leave the God I love;
Here's my heart, Lord, take and seal it,
Seal it from thy courts above.

103   **Rest. L. M.**

WM. B. BRADBURY

1. Asleep in Je - sus! blessed sleep, From which none ev - er wakes to weep;
2. Asleep in Je - sus! peaceful rest, Whose waking is su-preme-ly blest!

A calm and undisturbed re - pose, Unbroken by the dread of foes.
No fear, no foe shall dim that hour Which manifests the Saviour's pow'r

3 Asleep in Jesus! time nor space
Affects this precious hiding-place;
On India's plains or Lapland's snows
Believers find the same repose.

4 Asleep in Jesus! far from thee
Thy kindred and their graves may be;
But thine is still a blessed sleep,
From which none ever wakes to weep.

104

1 Afflicted saint, to Christ draw near;
Thy Saviour's gracious promise hear;
His faithful word declares to thee,
That as thy day thy strength shall be.

2 Let not thy heart despond and say,
"How shall I stand the trying day?"
He has engaged by firm decree
That as thy day thy strength shall be.

3 Thy faith is weak, thy foes are strong;
And if the contest should be long,
Thy Lord will make the tempter flee;
For as thy day thy strength shall be.

4 Should persecution rage and flame,
Still trust in thy Redeemer's name;
In fiery trials thou shalt see
That as thy day thy strength shall be.

—— o ——

105   **Can You Hate the Saviour?**

1. { Now the Saviour stands and pleading At the sin-ner's bolted heart; }
   { Now in heav'n he's in-ter - ced-ing, Un - der - tak-ing sinners' part. }

D.C. Once he died for your be - haviour, Now he calls you to his arms.

CHORUS.   D.C.

Sin - ners, can you hate the Saviour? Will you thrust him from your arms.

2 Now he's waiting to be gracious,
Now he stands and looks on thee;
See, what kindness, love and pity,
Shine around on you and me.
Sinners, can you hate, &c.

3 Open now your hearts before him,
Bid the Saviour welcome in;
Now receive, -and O, adore him,
Take a full discharge from sin.
Sinners, can you hate, &c.

4 Sinners, hear your God and Saviour,
Hear his gracious voice to-day;
Turn from all your vain behaviour,
O repent, return, and pray.
Sinners, can you hate, &c.

5 Come, for all things now are ready,
Yet there's room for many more;
O, ye blind, ye lame and needy,
Come to wisdom's boundless store.
Sinners, can you hate, &c.

106   Old Hundred. L. M.

I. WATTS, 1719.   G. FRANC, 1545.

1. Ye na-tions round the earth, rejoice Before the Lord, your sov'reign King!

Serve him with cheerful heart and voice; With all your tongues his glory sing.

2 The Lord is God; 'tis he alone
  Doth life, and breath, and being give;
We are his work, and not our own—
  The sheep that on his pastures live.

3 Enter his gates with songs of joy,
  With praises to his courts repair;
And make it your divine employ
  To pay your thanks and honors there.

107
4 Here, in thy name, eternal God,
  We build this earthly house for thee;
O, choose it for thy fixed abode,
  And guard it long from error free.

2 When here, O Lord, we seek thy face,
  And dying sinners pray to live,
Hear thou in heaven, thy dwelling-place,
  And when thou hearest, Lord, forgive.

3 When here thy messengers proclaim
  The gracious Gospel of thy Son,
Still by the power of his great name
  Be mighty signs and wonders done.

108
Be thou, O God, exalted high,
And, as thy glory fills the sky,
So let it be on earth displayed,
Till thou art here as there obeyed.

—0—

109   Praise. L. M.

By permission of O. DITSON & Co.   L. O. EMERSON.

Praise God, from whom all blessings flow; Praise him, all creatures here below;

Praise him a-bove, ye heav'nly host; Praise Father, Son, .. and Ho-ly Ghost.

110
1 Dismiss us with thy blessing, Lord;
  Help us to feed upon thy word;
All that has been amiss, forgive,
And let thy truth within us live.

2 Though we are guilty, thou art good;
  Wash all our works in Jesus' blood;
Give every burdened soul release,
And bid us all depart in peace.

69

111 The Beauteous Day.

Rev. W. O. Cushing, 1866.

G. F. Root.

1. We are watching, we are waiting, For the bright, prophetic day; When the shadows,
2. We are watching, we are waiting, For the beauteous King of day; For the chiefest

CHORUS

dreary shadows, From the world shall roll a-way. We are waiting for the morning,
of ten thousand, For the Light, the Truth, the Way. We are waiting for the morning,

When the beauteous day is dawning, We are waiting for the morning, For the golden

spires of day. Lo! he comes! see the King draw near; Zion, shout, the Lord is here.

3 We are watching, we are waiting
For the time so long foretold,
When with saved ones of all ages,
We shall walk the streets of gold.
We are waiting, &c.

4 We are watching, we are waiting
For an earth made free from strife,
Then, the pow'r of Satan ended,
We shall have eternal life.
We are waiting, &c.

—o—

112 Who's Like Jesus?

Of Him who did sal - va - tion bring, I could for - ev - er
D.S. died for you, and he died for me, He died to set poor

D.S.

think and sing, O, who's like Je - sus? He died on the tree. Yes, he
sin - ners free. O, who's like Je - sus? He died on the tree.

113 Nearer to Thee.

MRS. S. F. ADAMS.   By permission of O. DITSON & Co.   LOWELL MASON.

1. Near-er, my God, to thee, Near-er to thee; E'en though it

be a cross That rais-eth me, Still all my song shall be,

Near-er, my God to thee, Near-er, my God to thee, Near-er to thee.

114

2 Though like a wanderer,
  Daylight all gone,
Darkness be over me,
  My rest a stone,
Yet in my dreams I'd be
|: Nearer, my God, to thee, :|
  Nearer to thee.

3 There let my way appear,
  Onward to heaven;
All that thou sendest me,
  In mercy given:
Angels to beckon me
|: Nearer, my God, to thee, :|
  Nearer to thee.

4 Then with my waking thoughts,
  Bright with thy praise,
Out of my stony griefs
  Bethel I'll raise,
So by my woes to be
|: Nearer, my God, to thee, :|
  Nearer to thee.

5 And when the trumpet sounds,
  May I still wear
The righteousness of Christ,
  My garment fair:
Caught up with Him to be
|: Nearer, my God, to thee, :|
  Nearer to thee.

1 More love to thee, O Christ,
  More love to thee!
Hear thou the prayer I make,
  On bended knee;
This is my earnest plea,
||: More love, O Christ, to thee, :|
  More love to thee!

2 Once earthly joy I craved,
  Sought peace and rest;
Now thee alone I seek,
  Give what is best:
This all my prayer shall be,
|: More love, O Christ, to thee, :|
  More love to thee!

3 Then in my latest day,
  I will thee praise;
This be the constant cry
  My heart shall raise;
This still its prayer shall be,
|: More love, O Christ, to thee, :|
  More love to thee!

4 Then when thou com'st again,
  Thy saints to greet,
May I with all the blest
  Thee gladly meet:
And when thy face I see,
|: More love I'll have to thee, :|
  More love to thee.

MRS. ELIZABETH P. PRENTISS.

My Ain Countrie.

Miss M. A. Lee.

Scotch Song. Arr.

1. { I am far frae my hame, an' I'm wea-ry aft-en whiles, For the
An' I'll ne'er be fu' con-tent un-til my een do see The

D.C. But these sichts an' these soun's will as naething be to me, When I

lang'd-for-hame-bringing, an' my Father's welcome smiles, }
gowden gates of heav'n, an' my . . . . } ain . . countrie. *Fine.*

hear the an-gels singing in my . . . . ain . . countrie. *Fine.*

D.C.

{ The earth is fleck'd wi' flow-ers, mon-y-tint-ed, fresh and gay; }
{ The bird-ies war-ble blithely, for my Father made them sae; }

2

I've his gude word of promise, that some gladsome day the King
To his ain royal palace, his banished hame, will bring
Wi' een, an' wi' heart running owre we shall see
"The King in his beauty," an' our ain countrie.
My sins hae been mony and my sorrows hae been sair;
But there they'll never vex me, nor be remembered mair.
For his bluid hath made me white, and his hand shall dry my e'e,
When he brings me hame at last to my ain countrie.

3

He is faithfu' that hath promised, an' he'll surely come again,
He'll keep his tryst wi' me, at what hour I dinna ken;
But he bids me still to wait, an' ready aye to be,
To gang at ony moment to my ain countrie.
So I'm watching aye, and singing o' my hame as I wait,
For the soun'ing o' his footfa' this side the gowden gate..
God gie his grace to ilk ane wha listens noo to me,
That we a' may gang in gladness to our ain countrie.

116 The Eden City.

Music by AMANDA BAILEY.

1. We're look-ing for a ci-ty, When E-den is re-stor'd; A ci-ty of foundations, Whose builder is the Lord; Whose glories are unfading, Whose beauties are untold; Whose walls are built of jasper, With streets of finest gold.

Chorus.

Oh! hail, happy day, Oh! hail happy day, When nevermore we'll stray; O glorious sight! 'twill be delight, Within those walls to stay.

2 The length and breadth are equal,
  Twelve thousand furlongs square;
And nought unclean or hateful
  Shall ever enter there:
The kings of earth their glory
  And honor well may bring,
Within thy massy portals,—
  Great city of our King.—*Cho.*

3 No need of any temple,
  Or sun or moon to shine;
The Lord will it enlighten
  With glory all divine;
The nations of the saved
  Shall walk in glory bright
With Christ, the Son of David,
  Their everlasting light.—*Cho.*

4 The towering arches glitter
  With many a radiant stone;
And water, clear as crystal,
  Flows out from 'neath the throne;
The trees of life for healing,
  On either side are there,
Their leaves and branches waving,
  All stately, grand and fair.—*Cho.*

5 Ho, all ye weary, fainting,
  To this fair city come;
Come, drink from living fountains,
  And thirst no more nor roam:
O be constrained to enter
  Through Christ, the only Way,
And you he there will welcome,
  And bid you ever stay.—*Cho.*

Wonderful Grace.

W. H. BURRELL.   I. BALTZELL, by per.

1. 'Tis grace! 'tis grace! 'tis won-der-ful grace! This great sal-va - tion brings;
2. 'Tis grace! 'tis grace! 'tis won-der-ful grace! Which saves the soul from sin;
3. 'Tis grace! 'tis grace! 'tis won-der-ful grace! Its streams are full and free;

The soul, de - liv - er'd of its load, In sweetest rap - ture sings.
The pow'r of ris - ing e - vil slays, And reigns supreme with-in.
And flow - ing now for all the race—They ev - en flow to me.

CHORUS.

'Tis grace!...... 'tis grace!........ Wonder - ful, wonder - ful

'Tis wonderful grace! 'tis won-der-ful grace!

grace!........ 'Tis grace!........ 'tis grace!........

won-der-ful grace! 'Tis won-der-ful grace! 'tis won-der-ful grace!

Flowing still free-ly for me.

4
'Tis grace! 'tis grace! 'tis wonderful grace!
'Tis grace that will me save;
Will take me from Death's cold embrace,
And bring me from the grave.—*Cho.*

118 The Beautiful Vale.

Music by Asa Hull.
(By permission.)

1. My soul with rapture waits for thee, Beautiful vale of rest! My home beyond the

rolling sea, Beautiful vale of rest! I long to sing thy pleasures o'er, The

TRIO.

beauties of thy tranquil shore, sorrow come no more, Beautiful vale of rest.
Where pain and

Chorus.

Beautiful vale...... of rest, Beautiful vale........ of rest.

Beautiful vale of rest, Beautiful vale of rest.

rit. poco.

My soul with rapture longs for thee, O beauti - ful vale of rest.

2 Thy radiant fields and glowing skies,
   Beautiful vale of rest!
Too pure and bright for mortal eyes,
   Beautiful vale of rest!
Beside the living stream that flows,
The weary heart shall find repose,—
Thy pearly gates shall never close,
   Beautiful vale of rest!

3 The joys of earth, how soon they fade!
   Beautiful vale of rest!
Like morning dew or evening shade,
   Beautiful vale of rest!

Yet when we reach thy golden strand,
Our gentle Saviour's promised land,
We'll sing with all the angel band,
   Beautiful vale of rest!

4 Oh, who would dwell forever here,
   Beautiful vale of rest!
With joy, unfading joy so near,
   Beautiful vale of rest!
Oh, may I live, that I may wear
A starry crown forever there,
And breathe thy sweet and balmy air,
   Beautiful vale of rest!

119 Sweetly I'm Resting in Jesus.

Words and Music by WM. J. KIRKPATRICK.

1. Sweetly I'm resting in Je - sus, Trusting my Saviour and Lord;

Casting my soul on his mer-cy, Leaning up - on his word;

Bearing the cross thro' toil and pain, Counting as loss all earth-ly gain:

Fine.

Knowing the faithful a crown shall obtain, Sweetly I'm resting in Je - sus.
D.S. Blessed assurance, his name be adored, Sweetly I'm resting in Je - sus.

Chorus. D.S. 𝄋

Sweet - ly rest - ing, Firm - ly trusting his word;
Sweetly I'm resting in Jesus my Lord, Firmly I'm trusting, believing his word;

2 Sweetly I'm resting in Jesus,
    Plunged in the life-giving flood,
Bathed in the sea of redemption,
    Washed in the cleansing blood;
Passively lying at his feet,
Learning the bliss of love complete;
Waiting his pleasure, whatever is meet,
Sweetly I'm resting in Jesus.—*Cho.*

3 Sweetly I'm resting in Jesus;
    Glory-light beams on my way,
Bright'ning my path thro' the darkness,
    Chasing the clouds away,

Feeding in pastures green and fair,
Drinking from fountains flowing there,
Tenderly guarded by his loving care,
Sweetly I'm resting in Jesus.—*Cho.*

4 Sweetly I'm resting in Jesus,
    Safe on his bosom reclined;
Tokens of perfect salvation,
    Fullness of joy I find.
Purer and clearer all the way,
Shineth the light of perfect day;
Holy the rapture, triumphant the lay,
Sweetly I'm resting in Jesus.—*Cho.*

76

120 Whiter than Snow.

JAMES NICHOLSON.

WM. G. FISCHER, by per.

1. Lord Je - sus, I long to be per - fect - ly whole: I want Thee for -
2. Lord Je - sus, look down from Thy throne in the skies, And help me to
3. Lord Je - sus, for this I most humbly en - treat; I wait, blessed
4. Lord Je - sus, Thou see - est I pa - tient - ly wait; Come now, and with -

- ev - er to reign in my soul; Break down ev - 'ry i - dol, cast
make a complete sac - ri - fice; I give up my - self, and what
Lord, at Thy cru - ci - fied feet, By faith, for my cleansing, I
- in me a new heart cre - ate; To those who have sought Thee, Thou

out ev - 'ry foe; Now wash me, and I shall be whiter than snow.
ev - er I know—Now wash me, and I shall be whiter than snow.
see Thy blood flow—Now wash me, and I shall be whiter than snow.
nev - er said'st No—Now wash me, and I shall be whiter than snow.

CHORUS.

Whit - er than snow, yes, whit - er than snow;

Now wash me, and I shall be whit - er than snow.

77

121   **Mear. C. M.**

HARRIET AUBER.   WELSH AIR, AARON WILLIAMS.

1. With joy we hail the sa-cred day, Which God has call'd his own;

With joy the summons we o-bey, To wor-ship at his throne.

2 Thy chosen temple, Lord, how fair!
  As here thy servants throng
To breathe the humble, fervent prayer,
  And pour the grateful song.

3 Spirit of grace! O deign to dwell
  Within thy Church below;
Make her in holiness excel,
  With pure devotion glow.

122

1 Lord, in the morning thou shalt hear
  My voice ascending high;

To thee will I direct my prayer;
  To thee lift up mine eye:

2 Up to the heavens where Christ is gone
  To plead for all his saints,
Presenting at his Father's throne
  Our songs and our complaints.

3 O, may thy Spirit guide my feet
  In ways of righteousness:
Make every path of duty straight
  And plain before my face!

ISAAC WATTS.

——o——

123   **Golden Hill. S. M.**

1. Now is th'ac-cept-ed time; Now is the day of grace;

Then, sin-ners, come, without de-lay, And seek the Saviour's face.

2 Now is th'accepted time;
  The Saviour calls to-day;
To-morrow it may be too late:
  Then why will you delay?

3 Now is th'accepted time;
  The Spirit bids you come;
And every promise in his word
  Declares there yet is room.

Ariel. C. P. M.

C. WESLEY.   LOWELL MASON.

1. O, glo-rious hope of per-fect love! It lifts me up to things a-bove;

It bears on eagle's wings; It gives my ravish'd soul a taste, And

makes me for some moments feast With Jesus, priests and kings. With Jesus, priests and [kings.

2 Rejoicing now in earnest hope,
  I stand, and from the mountain top
    See all the land below:
  Rivers of milk and honey rise,
  And all the fruits of Paradise
    In endless plenty grow.

3 A land of corn, and wine, and oil,
  Favored with God's peculiar smile,
    With every blessing blest;
  There dwells the Lord our righteousness,
  And keeps his own in perfect peace
    And everlasting rest.

4 O, that I might at once go up;
  No more on this side Jordan stop,
    But now the land possess!
  This moment end my toilsome years,
  Sorrows, and sins, and doubts, and fears,
    A howling wilderness!

125

1 O could we speak the matchless worth,
  O, could we sound the glories forth,

  Which in our Saviour shine!
  We'd soar, and touch the heavenly strings
  And vie with Gabriel, while he sings,
    In notes almost divine.

2 We'd sing the precious blood he spilt,
  Our ransom from the dreadful guilt
    Of sin and wrath divine;
  We'd sing his glorious righteousness,
  In which all perfect heavenly dress,
    We shall forever shine.

3 We'd sing the characters he bears,
  And all the forms of love he wears,
    Exalted on his throne;
  In loftiest songs of sweetest praise
  We would to everlasting days
    Make all his glories known.

4 Yes, the delightful day will come,
  When Christ our Lord will bring us home,
    And we shall see his face!
  Then, with our Saviour, Brother, Friend,
  A blest eternity we'll spend,
    Triumphant through his grace.

Hamburg. L. M.

FROM A GREGORIAN CHANT.

1. Just as I am, with-out one plea, But that thy blood was shed for me,

And that thou bidst me come to thee, O, Lamb of God, I come, I come!

2 Just as I am, and waiting not,
    To rid my soul of one dark blot,
    To thee whose blood can cleanse each
        spot,
        O Lamb of God, I come, I come!

3 Just as I am, though tossed about
    With many a conflict, many a doubt,
    Fightings within, and fears without,
        O Lamb of God, I come, I come!

4 Just as I am—poor, wretched, blind;
    Sight, riches, healing of the mind,
    Yea, all I need in thee to find,
        O Lamb of God, I come, I come!

127

1 Around the table of our Lord,
    We come to eat with sweet accord;
    And thus obey his loving word,
        Until he come, until he come.

2 "Do this," he said: "Remember me:
    My grief and pain are all for thee;
    And this example thine shall be,
        Until I come, until I come."

3 In the lone garden, there he prayed;
    Upon the cross he bowed his head:
    Let us remember what he said,
        Until he come, until he come.

4 And when no more we gather here,
    Nor to this table may draw near,
    May we sit down with him so dear,
        When he shall come, when he shall
            come!

128

1 'Twas on that dark and doleful night,
    The powers of earth and hell arose
Against the Son of God's delight,
    And friends betrayed him to his foes.

2 Before the mournful scene began,
    He took the bread, and blessed, and
        brake:
What love through all his actions ran!
    What wondrous words of grace he
        spake!

3 "In memory of your dying Lord,
    Do this," he said, "till time shall end:
Meet at my table, and record
    The love of your departed Friend."

4 Jesus, thy feast we celebrate;
    We show thy death, we sing thy name,
    Till thou return, and we shall eat
    The marriage-supper of the Lamb.

129

1 Kingdoms and thrones to God belong;
    Crown him, ye nations, in your song;
    His wondrous name and power rehearse,
    His honors shall enrich your verse.

2 Proclaim him King, pronounce him blest,
    He's your defence, your joy, your rest;
    When terrors rise, when nations faint,
    God is the strength of every saint.

3 Jesus shall reign where'er the sun
    Does his successive journeys run;
    His kingdom stretch from shore to shore,
    Till moons shall wax and wane no more.

4 Blessings abound where'er he reigns;
    The prisoner leaps to loose his chains;
    The weary find eternal rest,
    And all the sons of want are blest.

5 Let every creature rise and bring
    Peculiar honors to our King!
    Angels descend with songs again,
    And earth repeat the loud Amen.

130 Wondrous Love.

MRS. M. STOCKTON.   WM. G. FISCHER, by per.

1. God lov'd the world of sinners lost And ruin'd by the fall ; Salvation full, at

highest cost, He offers free to all.

CHORUS.

O, 'twas love, 'twas wondrous love ! The love of God to me ; It bro't my Saviour from above, To die on Cal-va-ry.

2
E'en now by faith I claim Him mine,
The risen Son of God ;
Redemption by His love I find,
And cleansing through His blood.
    O, 'twas love, &c.

3
Love brings the glorious fullness in,
And to his saints makes known

The blessed rest, when freed from sin,
Through faith in Christ alone.
    O, 'twas love, &c.

4
Believing souls rejoice and sing ;
Sing as you forward go
To meet your glorious, coming King,
And all His love to know.
    O, 'twas love, &c.

———o———

131 Who'll Stand Up for Jesus?

L. HARTSOUGH.   L. HARTSOUGH.

Fine.

1. O, who'll stand up for Je-sus, The low-ly Naz-a-rene?
   And raise the blood-stain'd banner A-mid the............ hosts of sin?
D.C. All hail reproach or sorrow, If Je-sus............ leads me there.

CHORUS.   *D.C.*

The Cross for Christ I'll cher-ish, Its cru-ci-fix-ion bear ;

2 O, who will follow Jesus,
   Amid reproach and shame?
Where others shrink or falter,
Who'll glory in his name?
    The Cross for Christ, &c.

3 My all to Christ I've given,
   My talents, time, and voice,
Myself, my reputation,
The lone way is my choice.
    The Cross for Christ, &c.

132   Amazing Grace. C. M.

JOHN NEWTON.   ARR. by BRO. E. LEE.

1. A - maz-ing grace, how sweet the sound That sav'd a wretch like me!
     I once was lost, but now am found, Was blind, but now I see!

'Twas grace that taught my heart to fear, And grace my fears re - liev'd;..

How pre-cious did that grace ap-pear, The hour I first be - liev'd.

2 Thro' many dangers, toils and snares,
    I have already come;
    'Tis grace has brought me safe thus far,
    And grace will lead me home.
The Lord hath promised good to me,
    His word my hope secures;
He will my shield and portion be,
    As long as life endures.

3 Yes, when this flesh and heart shall fail,
    And mortal life shall cease,
I shall possess, within the veil,
    A life of joy and peace.
This earth will soon dissolve like snow,
    The sun forbear to shine;
But God, who called me here below,
    Will be forever mine.

——o——

133   Arise, my Soul.

1. Arise, my soul, arise! Shake off thy guilty fears;
   The bleeding sacri-fice In my behalf appears; Before the throne my Saviour

stands, My name is written on his hands, My name is writ-ten on his hands.

2 To God I'm reconciled;
    His pardoning voice I hear;
He owns me for his child;

I can no longer fear;
With confidence I now draw nigh,
And Father, Abba, Father, cry.

134 Beautiful Gates.

MISS V. M. SALTMARSH.   GEO. H. INGALLS.

1. Beau-ti-ful gates to the Cit-y of gold, Sparkling so bright, I would see;

O, when my pil-grim-age journey shall end, Then will they o-pen to me.

CHORUS.

Beau-ti-ful gates to the Cit-y of gold, Beau-ti-ful gates, Beau-ti-ful gates,

Beau-ti-ful gates I soon shall behold, Beau-ti - ful, beau-ti - ful gates!

2 Beautiful gates! now I know they are near,
  Brighter my pathway has grown;
  Light from the City begins to appear,
  Glorious light from His throne.
  Beautiful gates, &c.

3 Wash'd in the blood of the Lamb that was slain,
  Wash'd and made sinless and white,
  So shall I enter, and ever remain
  Safe in the city of light.
  Beautiful gates, &c.

——o——

135 Naomi. C. M.

1. { Father, whate'er of earthly bliss Thy sov'reign will denies,
     Accepted at thy throne of grace, Let.............this pe-ti-tion rise.

2 Give me a calm, a thankful heart,
  From every murmur free;
  The blessings of thy grace impart,
  And make me live to thee.

3 Oh, let the hope that thou art mine,
  Me everywhere attend;
  Thy presence thro' my journey shine,
  And crown my journey's end.

136 I My Cross Have Taken.

H. F. LYTE.

C. W. A. MOZART.

1. Je - sus, I my cross have ta-ken, All to leave and fol-low thee;

Na-ked, poor, despis'd, for-sa-ken.Thou, from hence, my all shalt be:

D.S.Yet how rich is my con-di - tion,While I make thee all my own.

Per - ish ev - 'ry fond am-bi-tion, All I've sought, and hop'd, and known;

2 Let the world despise and leave me,
  They have left my Saviour too;
  Human hearts and looks deceive me,
  Thou art faithful, thou art true.
  O, 'tis not in grief to harm me,
  While thy love is left to me!
  O, 'twere not in joy to charm me,
  If that love were hid from me!

3 Soul, then know thy full salvation;
  Rise o'er sin, and fear, and care;
  Joy to find, in every station,
  Something still to do or bear.
  Think what Spirit dwells within thee;
  Think what Father's smiles are thine;
  Think that Jesus died to win thee;
  Child of God, canst thou repine?

4 Haste thee on from grace to glory,
  Armed with faith and winged by
    prayer;
  An eternal day's before thee;
  God's own hand shall bring thee there;
  Soon shall close thy earthly mission,
  Soon shall pass thy pilgrim days;
  Hope shall change to glad fruition,
  Faith to sight, and prayer to praise.

137

1 Righteous God! whose vengeful vials
  All our fears and thoughts exceed,
  Big with woes and fiery trials,
  Hanging, bursting o'er our head;
  While thou visitest the nations,
  Thy selected people spare;
  Arm our cautioned souls with patience,
  Fill our humbled hearts with prayer.

2 If thy dreadful controversy
  With all flesh is now begun,
  In thy wrath remember mercy;
  Mercy first and last be shown.
  Plead thy cause with sword and fire;
  Shake us till the curse remove,
  Till thou com'st, the saints' desire,
  Crowning them with perfect love.

3 Every fresh alarming token
  More confirms the written word;
  Nature, for its Lord hath spoken,
  Must be suddenly restored.
  From this national confusion,
  From this ruined earth and skies,
  See the times of restitution,
  See the new creation rise!

138 Oh, How I Ought to Love Him.

Arr. by Geo. E. Lee.

1. { O, how I ought to love Him, O, how I ought to love Him,
{ O, how I ought to love Him, (Omit......................)

Be-cause He took me in, took me in, To his fa-vor, took me in,

To his fa-vor, took me in, To his favor, my Saviour took me in.

2 He saw me when a stranger,
‖: He saw me when a stranger, :‖
And kindly took me in;
‖: To his favor took me in, :‖
To his favor, my Saviour took me in.

3 I'll meet you in the morning,
‖: I'll meet you in the morning, :‖
When Jesus comes to reign;
‖: In his kingdom comes to reign, :‖
In his kingdom, my Saviour comes to reign.

4 I'll give Him all the glory,
‖: I'll give Him all the glory, :‖
When He shall come to reign;
‖: In his kingdom come to reign, :‖
In his kingdom, my Saviour comes to reign.

5 We'll sing the song of triumph,
‖: We'll sing the song of triumph, :‖
When Jesus comes to reign;
‖: In his kingdom comes to reign, :‖
In his kingdom, my Saviour comes to reign.

—o—

139   I'm a Traveler.

1. { I'm a lone-ly trav-'ler here, Wea-ry, op-press'd,
{ But my jour-ney's end is near, (Omit..................)

Soon I shall rest. Dark and dreary is the way, Toil-ing I've come,

Ask me not with you to stay. Yon-der's my home

140 Missionary Chant. L. M.

H. C. ZEUNER.

1. Go forth, ye heralds, in His name; Sweetly the Gospel trumpet sound;

The glorious ju - bi-lee pro-claim Where'er the hu - man race is found.

2 The joyful news to all impart,
And teach them where salvation lies;
With care bind up the wounded heart,
And wipe the tears from weeping eyes.

3 Be wise as serpents, as you go,
But harmless as the the peaceful dove;
And let your heav'n-taught conduct show
That you're commissioned from above.

4 Freely from Him ye do receive,
Freely, in love, to others give;
Thus they your doctrines will believe,
And, by the gospel they may live.

141

1 Shall I, for fear of feeble man,
The Spirit's course in me restrain?
Or undismayed in deed and word
Be a true witness for my Lord?

2 Awed by a mortal's frown, shall I
Conceal the word of God Most High?
How, then, before Him shall I dare
To stand, or how his anger bear?

3 Shall I, to soothe th' unholy throng,
Soften his truth, or smooth my tongue?

Shall I to gain earth's trifles, flee
The cross endured, my Lord, by thee?

4 What, then, is he whose scorn I dread?
Whose wrath or hate makes me afraid?
A man! an heir of death! a slave
To sin! a bubble on the wave!

142

1 Come, weary souls, with sin oppressed,
Come and accept the promised rest;
The Saviour's gracious call obey,
And cast your doubts and fears away.

2 Here mercy's boundless ocean flows,
To cleanse your guilt, and heal your woes;
Pardon and life, and endless peace;
How rich the gift! how free the grace!

3 Lord, we accept, with thankful heart,
The hope thy gracious words impart;
We come with trembling, yet rejoice,
And bless the kind inviting voice.

4 Dear Saviour! by thy power and love,
Confirm our faith—our fears remove;
O sweetly reign in every breast,
And guide us to eternal rest.

——0——

143 Come, My Brethren.

Fine.

1. Come, my breth-ren, let us try For a lit-tle sea-son,
Ev-'ry bur-den to lay by; Come, and let us rea-son.

D.C. Speak, and let the worst be known, Speak-ing may re-lieve you.

D.C.

What is this that casts you down? What is this that grieves you?

144   In God We Trust.

Lucy D. Harrington.   A. T. Gorham.

1. In God we trust, tho' dark the hour, And light be hid from view;

Tho' threat'ning clouds still o'er us lower, And screen our heaven's clear blue.

Each cloud is sil-ver-lin'd and bright, And beauty yet shall greet our sight.

REFRAIN.

We fear no more, but glad-ly sing, In God we trust, In God we trust;

We soar on Faith's tri-umphant wing—In God we trust, In God we trust.

2
Deep calleth unto deep, O Lord,
  The waves almost o'erwhelm;
Sweet comfort doth this thought afford,
  That thou dost guide the helm,
And angry waves shall cease to be,
For Jesus walks the raging sea.

3
Faith stronger grows in midnight hour,
  And waits the dawn of day;
Dark unbelief shall lose its pow'r,
  The shadows flee away.
His voice so sweet bids—'Peace, be still,'
And mountain waves obey His will.

145 Come Unto Me.

Miss E. Kellaway.

Geo. E. Lee.

1. Hark! 'tis the voice of Je-sus, Call-ing to thee, Wea-ry and burden'd one,

"Come un-to me." { For thee my blood was spilt, To take a-way thy.........guilt;

I'll cleanse thee, if thou wilt... But come to me.

2 Hark! 'tis the voice of Jesus
  Calling to thee;
"Speak for me while thou may'st;
  In me be free.
The world may mock and sneer,
But thou need'st never fear,
For I am always near;
  So speak for me."

3 Hark! 'tis the voice of Jesus,
  Calling to thee;
"I come again that thou
  Mayst come to me.
And when I come again,
Thou shalt be freed from pain,
And in my kingdom reign
  Eternally."

—o—

146 Christian's Triumph.

1. { Children of the heav'nly King, As we jour-ney, let us sing;
   { Sing our Saviour's wor-thy praise, Glo-rious in his works and ways.
D.C. Oh, how hap-py we shall be, When we've gain'd the vic-to-ry.

CHORUS.   D.C.

Vic-to-ry, vic-to-ry, When we've gain'd the vic-to-ry;

2 Fear not, brethren, joyful stand
  On the borders of our land;
Jesus Christ, our Father's Son,
Bids us undismayed go on.

3 Lord! obediently we'll go,
  Gladly leaving all below;
Only thou our leader be,
And we still will follow thee.

Balerma. C. M.

L. MASON.

1. Come, anx-ious sin-ner, in whose breast A thousand thoughts re-volve;

Come, with your guilt and fear op-press'd, And make this last.. re-solve:

2 "I'll go to Jesus, though my sin
    Hath like a mountain rose;
I know his courts, I'll enter in,
    Whatever may oppose.

3 "Prostrate I'll lie before his throne,
    And there my guilt confess;
I'll tell him I'm a wretch undone
    Without his pard'ning grace.

4 "Perhaps he will admit my plea,
    Perhaps will hear my prayer;
But if I perish, I will go,
    And perish only there."

148

1 Plung'd in a gulf of dark despair,
    We wretched sinners lay;
Without one cheerful beam of hope,
    Or spark of rising day.

2 With pitying eyes the Prince of Grace
    Beheld our helpless grief;
He saw, and, O, amazing love!
    He flew to our relief.

3 O, for this love let rocks and hills
    Their lasting silence break,
And all harmonious human tongues
    The Saviour's praises speak!

149

1 Return, O wand'rer, now return,
    And seek thy Father's face;
These new desires that in thee burn
    Were kindled by his grace.

2 Return, O wand'rer, now return,
    He hears thy humble sigh;
He sees thy softened spirit mourn,
    When no one else is nigh.

3 Return, O wand'rer, now return;
    Thy Saviour bids thee live;
Go to his feet, and gladly learn
    How freely he'll forgive.

4 Return, O wand'rer, now return,
    And dry the falling tear;
Thy Father calls, no longer mourn,
    'Tis love invites thee near.

—o—

150   What I Want.

1. { Here, as I go o'er life's rough way, I want more faith in Je-sus; }
   { In ev-'ry thing I do or say, I want more faith in Je-sus: }

Cho. What I want, what I want, what I want, Is more faith in Je-sus.

2 When trials come, and troubles rise,
   I want more faith, &c.
'Neath cloudless heav'ns or stormy skies,
   I want more faith, &c.—Cho.

3 While here the cross I have to bear,
   I want more faith, &c.

And at all times and everywhere
   I want more faith, &c.—Cho.

4 I want more love for Jesus near,
   I want more faith in Jesus,
To wait for him till he appear,
   I want more faith in Jesus.--Cho.

Frederick. 11s.

GEORGE KEITH, 1787.　　　　　　　　　　　　　　GEORGE KINGSLEY.

1. How firm a foundation, Ye saints of the Lord, Is laid for your

faith in his ex-cel-lent word; What more can he say than to

you he hath said, You, who un-to Je-sus for ref-uge hath fled!

2 In every condition, in sickness, in health,
In poverty's vale, or abounding in wealth,
At home and abroad, on the land, on the sea,
As thy days may demand shall thy strength ever be.

3 "Fear not, I am with thee, O be not dismayed!
For I am thy God, and will still give thee aid;
I'll strengthen thee, help thee, and cause thee to stand,
Upheld by my gracious omnipotent hand.

4 "When through the deep waters I call thee to go,
The rivers of woe shall not thee overflow;
For I will be with thee thy troubles to bless,
And sanctify to thee thy deepest distress.

5 "When through fiery trials thy pathway shall lie,
My grace all-sufficient shall be thy supply;
The flame shall not hurt thee; I only design
Thy dross to consume, and thy gold to refine.

6 "The soul that on Jesus doth lean for repose,
I will not, I will not desert to his foes:
That soul, though all hell should endeavor to shake,
I'll never, no, never, no, never forsake."

152
——o——

1 Thou sweet gliding Kedron, by thy silver stream,
The Saviour at midnight, when moonlight's pale beam
Shone bright on the waters, would frequently stray,
And lose, in thy murmurs, the toils of the day.

2 O garden of Olivet, thou dear honored spot,
The fame of thy wonders shall ne'er be forgot;
The theme most transporting to seraphs above,
The triumph of sorrow, the triumph of love.

1. { Hark! ten thousand, thousand voices, Sound the note of ju - bi - lee;
Je - sus reigns, and earth re - joices, End-ed her cap - tiv - i - ty. }

See, He sits up-on his throne,   Jesus rules the world a - lone,

See, He sits   up-on his throne,   Je-sus rules   the world a - lone.

Hal - le - lu - jah! Hal - le - lu - jah! Hal - le - lu - jah! A - men.

2 King of glory, reign forever,
  Thine an everlasting crown;
Nothing from thy love shall sever
  Those whom thou shalt call thine own;
Happy objects of thy grace,
  Destined to behold thy face.—
    Hallelujah! Hallelujah! &c.

3 Saviour, hasten thine appearing;
  Bring, O bring the glorious day,
When, the awful summons hearing,
  Heaven and earth shall pass away;
Then with golden harps we'll sing,
  "Glory, glory to our King."—
    Hallelujah! Hallelujah! &c.

154

1 Love divine, all love excelling,
  Joy of heaven, to earth come down;
Make with us thy glorious dwelling;
  All thy faithful people crown.
Jesus, thou art all compassion;
  Pure, unbounded love thou art;
Visit us with thy salvation;
  Come, and nevermore depart.

2 Breathe, O breathe thy peaceful Spirit
  Into every troubled breast;
Let us all thy grace inherit;
  Bring us to the promised rest.
Take away the love of sinning;
  Take our doubts and fears away;
End the work of thy beginning;
  Bring us to th' eternal day.

155

1 Hark! what mean those holy voices,
  Sweetly sounding through the skies?
Lo, th' angelic host rejoices;
  Heavenly hallelujahs rise.
Hear them tell the wondrous story;
  Hear them chant in hymns of joy,—
"Glory in the highest, glory!
  Glory be to God most high!

2 "Peace on earth, good will from heav'n,
  Reaching far as man is found;
Souls redeemed, and sins forgiven!
  Loud our golden harps shall sound.
Christ is born, the great Anointed;
  Heaven and earth his praises sing;
O, receive whom God appointed
  For your Prophet, Priest, and King."

CAWOOD.

Comfort in Affliction

MRS. M. A. KIDDER.—*used by per. Biglow & Main.*   S. C. HANCOCK.

1. Though we sleep, 'tis not for-ev - er, There will be a glorious dawn!
2. When we see a precious blossom, That we tended with such care,

We shall meet to part, no, nev - er, On the res - ur - rec-tion morn!
Rudely ta - ken from our bo - som, How our hearts al-most despair!

From the deepest caves of o - cean, From the desert and the plain,
Round its lit-tle grave we lin - ger Till the setting sun is low,

From the val - ley and the mountain, Countless throngs shall rise a - gain!
Feel - ing all our hopes have perished With the flow'r we cherished so.

CHORUS.

Though we sleep, 'tis not for-ev - er, There will be a glorious dawn;

Comfort in Affliction.

We shall meet to part, no, nev-er, On the res-ur-rec-tion morn.

3 Though we sleep, 'tis not forever
In the lone and silent grave;
Blessed be the Lord that taketh,
Blessed be the Lord that gave.

In the bright eternal city,
Death can never, never come;
In his own good time he'll call us
From our rest to home, sweet home.

——o——

157   Sabbath Morn.   7s.

JOHN NEWTON.   LOWELL MASON.

1. { Safe-ly through an-oth-er week, God has brought us on our way;
{ Let us now a blessing seek, (Omit..........................)

Wait-ing in his courts to-day: { Day of all the week the best,
{ Day of all the week the best,

Em-blem of e-ter-nal rest. }
(Omit..........................)   Em-blem of e-ter-nal rest.

2 While we seek supplies of grace,
Through the dear Redeemer's name,
Show thy reconciling face,
Take away our sin and shame;
|: From our worldly cares set free,
May we rest this day in thee. :|

3 Here we come thy name to praise;
May we feel thy presence near:
May thy glory meet our eyes,
While we in thy house appear;
|: Here afford us, Lord, a taste
Of our everlasting feast. :|

Migdol. L. M.

L. MASON.

1. Soon may the last glad song a-rise, Thro' all the millions of the skies,

That song of triumph which records That all the earth is now the Lord's.

2 Let thrones and pow'rs and kingdoms be
Obedient, mighty God, to thee!
And over land, and stream, and main,
Now wave the scepter of thy reign.

3 O let that glorious anthem swell;
Let host to host the triumph tell,
That not one rebel heart remains,
But over all the Saviour reigns.

159

1 Jesus! thy church, with longing eyes,
For thine expected coming sighs,
When will the promised light arise,
And glory beam on Zion's gates?

2 O come and reign o'er every land,
Let Satan from his throne be hurled,
All nations bow to thy command,
And grace revive a dying world.

3 Teach us in watchfulness and prayer,
To wait for thine appointed hour;
And fit us, by thy grace, to share
The triumphs of thy conqu'ring power.

160

1 Awake, my soul, lift up thine eyes,
See where thy foes against thee rise,
In long array, a numerous host;
Awake, my soul, or thou art lost.

2 Thou tread'st upon enchanted ground;
Perils and snares beset thee round;
Beware of all, guard every part,
But most the traitor in thy heart.

3 Come, then, my soul, now learn to wield
The weight of thine immortal shield;
Put on the armor from above
Of heavenly truth and heavenly love.

—o—

161   Grace is Free.

1. { By faith I see the Saviour dy-ing On the tree, on the tree; }
{ To ev-'ry one I hear him cry-ing, "Look to me, look to me." }

He bids the guilty now draw near, Re-pent, believe, dis-miss their fear;

Hark! hark! what precious words I hear, "Grace is free, grace is free!"

162   Jesus is Coming Again.

Miss. JESSIE E. STROUT.   GEO. E. LEE.

1. Lift up the trumpet, oh, loud let it ring! Je-sus is coming a-gain!

Cheer up, ye pilgrims, be joy-ful and sing, Je-sus is coming a-gain!

CHORUS.

Com-ing a-gain, Com-ing a-gain, Je-sus is com-ing a-gain!

2 Echo it, hill-tops, proclaim it, ye plains, Jesus, &c.
   Coming in glory, the Lamb that was slain, Jesus, &c.—*Cho.*
3 Sound it, old ocean, in thy mighty wave, Jesus, &c.
   Break on the sands of the shores that ye lave, Jesus, &c.—*Cho.*
4 Heavings of earth, tell the vast, wond'ring throng, Jesus, &c.
   Tempests and whirlwinds, the anthem prolong, Jesus, &c.—*Cho.*
5 Nations are angry,—by this we do know, Jesus is coming again!
   Knowledge increases ; men run to and fro, Jesus, &c.—*Cho.*

—o—

163   I Am on My Way.

1. Christians, I am on my journey! Ere I reach the crystal sea,   *Fine.*

I would tell the wondrous sto-ry, What the Lord has done for me.

D.S. I am on my way to Zi-on, I'm a pil-grim go-ing home.

CHORUS.   **D.S.**

Glo-ry, glo-ry, hal-le-lu-jah, Tho' a stran-ger here I roam,

2 I was lost, but Jesus found me,   Looks beyond a world of sorrow,
   Taught my heart to seek his face ;   To the city from above.
From a wild and lonely desert,
   Brought me to his fold of grace.   4 I shall soon behold my Saviour,
       When this dreary day is o'er ;
3 Now my soul with rapture glowing,   I shall cast my crown before him
   Sings aloud his pard'ning love ;   I shall praise him evermore.

Bridgewater. L. M.

C. WESLEY.   L. EDSCR.

1. Come, sin-ners, to   the gos-pel feast; Let ev-'ry soul be Ye need not one be   left be-hind, Ye

Je-sus' guest; Ye need not one be   left be-hind, Ye   need not one be

need not one   be left   be-hind, For God hath bid-den all   man-kind.
left be-hind, For God   hath bid - - - den all man-kind.

2 Sent by my Lord, on you I call;
The invitation is to all;
Come, all the world! come, sinner, thou!
All things in Christ are ready now.

3 Come, all ye souls by sin oppressed,
Ye restless wanderers after rest,
Ye poor, and maim'd, and halt, and blind,
In Christ a hearty welcome find.

4 My message as from God receive:
Ye all may come to Christ and live;
O, let his love your hearts constrain,
Nor suffer him to die in vain.

165

1 Great God, attend while Zion sings
The joy that from thy presence springs;
To spend one day with thee on earth
Exceeds a thousand days of mirth.

2 Might I enjoy the meanest place
Within thy house, O God of grace,
Not tents of ease or thrones of power
Should tempt my feet to leave thy door.

3 God is our Sun—he makes our day;
God is our Shield—he guards our way
From all assaults of hell and sin,
From foes without and foes within.

4 All needful grace will God bestow,
And crown that grace with glory, too;
He gives us all things, and withholds
No real good from upright souls.
I. WATTS.

DOXOLOGY.

Praise God, from whom all blessings flow ·
Praise him, all creatures here below;
Praise him above, ye heavenly host,
Praise Father, Son, and Holy Ghost.

166

1 Jesus, thy blood and righteousness
My beauty are, my glorious dress;
'Midst flaming worlds, in these arrayed,
With joy shall I lift up my head.

2 Bold shall I stand in that great day,
For who aught to my charge shall lay!
Fully, through thee, absolved I am
From sin's tremendous curse and shame.

3 This spotless robe the same appears
When ruined nature sinks in years;
No age can change its glorious hue;
The robe of Christ is ever new.

4 O, let the dead now hear thy voice!
Now bid thy banished ones rejoice!
Their beauty this, their glorious dress,
"Jesus, the Lord our Righteousness."

167   Sweet Home.   11s.

1. Mid scenes of confusion and creature complaints, How sweet to my soul is communion with saints!
2. Sweet bonds that unite all the children of peace; And thrice precious Jesus, whose love cannot cease,
3.   I sigh from this body   of sin to be free, Which hinders my joy and communion with thee;
4.   While here in this valley of conflict I stay, O give me submission and strength as my day;

To find at the banquet of mercy there's room, And feel in the presence of Je - sus at home!
Tho' oft from thy presence in sadness I roam, I long to behold thee, in glo - ry, at home!
Tho' now my temptations like billows may foam, All, all will be peace, when I'm with thee at home.
In all my afflictions to thee would I come, Re - joic-ing in hope of my glo - ri - ous home.

Home, home, sweet, sweet home, Pre-pare me, dear Saviour, for glo - ry, my home.

168

——o——

1 The pleasures of earth I have seen fade away;
   They bloom for a season, but soon they decay;
   But pleasures more lasting in Jesus are given,
   Salvation on earth, and the kingdom of heaven.
     Home, home, sweet, sweet home—
     The saints in those mansions are ever at home.

2 Allure me no longer, ye false, glowing charms;
   The Saviour invites me, I'll go to his arms;
   At the banquet of mercy I hear there is room;
   O there may I feast with his children at home!
     Home, home, sweet, sweet home—
     O Jesus, conduct me, I pray, to my home!

3 Farewell, vain amusements, my follies, adieu,
   While Jesus, his kingdom and glory I view;
   I feast on the pleasures that flow from his throne,
   The foretaste divine of my heavenly home.
     Home, home, sweet, sweet home—
     O when shall I share the fruition of home?

4 Affliction and sorrow, and death shall be o'er;
   The saints shall unite to be parted no more;
   Their loud hallelujahs fill heaven's high dome;
   They dwell with the Saviour, forever at home.
     Home, home, sweet, sweet home—
     They dwell with the Saviour forever at home.

169 The Shining Shore. 8s & 7s.

By permission of O. Ditson & Co.

G. F. Root.

1. My days are glid-ing swiftly by, And I, a pilgrim stranger,

Would not de-tain them as they fly! Those hours of toil and dan-ger;

CHORUS.

For oh! we stand on Jordan's strand, And soon we'll all pass o-ver,

And just be-fore, the shin-ing shore We may al-most dis-cov-er.

2 We'll gird our loins, my brethren, dear,
Our distant home discerning:
Our absent Lord has left us word,
"Let every lamp be burning."—*Cho.*

3 Should coming days be cold and dark,
We need not cease our singing;

That perfect rest nought can molest,
Where golden harps are ringing.–*Cho.*

4 Let sorrow's rudest tempest blow,
Each chord on earth to sever, [home
Our King says "come," and there's our
Forever, oh! for ever!—*Cho.*

——o——

170 Glory to the Lamb.

Fine. D.C.

{ The world is o-ver-come by the blood of the Lamb, }
{ The world is o-ver-come by the blood of the Lamb. } Glory to the Lamb.

D.C. Glo-ry to the Lamb, Glory to the Lamb.

171 Ganges. C. P. M.

1. Come on, my partners in dis - tress, My comrades thro' this wilderness,

Who still your bodies feel: A - while for - get your griefs and fears,

And look be - yond this vale of tears, To that ce - les - tial hill.

2 Who suffer with our Master here,
Shall soon before his face appear,
And by his side sit down ;
To patient faith the prize is sure,
And all that to the end endure
The cross, shall wear the crown.

3 Thrice blessed, bliss-inspiring hope,
It lifts the fainting spirit up,
It brings to life the dead ;
Our conflicts here shall soon be past,
And you and I ascend at last,
To meet our living Head.

172 "Are We Almost There?" P. M.

1. "Are we almost there? are we al - most there?" Says the weary saint as he sighs for home;
2. Then he talks of the flow'rs, the unsullied stream, That flows thro' the Para - dise of God;
3. He is weary and sick of this world's rude strife, And pants for a ho - ly, peace-ful clime:

"Are those the ver-dant trees that rear Their stately forms 'mid heaven's bright dome?"
And he longs to wake from life's troubled dream, To walk those gold-en streets a-broad.
To glow with the vig-or of end-less life, And be compass'd no more by the scenes of time.

4 His eye is fixed on the world to come,
He walks by faith through this vale of care,
And oft inquires as he draws near home,
With anxious heart, "Are we almost there?"

5 He is waiting to hear the trumpet sound,
And to meet his Saviour in the air;
The day-star dawns—soon with joyous bound,
He can say indeed—"We are almost there!"

173 Sweet the Moments. 8s & 7s.

J. W. DADMAN.

1. Sweet the mo-ments, rich in blessing, Which be - fore the cross I spend,

Life and health and peace possessing, From the sinner's dy - ing Friend.

Love and grief my heart di - vid-ing, With my tears his feet I'll bathe;

Still in faith and hope a-bid-ing, Life de - riv - ing from his death.

2 O how blessed is this station!
  Low before the cross I'll lie,
  While I see divine compassion
  Pleading in the Saviour's eye:
  Here I'll sit, forever viewing
  Mercy streaming in his blood;
  Precious drops, my soul bedewing,
  Plead and claim my peace with God.

3 Here it is I find a heaven,
  While upon the Lamb I gaze;
  Here I see my sins forgiven,
  Lost in wonder, love and praise.
  May I still enjoy this feeling,
  In all need to Jesus go;
  Prove each day his blood more healing,
  And Himself more deeply know.

— o —

174 I will Sing for Jesus.

PHILIP PHILLIPS.

I will sing for Je-sus, With his blood he bought me; And all a-long my

CHORUS.

pilgrim way His loving hand has brought me. O ! help me sing for Jesus, Help me

tell the sto - ry Of Him who did re-deem us, The Lord of life and glo-ry.

175　Dundee.　C. M.

GUILLAUME FRANC.

1. Fath-er of mercies, in thy Word, What end-less glo-ry shines;

For-ev-er be thy name a-dor'd For these ce-les-tial lines.

2 'Tis here the Saviour's welcome voice
　　Spreads heavn'ly peace around;
　And life, and everlasting joys
　　Attend the blissful sound.

3 O, may these heavenly pages be
　　My ever sweet delight;

And still new beauties may I see,
　And still increasing light!

4 Divine Instructor, gracious Lord,
　　Be thou forever near;
　Teach me to love thy sacred word,
　　And view my Saviour here.

———o———

176　Brown.　C. M.

WM. B. BRADBURY.

1. Try us, O God, and search the ground of ev-'ry sin-ful heart;

Whate'er of sin in us is found, O! bid it all de-part.

2 If to the right or left we stray,
　　Leave us not comfortless,
　But guide our feet into the way
　　Of everlasting peace.

3 Help us to help each other, Lord,
　　Each other's cross to bear;
　Let each his friendly aid afford,
　　And feel his brother's care.

4 Help us to build each other up;
　　Our little stock improve;
　Increase our faith, confirm our hope,
　　And perfect us in love.

5 Up into thee, our living Head,
　　Let us in all things grow,
　Till thou hast made us free indeed,
　　And spotless here below.

Martyn. 7s.

WESLEY.

SIMEON B. MARSH.

Fine.

1. { Je - sus, ref - uge of my soul, Let me to thy bo-som fly, }
   { While the ra - ging billows roll, While the tem-pest still is high; }

D.C. Safe in - to the ha-ven guide, O, re-ceive me home at last.

Hide me, O my Sav - iour hide, Till the storm of life is past!

D.C.

2 Other refuge have I none;
  Hangs my helpless soul on thee;
Leave, oh, leave me not alone
  Still support and comfort me;
All my trust on thee is stayed.
  All my help from thee I bring;
Cover my defenceless head
  With the shadow of thy wing.

3 Thou, O Christ, art all I want;
  All in all in thee I find;
Raise the fallen, cheer the faint,
  Heal the sick, and lead the blind.
Just and holy is thy name,
  I am all unrighteousness;
Vile and full of sin I am,
  Thou art full of truth and grace.

4 Plenteous grace with thee is found,
  Grace to cover all my sin :
Let the healing streams abound;
  Make and keep me pure within.

Thou of life the fountain art!
  Freely let me take of thee:
Spring thou up within my heart,
  Rise to all eternity.

178

1 Son of God, thy people's shield,
  Must we still thine absence mourn!
Let thy promise be fulfilled ;
  Thou hast said, "I will return."
Gracious Master, soon appear ;
  Quickly bring thy morning light ;
Then will cease the constant tear,
  Hope be turned to joyful sight.

2 As a woman counts the days
  Till her absent lord she sees,
Longs and watches, weeps and prays,
  So the church must long for thee.
Come, that we may see thee nigh,
  Then thy sheep shall feed in peace;
Hush forever trouble's sigh,
  Sin and sorrow's triumphs cease.

——0——

179   Christ All the World to Me.

1

2

1. { My soul is now u - ni-ted To Christ the liv-ing vine;
   { His grace I long had slighted, But now I (*Omit*........ feel him mine.

CHORUS.

Christ is all the world to me, And his glo - ry I shall see:

And be - fore I'd leave my Saviour I would lay me down and die.

180 Long Time Ago. 8s & 4s.

1. Je - sus died on Calv'ry's mountain, Long time a - go; And sal-va - tion's

healing fountain Doth freely flow.

3 Jesus died, but lives forever—
　No more to die;
　Blessed Jesus, precious Saviour,
　Now sits on high.

4 Now in heav'n he's interceding
　For dying men;
　Soon he'll finish there his pleading,
　And come again.

2 Once his voice, in tones of pity,
　Was heard below;
　And he wept o'er Judah's city,
　Long time ago.

5 When he comes a voice from heaven
　Shall pierce the tomb:
　"Come ye blessed of my Father,
　Children—come home."

—o—

181 Jesus Saves Me All the Time.

JAS. NICHOLSON.　　　　　　　　　　　　J. A. DUNCAN.

1. Je - sus saves me ev - 'ry day, Je - sus saves me ev - 'ry night;

Je - sus saves me all the way—Thro' the dark - ness, thro' the light.

CHORUS.

Je - sus saves, O bliss sub-lime—Je - sus saves me all the time.

2 Jesus saves when I repine,
　Jesus saves when I rejoice;
Jesus saves when hopes decline—
　Faith can always hear his voice.

3 Jesus saves me, He is mine;
　Jesus saves me, I am His;

Jesus saves while I recline—
　On his precious promises.

4 Jesus saves, He saves from sin,
　Jesus saves, I feel Him nigh;
Jesus saves, He dwells within,
　Gladly do I testify.

182 What a Friend We Have.

ANON.   Western Melody.

1. What a friend we have in Je - sus, All our sins and griefs to bear;

What a pri - vi - lege to car - ry, Ev - ery-thing to God in pray'r.

O, what peace we of - ten for - feit, O, what need - less pain we bear,

Bis.

All because we do not carry, Every-thing to God in pray'r.
All because we do not carry, Every - - - - - thing to God in prayer.

2 Have we trials and temptations?
Is there trouble anywhere?
We should never be discouraged,
Take it to the Lord in prayer.
Can we find a friend so faithful,
Who will all our sorrows share,
|: Jesus knows our every weakness,
Take it to the Lord in prayer. :||

3 Are we weak and heavy laden,
Cumbered with a load of care,
Precious Saviour, still our refuge,
Take it to the Lord in prayer.
Do thy friends despise, forsake thee?
Take it to the Lord in prayer,
|: In his arms he'll take and shield thee,
Thou wilt find a solace there. :||

183 We Are Hasting Away.

1. { To - day, if you will hear his voice, Now is the time to make your choice; }
   { Say, will you to Mount Zi - on go? Say, will you have this Christ or no? }

CHORUS.

We are hasting away, we are hasting away, We are hasting away to the great

104   [judgment day.

184 **Zerah. C. M.**

L. Mason.

1. To us a Child of hope is born, To us a Son is giv'n;

Him shall the tribes of earth o - bey, Him all the hosts of heav'n.

Him shall the tribes of earth o - bey, Him all the hosts of heav'n.

2 His name shall be the Prince of peace,
   Forevermore ador'd;
‖: The Wonderful, the Counsellor,
   The great and mighty Lord. :‖

3 His pow'r, increasing, still shall spread;
   His reign no end shall know;
‖: Justice shall guard his throne of love,
   And peace abound below. :‖

4 To us a Child of hope is born;
   To us a Son is given;
‖: The Wonderful, the Counsellor,
   The mighty Lord of heaven. :‖

185

1 Soon all shall hear our Jesus' name,
  Angels shall prostrate fall;

‖: For him the brightest glory claim,
   And hail him Lord of all. :‖

2 The risen saints shall sound the lyre,
   And, as they sound it, fall
‖: Before his face, who formed their choir,
   And hail him Lord of all. :‖

3 The remnant saved from Israel's race,
   Redeemed from Israel's fall,
‖: Shall praise him for his wondrous grace,
   And hail him Lord of all. :‖

4 Gentiles shall come from every land,
   O'er all this earthly ball—
‖: Shall come, and on Mount Zion stand,
   And hail him Lord of all. :‖

—o—

186   Only Jesus Will I Know.

Fine.

1. { Vain, de - lu - sive world, a - dieu, With all.. of crea - ture good; }
   { On - ly Je - sus I pur - sue, Who bought me with his blood. }

D.C. On - ly Je - sus will I know, And Je - sus cru - ci - fied.

D.C.

All thy pleasures I.. fore-go, I tram-ple on thy wealth and pride:

105

187   The Alarm.   8s & 7s.

Slow.

1. We are liv-ing, we are dwelling, In a grand and aw-ful time;

In an age on a-ges tell-ing, To be liv-ing is sub-lime.

Lively.

Hark! the waking up of na-tions, Gog and Ma-gog to the fray;

Hark! what soundeth? is cre-a-tion Groaning for its lat-ter day!

2 Will ye play, then, will ye dally
With your music and your wine?
Up! it is Jehovah's rally!
God's own arm hath need of thine.
Hark! the onset! will ye fold your
Faith-clad arms in lazy lock?
Up! O up, thou drowsy soldier;
Worlds are charging to the shock!

3 Worlds are charging, heaven beholding,
Thou hast but an hour to fight;
Now the blazoned cross unfolding,
On—right onward for the right.
On! let all the soul within you,
For the truth's sake go abroad!
Strike! let every nerve and sinew
Tell on ages—tell for God!

——o——

188   Marching to Jerusalem.

1. { O brethren, will you meet me On that im-mor-tal shore?
{ O brethren, will you meet me Where part-ing is no more? }

CHORUS.

We are marching to Je-ru-sa-lem, We're marching to Je-

-ru-salem, We're marching to Je-ru-sa-lem, And soon shall be at home.

189 Salvation. 8s, 7s & 4s.

T. M. TOWNE.

O thou God of my sal-va-tion, My Redeem-er from all sin;
Mov'd by thy divine com-pas-sion, Who hast died my heart to win.

I will praise thee, I will praise thee, Where shall I thy praise be-gin?

2 While the angel choirs are crying,
Glory to the great I AM,
I with them will still be vieing,
Glory, Glory to the Lamb.
O how precious, O how precious,
Is the sound of Jesus' name.

3 Angels now are hov'ring round us,
Unperceived they near us throng,
Wond'ring at the love that crowned us,
Glad to join us in our song.
Hallelujah! Hallelujah!
Love and praise to Christ belong.

——o——

190 Melmore. L. M.

C. WESLEY.

1. Stay, thou in-sult-ed Spir-it, stay, Tho' I have done thee such despite;

Cast not a sin-ner quite a-way, Nor take thine ev-er-lasting flight.

2 Though I have most unfaithful been
Of all whoe'er thy grace received,
Ten thousand times thy goodness seen,
Ten thousand times thy goodness griev'd.

3 Yet, O, the chief of sinners spare,
In honor of my great High Priest;

Nor, in thy righteous anger, swear,
I shall not see thy people's rest.

4 My weary soul, O God, release;
Uphold me with thy gracious hand;
O, guide me into perfect peace,
And bring me to the promised land.

191   Dennis. S. M.

1. "Blest are the meek," he said, Whose doc - trine is.. di - vine;
"The hum-ble minds earth shall pos - sess, And brightly there shall shine.

2
"While on this earth they stay,
Sweet peace with them shall dwell;
And cheerful hope and heavenly joy,
Beyond what tongue can tell.

3
"The God of peace is theirs;
They own his gracious sway;
And, yielding all their wills to him,
His sov'reign laws obey.

4
"No angry passions move,
No envy fires the breast;
The prospect of eternal peace
Bids every trouble rest."

5
O gracious Father, grant
That we this influence feel,
That all we hope, or wish, may be
Subjected to thy will.

192   1
Blest be the tie that binds
Our hearts in Christian love;
The fellowship of kindred minds
Is like to that above.

2
Before our Father's throne,
We pour our ardent prayers;
Our fears, our hopes, our aims are one,
Our comforts and our cares.

3
We share our mutual woes,
Our mutual burdens bear;
And often for each other flows
The sympathizing tear.

4
When we asunder part,
It gives us inward pain;
But we shall still be joined in heart,
And hope to meet again.

5
This glorious hope revives
Our courage by the way,
While each in expectation lives,
And longs to see the day.

6
From sorrow, toil, and pain,
And sin we shall be free;
And perfect love and friendship reign
Through all eternity.

193   1   JOHN FAWCETT.
And are we yet alive,
And see each other's face?
Glory and praise to Jesus give,
For his redeeming grace.

2
Preserved by power divine
To full salvation here,
Again in Jesus' praise we join,
And in his sight appear.

3
What troubles have we seen,
What conflicts have we passed,
Fightings without, and fears within,
Since we assembled last!

4
But out of all the Lord
Hath brought us by his love;
And still he doth his help afford,
And hides our life above.

5
Then let us make our boast
Of his redeeming power,
Which saves us to the uttermost,
Till we can sin no more:

6
Let us take up the cross,
Till we the crown obtain;
And gladly reckon all things loss,
So we may Jesus gain.

194 Wentworth. C. M.

F. A. BLACKMER, by xr.

1. And must I be to judgment brought, And answer in that day

For ev - 'ry vain and i - dle thought, And ev - 'ry word I say?

Yes, ev - 'ry se - cret of my heart Shall short - ly be made known,

And I re - ceive my just de - sert For all that I have done.

2 How careful then ought I to live!
With what religious fear,
Who such a strict account must give
For my behaviour here!

If now thou standest at the door,
O let me feel thee near!
And make my peace with God, before
I at thy bar appear.

——o——

195 He Will Provide.

1. Tho' troubles as - sail and dan-gers af-fright, Tho' friends should all fail

D.S. The promise assures us

Fine.

and foes all u - nite, Yet one thing secures us what-ev - er be - tide,
The Lord will pro-vide.

109

Pleyel's Hymn. 7s.

C. WESLEY.

IGNACE PLEYEL 1800.

1. Sin-ners, turn, why will you die? God, your Ma - ker, asks you why;
2. Sin-ners, turn, why will you die? 'Tis your Sav - iour asks you why;

God, who did you be - ing give, Made you with him - self to live.
He who would your souls re - trieve, Died him-self that you might live.

3 Will you let him die in vain
Crucify your Lord again?
Why, ye ransom'd sinners, why,
Will ye slight his grace, and die?

4 Will you not his grace receive?
Will you still refuse to live?
O ye dying sinners, why,
Why will ye forever die?

— o —

197 **Entreaty. 8s, 7s & 4s.**

STEPHEN JENKS, 1808.

Hear, O sin-ner! Mer-cy hails you, Now with sweetest voice she calls;

{ Bids you haste to seek the Saviour, Ere the hand of jus - tice falls; }
{ Hear, O sin - ner! Hear, O sin-ner! 'Tis the voice of mer - cy calls. }

2 See the storm of vengeance gathering
O'er the path you dare to tread;
Hark! the awful thunders ro ling
Loud, and louder o'er your head;
|: Turn, O sinner! :|
Dost thou not His vengeance dread?

3 Haste! O sinner! to the Saviour,
Seek his mercy while you may;
Soon the day of grace is over;
Soon your life will pass away!
|: Haste, O sinner! :|
You must perish—if you stay!

198 Jesus is Mine.

Mrs. Catherine J. Bonar.   T. E. Perkins, by per.

1. Fade, fade, each earth-ly joy, Je - sus is mine! Break ev'ry
mor - tal tie,.. Je - sus is mine! Dark is the wil - der-ness,
Earth has no resting place, Je - sus a - lone can bless, Je - sus is mine!

2 Tempt not my soul away,
  Jesus is mine!
Here would I ever stay,
  Jesus is mine!
Perishing things of clay,
Born but for one brief day,
Pass from my heart away,
  Jesus is mine!

3 Farewell, ye dreams of night,
  Jesus is mine!
Lost in this dawning light,
  Jesus is mine!

All that my soul has tried,
Left but a dismal void,
Jesus has satisfied,
  Jesus is mine!

4 Farewell, mortality,
  Jesus is mine!
Welcome eternity,
  Jesus is mine!
Welcome, O loved and blest,
Welcome, sweet scenes of rest,
Welcome, my Saviour's breast,
  Jesus is mine!

——o——

199 Lord, Revive Us.

1. { Saviour, vis - it thy plan - ta - tion, Grant us, Lord, a gra-cious rain; }
   { All will come to des - o - la - tion, Un - less thou re - turn a - gain. }

CHORUS.

Lord, re - vive us, O re - vive us; Lord, re - vive thy work in me; Good

Lord, re - vive us, O, re - vive us, All our help must come from thee.

111

200 My Saviour, I Love Thee.

Music by W. WILLIAMS.

1. My Sav - iour, I love Thee, I know Thou art mine, For

Thee all the fol - ly of sin I re - sign; My gra - cious Re-

- deem - er, for - ev - er art Thou, If ev - er I lov'd Thee, my

Sav - iour, 'tis now, If ev - er I lov'd Thee, my Saviour, 'tis now.

2

I love Thee because Thou hast first loved me,
And purchased my pardon on Calvary's tree;
I love Thee for wearing the thorns on Thy brow,
|: If ever I loved Thee, my Saviour, 'tis now. :|

3

I'll love Thee in life, I will love Thee till death,
And praise Thee as long as Thou lendest me breath,
And say when the death-dew lies cold on my brow,
|: "If ever I loved Thee, my Saviour, 'tis now." :|

4

In mansions of glory and endless delight,
I'll ever adore Thee, entranced with the sight;
I'll sing with the glittering crown on my brow,
|: "If ever I loved Thee, my Saviour, 'tis now."

201 Give. C. M.

J. Griggs.

1. I know that my Re - deem - er lives, And ev - er prays for me;
2. Je - sus, I hang up - on thy word; I stead-fast - ly be - lieve

A to - ken for his love he gives, A pledge of lib - er - ty.
Thou wilt re - turn, and claim me, Lord, And to thy - self re - ceive.

3 Joyful in hope, my spirit soars
   To meet thee from above;
   Thy goodness thankfully adores,
   And sure I taste thy love.

4 When God is mine, and I am his,
   Of paradise possessed,
   I taste unutterable bliss
   And everlasting rest.

—o—

202 The Lovely Morning. 6s & 5s.

Fine. CHORUS.

1. { To that love - ly morn-ing, All shin-ing and fair, }
   { We're fast on - ward hast-'ning, And soon shall be there. } When the

D.C. O, may we be read - y To hail that glad day.

D.C.

mighty, mighty, mighty trump Sounds "Come, come a - way,"

2 And when that bright morning
  In splendor shall dawn,
  Our toil will be ended,
  Our sorrows all gone.
    When the mighty, &c.

3 The Bridegroom trom glory
  To earth shall descend;
  Ten thousand bright angels
  Around him attend.
    When the mighty, &c.

4 The graves will be open'd,
  The dead will arise.
  And with the Redeemer
  Mount up to the skies.
    When the mighty, &c.

5 The saints then immortal,
  In glory shall reign;
  The Bride with the Bridegroom
  Forever remain.
    When the mighty, &c.

118

203 I am Coming to the Cross.

WM. MCDONALD.   WM. G. FISCHER, by per.

1. I am com-ing to the cross; I am poor, and weak, and blind;
Cho.—I am trust-ing, Lord, in Thee, Blest Lamb of Cal-va-ry;

I am count-ing all but dross, I shall full sal-va-tion find.
Humbly at Thy cross I bow, Save me, Je-sus, save me now.

2 Long my heart has sighed for Thee,
  Long has evil reigned within;
Jesus sweetly speaks to me,—
  "I will cleanse you from all sin."—Cho.

3 Here I give my all to Thee,
  Friends, and time, and earthly store;
Soul and body Thine to be,—
  Wholly Thine for evermore.—Cho.

4 In thy promises I trust,
  Now I feel the blood applied:
I am prostrate in the dust,
  I with Christ am crucified.—Cho.

5 Jesus' love—it fills my soul!
  Perfected in Him I am;
I am every whit made whole:
  Glory, glory to the Lamb.—Cho.

———o———

204 Cross and Crown.

Words Arranged by I. I. L.   A. CHAPIN.

1. Must Je-sus bear the cross a-lone, And all the world go free?
2. The con-se-cra-ted cross I'll bear, Un-til my Lord I see,

No, there's a cross for ev-'ry-one, And there's a cross for me.
And then with him the crown I'll wear, For there's a crown for me.

3 How happy then the saints will be,
  Who now are sorrowing here!
Joy will be theirs eternally,
  Without a sigh or tear.

4 Then let us bear the heavy cross,
  Till from the cross we're free;
Then when He comes, we'll wear the
  The crown for you and me. [crown

114

205 The Cleansing Wave.

Mrs. Phœbe Palmer.   Mrs. Jos. F. Knapp, by per.

1. Oh, now I see the crimson wave, The fountain deep and wide;
2. I see the new cre - a - tion rise, I hear the speaking blood;

Je - sus my Lord, migh - ty to save, Points to His wounded side.
It speaks! pol-lu - ted na-ture dies! Sinks! 'neath the cleansing flood.

CHORUS.

The cleansing stream, I see! I see! I plunge, and oh, it cleanseth me!

Oh, praise the Lord, it cleanseth me! It cleanseth me, yes, cleanseth me!

3
I rise to walk in heaven's own light,
  Above the world and sin,
With heart made pure, and garments white,
  And Christ enthron'd within.—*Cho.*

4
Amazing grace! 'tis heaven below
  To feel the blood applied;
And Jesus, only Jesus know,
  My Jesus crucified—*Cho.*

—o—

206 Gethsemane. P. M.

Fine.

The day of bright glo - ry is roll-ing a - round, When Je-sus de -

D.C. To gaze on the Saviour with unclouded eyes.

D. C.

- scending-the trumpet shall sound ; My soul then in raptures of glo-ry shall rise

207 I've Been Redeemed.

E. A. H.

Arr. by Dr. T. H. Peacock, by per.

Southern Melody.

1. All glo - ry to the bleeding Lamb Who died on Cal - va - ry!.... Yes,
2. The blood that my Re - deemer spilt, The blood, so rich and free,.... That
3. I am redeem'd - O blessed state! I am redeem'd from sin:.... O

glo - ry to the bleed - ing Lamb Who saves and ran - soms me!
clean - ses sin - ful hearts from guilt, Now saves and clean - ses me.
love so in - fi - nite - ly great! The blood has made me clean.

CHORUS.

I've been re-deem'd,.... I've been re-deem'd,.... I've been re-deem'd, I've been re-
I've been redeem'd, I've been redeem'd, I've been redeem'd,

Fine.

- deem'd, I've been redeem'd, I've been redeem'd, Been wash'd in the blood of the Lamb.
I've been redeem'd, I've been redeem'd, I've been redeem'd,

Been redeem'd by the blood of the Lamb, Been redeem'd by the blood of the Lamb.
Been redeem'd by the blood of the Lamb, Been redeem'd by the blood of the Lamb.

I've been Redeemed. Concluded.

Been redeem'd by the blood of the Lamb...... That flow'd on Cal-va-ry.
Been redeem'd by the blood of the Lamb,

D.S.

—0—

208 Come, Drink at the Fountain.

J. E. H.   J. E. HALL.

From "Bible Ballads," by permission.

Earnestly.

1. Come, drink at the fountain, my brother, The fountain of life, flowing free;
2. Come, drink at the fountain, my sis-ter, You'll find it sweet wa-ter, and pure;
3. Come, drink at the fountain, dear sin-ner, This fountain will cleanse you from sin;
4. Come, drink at the fountain, ye low-ly, Your sorrows bring there and be free;

Come, drink of the life-giv-ing wa-ter, 'Tis flowing, blest fountain, for thee.
Come, drink of the clear flowing wa-ter, And drinking, you'll thirst never-more.
Come, drink of the sin-cleansing wa-ter, 'Tis flowing, dear sin-ner, drink in.
Come, drink if you feel you are need-y, 'Tis flowing, thy comfort to be.

CHORUS.
ad lib.   f a tempo.   rit.

Come, drink, drink, drink and thirst no more, Drink at the fountain and live.

tempo.   rit.

Come, drink at the sweet flowing fountain, Oh! drink of the wa-ter, and live.

Trusting in the Promise.

H. B. HARTZLER.

From "Songs of Grace," by per.

E. S. LORENZ.

1. I have found re - pose for my wea - ry soul, Trusting in the
2. I will sing my song as the days go by, Trusting in the
3. O, the peace and joy of the life I live, Trusting in the

prom-ise of the Sav - iour; And a har - bor safe when the
prom-ise of the Sav - iour; And re - joice in hope, while I
prom-ise of the Sav - iour; O, the strength and grace on - ly

bil-lows roll, Trust-ing in the promise of the Sav - iour. I will
live or die, Trust-ing in the promise of the Sav - iour. I can
God can give, Trust-ing in the promise of the Sav - iour. Who-so -

fear no foe in the dead-ly strife, Trusting in the promise of the
smile at grief, and a - bide in pain, Trusting in the promise of the
- ev - er will may be sav'd to - day, Trusting in the promise of the

Sav-iour; I will bear my lot in the toil of life, Trusting in the
Sav-iour; And the loss of all shall be high-est gain, Trusting in the
Sav-iour; And be - gin to walk in the ho - ly way, Trusting in the

118

Trusting in the Promise. Concluded.

REFRAIN.

prom-ise of the Sav - .our. Rest-ing on his mighty arm for -

- ev - er, Nev-er from his lov-ing heart to sev - er, I will rest by

grace In his strong embrace, Trusting in the promise of the Saviour.

—o—

210   Even Me.   8s, 7s & 3s.

Mrs. Elizabeth Codner.   Wm. B. Bradbury.

1. { Lord, I hear of show'rs of bless-ing Thou art scatt'ring full and free;
   Show'rs, the thirsty land re-fresh-ing; Let some drops now fall on me. }

2. { Pass me not, O God, my Father, Sin - ful though my heart may be;
   Thou mightst leave me, but the rather Let thy mer-cy light on me. }

E - ven me, E - ven me, Bless me, Sav - iour, e - ven me.

3 Pass me not, O gracious Saviour,
   Let me live and cling to thee;
   I am longing for thy favor;
   Whilst thou'rt calling, O call me.

4 Love of God, so pure and changeless,
   Blood of Christ, so rich, so free,
   Grace of God, so strong and bound-
   Magnify them all in me. [less.

211 Open the Windows of Heav'n to Me.

J. B. ATCHINSON. *By Permission.* W. S. MARSHALL.

1. In - to thy store-house, O Lord, I come, Bringing my tithes to thee;
2. Now I will prove thee, herewith, O Lord; Empty I come to thee,
3. Glo - ry to Je-sus! he hears my prayer; Blessings of peace have come!

O-pen the windows of heav'n, O Lord, And pour out a blessing on me.
All that I have I now consecrate, Thine, evermore, Lord, I would be.
Showers of blessing now fall on me; I o-pen my heart to make room.

CHORUS.

O - pen the windows of heav'n, O Lord, O-pen the windows to me;

rit.

Pour out rich blessings of peace and love, And let me catch glimpses of thee.

——o——

212 Look to Jesus.

JOSEPHINE POLLARD. *By Permission.* C. E. POLLOCK.

1. Look to Je - sus wea - ry one, Full of an-guish, full of grief;
2. See! the lov - ing Sav-iour stands, Pleading for thy fond em - brace;
3. Look to Je - sus; not in vain Do the wea-ry seek for rest:

Look to Jesus. Concluded.

He will com-fort, he a-lone, Has the balm for thy re-lief.
Trust thy-self to Je-sus' hands, In his bo-som hide thy face:
Weep a-way thy tears and pain, Like a child up-on his breast.

Look to him in thy despair, Rest and ref-uge he will give,
All thy sick-ness he can cure, All thy sins he will for-give,
Breathe thy sor-row in his ear, Strength for ev-'ry day re-ceive;

rit..................

All thy bur-dens he will bear, Look to Je-sus, look and live.
He will make his promise sure, Look to Je-sus, look and live.
Light in dark-ness will ap-pear, If thou wilt but look and live.

——o——

213   I Will Arise.   8s & 7s.

1. Come, thou Fount of ev-'ry blessing, Tune my heart to sing thy grace;
Cho.—I will a-rise and go to Je-sus, He will embrace me in his arms;

Streams of mer-cy, nev-er ceas-ing, Call for songs of loud-est praise.
In the arms of my dear Saviour, Oh! there are ten thousand charms.

Uxbridge. L. M.

L. MASON.

1. Afflicted saint, to Christ draw near; Thy Saviour's gracious promise hear;
2. Let not thy heart despond and say "How shall I stand the try-ing day?"

His faithful word declares to thee, That as thy day thy strength shall be.
He has engaged by firm de - cree That as thy day thy strength shall be.

3 Though thou be weak, and foes be strong,
The conflict fierce, the contest long.
Thou shalt o'ercome, the foe shall flee,
For as thy day thy strength shall be.

4 Though persecution, flood and flame
Arise, and thou shouldst suffer shame,
In every trial thou shalt see
That as thy day thy strength shall be.

——0——

215
Communion. C. M.

ISAAC WATTS.

STEPHEN JENKS.

1. A - las! and did my Saviour bleed? And did my Sov'reign die?

Would he de - vote that sa - cred head For such a worm as I?

2 Was it for crimes that I have done,
He groaned upon the tree?
Amazing pity! grace unknown!
And love beyond degree!

3 Well might the sun in darkness hide,
And shut his glories in,
When Christ, the mighty Maker, died,
For man, the creature's sin.

4 Thus might I hide my blushing face,
While his dear cross appears;
Dissolve my heart in thankfulness,
And melt mine eyes to tears.

5 But drops of grief can ne'er repay
The debt of love I owe:
Here, Lord, I give myself away,—
'Tis all that I can do

Bethany. C. M.

Arr. by A. Ross.

Why

1. Death may dissolve my body now, And bear me to the tomb;

Why do my minutes

Why do my minutes move so slow,

do my minutes move so slow,.... move so slow, move so slow,

Why do my minutes move so slow,.. move so slow,..

move so slow,.. move so slow,.. move so slow,.. *Why*

...... move so slow,.... move so slow, *Why do my minutes*

...... Why do my minutes move so slow,........ Nor my salvation come?

move so slow,.. Why do my minutes move so slow, Nor my salvation come?

do my minutes move so slow, Nor my.................. sal-va - - tion come?

move so slow,.... Nor my............ sal - va - - tion come?

2 With heav'nly weapons I have fought
The battles of the Lord;
Finish'd my course, and kept the faith,
And wait the sure reward.

3 God has laid up in heav'n for me
A crown which cannot fade;
The righteous Judge, at that great day
Shall place it on my head!

4 Nor hath the King of grace decreed
This prize for me alone;
But all that love and long to see
Th' appearance of his Son!

5 God is my everlasting aid,
And hell shall rage in vain:
To him be highest glory paid,
And endless praise. —*Amen*

1. O Sav-iour of sin-ners, when faint and de - press'd, With man-i - fold
3. When judgments, O Lord, are a - broad in the land, And mer-it - ed

tri - als and sor - rows op-press'd, I'll bow at thy feet, and with
ven-geance descends from thy hand! O'erwhelm'd with the sight, for pro -

con - fi - dence cry, "Lead me to the Rock that is high-er than I!"
- tec - tion I'll fly, And hide in the Rock that is high-er than I!

2. When tempted by Sa - tan the Spir-it to grieve, The ser-vice of
4. At home, with the cho-sen of Je - sus, I long To dwell, and e -

Christ, my Re - deem-er, to leave, I'll claim my re - la - tion to
e - ter - nally join in the song Of praise and of bless-ing, while

Je - sus on high, The Rock of sal - va-tion that's high-er than I!
a - ges pass by, Christ Je-sus. the Rock that is high-er than I!

—o—

218   Beautiful Land of Light.

From "Golden Sunbeams."

1. There's a beautiful land, a land of light, Which lies just o-ver the way;
2. O, those sweet loving eyes we clos'd at night 'Mid sorrows bit-ter-est tears;
3. Look ye up, then, ye poor and suff'ring ones, Whose troubles rise on each hand;

Where the night of life, with its gloom and strife, Fades out into golden day.
Will be beaming there, 'neath their brows of light, Untouch'd by the frost of years.
For   Jesus' grace saves in each dark place, And guides to that better land.

CHORUS.

For   o-ver the riv-er in that beautiful land, The beautiful land ever bright;

No heart-ache or pain ev-er saddens the band In that beautifu. land of light.

Refuge of my Soul. 7s.

C. WESLEY.   L. MASON.

1. Je - sus, Ref - uge of my soul, Let me to thy bo - som fly,

While the ra - ging bil - lows roll, While the tem-pest still is high;

Hide me, O my Sav-iour, hide, Till the storm of life is past;

Safe in - to the ha - ven guide—Oh! re-ceive me home at last.

2
Other refuge have I none,
  Hangs my helpless soul on thee;
Leave, oh, leave me not alone,
  Still support and comfort me:
All my trust on thee is stay'd;
  All my help from thee I bring;
Cover my defenseless head
  With the shadow of thy wing.

3
Thou, O Christ, art all I want;
  All in all in thee I find;
Raise the fallen, cheer the faint,
  Heal the sick, and lead the blind.

Just and holy is thy name—
  I am all unrighteousness;
Vile and full of sin I am—
  Thou art full of truth and grace.

4
Plenteous grace with thee is found,
  Grace to cover all my sin;
Let the healing streams abound;
  Make and keep me pure within.
Thou of life the Fountain art—
  Freely let me take of thee;
Spring thou up within my heart;
  Rise to all eternity.

220 My Mission Field.

W. O. CUSHING.

From "Heavenly Carols," by permission.

E. S LORENZ.

1. I would toil in the field where he calleth me to go, Tho' hum-ble my

work may be; I would ask no more; I on - ly care to know,'Tis the

I would ask no more: I on - ly care to know,'Tis the

Fine. CHORUS.

way my Lord lead - eth me. 'Tis the way.......... my Lord

'Tis the way my

way my Lord lead - eth me.

D.S.

lead- - eth me, 'Tis the way........ my Lord lead - eth me;

Lord lead-eth me, 'Tis the way my Lord lead-eth me;

2

I would walk in the path where it leadeth unto day,
  Though lonely the path might be;
I would take my staff and follow all the way,
  'Tis the way my Lord leadeth me.—*Cho.* 'Tis the way, &c.

3

I would toil in the field where he calleth me to go,
  Though barren the soil might be;
Though the way be hard, 'tis sweet enough to know,
  'Tis the way my Lord leadeth me.—*Cho.* 'Tis the way, &c.

221 Laban. S. M.

GEO. HEATH, 1781.   LOWELL MASON, 1830.

1. My soul, be on thy guard, Ten thousand foes a-rise;

The hosts of sin are press-ing hard, To draw thee from the prize.

2 O watch, and fight, and pray;
The battle ne'er give o'er;
Renew it boldly every day,
And help divine implore.

3 Ne'er think the vict'ry won,
Nor lay thine armor down:
The work of faith will not be done,
Till thou obtain the crown.

222

1 In every trying hour
My soul to Jesus flies;
I trust in his Almighty power
When swelling billows rise.

2 His comforts bear me up;
I trust a faithful God;
The sure foundation of my hope
Is in my Saviour's blood.

3 Loud hallelujahs sing
To our Redeemer's name;
In joy or sorrow, life or death,
His love is still the same.

— o —

223 Land of Rest. C. M.

1. O land of rest, for thee I sigh, When will the mo-ment come,
And dwell with Christ at home, ... And dwell with Christ at home,

End.

When I shall lay my ar-mor by, And dwell with Christ at home.
When I shall lay my ar-mor by, And dwell with Christ at home.

2 No tranquil joys on earth I know;
No peaceful, sheltering dome;
This world's a wilderness of woe;
This world is not my home.

3 To Jesus Christ I sought for rest,
He bade me cease to roam;

And fly for succor to his breast,
And he'd conduct me home.

4 Weary of wand'ring round and round
This vale of sin and gloom,
I long to leave the unhallow'd ground,
And dwell with Christ at home.

224　He Will Gather the Wheat.

HARRIET B. M'KEEVER.　　JNO. R. SWENEY.

From "The Garner," by per.

1. When Je-sus shall gath-er the na - tions Be-fore him at last to ap-pear,

Then, oh! how shall we stand in the judgment, When summon'd our sentence to hear?

CHORUS.

He will gather the wheat in his gar - ner, But the chaff will he scatter a - way;

Then, oh! how shall we stand in the judgment Of the great Res-ur-rec-tion Day?

2
Shall we hear, from the lips of the Saviour,
　The words, "Faithful servant, well
　　done;"
Or, trembling with fear and with anguish,
　Be banished away from his throne.
　　Cho.—He will gather, &c.

3
He will smile when he looks on his children,
　And sees on the ransomed his seal;
He will clothe them in heavenly beauty,
　As low at his feet they shall kneel.
　　Cho.—He will gather, &c.

4
Then let us be watching and waiting,—
　Our lamps burning steady and bright,—
When the Bridegroom shall come to the
　　marriage,
We'll enter with Him with delight.
　　Cho.—He will gather, &c.

5
Thus living with hearts fixed on Jesus,
　In patience we wait for the time,
When, the days of our pilgrimage ended,
　We'll bask in his presence divine.
　　Cho.—He will gather, &c.

225 My Beloved. 11s & 8s.

Jos. Swain, 1792.   (*Arr. by Hubert P. Main, 1869.*)   Freeman Lewis, 1813.

1. O Thou, in whose pres-ence my soul takes de - light, On
2. Where dost thou at noon-tide re - sort with thy sheep, To

whom, in af - flic - tion I call; My com - fort by day, and my
feed in the pas - tures of love? And why in the val - ley of

song in the night, My hope, my sal - va - tion, my all.
death should I weep, Or a - lone in the wil - der - ness rove?

3 O, why should I wander, an alien from
thee.
Or cry in the desert for bread?
Thy foes will rejoice when my sorrow's
they see,
And smile at the tears I have shed.

4 He looks, and ten thousands of angels
rejoice,
And myriads wait for his word;
He speaks, and eternity, fill'd with his
voice,
Re-echoes the praise of the Lord.

———o———

226   Give Me Jesus.

1. When I'm hap - py, hear me sing, When I'm hap-py, hear me sing,
2. When in sor - row, hear me pray, When in sor-row, &c.

CHORUS.

When I'm hap - py, hear me sing, Give me Je - sus. Give me Je - sus,

Give me Je - sus: You may have all the world: Give me Je - sus.

3 When I'm dying, hear me cry,
4 When I'm in the Judgment day,

5 When I stand before the throne,
6 When among the ransomed throng,

Warren. L. M.

V. C. TAYLOR.

1. Je-hovah reigns, ex-alt-ed high, O'er all the earth, o'er all the sky;

Though clouds and darkness veil his feet, His dwelling is the mer-cy-seat.

2 O ye that love his holy name,
Hate every work of sin and shame;
He guards the souls of all his friends,
And from the snares of sin defends.

3 Immortal light, and joys unknown,
Are for the saints in darkness sown;

Those glorious seeds shall spring and rise,
And the bright harvest bless our eyes.

4 Rejoice, ye righteous, and record
The sacred honors of the Lord;
None but the soul that feels his grace,
Can triumph in his holiness.

—o—

228 Come, My Brethren. 7s & 6s.

Fine.

1. { Come, my brethren, let us try, For a lit-tle sea-son,
Ev-'ry bur-den to lay by; Come and let us rea-son. }
D.C. Speak, and let the worst be known, Speak-ing may re-lieve you.

D.C.

What is this that casts you down? What is this that grieves you?

2 Think on what your Saviour bore,
In the gloomy garden;
Sweating blood at every pore,
To procure thy pardon.
See him nailed upon the tree,
Bleeding, groaning, dying!
See, he suffered this for thee!
Therefore be believing.

3 Joseph took the Saviour down,
Shrouded him in linen:
Laid him in the silent tomb!
And returned in mourning.
Jesus rises from the tomb!
Angels come from glory!
See! that glory shines around!
Hallelujah, glory!

229   We Shall Know.

ANNIE HERBERT.   J. H. ANDERSON.

1. When the mists have roll'd in splen-dor From the beau-ty of the hills,
2. If we err in hu-man blindness, And for-get that we are dust;
3. When the mists have ris'n a-bove us, As our Father knows his own,

And the sun-shine, warm and ten-der, Falls in kiss-es on the rills,
If we miss the law of kind-ness, When we struggle to be just,
Face to face with those that love us, We shall know as we are known;

We may read love's shin-ing let-ter In the rainbow of the spray,
Snow-y wings of peace shall cov-er All the plain that hides away,—
Love, be-yond the o-rient meadows Floats the golden fringe of day,

We shall know each oth-er bet-ter When the mists have clear'd away.
When the wea-ry watch is o-ver, And the mists have clear'd away.
Heart to heart, we bide the shad-ows, Till the mists have clear'd away.

CHORUS.

We shall know... as we are known,.... Never more.... to walk a-
We shall know   as we are known,   Never more

From "The Welcome," by per. of Messrs. S. Brainard's Sons.
132

-lone, In the dawn - - ing of the morn-ing, When the
to walk a-lone, In the dawning of the morn-ing,

mists.... have clear'd a - way; In the dawn - - ing of the
When the mists have clear'd a-way; In the dawning

morn - ing, When the mists........ have clear'd a-way,
When the mists have clear'd away.

—o—

230   DAY-BREAK.

1

When the clouds have left the hill-tops,
  And the beauty of the day
Gleams through shining, golden portals,
  Melting all the mists away;
Then this earth will be all joy-land,
  Blessed day of jubilee!
Oh, for thee our hearts are yearning,
  Sunshine of Eternity.

2

When the darkness rolls from ocean,
  And the light beams brightly o'er
Every wave and foaming billow
  Dashing 'gainst this mortal shore;
Then the heart will sing with rapture,
  And the voice break forth in praise
To the God that rules the tempest:
  "Just and true are all thy ways."

3

When the pain and wasting fever,
  And the thousand ills of life
All are healed by one Physician,
  And forever hushed the strife;

Then sweet peace and holy comfort
  Will possess the inmost soul,
For the weary, homesick pilgrim
  Will have reach'd the long'd-for goal

4

When the graves of earth are opened,
  And the fair, lov'd forms arise,
Springing up from dusty chambers,
  Soaring upward to the skies;
Then sweet waves of thrilling music
  Will entrance the listening ear,
"Like the sound of many waters,"
  Murmuring gently, soft and clear.

5

When the city, grand, eternal,
  Comes to earth 'mid clouds of light,
And the King bids saints to enter
  Mansions filled with holy light;
Then the life-work of all ages
  Will receive a just reward—
Home with Jesus, sweet rest given,
  In the kingdom of our Lord.

231 Linger Not.

I. BALTZELL, by per.

1. 'Tis not the Sav-iour makes de-lay, For, oh! how long he's waited;
2. How long will you thus slight his love, And still the vain pur-su-ing—
3. Come, then, while yet the Spir-it strives, Come, all your sins confessing;

And while you've lin-ger'd day by day, His love has ne'er a-ba-ted.
Re-gard-less of the things a-bove, Seem bent on your un-do-ing?
Come, learn how free-ly Christ forgives, And share sal-va-tion's blessing.

CHORUS.

"Turn ye, oh, turn ye." Oh! hear him re-peat-ing the cry:

turn you, poor sinner,

"Haste, sin-ner, haste, sinner, Oh! why will you die?"

"Hasten, oh, sin-ner, I'm waiting to save you,

—0—

232 Why Not Be Saved To-Night?

From "Songs of Grace."   I. BALTZELL, by per.

1. Oh, do not let the word de-part, And close thine eyes against the light;
2. To-mor-row's sun may nev-er rise To bless thy long-de-luded sight;
3. Our God in pit-y lingers still; And wilt thou thus his love requite?
4. The world has nothing left to give; It has no new, no pure delight;

134

Why not be Saved To-night?

Poor sin-ner, harden not thy heart; Thou wouldst be sav'd, why not to-night!
This is the time; oh, then be wise! Thou wouldst be sav'd, why not to-night!
Renounce at length thy stubborn will; Thou wouldst be sav'd, why not to-night!
Oh, try the life which Christians live; Thou wouldst be sav'd, why not to-night!

REFRAIN.

Why not be sav'd to - night,.... Why not be sav'd to - night?
to-night?

Rit. to the end. p pp

Why not to - night? Why not to - night?
Why not be sav'd to - night? Why not be sav'd to - night?

233 How Precious is the Name.

1. How precious is the name, brethren sing, brethren sing, How precious is the
bore our sin and shame, on the tree, on the tree, Who bore our sin and

2. I've giv-en all for Christ, he's my all, he's my all, I've giv-en all for
less he's in my breast, reigning there, reigning there, Unless he's in my

3. His ea-sy yoke I'll bear, with de-light, with de-light, His ea-sy yoke I'll
name I will de - clare ev-er - more, ev-er - more, His name I will de-

Fine. D.C.

name, brethren sing, How precious is the name Of Christ, our Paschal Lamb, Who
shame on the tree.
Christ, he's my all; I've giv-en all for Christ, And my spirit cannot rest, Un -
breast, reigning there.
bear with de-light; His ea-sy yoke I'll bear, And his cross I will not fear; His
- clare ev - er-more.

234 Springfield. S. M.

C. WESLEY.   J. C. STODDARD.

1. Soldiers of Christ, a - rise, And put your arm - or on,

Strong in the strength which God supplies Thro' his E - ter - nal Son;

Strong in the Lord of Hosts,...... And in his mighty pow'r;

Who in the strength of Je - sus trusts, Is more than con-quer-or.

2 Stand then in his great might,
   With all his strength endued;
But take, to arm you for the fight,
   The panoply of God;
That having all things done,
   And all your conflicts past,
Ye may o'ercome, through Christ alone,
   And stand entire at last.

3 From strength to strength go on;
   Wrestle, and fight, and pray;
Tread all the powers of darkness down,
   And win the well-fought day:
Still let the Spirit cry
   In all his soldiers, "Come!"
Till Christ, descending from on high,
   Shall take the conquerors home.

———o———

235 Joy and Rest.

1. { I have sought round the verdant earth For unfading joy; }
     { I have tried ev'ry source of mirth, But all, all will cloy. } Lord, bestow on me

Grace to set the spir - it free; Thine the praise shall be, Mine, mine the joy.

2 I have turned to thy gospel, Lord,
   From folly away;
I have trusted thy holy word
   That taught me to pray.

Here my soul is blessed,
Here my spirit finds a rest,
Jesus is my guest,
   With me to stay.

141

Turner. C. M.

C. WESLEY.

ABRAHAM MAXIM.

1. O for a thousand tongues to sing The great Re-deem-er's praise, The glo-ries of our God and King, The glo - ries of our God and King, The tri - umphs of his grace. The tri-umphs of his grace, The tri - umphs of his grace.

The glo - ries of our God..... and King, The God and King, The tri - - - umphs of.......... his grace.

glo-ries of our God and King, The tri - - umphs of his grace!

2 Jesus! the name that soothes our fears,
That bids our sorrows cease;
'Tis music in the sinner's ears,
'Tis life, and health, and peace.

3 He breaks the power of reigning sin,
And sets the prisoners free;
His blood can make the foulest clean;
His blood availed for me.

4 He speaks—and, list'ning to his voice,
New life the dead receive;
The broken, contrite hearts rejoice;
The humble poor believe.

237

1 My God, the spring of all my joys,
The life of my delights,
The glory of my brightest days,
And comfort of my nights!

2 In darkest shades, if thou appear,
My dawning is begun;
Thou art my soul's bright morning star,
And thou my rising sun.

3 The opening heavens around me shine
With beams of sacred bliss,
If Jesus shows his mercy mine,
And whispers I am his.

4 My soul would leave this heavy clay
At that transporting word,
Run up with joy the shining way,
To see and praise my Lord.

ISAAC WATTS.

238 Scarcely Saved.

L. B.

I. BALTZELL, by per.

1. Scarce-ly sav'd! oh, what a word! 'Tis the lan-guage of the Lord;
2. Scarce-ly sav'd! a warn-ing hear! Rouse thee, sin - ner! judgment's near;
3. Scarce-ly sav'd! if sav'd at all; Sin - ner, hear the Saviour's call;
4. Scarce-ly sav'd! oh, sin - ner, hear! Christ, the great Phy-si - cian's near;

Scarce-ly sav'd the right-eous are; Sin-ner, where wilt thou ap-pear?
Je - sus waits to save thee now, At his foot-stool hum-bly bow.
Come with all your guilt and sin, Christ will free-ly take you in.
Wilt thou now this truth be - lieve? "On-ly look to Christ and live."

CHORUS.

Scarcely sav'd! oh, sinner, hear it! Scarcely sav'd! oh, sin - ner, fear it!

Fly to Je - sus, while you may, He will wash your sins a - way.

—o—

239 Sweet was the Time.

1. { Sweet was the time when first I felt The Saviour's pard'ning blood }
   { Ap - plied to cleanse my soul from guilt, And bring me home to God. }

D.C. And when the evening shades prevail'd, His love was all my song.

D.C.

Soon as the morn the light re-veal'd, His praises tun'd my tongue; ....

New Jerusalem. C. M.

J. INGALLS, 1790.

1. From the third heav'n, where God resides, That holy, happy place;

The new Jerusalem comes down, A-dorn'd . . . . with shining grace,

The new Jerusalem comes down, A-dorn'd . . .

new Jerusalem comes down, A-dorn'd . . . . with shining grace, The

-lem comes down, Adorn'd . . . . . . with shining grace, The new Jerusa -

The new Je-ru-sa-lem, &c.

. . . . . . with shin - ing grace, Adorn'd with shining grace, Adorn'd, &c.

new Jerusalem, &c.

-lem comes down, Adorn'd, &c.

2 Attending angels shout for joy,
And the bright armies sing,—
"Mortals, behold the sacred seat
Of your descending King.

3 "The God of glory down to men
Removes his blest abode;
Men are the objects of his grace,
And he their gracious God.

4 "His own kind hand shall wipe the tears
From every weeping eye; [fears,
And pains, and groans, and griefs, and
And death itself, shall die."

5 How long, dear Saviour, O how long
Shall this bright hour delay?
Fly swifter round, ye wheels of time,
And bring the welcome day.

241   Hallelujah! I'm Saved!

CHARLES WESLEY.

ISA. BALTZELL, by per.

Lively.

1. Oh, how hap-py are they Who their Saviour o-bey,
2. That sweet com-fort was mine, When the fa-vor di-vine
3. 'Twas a heav-en be-low My Re-deem-er to know,

And have laid up their treasures a-bove; Tongue can nev-er ex-press
I first found in the blood of the Lamb; When my heart it be-liev'd,
And the an-gels could do noth-ing more Than to fall at his feet,

The sweet comfort and peace Of a soul in its ear-li-est love.
What a joy I re-ceiv'd, What a heav-en in Je-sus' dear name.
And the sto-ry re-peat, And the lov-er of sin-ners a-dore.

CHORUS.

Hal-le-lu-jah! I'm sav'd! Hal-le-lu-jah! I'm sav'd!

Hal-le-lu-jah! I'm sav'd Through the blood of the Lamb!

242   Shirland. S. M.

SAMUEL STANLEY.

1. A - rise, ye saints, a - rise! The Lord your lead - er is; The foe be - fore his ban - ner flies, And vic - to - ry is his.

2 We follow him, our Guide,
  Our Captain, and our King;
We follow him, through grace supplied
  From heaven's eternal spring.

3 We soon shall see the day
  When all our toils shall cease;

When we can cast our cares away,
  And dwell in endless peace.

4 This hope supports us here;
  It makes our burden light;
'Twill serve our drooping hearts to cheer
  Till faith shall end in sight.

——0——

243   Union Hymn. 8s.

1. From whence doth this union a - rise, That ha - tred is conquer'd by love? That fast - ens our souls in such ties As nature and time can't re - move?

2 It cannot in Eden be found,
  Nor yet in a paradise lost;
It grows on Immanuel's ground,
  And Jesus' rich blood it did cost.

3 The saints are so dear unto me—
  Our hearts all united in love;

When Jesus shall come we shall see
  Those bright shining mansions above.

4 Then with Him forever we'll reign,
  And all his great glory behold;
We'll never be parted again,
  But live through the ages untold.

146

244. Cowper. P. M.

WM. COWPER.   GERMAN.

1. To Jesus, the crown of my hope, My soul is in haste to be gone;

O, bear me, ye cherubim, up, And waft me a-way to His throne:
D.S. Whose name is ex-al-ted a-bove, With glo-ry, do-min-ion and pow'r.

My Saviour whom ab-sent I love, Whom not hav-ing seen I a-dore;

1 O, come! break these bonds that detain
My soul from its portion in thee;
Come, break off this wearisome chain,
And make me eternally free.
When that happy era begins,
Arrayed in thy glories I'll shine,
Nor grieve any more by my sins
The bosom on which I recline.

2 O, then shall the veil be removed,
And round me thy brightness be pour'd;
I'll meet thee whom, absent, I loved,
Whom having not seen, I adored.
O, then nevermore shall the fears,
The trials, temptations and woes,
Now dark'ning this valley of tears,
Intrude on that blissful repose.

245

1 How tedious and tasteless the hours,
When Jesus no longer I see;
Sweet prospects, sweet birds and sweet
flowers,
Have lost all their sweetness to me;
The mid-summer sun shines but dim,
The fields strive in vain to look gay:
But when I am happy in him
December's as pleasant as May.

2 His name yields the richest perfume,
And sweeter than music his voice;
His presence disperses my gloom,
And makes all within me rejoice;
I should, were he always thus nigh,
Have nothing to wish or to fear;
No mortal so happy as I,
My summer would last all the year.

3 Content with beholding his face,
My all to his pleasure resigned;
No changes of season or place
Would make any change in my mind;
While blest with a sense of his love,
A palace a toy would appear;
And prisons would palaces prove,
If Jesus would dwell with me there.

4 My Lord, if indeed I am thine,
If thou art my sun and my song,
Say, why do I languish and pine?
And why is the winter so long?
O, drive these dark clouds from the sky,
Thy soul-cheering presence restore;
Come, Saviour, to me from on high;
Let winter and clouds be no more.

147

The Whole Burnt Offering.

J. C. MORGAN.   *By Permission.*   A. H.

1. Je - sus! I hear thee knocking, And gladly yield to thee; The gates of

Will un-lock-ing, Thy tem-ple hence to be. I give to thee my

treasures, My bur-dens, hopes and fears; Re-nounce all sel - fish

CHORUS.

pleasures, All trust in works or tears. My all is on the al-tar;

rit. ad lib:

I'm waiting for the fire, Waiting, waiting, I'm waiting for the fire.

2 In heavenly love abiding,
  No change my heart shall **fear**;
And safe is such confiding,
  For nothing changes here.
The storm may roar without me,
  My heart may low be laid,
But God is round about me,
  And can I be dismayed?

3 Wherever he may guide me,
  No want shall turn me **back**;
My Shepherd is beside me,
  And nothing can I lack.
His wisdom ever waketh,
  His sight is never dim,
He knows the way he taketh,
  And I will walk with him.

247 There is Glory.

I. I. LESLIE.　　　　　　　　JNO. R. SWENEY.

1. To thee, Saviour, I am clinging; With my faith I cling to Thee;

Of Thy love and grace I'm sing-ing, For they sure-ly have reach'd me.

CHORUS.

There is glo-ry! There is glo-ry! Oh, there's joy with-in my soul!

For I've felt the touch of His mer-cy, And He sure-ly makes me whole.

2 All unworthy of the calling,
  Without merit, without plea;
But Thy grace, upon me falling,
  Draws my wand'ring heart to Thee.

3 Now I'm trusting—now believing
  That however weak I be,

Of Thy strength and grace receiving,
  I shall gain the victory.

4 Yes, dear Saviour, I am clinging,
  Clinging closely to Thy side;
All my joy from Thee is springing,
  And with Thee I will abide.

——o——

248 The Lamb of God.

1. Je - sus was the Lamb of God, Je - sus was the Lamb of God,
2. Glo - ry to the Lamb of God, Glo - ry to the Lamb of God.

Je - sus was the Lamb of God That was slain.
Glo - ry to the Lamb of God That was slain.

3 I believe in that dear Lamb
  That was slain,

4 He will take my sins away,
  That dear Lamb

Northfield. C. M.

1. O, for a faith that will not shrink, Tho' press'd by many a foe;

That will not trem - ble on the brink, That
That will not tremble, &c.

That will not trem-ble on the brink That will not trem - ble

pov - er - ty or woe,
will not trem - ble on the brink Of pov - - er - ty or woe;

on the brink

250

2
That will not murmur nor complain
Beneath the chastening rod;
But in the hour of grief and pain,
Will lean upon its God;

3
A faith that shines more bright and clear
When tempests rage without;
That when in danger knows no fear,
In darkness feels no doubt;

4
A faith that keeps the narrow way,
By truth restrained and led,
And with a pure and heavenly ray
Lights up a dying bed.

5
Lord, give me such a faith as this,
And then, whate'er may come,
I'll taste e'en here the hallowed bliss
Of an eternal home.

1
O, glorious day of endless rest!
We hail each sign of thee,
With longing hearts and waiting eyes,
We pray, expecting thee.

2
Thy piercing rays of glory, bright
Beyond the mid-day sun,
Will soon to every eye reveal
The mighty, coming One.

3
With cheerful hope and earnest prayer,
Confiding in His word.
We look to see thy morning dawn,
Which brings our absent Lord.

4
O, blissful day of promised rest!
We yet shall share thy peace;
And every sorrow, pain and care
Shall in thy radiance cease.

251 Beautiful Mansions of Rest.

C. C.   "CARL CLEVELAND."

1. Beau-ti-ful mansions of rest, Home of the spot-less and fair!
2. Beau-ti-ful mansions of rest, Joy of the cit-y of gold,
3. Beau-ti-ful mansions of rest, Ev-er I'm sigh-ing for thee—

O, to be far from this wild un-rest, And dwell with my Saviour there!
Endless a-bode of the vic-tor blest, Ere long may those gates un-fold!
Longing to reign with the white-rob'd blest, From sorrow and sin set free;

Glad-ly I haste on my way, Care-worn, with sor-row op-prest,
Pil-grim and stranger I roam On at the Master's be-hest,
Saviour, oh, hasten the day When at thy welcome be-hest,

To the beau-ti-ful mansions, the beau-ti-ful mansions, the
To the beau-ti-ful mansions, the beau-ti-ful mansions, the
We shall meet in the mansions, shall meet in the mansions, the

beau-ti-ful mansions of rest.

REFRAIN.

Beautiful mansions, beautiful mansions,

Beautiful Mansions of Rest. Concluded.

beau-ti-ful mansions, home of the blest, O the beau-ti-ful mansions,

beau - ti - ful mansions, beau - ti - ful mansions, mansions of rest.

—o—

252 Alone, Yet Not Alone.

From "Living Waters." D. F. HODGES.

1. When no kind earthly friend is near, With gentle words my heart to cheer, Still

REFRAIN.

I am with my Saviour dear, "Alone, yet not a-lone." A - lone, yet not alone;

A-lone, yet not a-lone. So happy, so content am I, Alone, yet not a-lone.

2 Though no lov'd forms my path attend,
  With tender looks o'er me to bend,
  Yet I am with my unseen Friend;
  "Alone, yet not alone."—*Refrain.*

3 When sorely racked with pain and grief,
  Here I can find a sure relief;
  And I rejoice in the belief!
  "Alone, yet not alone."—*Refrain.*

4 'Tis on His strength that I rely,
  And doubts and fears at once defy,
  So happy, so content am I;
  "Alone, yet not alone."—*Refrain.*

5 Whate'er may now to me betide,
  I have a place wherein to hide,
  By faith, 'tis e'en at His blest side;
  "Alone, yet not alone."—*Refrain.*

147

253 That Glorious Day.

Dr. L. Mason.

1. That glorious day is coming, The hour is hast'ning on; Its radiant light is near-ing, Far brighter than the sun; In yonder clouds of heaven The Saviour will ap-pear, And gather all his chosen, To meet him in the air.

2 Then fire, from heav'n descending,
 Shall sweep this wide earth o'er;
And nations, loud lamenting,
 Shall sink to rise no more—
Though tears with prayers are blended,
 In vain, in vain they cry:
The day of grace is ended,
 The sinner now must die.

3 The saints, then all victorious,
 Will go to meet their Lord;
An earth both bright and glorious,
 Will then be their reward;

And God himself there reigning,
 Will wipe all tears away;
Nor clouds nor night remaining,
 But one eternal day.

4 O, Christian, keep from sleeping,
 And let your love abound;
Be watchful, prayerful, faithful,
 The trumpet soon will sound!
O, sinner, hear the warning!
 To Jesus quickly fly!
Then you, in that blest morning,
 May meet Him in the sky.

———o———

254 In the Strength of Grace.

1. Lord, in the strength of grace, With a glad heart and free, My-self, my res-i-due of days, I consecrate to thee, I con-se-crate to thee.

2 Thy ransomed servant, I
 Restore to thee thine own;

And from this moment live or die
[: To serve my God alone.:]

255 The Garden Hymn. C. P. M.

1. The Lord in - to his gar - den comes; The spi - ces yield a
rich per-fume, The lil - ies grow and thrive; The lil - ies grow and thrive;
Re - freshing show'rs of grace di - vine, From Je - sus flow to ev - 'ry vine,
Which makes the dead re - vive, Which makes the dead re - vive.

2
O, that this dry and barren ground
In springs of water may abound,
||: A fruitful soil become! :||
The desert blossoms as the rose,
When Jesus conquers all his foes,
||: And brings his people home. :||

3
That glorious time is hast'ning on,
The mighty work will be begun,
||: When all the saints shall live. :||

Who comes to Jesus now may be
From death and sorrow ever free,
||: For he them life will give. :||

4
Amen, amen, my soul replies,
We soon shall meet in paradise,
||: And claim our mansions there; :||
Now here's my heart and here's my hand,
To meet you in that heavenly land,
||: And all its glories share. :||

149

Are You Ready?

MARY D. JAMES.

JNO. R. SWENEY.

1. Should the summons, quickly fly - ing, On the slumb'ring nations fall,—
2. What if now the startling mandate Should the sleeping vir-gins hear,—
3. Is there oil in all your ves-sels? Are your garments pure and white?
4. Rise! ye virgins,—sleep no long-er,—Lest the call your souls sur-prise!

Lo! the Heav'nly Bridegroom com-eth, Would the sound your souls ap-pal?
Are your lamps all trimm'd and burning, Should the Bridegroom now appear?
Are they wash'd in the cleansing Fountain, Fit to stand in Je - sus' sight?
Lest ye fail to meet the Bridegroom, When he com-eth from the skies.

CHORUS.

Are you rea - dy?.... Are you rea - dy, ... Should you
Are you rea - dy?.... Are you rea - dy, ... Now to
Are you rea - dy?.... Are you rea - dy?.... Are your
Oh! be rea - dy!.... Oh! be rea - dy!.... When he

hear the mid - night call?.... Are you rea - dy?...... Are you
see your Lord ap - pear!.... Are you rea - dy?...... Are you
lamps all clear and bright?.. Are you rea - dy?...... Are you
com - eth from the skies;... Oh! be rea - dy!...... Oh! be

Should you
Now to
Are your
Hasten,

Are You Ready?

rea - dy?.......... Should you hear the mid - night call?
rea - dy?.......... Now to see your Lord ap - pear?
rea - dy?.......... Are your lamps all clear and bright?
rea - dy!.......... Hasten, from your slum - bers rise!

hear the midnight call? Should you hear the mid - night call?
see your Lord ap-pear? Now to see your Lord ap - pear?
lamps all clear and bright? Are your lamps all clear and bright?
from your slumbers, rise! Hasten, from your slum - bers, rise!

257 I'm Redeemed by His Blood.

From "Gates of Praise."   I. BALTZELL, by per.

1. O, Jesus, full of truth and grace, Oh, all-a-toning Lamb of God! I
2. Thou art the anchor of my hope, Thy faithful promise I receive; Sure-
3. Sa - tan, with all his arts, no more Me from the gospel-hope can move; I

CHORUS.

wait to see thy glorious face, I seek redemption in thy blood. I'm re-
- ly thy death will raise me up, For thou hast died that I might live.
shall receive the gracious pow'r, And find the pearl of perfect love.

- deem'd by his blood, I'm re-deem'd by his blood! Now I
I'm redeem'd by his blood! I'm redeem'd by his blood!

Repeat pp

know, now I feel that his precious blood was shed To redeem my soul from sin.

258 Beyond the Swelling Flood.

A. E. C.

J. H. KINNEY.

1. Yes, we shall meet be-yond the flood, In robes made white thro' Je-sus' blood,

And hold sweet converse, free from pain, Nor ev-er fear to part a - gain, Be-

CHORUS.

- yond the swelling flood! Be - yond... the swelling flood, Be-yond... the
We'll meet... to part no more, We'll meet.. to

Beyond the swelling flood... Beyond the swelling
We'll meet to part no more,.. We'll meet, &c.

swelling flood, Be - yond... the swelling flood, We'll meet to part no more.
part no more, We'll meet... to part no more, Be-yond the swelling flood.

flood.... Beyond the swelling flood... We'll meet to part no more.

2 I care not now what ills may come,
  Since hope sustains this thought of home,
  And God's own word doth plainly say
  "Thy God shall wipe all tears away
    Beyond the swelling flood!"
  Cho.—Beyond the swelling flood, &c.

3 That meeting, O, how sweet, dear!
  What sounds shall greet the list'ning ear!
  What thrills of rapture wake the soul,

As back those pearly gates shall roll,
  Beyond the swelling flood.
  Cho.—We'll meet to part no more, &c.

4 Dear Saviour! guide my willing feet,
  That I may have that joy complete;
  And live to praise thro' endless day
  The love that dries all tears away,
    Beyond the swelling flood.
  Cho.—We'll meet to part no more, &c.

259 The Porter.

"He commanded the Porter to Watch."

Arr. by A. Ross.

1. I am waiting for the Mas-ter, Who will rise and bid me come
To the glo-ry of his presence, To the gladness of his home.

REFRAIN.

I am watch - - ing at the por-tal, I am
I am watching, I am watching,

wait - - - ing at the door, On-ly wait
waiting, I am waiting   waiting, on-ly

- ing for his coming, My Re-deem - - er gone be-fore.
waiting   My Re-deemer, my Re-deemer

2 Many a weary path I've travelled
  In the darkness, storm and strife,
Bearing many a heavy burden,
  Often struggling for my life.

3 Many friends, who travelled with me,
  Reached the valley long ago;
One by one they left me battling
  With the dark and crafty foe.

4 Yes, their pilgrimage was shorter,
  And their journey sooner done;
O, how lovingly they'll greet me,
  When the battle shall be won.

5 I shall soon be there and with Him,
  I shall join the glorious throng,
There to mingle in his worship,
  And help swell the mighty song.

260   Turn to the Lord.

1. { Come, ye sin-ners, poor and needy, Weak and wounded, sick and sore; }
{ Je-sus ready stands to save you, Full of pit-y, love, and pow'r. }

D.C. Glo-ry, hon-or, ad-o-ration, Christ, the Lord, will come to reign.

CHORUS.   *D.C.*

Turn to the Lord, and seek sal-va-tion; Sound the praise of his dear name;

2 Now, ye needy, come and welcome,
    God's free bounty glorify;
True belief and true repentance—
    Every grace that brings you nigh.

3 Let not conscience make you linger,
    Nor of fitness fondly dream
All the fitness he requireth
    Is to feel your need of him.

4 Come, ye weary, heavy-laden,
    Bruised and mangled by the fall,
If you tarry till your better,
    You will never come at all.

5 Agonizing in the garden,
    Lo! your Saviour prostrate lies;
On the bloody tree behold him;
    Hear him cry before he dies.

——o——

261   Evening Hymn. S. M.

1. The day is past and gone, The evening shades ap-pear;

O, may we all re-mem-ber well, The night of death draws near!

2 Lord, keep us safe this night,
    Secure and free from fear;
May angels guard us till the light
    Of morning shall appear.

3 And then when we arise
    And view the unwearied sun,

May we press on to win the prize—
    For heavenly glory run.

4 And when life's day is past,
    And time shall be no more,
O, may we in thy presence rest,
    Where night will come no more.

262 The Pleading Voice.

JOEL SWARTZ.   I. BALTZELL, by per.

Moderato.

1. I oft - en heard a pleading voice, My in-most soul with - in;
2. A - las! I oft - en clos'd my ear, And steel'd my stubborn heart;
3. My out-ward life seem'd glad and gay, But still I had no rest;

It bade me make my God my choice, And flee the ways of sin.
The ten - der voice I would not hear, Nor from my sins de - part.
And still the slighted voice would say, "In God thou may'st be blest."

CHORUS. *Not too Loud.*

How ten - - der its tone,.......... Like a whis - - -

How ten-der its tone, How ten-der its tone, Like a whis-per, Like a

- per it came; Wheth - er throng'd or a - -

whis - per it came; Wheth-er throng'd or a - lone, Whether

Softly.

- lone,......... It was ev - - - er the same.

throng'd or a - lone, It was ev - er, it was ev - er the same.

4 At length I yielded, and found peace,
   And He forgave my sin;
And now, soft whispers never cease,
   Of peace and joy within.—*Cho.*

5 O bring to Him thy burdened soul,
   However much oppressed; [whole,
His whisp'ring voice will make thee
   And give thy conscience rest.—*Cho.*

263 The Chariot. 12s.

MILMAN.   J. WILLIAMS.

1. The Chariot! the Chariot! its wheels roll in fire, As the Lord com-eth
down in the pomp of His ire; Lo, self - moving, it drives on its
path-way of cloud, And the heav'ns with the burden of God - head are bow'd.

2 The glory! the glory! around Him are poured
Mighty hosts of the angels that wait on the Lord;
And the glorified saints, and the martyrs are there,
And there all who the palm-wreaths of victory wear.

3 The trumpet! the trumpet! the dead have all heard;
Lo, the depths of the stone-covered charnel are stirred!
From the sea, from the earth, from the south, from the north,
All the vast generations of men are come forth.

4 The Judgment! the Judgment! the thrones are all set,
Where the Lamb, and the white-vested elders are met;
There all flesh is at once in the sight of the Lord,
And the doom of eternity hangs on His word.

5 In mercy, in mercy, look down from above,
Great Creator, on us, thy sad children, with love!
When the wicked away from thy glory are driven,
May we find in thy presence a home and a heaven.

——o——

264 Fullness of Mercy.

H. W. FABER.   Arr. by S. J. VAIL.

1. There's a full-ness in God's mercy, Like the full-ness of the sea;

Fullness of Mercy. Concluded.

There's a kind-ness in His justice, Which is more than lib - er - ty.

REFRAIN.

He is call-ing, "Come to me;" Lord, I'll gladly haste to Thee.

2 For the love of God is broader
   Than the measure of man's mind;
   And the heart of the Eternal
   Is most wonderfully kind.—*Refr.*

3 Pining souls! come nearer Jesus;
   Come, but come not doubting thus.

Come with faith that trusts more freely
   His great tenderness for us.—*Refr.*

4 If our love were but more simple
   We should take him at his word;
   And our lives would be all sunshine
   In the sweetness of our Lord.—*Refr.*

—o—

265 Wesley.

C. WESLEY.

1. Come, let us a - new, Our journey pur-sue, Roll round with the

year, { And nev-er stand still Till the Master ap-pear,
       { And nev-er stand still Till the.............. Mas-ter ap-pear.

2 His adorable will
   Let us gladly fulfil,
   And our talents improve
‖: By the patience of hope
   And the labor of love. :‖

3 Our life as a dream,
   Our time as a stream,
   Glides swiftly away,
‖: And the fugitive moment
   Refuses to stay. :‖

4 Oh! that each, in the day
   Of his coming, may say:
   I have fought my way through,
‖: I have finished the work
   Thou didst give me to do. :‖

5 Oh! that each from the Lord
   May receive the glad word:
   Well and faithfully done!
‖: Enter into my joy
   And sit down on my throne! :‖

157

266   It Is I, Be Not Afraid.

"Be of good cheer; it is I, be not afraid."—Matt. xiv: 27.

I. BALTZELL.

A. S. KIEFFER, by per.

1. When the storm in its fu - ry on Gal - i - lee fell, And
2. The storm could not bur - y that word in the wave, 'Twas

lift- ed its wa - ters on high, And the faith-less dis - ci - ples were
taught thro' the tem-pest to fly; It shall reach his dis - ci - ples in

D.S. In the midst of the storm, In the

Fine.

bound in the spell, Je - sus whis-per'd, "Fear not, it is I."
ev - er - y clime, Say-ing, "Be not a - fraid, it is I."

midst of the gloom, Fear not, trem-bling one, "It is I."

CHORUS.

D.S

"It is I,...... It is I,".... Fear not, trembling ones, "It is I."

"It is I,"   "It is I,"   "It is I."

3 When the spirit is broken with sorrow and care,
   And comfort is ready to die;
  Then the darkness shall pass, and the sunshine appear
   By the life-giving word, "It is I."—*Cho.*

4 When the Judgment is nearing, and dark is the day;
   When clouds have o'er-shaded the sky;
  In the darkness and gloom, unto thee He will say,
   "Fear not now, look and see, "It is I."—*Cho.*

158

I'm a Traveller. **7s & 4s.**

I. I. LESLIE, 1843.   F. A. BLACKMER, by per.

1. I'm a lone-ly travel-ler here, Sad and op-press'd;

But my journey's end is near, Soon I shall rest.

Dark and drea-ry is the way, Wea-ry I've come;

Ask me not with you to stay; Yon-der's my home.

2 I'm a weary traveller here,
    I must go on;
For my journey's end is near;
    I must be gone.
Brighter joys than earth can give,
    Win me away;
Pleasures that forever live;
    I cannot stay.

3 I'm a traveller to a land
    Where all is fair;
Where is seen no broken band;
    All, all are there.—
Where no tear shall ever fall,
    Nor heart be sad;
Where the glory is for all,
    And all are glad.

4 I'm a traveller, and I go
    Where all is fair;
Farewell all I've loved below—
    I must be there.
Worldly honors, hopes and gain,
    All I resign;
Welcome sorrow, loss and pain,
    If Christ be mine.

5 I'm a traveller—call me not—
    Onward's my way;
Yonder is my rest and lot,
    I cannot stay.
Farewell earthly pleasures all,
    Pilgrim I'll roam;
Hail me not—in vain you call,
    Yonder's my home.

268 Hail to the Brightness. 11s & 10s.

By permission of O. DITSON & Co.

DR. L. MASON.

1. Hail to the brightness of Zi - on's glad morning! Joy to the lands that in dark-ness have lain; Hush'd be the ac - cents of sor-row and mourning, Zi - on in tri - umph be-gins her blest reign.

2 Hail to the brightness of Zion's glad morning,
 Long by the prophets of Israel foretold;
 Hail to the millions from bondage returning,
 Gentiles and Jews the blest vision behold.

3 Lo! in the desert rich flowers are springing,
 Streams ever copious are gliding along;
 Loud from the mountain-tops echoes are ringing,
 Wastes rise in verdure and mingle in song.

4 Hear, from all lands, from the isles of the ocean,
 Praise to Jehovah ascending on high;
 Fall'n are the engines of war and commotion;
 Shouts of salvation are rending the sky.

—o—

269 Win on the Field of Battle.

1. Firmly, brethren, firmly stand, All u - ni - ted, heart and hand, One unbroken,

2. In our Captain's name we boast, Christ it is who leads the host; Firmly then stand

CHORUS.

valiant band, Dauntless, brave and true. Win on the field of bat-tle, Win on the
at your post—Brethren, firmly stand.

field of bat-tle, Win on the field of bat - tle.—Glo-ry is in view.

270 Saviour, Comfort Me.

F. A. B.   F. A. BLACKMER, by per.

1 In the dark and gloomy day, When earth's rich-es fly a - way,

And the last hope will not stay, Then, Sav - iour, com - fort me.

2 When the dear, loved ones are gone,
· That my poor heart leaned upon,
· Desolate, bereft, alone,
    O, Saviour, comfort me.

3 Thou, who wast so sorely tried,
    And for me wast crucified,

Bid me in thy love confide—
    My Saviour, comfort me.

4 So it shall be good for me,
    Much afflicted now to be,
    If thou wilt but tenderly,
    My Saviour, comfort me.

——o——

271 Salvation's Free.

1. Come, ye that love the Lord, And let your joys be known;
Cho.—I'm glad sal - va - tion's free, I'm glad sal - va - tion's free;

Join in a song with sweet ac - cord, While ye sur-round his throne.
Sal - vation's free for you and me; I'm glad sal - va - tion's free.

2 Let those refuse to sing
    Who never knew our God,
    But servants of the heav'nly King
    May speak his praise abroad.—Cho.

3 There we shall see his face,
    And never, never sin ;
    There, from the rivers of his grace,
    Drink endless pleasures in.—Cho.

4 Yea, and before we rise
    To that immortal state,

The thoughts of such amazing bliss
    Should constant joys create.—Cho.

5 The men of grace have found
    Glory begun below ;
    Celestial fruit on earthly ground
    From faith and hope may grow.—Cho.

6 Then let our songs abound,
    And every tear be dry ;
    We're marching to Immanuel's ground—
    To it we're drawing nigh.—Cho.

272 Let Us Praise Him.

"Let all the people praise thee, O God, let all the people praise thee."—Psa. lxvii: 5.

I. B., by per.

Spirited.

1. To thee, my God and Sav-iour, My heart ex-ult-ing springs:
2. We cel-e-brate thy glory, With all the hosts a-bove,
3. By thee, through life sup-port-ed, We pass the dang-'rous road,
4. We'll cast our crowns be-fore thee, Our toils and con-flicts o'er,

Re-joic-ing in thy fa-vor, Al-mighty King of kings.
And tell the won-drous sto-ry Of thy re-deem-ing love.
By heav'nly hosts es-cort-ed, On to that bright a-bode.
And ev-er-more a-dore thee On Ca-naan's hap-py shore.

CHORUS.

Let us praise him, praise him, Praise his ho-ly
praise him, praise him, praise him, praise him,

name; Let us praise him, praise him,
praise him, praise him, praise him, praise him,

Praise his ho-ly name Hal-le-lu-jah! Hal-le-lu-jah! A-men.

273   Evergreen Plain.

I. BALTZELL, by per.

Moderato.

1. Shall we meet be-yond the riv - er, In that clime where saints will dwell?
2. Shall we meet where flow'rs are blooming, Ev - er fadeless, ev - er fair?

Shall we meet where friendship nev-er Will the tale of sor - row tell?
Where the light of day, il - lum-ing, Falls on all who en - ter there?

CHORUS.

Shall we meet,.......... shall we meet.......... shall we
Shall we meet,   Shall we meet,

meet on the ev - er - green plain?   Shall we
Shall we meet,

meet and know each oth-er ev - er? Shall we nev - er part a - gain?

3 Shall we meet our loved companions,
  On that brighter, fairer shore?
When the work of faith is ended,
Shall we meet to part no more?
    Cho.—Shall we meet, &c.

4 Yes! we'll meet beyond the river,
  Yes! we'll meet upon that shore,
Yes! we'll meet our lov'd and lost ones—
There we'll meet to part no more.
    Cho.—Shall we meet, &c.

163

274   **Holley. 7s.**

W. HAMMOND.
GEO. HEWS.

1. Lord, we come be - fore thee now, At thy feet we hum-bly bow;

Oh, do not our suit dis - dain; Shall we seek thee, Lord, in vain?

2 Lord, on thee our souls depend;
In compassion now descend;
Fill our hearts with thy rich grace,
Tune our lips to sing thy praise.

3 Send some message from thy word,
That may joy and peace afford;
Let thy spirit now impart
Full salvation to each heart.

4 Comfort those who weep and mourn;
Let the time of joy return;
Those that are cast down, lift up;
Make them strong in faith and hope,

5 Grant that all may seek and find
Thee a gracious God, and kind:
Heal the sick, the captive free;
Let us all rejoice in thee.

——o——

275   **Omega. 12s & 11s.**

A. A. HOYT.
ARR. by F. A. BLACKMER.

1. { The day of our God in its grandeur is com - ing,
Earth's vin - tage all ri - pen'd, the reap - ers de - scend - ing,

Cho.—O, Saviour, Re - deem - er, ride on in thy pow - er,

Fine.

Time's re - cord is clos - ing, the Judg - ment is near;.... }
Will reap the dread har - vest—Death's sick - le they bear...... }

De - scend in thy glo - ry, and reign on thy throne.

164

The Saviour de-scend-ing will come with all pow - er, The

trump of Je - ho - vah will sound thro' the air; And ter-ri-fied millions will

rit.   D. C.

wail in their anguish, Their hearts fail with ter-ror, and sink in de - spair.

2 Then will the great Judge on his throne be exalted,
   While heaven and earth see his banner unfurled;
The saints stand rejoicing, their vict'ry completed—
   Their mighty Deliv'rer is King of the world.
Oh, glorious day of the saints' resurrection!
   From land and from ocean again they will come,
And greet one another in holy relation,
   And then dwell, forever, in Eden, their home,

3 Creation is groaning, and travails with danger,
   The "wise" see its peril, and look for the end;
The Bride is in exile, a pilgrim and stranger,
   Expecting the Bridegroom will soon her defend.
She longs to lay by her sad garments of mourning,
   And put on the robe which her Lover will bring;
To strike the key-note of the loud, choral anthem
   At the coronation of Jesus, her King.

4 Our Father in heaven, we pray for the Kingdom
   Appointed to Jesus, our Saviour and Lord;
Where all thy redeemed ones will eat at his table,
   And dwell in his presence, their glorious reward.
Then come, O thou Blessed! with that shining city,
   Whose walls are of jasper, whose streets are of gold;
O, come with the mansions, for us, thou didst promise—
   We're watching and longing thy face to behold!

276 Waiting For Thee.

"To wait for his Son from Heaven."—1 Thess. i: 10.

I. I. LESLIE.   I. BALTZELL, by per.

1. Saviour, we are long-ing, waiting, For the com-ing of the day,
2. All our earthly name and treasure We have left to wel-come thee,
3. Lov-ing Saviour, come and save us, Save us from our dreadful foe;
4. Je - sus, come! O, bring thy glo-ry! We are look-ing it to see;

When thou wilt re - turn and bless us, Taking all our pains a - way.
And to do thy will and pleasure, Waiting till thy face we see.
In this des - ert do not leave us—Here we know not where to go.
We are tell-ing o'er the sto - ry, While we're waiting, Lord, for thee.

CHORUS.

We are waiting now for thee, We are wait-ing now for thee, We are
waiting, we are waiting for thee; We are waiting now for thee, We are
wait-ing now for thee, We are waiting, we are wait-ing for thee.

The Better Land.

1. We have heard of a bright, a better land; We have heard, and our hearts are glad,

For we were a lonely pilgrim band, And weary, and worn, and sad.

They tell us we pilgrims shall ever dwell there, No longer be homeless ones;

They say that the land is bright and fair, And clear, living water there runs.

2

They say green fields are waving there,
　That never a blight will know;
That hills and vales are blooming fair,
　And flowers, unfading, grow
And lovely birds in bowers green,
　Their melodies ever repeat;
While voices mingle in every scene
　With harpings of seraphim sweet!

3

We have heard of the robe, the palm, the
　crown,
　And the countless throng in white;
The city of gems of a high renown,
　Illumin'd with heavenly light.
The King in his beauty there will be,
　His presence the joy of the land;
A little while, and his face we'll see,
　And be with that beautiful band.

Watching and Waiting.

"Wait till my change come."—Job xiv: 14.

I. B.   I. BALTZELL, by per.

1. I will watch and wait for the morning's dawn, That will end the night of each weary [one;

I will sing my song as the days go by, Marching onward still to my home, so nigh.

CHORUS.

I am wait - - - ing for the dawn - - ing,
I am waiting for the dawning of that bright and glorious day, When the

wait - - - ing for the dawn - - ing,
storm of life is o - ver, and the mists have roll'd a - way; I am

wait - - ing for the dawn - - ing,
waiting for the summons that shall call me to my home, Waiting for the break of day.

2 I will watch and wait till the storm is o'er,
And a light shines out from the golden shore;
Then the Lord will say, "Weary wand'rer, come
To the land of rest, to thy blissful home."

3 I will watch and wait, for 'twill not be long
Ere I strike glad hands with the blood-washed throng;
Then I'll shout and sing while the ages roll,
Hallelujah! Christ hath redeemed my soul!

C. WESLEY.

Fine.

1. Vain, de-lu-sive world, a-dieu, With all of creature good;
Only Je-sus I pursue, Who bought me with his blood:
D.C. On-ly Je-sus will I know, And Je-sus cru-ci - - fied.

All thy pleasures I fore-go, I trample on thy wealth and pride,

2 Him to know is life and peace,
And pleasure without end;
This is all my happiness,
On Jesus to depend;
Daily in his grace to grow,
And ever in his love abide,
Only Jesus will I know,
And Jesus crucified!

3 O, that I could all invite,
This saving truth to prove;
Show the length, the breadth, the height,
And depth of Jesus' love;
Fain I would to sinners show,
His blood by faith alone applied;
Only Jesus will I know,
And Jesus crucified!

280

1 To the haven of thy breast,
O Son of Man, I fly!
Be my refuge and my rest,
For, O! the storm is high;
Save me from the furious blast;
A covert from the tempest be;
Hide me, Jesus, till o'erpast
The storm of wrath I see.

2 Welcome as the water-spring
To a dry and barren place;
O, descend to me and bring
Thy sweet refreshing grace;
O'er a parched and weary land,
As a great rock extends its shade,
Hide me, Saviour, with thy hand,
And screen my naked head.

3 In the time of my distress
Thou hast my succor been,
In my utter helplessness
Restraining me from sin;
O, how swiftly didst thou move
To save me in the trying hour!
Still protect me with thy love,
And shield me with thy power.

4 First and last in me perform
The work thou hast begun;
Be my shelter from the storm,
My shadow trom the sun;
Weary, parched with thirst, and faint,
Till thou th' abiding Spirit breathe,
Every moment, Lord, I want
The merit of thy death. C. WESLEY.

281   I'm a Pilgrim.

1. I'm a pilgrim and I'm a stranger, I can tar-ry, I can tar-ry bnt a night!

D.C.

Do not de-tain me, for I am go-ing To where the fountains are ev-er flowing.

169

282   We'll Await His Coming.

"For yet a little while he that shall come will come, and will not tarry."—Heb. ■ ɪ. 쪽

I. B., by per.

1. Oh, land of rest, for thee I sigh; When will the mo - ment come,
2. No tran-quil joys on earth I know, No peace-ful, shelt-'ring dome;
3. To Je - sus Christ I sought for rest; He bade me cease to roam,
4. Wea-ry of wand-'ring round and round This vale of sin and gloom,

When I shall lay my ar - mor by, And dwell in peace at home?
This world's a wil - der - ness of woe, This world is not my home.
And fly for suc - cor to his breast, And he'd con - duct me home.
I long to leave th' un-hallow'd ground, And dwell with Christ at home.

CHORUS.

We will wait the com-ing of the Lord,............ We will
We will wait the com-ing of the Lord,

wait the com-ing of the Lord, We will wait the
We will wait the coming of the Lord, We will

com-ing of the Lord,........... And we'll be gather'd home.
wait the coming of the Lord,

283   Federal Street. L. M.

H. K. OLIVER.

[Musical notation]

1. Asleep in Je - sus! blessed sleep, From which none ever wakes to weep;

A calm and un - dis - turb'd re - pose, Un-broken by the dread of foes.

2 Asleep in Jesus! peaceful rest,
Whose waking is supremely blest!
No fear, no foe shall dim that hour
Which manifests the Saviour's power.

3 Asleep in Jesus! time nor space
Affects this precious hiding-place;
On India's plains or Lapland's snows
Believers find the same repose.

4 Asleep in Jesus! far from thee
Thy kindred and their graves may be;
But thine is still a blessed sleep,
From which none ever wakes to weep.

284

1 Show pity, Lord! O Lord, forgive!
Let a repenting rebel live;
Are not thy mercies large and free?
May not a sinner trust in thee?

2 My crimes are great, but don't surpass
The pow'r and glory of thy grace;
Great God, thy nature hath no bound;
So let thy pard'ning love be found.

3 Oh, wash my soul from every sin,
And make my guilty conscience clean;
Here, on my heart, the burden lies,
And past offences pain my eyes.

4 My lips with shame my sins confess,
Against thy law, against thy grace;
Lord, should thy judgments grow severe,
I am condemned, but thou art clear.

5 Should sudd'n vengeance seize my breath,
I must pronounce thee just in death;
And if on thy left hand I stand,
It will be by thy just command.

6 Yet save a trembling sinner, Lord,
Whose hope still hov'ring round thy word
Would light on some sweet promise there,
Some sure support against despair.

——0——

285   Happy Man. 6s & 7s.

[Musical notation]

1. How happy is the man who has cho-sen wisdom's ways, And measur'd
D.C. In pov-er-ty he's happy, for he knows he has a Friend Who nev-er

Fine.

out his span to his God in pray'r and praise; His God and his Bi - ble are
will forsake him, and on whom he can depend.

D.C.

all that he de-sires, To ho-li-ness of heart he con - tin-ual-ly aspires;

The Good Old Way. 8s.

1. Lift up your heads, Immanuel's friends, And taste the pleasure Je - sus sends;

Let nothing cause you to de-lay, But hasten in the good old way.

CHORUS.

O, good old way! how sweet thou art, May none of us from thee de-part.

2 Our conflicts here, though great they be,
Shall not prevent our victory;
If we but watch, and strive, and pray,
Like soldiers in the good old way.

Chorus.
O, praise the Lord! we shall gain the day,
By marching in the good old way.

3 O, good old way! how sweet thou art,
May none of us from thee depart,
But may our actions always say,
We're marching in the good old way.

4 Though Satan may his arts employ,
Our heavenly prospects to destroy,

Yet never fear, we'll gain the day,
By marching in the good old way.

5 And when on Pisgah's top we stand,
And view by faith the promised land,
Then we will sing, and shout, and pray,
And march along the good old way.

6 Ye valiant souls, for Christ contend,
Remember glory's at the end;
Our God will wipe all tears away,
When we have run the good old way.

7 When far beyond this mortal shore,
We meet with those we've loved before,
We'll shout to think we've gain'd the day,
By marching in the good old way.

287 All the Way 'Long it is Jesus.

1. { Oh, good old way, how sweet thou art, All the way 'long it is Je - sus. }
{ May none of us from thee de - part, All the way 'long it is Je - sus. }

CHORUS.

Je - sus, Je - sus, Why, all the way 'long it is Je - sus.

2 But may our actions always say
We're marching in the good old way. [173]

3 This note above the rest shall swell,
That Jesus doeth all things well.

288   Homeward Bound.

1. Out on an o-cean all boundless we ride, We're homeward bound,
Toss'd on the waves of a rough, restless tide, We're homeward bound,

home-ward bound:
home-ward bound; Far from the safe, qui-et har-bor we've rode,

Seek-ing our Father's ce-les-tial a-bode, Prom-ise of

which on us each he bestow'd, We're homeward bound, homeward bound.

2 Wildly the storm sweeps us on as it roars,
  We're homeward bound, homeward bound:
Look! yonder lie the bright, heavenly shores,
  We're homeward bound, homeward bound.
Steady, O pilot! stand firm at the wheel,
Steady! we soon shall outweather the gale;
O, how we fly 'neath the loud creaking sail!
  We're homeward bound, homeward bound.

3 Into the harbor of Eden now we glide,
  We're home at last, home at last;
Softly we drift on its bright, silver tide,
  We're home at last, home at last.
Glory to God! all our dangers are o'er,
We stand secure on the glorified shore.
Glory to God we shall shout evermore,
  We're home at last, home at last.

289 Praise the Lord.

JOHN MAXIM.

1. { Come, brethren, let us join and sing, Praise the Lord! Praise the Lord!
   { Christ is our Prophet, Priest and King, Praise the Lord! Praise the Lord!

Come, let us speak, and sing and pray, And help each oth-er on the way Till

dawns the bright, e-ter-nal day, Praise the Lord! Praise the Lord!

2 Jesus is on the mercy-seat,
  ‖: Praise the Lord! :‖
Come, bow and worship at his feet,
  ‖: Praise the Lord! :‖
He's promis'd that when two or three
Meet in His name, there He will be,
And His salvation they shall see,
  ‖: Praise the Lord! :‖

3 Then, brethren, let us bear the cross,
  ‖: Praise the Lord! :‖
And count all things below as dross,
  ‖: Praise the Lord! :‖
If Jesus Christ you follow here, [fear,
There's naught on earth you need to
Tho' in the clouds He should appear,
  ‖: Praise the Lord! :‖

——O——

290 Ne'er to Sever. 6s & 5s.

1. When shall we meet a-gain—Meet ne'er to sev-er? When will peace

wreathe her chain Round us for-ev-er? Our hearts will ne'er re-pose, Safe

from each blast that blows, In this dark vale of woes—Never, no, nev-er!

291   **Talmar.**   **8s & 7s.**

By permission of O. Ditson & Co.   I. B. WOODBURY.

1. Hail! thou once re-ject-ed Je-sus, Now the ev-er-last-ing King!

Thou didst suf-fer to re-deem us, Thou didst our sal-va-tion bring

2 Once the agonizing Saviour,
    Bearing all our sin and shame!
By thy merits we find favor;
    Life is given through thy name.
3 Paschal Lamb, by God appointed!
    All our sins on thee were laid;

With the Spirit's power anointed,
    Thou hast full atonement made.
4 All thy people are forgiven
    Through the virtue of thy blood;
Thou didst come to earth from heaven,
    Here to make our peace with God.

—— o ——

292   **St. Thomas.**   **S. M.**

A. WILLIAMS.

1. In ev-'ry try-ing hour My soul to Je-sus flies;

I trust in his Al-mighty pow'r When swell-ing bil-lows rise.

2 His comforts bear me up;
    I trust a faithful God:
The sure foundation of my hope
    Is in my Saviour's blood.
3 Loud hallelujahs sing
    To our Redeemer's name;
In joy or sorrow, life or death,
    His love is still the same.

293
1 With willing hearts we tread
    The path the Saviour trod;

We love th' example of our Head,
    The glorious Lamb of God.

2 On thee, on thee alone,
    Our hope and faith rely;
O, thou who didst for sin atone,
    Who didst for sinners die!

3 We trust thy sacrifice;
    To thy dear cross we flee;
O, may we die to sin, and rise
    To life and bliss in thee!

294 Precious is the Promise.

A. T. G.   FRANK M. DAVIS.

1. Precious is the promise, Faith-ful is the word Giv-en to the
sons of men By the lov-ing Lord; Hear Him gently pleading—
Heed his mild be - hest: Come to me, ye wea-ry ones, I will give you

REFRAIN.

rest. Pre-cious, precious promise, Faith-ful, faith-ful word;

Ev - er-more, oh Saviour dear, Be Thy name a - dored!

2 Lo! the cleansing fountain
   Flows for you and me;
From the deadly ban of sin
   Christ will set you free.
Come, ye weak and erring—
   Come, oh, weary soul!
Seek the Great Physician now,
   He will make you whole.—*Refrain.*

3 Precious is the promise,
   Faithful is the word;
Sinner, turn—why will you die?
   Seek your waiting Lord.
While the blessing lingers,
   To the refuge come;
Win a fadeless crown of life—
   Gain a deathless home.—*Refrain.*

295   Shirland. S. M.

ISAAC WATTS.   SAMUEL STANLEY.

1. My soul! re - peat his praise, Whose mer-cies are so great;

Whose an - ger is so slow to rise, So read-y to a - bate.

2 High as the heavens are raised
  Above the ground we tread;
So far the riches of his grace
  Our highest thoughts exceed.

3 His power subdues our sins;
  And his forgiving love,

Far as the east is from the west,
  Doth all our guilt remove.

4 The pity of the Lord,
  To those who fear his name,
Is such as tender parents feel;
  He knows our feeble frame.

—o—

296   Faith. L. M.

C. WESLEY.   JEREMIAH INGALLS.
                            Fine.

1. { A-way, my un-be-liev-ing fear! Fear shall in me no more have place; }
   { My Saviour doth not yet ap-pear, He hides the brightness of his face: }
D.C. No, in the strength of Je-sus, no! I nev-er will give up my shield.

But shall I there-fore let him go, And base-ly to the tempter yield?

2 Although the vine its fruit deny,
  Although the olive yield no oil,
The with'ring fig-trees droop and die,
  The fields elude the tiller's toil;
The empty stall no herd afford,
  And perish all the bleating race;
Yet will I triumph in the Lord,
  The God of my salvation praise.

3 In hope, believing against hope.
  Jesus, my Lord, my God, I claim;
Jesus, my strength, shall lift me up;
  Salvation is in Jesus' name.
To me he soon shall bring it nigh;
  I shall with joy outstrip the wind;
On wings of love mount up on high,
  And leave the world and sin behind.

177

Heber. C. M.

Geo. Kingsley.

1. Je - ru - sa-lem, our heav'nly home, Name to us ev - er dear,

When will the Saviour come, and thou To us, his saints ap - pear.

2 When shall these eyes thy jasper walls
  And gates of pearl survey:
  The fabric reared on precious stones
  Of every brilliant ray?

3 Transparent as the crystal glass,
  And formed of purest gold;

Perfection's height art thou, of all
  That man can e'er behold.

4 O when, thou city of our God,
  Wilt thou for us descend,
  And our eternal Sabbath come,
  When praise shall never end?

——0——

298 Sicilian Hymn. 8s & 7s.

1. Lord, dis - miss us, with thy bless-ing, Fill our hearts with joy and peace,

{ Let us each, thy love pos-sess-ing, Tri-umph in re - deeming grace: }
{ Oh, re-fresh us, Oh, re - fresh us, Trav'ling thro' this wilder-ness. }

2 Thanks we give, and adoration,
  For the gospel's joyful sound;
  May the fruits of thy salvation
  In our hearts and lives abound;
  ‖: May thy presence :‖
  With us evermore be found.

3 So, whene'er the signal's given
  Us from earth to call away,
  Borne on angels' wings to heaven,
  Glad the summons to obey,
  ‖: May we ever :‖
  Reign with Christ in endless day.

Good News.

Words by M. G.
Moderato.

I. BALTZELL, by per.

1. Good news, good news, I hear; 'Tis sounding far and wide, The Lord will soon ap-pear, To take His lov-ing Bride. She's wait-ed long to see The hap-py morning dawn, When death no more will be, And sin for-ev-er gone.

CHORUS.
Lively.

Re-joice,.... re-joice,.... Good news, good news I hear;...
Re-joice, re-joice, re-joice, re-joice, I hear;

Re-joice,.... re-joice,.... Good news, good news I hear.
Re-joice, re-joice, re-joice, re-joice,

2 The joyful news I love,
 That Jesus soon will come
In glory from above,
 To take his people home.
Then all our grief will cease,
 And partings be no more;
We'll greet our friends in peace,
 On Canaan's happy shore.

3 Dear Jesus, come again,
 We'll gladly welcome thee,
O, come on earth to reign,
 And set Death's captives free.
'Till then direct our way;
 With Thee we would agree;
For this we humbly pray,
 Come bring the jubilee.

Pilgrim. 7s.

GEO. CRABBE.

J. C. STODDARD.

Andante.

1. Pil-grim, bur-den'd with thy sin, Come the way to Zi-on's gate:

There, till mer-cy lets thee in. Knock, and weep, and watch, and wait.

Knock—he knows the sin-ner's cry; Weep—he loves the mourner's tears;

Watch, for sav-ing grace is nigh; Wait, till heav'nly light ap-pears.

2

Hark, it is the Bridegroom's voice:
  "Welcome, pilgrim, to thy rest!"
Now within the gate rejoice,
  Safe, and seal'd, and bought, and blest:
Safe, from all the lures of vice;
  Sealed, by signs the chosen know;
Bought by love, and life the price;
  Blest, the mighty debt to owe

3

Holy pilgrim, what for thee
  In a world like this remain?
From thy guarded breast shall flee
  Fear, and shame, and doubt, and pain;
Fear, the hope of heaven shall fly;
  Shame, from glory's view retire;
Doubt, in certain rapture die;
  Pain, in endless bliss expire.

301   Wilmot.   8s & 7s.

From C. M. Von WEBER.

1. Je - sus, while our hearts are bleeding O'er the spoils that death has won,

We would, at this sol - emn meeting, Calm-ly say, Thy will be done.

2 Though cast down, we're not forsaken;
   Though afflicted, not alone;
Thou didst give, and thou hast taken;
   Blessed Lord, Thy will be done.

3 Tho' to-day we're fill'd with mourning,
   Mercy still is on the throne;
With thy smiles of love returning,
   We can sing, Thy will be done.

4 By thy hands the boon was given;
   Thou hast taken but thine own;
Lord of earth and God of heaven,
   Evermore, Thy will be done.

302

1 Lo! the Lord Jehovah liveth!
   He's my rock, I bless his name;
He, my God, salvation giveth;
   All ye lands, exalt his fame

2 God, Messiah's cause maintaining,
   Shall his righteous throne extend:
O'er the world the Saviour reigning,
   Earth shall at his footstool bend.

3 O'er his enemies exalted,
   Great Redeemer! see him rise!
Though by powers of hell assaulted,
   God supports him to the skies.

4 Jesus, hail! enthroned in glory,
   Through all ages to abide;
All the heavenly host adore thee,
   Seated at thy Father's side.

—0—

303   The Band Hymn.

L. H.

1. { We are a band of brethren dear, I belong to this band, Halle - lu - jah! }
{ Who live as pilgrim strangers here, I belong to this band, Halle - lu - jah! }

Hal-le-lu - jah! hal-le-lu - jah! I be - long to this band, Halle - lu - jah!

2 The prophets and apostles too
   Did belong, &c.
And all God's children here below
   Do belong, &c.

3 King David on his throne of state
   Did belong, &c.
And Lazarus at the rich man's gate
   Did belong, &c.

4 And Jews and Gentiles, free and bond,
   May belong, &c.
And rich and poor the world around
   May belong, &c.

5 I hope to meet my brethren there,
   They belong, &c.
Who often joined with me in prayer,
   They belonged, &c.

304 **I Have Found Him.**

JOHN BARBOUR.   Prof. WM. A. McNEAL, by per.

1. I have found him! O, how precious Jesus now appears to me; He has heard my
pray'r and bless'd me, And from sin has set me free; Oh, how hap-py it has made me,
To surrender all to thee: Blessed Saviour, thine the glory, Shall my song for-

CHORUS.

- ev - er be. Yes, I've found him, and his glory Has complete-ly fill'd my soul!

Glo - ry in the high-est, glo - ry, For the half was nev - er told!

2 Now no more I pine with sorrow,
Heavy burden'd with my sin;
For I am an heir of glory,
And his praise I'll now begin:
Blessed be the name of Jesus;
Glory to the Lamb above;
I am saved, all through his mercy
And the fullness of his love.

3 Would you find him, seek his mercy;
Sinner, wont you come just now?
He will listen to your pleadings,
At the throne of grace now bow.
O, what joy his grace will give you,
You will sing with joy the Song—
Hallelujah! I have found him,
Glory, glory to the Lamb!

305 The Saviour Calling. 7s & 6s.

I. I. LESLIE.   By permission of O. Ditson & Co.   L. O. EMERSON.

1. I hear the Sa - viour call - ing, He calls my heart a - way

From ev - 'ry fad - ing ob - ject, From all that will de - cay.

No more to earth - ly treas - ures, No more to friends I'll cling;

No more I'll seek earth's pleasures— To Him my heart I bring.

2 The day of life is passing,
  And I shall soon be gone;
What then are earthly treasures,
  Or all I've looked upon?
If He but call me to him,
  If I by grace can go,
I shall be rich, and never
  A loss or trial know.

3 Farewell to all that holds me
  Away from His dear arms;
Adieu to earthly pleasures,
  And all earth's gilded charms;
I hear the Saviour calling,
  Earth's treasures all grow dim;
Farewell to all its pleasures—
  I'm going now to Him.

—o—

306 Why, it's all Glory. 8s & 7s.

1. { Je-sus sought me when a stranger, Wand'ring from the fold of God;
   { He, to res - cue me from danger, In - ter-pos'd his precious... blood. }

CHORUS.

Why, its all glory, glory, Glory, hallelujah, We're going where pleasures never die.

188

307 I Will Guide Thee with Mine Eye.

"I will guide thee with mine eye."—Ps xxxii: 8.

Words arr. by I. I. Leslie.

Wm. W. Bentley, by per.

With Feeling.

1. Sweet and precious is the promise God has giv'n each pass-er by,
On the way to rest and glo-ry, "I will guide thee with mine eye."

CHORUS.

I will guide thee, I will guide thee, I will guide thee with mine eye;
On the way to rest and glo-ry, I will guide thee with mine eye.

2 In thy trouble, care and sorrow,
And when hope is near to die;
Let this promise keep thee steadfast.
"I will guide thee with mine eye."
Cho.—I will guide thee, &c.

3 When the tempter comes to 'lure thee
From the way, and foes are nigh,
Let this promise then assure thee
"I will guide thee with mine eye."
Cho.—I will guide thee, &c.

4 When thy last fond hope is numbered,
And thy present comforts fly,
Let this promise be remembered,
"I will guide thee with mine eye."
Cho.—I will guide thee, &c.

5 When thro' deeper shades and darkness,
Onward still thy path may lie,
Hear Him say, "I will be with thee,"
"I will guide thee with mine eye."
Cho.—I will guide thee, &c.

308 Hendon. 7s.

Dr. Malan,

1. Children of the heav'nly King, As ye journey, sweetly sing; Sing your Saviour's

worthy praise, Glorious in his works and ways, Glorious in his works and ways.

2 Fear not, brethren, joyful stand
On the borders of the land;
Jesus Christ, your Father's Son,
|: Bids you undismayed go on. :|

3 Lord, submissively we'll go,
Gladly leaving all below;
Only thou our leader be,
|: And we still will follow thee. :|

309 None but the Righteous. L. M.

From "Devotional Melodies."

1. Come, sinners, to the gos-pel feast, None but the righteous will be sav'd,
Let ev-'ry soul be Jesus' guest: None but the righteous will be sav'd.
Ye need not one be left behind. None but the righteous will be sav'd,
For God hath bid-den all mankind. None but the righteous will be sav'd.

CHORUS.

Oh, no! oh, no! None but the right'ous will be sav'd:
Oh, no! oh, no! None but the right'ous.............. will be sav'd.

2 Sent by my Lord, on you I call;
The invitation is to all;
Come, all the world! come, sinner, thou!
All things in Christ are ready now.

3 My message as from God receive;
Ye all may come to Christ and live;
O let his love your hearts constrain,
Nor suffer him to die in vain!

310 We'll Stand by That Stream.

Words arr. by I. L. L.   I. BALTZELL, by per.

1. I'll sing of that stream, of that beau-ti-ful stream, That flows thro' the
2. I'll sing of that stream, of that beau-ti-ful stream, Which gladdens the

sweet E - den land: Its wa - ters gleam bright in the heav-en-ly light, And
cit - y of God; It flows from the throne of the Fa - ther a - lone, And

CHORUS.

rip - ple o'er bright, gold-en sand. We'll stand by that beau-ti-ful
spreads its sweet wa - ters a - broad.   Stand by the

stream,...... We'll stand by that beau-ti-ful stream,...... Its
beau-ti-ful stream,   Stand by the beau-ti-ful stream,

wa - ters so brightly flowing, so free; We'll stand by that beauti - ful stream.

3 I'll sing of that stream, of that beautiful stream,
    Where never a sorrow is known;
    Where angels shall stand with the ever-saved band,
    And walk in the light of the Throne.—*Cho.*

4 I'll sing of that stream, of that beautiful stream,
    The River of Life is its name;
    When our sorrows are o'er, we will stand on its shore,
    And loud our salvation proclaim.—*Cho.*

1. The Lord will come; the earth shall quake, The hills their fix-ed seat for-sake; And, with'ring, from the vault of night, The stars withdraw their feeble light.

2 The Lord will come, but not the same
As once in lowly form he came—
A silent Lamb to slaughter led,
The bruis'd, the suff'ring, and the dead.

3 The Lord will come—a glorious form—
Come as the lightning and the storm;
On radiant clouds, swift as the wind,
He'll come the Judge of all mankind.

4 Can this be he who, once did stray
A pilgrim on the world's highway,
By pow'r oppress'd, and mock'd by pride?
O God! is this the crucified?

5 While sinners in despair shall call
"Rocks, hide us! mountains, on us fall!"
The saints ascending from the tomb,
Shall joyful sing, "The Lord is come!"

312 Keep Your Lamps Burning.

"Then all those virgins arose and trimmed their lamps."—Matt. xxv: 7.

Arranged by I. I. LESLIE.   Arranged by I. B.

Spirited.

1. We're a band of pilgrim strangers, Trav'ling thro' a land of dangers;
2. Now by faith we do discover That the journey's al-most o-ver,

But the Saviour is our Lead-er, And he'll sure-ly bring us through.
And we're nearing now the bor-der Of the bright and hap-py land.

CHORUS.

ff

Keep your lamps trimm'd and burning, Keep your lamps trimm'd and burning,

Keep your lamps trimm'd and burning, Keep your ves-sels fill'd with oil.

3 Long the journey's been, and weary,
And the way both dark and dreary;
But we soon shall see the city
And be there forevermore.

4 From the wilderness we're coming,
And we soon shall cease our roaming;
Now the Jordan's just before us,
And we soon shall o'er it go.

—o—

313   Oh, Tell Me No More.   11s.

Oh, tell me no more of this world's vain store, The time for such tri-fles with
With me now is o'er, with me now is o'er; The time for such tri-fles with

me now is o'er;
me now is o'er.

The souls that believe, will in Paradise live,
And me in that number will Jesus receive;
My soul, don't delay, he calls thee away,
Rise, follow thy Saviour, and hail the glad day.

WM. BILLINGS, 1770.

1. Oh! for... a thousand tongues to sing My great Re-deem-er's praise,

The glo-ries of my God and King, The tri - - - umphs of .. his grace

2. My gra-cious Mas-ter, and my God, As - sist me to pro - claim—

To spread thro' all the earth a - broad The hon-ors of thy Name;

To spread thro' all the earth a-broad The hon - ors of thy Name.

3 Jesus! the Name that charms our fears,
   That bids our sorrows cease;
   'Tis music in the sinner's ears,
   'Tis life, and health, and peace.

4 He breaks the power of cancell'd sin,
   He sets the pris'ner free;
|: His blood can make the foulest clean;
   His blood avail'd for me. :||

5 He speaks,—and, list'ning to His voice,
   New life the dead receive;
   The mournful, broken hearts rejoice;
   The humble poor believe.

6 Hear Him, ye deaf; His praise, ye dumb,
   Your loosen'd tongues employ;
|: Ye blind, behold your Saviour come;
   And leap, ye lame, for joy :||

315 Fly to the Fountain.

"In that day there shall be a fountain opened."—Zech. xiii: 1.

F. E. PITTS.   I. BALTZELL, by per.

1. There is   a fountain pure and free, It flows for you, It flows for me:
2. To   ev-'ry land, to   ev-'ry race, In "ev-'ry dry and barren place,"
3. To   wake the world, and all in-vite, The Spir-it and the Bride u-nite;

Now ev-'ry tribe be-neath the sun May to   this flow-ing fountain run.
The wa-ter's free, and free the call; None are de-nied, but welcom'd all.
And let the news be car-ried home, And ev-'ry one that hears it, come.

CHORUS.

Fly   to the fount-ain,   Flow-ing   free-ly,
Will you fly with me to the cleansing fountain, Flowing ev-er pure and free;

Fly   to the fount - ain,   Flowing for you and for me?
Will you fly with me to the cleansing fountain?

4	5
The thirsty, in the desert place,	"Ho! every one," the prophet cries—
May hear the welcome word of grace;	And every one, my soul replies—
Though dying, if he will believe	For every one there's ample room;
Eternal life he shall receive.	Then freely to the waters come.
Cho.—Will you fly with me, &c.	*Cho.*—Will you fly with me, &c.

From "Songs of Grace," by permission.

190

316   Coming to the Saviour.

E. A. H.

ASA HULL

1. I am com-ing to the Saviour, At His feet I bow;
2. All my sin and guilt con-fess-ing, At His feet I bow;
3. In con-tri-tion hum-bly kneel-ing, At His feet I bow;

I am plead-ing for His fa-vor, Just now, just now.
I am wait-ing for His bless-ing, Just now, just now.
I am seek-ing grace and heal-ing, Just now, just now.

CHORUS.

I am com-ing, I am com-ing, I am com-ing just now,
com-ing, com-ing,

I am com-ing, I am com-ing, I am com-ing just now.
com-ing, com-ing,

4
I believe Him, I believe Him,
At His feet I bow;
I receive Him, I receive Him,
Just now, just now.
  Cho.—I am coming, &c.

5
Hallelujah! Hallelujah!
To the Lamb once slain;
Hallelujah! Hallelujah!
Amen! Amen!
  Cho.—I am coming, &c.

From "Songs of Faith," by permission.

Going Forth. 7s.

"And went forth to meet the Bridegroom."—Matt. xxv: 1.

1. Ye who rose to meet the Lord, Ventured on his faithful word,

Faint not now for your re-ward Will be quickly giv'n.

Faint not now, still watch and pray; Je - sus will not long de - lay;

E - ven now 'tis dawn of day; Day's star shines from heav'n.

2 Would you evermore endure,
Keep the garment spotless, pure;
Claim the promise, ever sure—
Faithful is the Lord.
Let your lamps be burning bright,
In God's word is radiant light,
Walk by faith and not by sight—
Crowns are the reward.

3 'Mid the darts of every foe,
Onward, fearless, onward go,
The good soldier's courage show—
On to victory!

"Let thine eyes be turned on me,"
Jesus says—"I'll rescue thee;
Overcome, and faithful be—
Thou shalt glory see."

4 Tokens now are in the sky,
Angel voices, sounding high,
Echo there the mighty cry,—
"Jesus claim thy own."
Saints on earth take up the strain,
"Quickly come, O come to reign!"
Heaven and earth resound, "Amen!
Welcome to thy throne!"

—o—

318 Save, or We Perish. 12s.

1. When thro' the torn sail the wild tempest was streaming, When o'er the dark

Save, or we Perish. Concluded.

wave the red light'ning was gleaming, Nor hope lent a ray, the dis-

- ci-ples to cherish, They flew to their Master, "Save, Lord, or we perish!"

2 O, Jesus, once tossed on the breast of the billow,
Aroused by the cry of despair from thy pillow,
Now, seated in glory, the poor sinner cherish,
Who cries in his danger, "Save, Lord, or I perish!"

3 And oh! when the whirlwind of passion is raging,
When sin in our hearts its wild warfare is waging,
Arise in Thy strength, thy redeemed ones to cherish!
Rebuke the destroyer,—"Save, Lord, or we perish!"

——o——

319   Coming to the City.

Words by I. I. L.   Southern Melody, arr.

1. Tho' the way grow dark and drear-y, And the tempests harder blow;..

Cho.—We are com-ing to the Cit - y, We can almost see its light;...

D.C.

Tho' thou hast grown faint and wea - ry, Courage, now! and forward go!

We are com-ing to the Cit - y, Now it is al-most in sight.

2 Though the foe be all around us,
  And our friends be weak and few,
He who sought us here and found us,
  He will lead us safely through.—Cho.

3 Captain now of our salvation,
  He our King is soon to be;
He will rule o'er every nation—
  He will set his people free.—Cho.

4 Hasten on ye pilgrims weary,
  Hasten on, though rough the way;
Though it darker grow and dreary,
  Soon we'll see the shining day.—Cho

5 Soon He cometh in his glory,
  Soon the journey will be o'er;
We shall then begin the story
  To be told forevermore.—Cho.

320   The Solid Rock. L. M.

WM. B. BRADBURY.

1. My hope is built on nothing less Than Je - sus and his

righteousness; I dare not trust the sweetest frame, But wholly lean on

Je - sus' name; On Christ, the sol - id Rock, I stand; All

oth - er ground is sinking sand, All oth - er ground is sinking sand.

2 When darkness seems to veil his face,
  I rest on his unchanging grace;
  In every high and stormy gale,
  My anchor holds within the vail:
    On Christ, the solid Rock, I stand;
    All other ground is sinking sand.

3 His oath, his covenant, and blood,
  Support me in the whelming flood,
  When all around my soul gives way,
  He then is all my hope and stay!
    On Christ, the solid Rock, I stand;
    All other ground is sinking sand.

No. 2.

1 The smitten Rock, whence water flows,
  To quench my thirst and heal my woes;
  From it a stream, on every hand,
  Runs free through all the desert land:
  This Rock, my spring, to which I fly
  When other springs are parched and dry.

2 When clouds and tempests fill the sky,
  Within this Rock I calmly lie;
  Safe from the blast and beating rain,
  I am secure, and here remain:
  Within this Rock, my hiding-place,
  I rest secure, and trust His grace.

3 When friends forsake, and foes are near,
  When earthly help shall disappear;
  Then will I trust this Rock so high,
  And in its strength more firm rely:
  This Rock my life and all shall be
  Through time and in eternity.

4 When earth shall shake and nature rend,
  This Rock shall stand and me defend;
  Beneath its calm, majestic form,
  I shall be safe amid the storm:
  O, Rock of my salvation, Thou
  Shalt be my shelter then as now!

I. I. LESLIE

Malvern. L. M.

By permission of O. Ditson & Co.

L. Mason.

1. Awake! our souls, a - way! our fears, Let ev'ry trembling thought be gone;

Awake! and run the heav'nly race, And put a cheerful courage on.

2 True,—'tis a straight and thorny road,
And mortal spirits tire and faint;
But they forget the mighty God,
Who feeds the strength of every saint:

3 The mighty God, whose matchless pow'r
Is ever new and ever young;

And firm endures while endless years
Their everlasting circles run.

4 From thee, the overflowing spring,
Our souls shall drink a full supply;
While such as trust their native strength,
Shall melt away, and droop, and die.

——o——

322 Prayer and Mercy-Seat.

1. What va-ri-ous hin-d'ran-ces we meet In coming to the mer-cy-seat;

Yet who that knows the worth of pray'r, But wishes to be of-ten there

2 Pray'r makes the darkest cloud withdraw,
Pray'r climbs the ladder Jacob saw;
Gives exercise to faith and love,
Brings every blessing from above.

3 Restraining prayer, we cease to fight,
Pray'r makes the christian's armor bright,
And Satan trembles when he sees
The weakest saint upon his knees.

4 When Moses stood with arms spread wide,
Success was found on Israel's side;

But when through weariness they failed,
That moment Amalek prevailed.

5 Have you no words? Ah! think again,
Words flow apace when you complain,
And fill your fellow creature's ears
With a sad tale of all your cares.

6 Were half the breath thus vainly spent,
To Heaven in supplication sent,
Your cheerful song would often be,
Hear what the Lord hath done for me.

323   The Beautiful City.

T. J. Cook.

1. Beautiful Zi - on, now a - bove, Beautiful cit - y that I love;

Beautiful gates of pear-y white, Beautiful temple—God its light!

He who was slain on Cal - va - ry, Opens those pearly gates to me.

REFRAIN.   *Repeat pp.*

Zi - on, Zi-on, love-ly Zi-on, Beau-ti-ful Zi - on, cit-y of our God.

2 Beautiful crowns on every brow
Beautiful palms the conquerors show;
Beautiful robes the ransom'd wear,
Beautiful all who enter there.
Thither I press with eager feet,
There shall my rest be long and sweet.

3 Beautiful throne of Christ our King,
Beautiful songs the saints will sing;
Beautiful rest—all wand'rings cease,
Beautiful home of perfect peace;
There shall my eyes the Saviour see—
Haste to that heavenly home with me.

—o—

324   The Pilgrim Stranger.   L. M.

1. { Whith - er goest thou, pil - grim stranger, Wand'ring thro' this
Know'st thou not 'tis full of dang-er, And will not thy

190

The Pilgrim Stranger. Concluded.

CHORUS.

gloom - y vale?
cour - age fail? "No! I'm bound for the kingdom; Will you

go to glo-ry with me? Hal - le - lu - jah! Praise ye the Lord."

2
"Pilgrim thou dost justly call me,
Trav'ling through this lonely void;
But no ill shall e'er befall me,
While I'm blest with such a *Guide*.
"Oh, I'm bound, &c."

3
Such a Guide! no guide attends thee,
Hence for thee my fears arise;

If some guardian power defend thee,
'Tis unseen by mortal eyes.
"Oh, I'm bound, &c."

4
"Yes, unseen; but still believe me,
Such a guide my steps attend;
He'll in every strait relieve me,"
He will guide me to the end.
"I am bound, &c."

——o——

325   Essex.   7s.   D. or 7s, 6 l.

Arranged from a Spanish Melody.

Slow and expressive.   *Fine.*

1. { Rock of A - ges, cleft for me,   Let me hide my - self in thee;
   { Let the wa - ter and the blood,   From thy wounded side which flow'd,
D.C. Be of sin the dou - ble cure,   Save from wrath and make me pure.

D.C.

Be of sin the double cure,   Save from wrath and make me pure;

2 Could my tears forever flow,
Could my zeal no languor know,
These for sin could not atone,
Thou must save, and thou alone:
{: In my hand no price I bring,
Simply to thy cross I cling. :}

3 While I draw this fleeting breath,
When my eyes shall close in death,
When I with the throng unknown
See thee on thy judgment throne—
|: Rock of Ages, cleft for me,
Let me hide myself in thee. :|

326 Only Waiting.

"They that watch for the morning."—Ps. cxxx 6.

Words Arranged by I. I. L.   Author Unknown.

1. On-ly wait-ing till the dawning; Till the drear-y night has flown;

On-ly wait-ing till the twi-light In-to the full day has grown;

Till the shadows are all scatter'd, And the earth is bright a-gain;

And He com-eth who for-ev-er O-ver all the world shall reign.

2 Only waiting till the dawning
  Of the grand, eternal day;
Waiting for the beams of glory
  That shall drive the night away.
Waiting for the angels' voices,
  To be heard along the skies;
Waiting for the trumpet's sounding,
  That shall bid the dead arise.

3 Only waiting till the heavens
  Are aglow with radiant light,
And the clouds shall bear Him hither
  With attending angels bright;

Waiting till we see the shining
  And the glory of His throne;
Till He smiles upon his people,
  And shall come to take his own.

4 Only waiting till the reapers
  Shall appear to gather home
All His loved ones, who are longing
  For their Saviour, King to come.
Quickly, Reapers! O, come quickly!
  Is the cry of many a heart;
Come and gather all the waiting;
  They are longing to depart.

———o———

327 My Beloved.

1. O, thou in whose presence my soul takes delight, On whom in affliction I call;

My comfort by day, and my song in the night, My hope, my sal-va-tion, my all.

198

328 **Virginia. L. M.**

H. Stowell. J. Griggs.

Slow and connected.

1. From ev-'ry stormy wind that blows, From ev-'ry swell-ing tide of woes,

There is a calm, a sure retreat; 'Tis found be-neath the mer-cy-seat.

2 There is a place, where Jesus sheds
The oil of gladness on our heads;
A place than all besides more sweet;
It is the blood-bought mercy-seat.

3 Ah! whither could we flee for aid,
When tempted, desolate, dismayed!

Or how the hosts of sin defeat,
Had suffering saints no mercy-seat?

4 There, as on eagles' wings we soar,
And sin and sense molest no more;
And heav'n comes down our souls to greet,
While glory crowns the mercy-seat.

329 **Newton. 8s & 7s. Double.**

Bold and spirited. *Fine.*

1. Lift the voice, and sound the trum-pet, Watcher on the mountain height;
Roll the clar-ion notes a-round thee, Shout, as flees the pass-ing night.
D.C. Cry a-loud, "Be-hold the dawn-ing, Rouse and gird to meet the foe!"

D.C.

Lift the voice in words of warn-ing; Wake the slumb'ring hosts below;
Lift the voice, &c. Wake the slumb - 'ring hosts be - low.

2 Lift the voice! Lo, weak and dying,
Warriors, struggling, faint and fall;
Bid them fight, on God relying;
Jesus comes to conquer all!
Lift the voice in notes of gladness,
Ring the shout along the sky;
"Cease your tears, ye sons of sadness,
Sing! rejoice! your God is nigh."

3 Lift the voice, like music blended,
With heart-healing minstrelsy;
Cry "Thy warfare now is ended;
Lo, thy Saviour comes to thee!"
Soon, beyond time's night of sadness,
Watchmen, ye shall joyful sing;
Eye to eye shall see with gladness,
When the Lord shall Zion bring.

Knocking at the Door.

"Behold I stand at the door and knock."—Rev. iii: 20.

E. J. CARR.   I. BALTZELL, by per.

1. The voice of my Be - lov - ed calls, "O - pen, my love, my bride;"
2. The door is clos'd—why should it be, When he is standing there?
3. So late, so cold, so drear without! His hair with dew is wet;
4. "A - rise!" I hear him call a - gain; I yield him all my heart;

I hear him knock-ing at the door, A sound I've oft - en
Oh, could I hear that plaintive cry! Oh, could I see that
The shades of eve - ning o'er him fall; How can I stand and
No long - er will I make de - lay; En - ter, O Lord, with -

CHORUS.

heard be - fore, Yet keep him still out - side.
pity - ing eye! That look I could not bear.   } Oh, the Sav - iour is
hear him call In tones of deep re - gret?
- in I pray, And nev - er-more de - part.

stand-ing at the door, (at the door) Gently knock-ing as he

knock'd be - fore; (at the door) Let him now en - ter in; He will

From "Songs of Grace," by permission.

Knocking at the Door. <small>Concluded.</small>

cleanse the heart from sin: O, sin-ner, let the Saviour en - ter in.

—o—

331 The Thrilling Cry.

Words Arranged by I. I. L.

1. A thrilling cry—we hear the sound; The faithful watchmen lift their voice;

From land to land the world a - round— It bids the saints re - joice:

"Ye virgins, rise, break forth and sing The glorious com-ing of your King

The thrilling cry—we hear it sound, "Go forth to meet your Lord."

2 Blow, watchmen, blow the certain sound,
  For dark and dang'rous is the night;
And daring scoffers gather round—
  The evil servants smite.
Ye faithful ones the strict watch keep,
  With lamps well trimm'd, and do not
The thrilling cry, we hear it sound, [sleep—
  "Go forth to meet your Lord."

3 In darkest hours God's word gives light,
  Its rays dispel the thick'ning gloom;
The path to glory now is bright—
  The Bridegroom soon will come.

Then lift your voices, saints, and sing
  Your sweetest strains to Zion's King—
The thrilling cry—we hear it sound,
  "Go forth to meet your Lord."

4 Behold! He comes, the mighty One!
  Ye virgins, haste! Him now you'll meet;
The watching and the waiting done,
  He comes his bride to greet.
The trumpet sounds along the skies,
  The earth it shakes, the dead arise;
The thrilling cry the world around,
  "The Lord, the Lord has come!"

201

332 Mount Vernon. 8s & 7s.
L. MASON.

1. Sis - ter, thou wast mild and love-ly, Gen-tle as the summer breeze,

Pleasant as the air of evening, When it floats a - mong the trees.

2 Peaceful be thy silent slumber,
  Peaceful in the grave so low;
  Thou no more wilt join our number,
  Here no more our songs shalt know.

3 Dearest sister, thou hast left us;
  Here thy loss we deeply feel
  But 'tis God that hath bereft us;
  He can all our sorrows heal.

4 Yet again we hope to meet thee,
  When mortality has fled,
  Then with all the blest to greet thee,
  Where no farewell tear is shed.

333

1 Brother, thou wast true and faithful,
  Kind and patient all the day

Cheerful as the skies of evening,
When the mists have passed away.

2 Peaceful be thy dreamless slumber,
  Where we lay thee down to rest;
  Thou wilt be among our number,
  When we meet with all the blest.

3 Dearest brother, we shall miss thee—
  Now no more thy voice we hear;
  But though gone we still shall bless thee,
  For to us thou wast most dear.

4 Yes, we know that we shall meet thee,
  And again stand by thy side;
  Shall in heavenly mansions greet thee,
  Where no tomb can us divide. I. I. L.

——o——

334 Shawmut. S. M.
L. MASON.

1. Sub - mis - sive-ly, my God, I all to thee re - sign,

And bow be - fore thy chast-'ning rod; Nor will I, Lord, re - pine.

2 Why should my heart complain,
  When wisdom, truth, and love
  Direct the stroke, inflict the pain,
  And point to thee above?

3 How short my sufferings here;
  How needful every cross:

Away with doubt, distrust, and fear,
Nor call my gain my loss.

4 Then give, or take away,
  I'll bless thy sacred Name;
  Jesus to-day, and yesterday,
  And ever, is the same.

Bright Eden.

Mrs. M. V. Seward.   P. P. Bliss.

DUET and CHORUS.

1. We've heard of a hap-py, a beau-ti-ful land, Where Saints all shall

dwell, a bright sin-less band; With Christ their Re-deem-er for-

-ev-er to reign, Se-cure from temp-ta-tion, sor-row and pain.

CHORUS.

Beau-ti-ful land, beautiful land, Eden, bright Eden, beau-ti-ful land.

2 We've heard there are beautiful crowns to be given
When Jesus our Saviour shall come down from heaven;
If here every cross we do patiently bear,
Bright crowns in that beautiful land we'll wear.
Cho.—Beautiful land, &c.

3 Dear Saviour, O when wilt thou take us all there?
When, when shall thy children these joys ever share?
O, come and redeem us from earth's bitter strife,
And give us in Eden unending life.
Cho.—Beautiful land, &c.

4 Thy children are waiting and watching for thee,
Now, now they are sighing from sin to be free;
They're longing with angels of glory to stand
In Paradise fair,—that beautiful land.
Cho.—Beautiful land, &c.

Victor. 8s, 7s & 4s. M. S.

1. Look, ye saints: the sight is glorious; See the Man of sorrows now;
   From the fight returned victo - rious, Ev-'ry knee to him shall bow;
2. Crown the Saviour, saints and angels, Rich the trophies Je - sus brings;
   In the seat of pow'r enthrone him, While the heav'nly concave rings;

[brow.
Crown him, Crown him; Crowns become the Victor's brow, Crowns become the Victor's
Crown him, Crown him; Crown the Saviour King of kings, Crown the Saviour King of
[kings.

337

1 On the mountain's top appearing,
    Lo! the sacred herald stands,
  Welcome news to Zion bearing,
    Zion, long in hostile lands.
      Mourning captive,
    God himself shall loose thy bands.

2 Has thy night been long and mournful?
    Have thy friends unfaithful proved?
  Have thy foes been proud and scornful?
    By thy sighs and tears unmoved?
      Cease thy mourning:
    Zion still is well beloved.

3 God, thy God, will now restore thee;
    He himself appears thy Friend;
  All thy foes shall flee before thee;
    Here their boasts and triumphs end;
      Great deliv'rance
    Zion's King will surely send.

4 Peace and joy shall now attend thee;
    All thy warfare now be past:
  God thy Saviour will defend thee;
    Victory is thine at last;
      All thy conflicts
    End in everlasting rest.

——o——

338 Watchman. S. M.

1. The harvest - time is near, The year de - lays not long;

And he who sows with many a tear, Shall reap with many a song.

2 Sad to his toil he goes,
    His seed with weeping leaves;
  But he shall come at twilight's close,
    And bring his golden sheaves.

3 But fearful vengeance falls
    On that rebellious race,
  Who will not hear when Jesus calls,
    And dare to slight his grace.

339 The Land Just Across the River.

T. C. O'KANE, by per.

1. On Jordan's storm-y banks I stand, And cast a wish-ful eye
2. O'er all these wide-ex-tend-ed plains Shines one e-ter-nal day;
3. When shall I reach that hap-py place, And be for-ev-er blest?
4. Fill'd with de-light my raptured soul Would here no long-er stay;

To Canaan's fair and hap-py land, Where my pos-ses-sions lie.
'There God the Son for-ev-er reigns, And scatters night a-way.
When shall I see my Father's face, And in his bo-som rest?
Tho' Jordan's waves a-round me roll, Fear-less I'd launch a-way.

CHORUS.

We will rest in the fair and hap-py land, Just a-
by and by,

-cross on the ev-er-green shore;........... Sing the
ev-er-green shore.

song of Mo-ses and the Lamb, by and by, And dwell with Je-sus ev-er-more.

205

Sing, Oh, Sing the Praise of Jesus.

"He was crucified through weakness, yet he liveth by the power of God."—2 Cor. xiii: 4.

A. R. THOMPSON.　　　　　　　　　　　　I. BALTZELL, by per.

1. The morn-ing tinges all the sky, The air with praises rings;
2. The shin-ing an-gels cry, "A - way With grief, no spi - ces bring;
3. That thou our Paschal Lamb mayst be, And end-less joy be - gin,
4. Glo - ry to God! our glad lips cry; All praise and wor - ship be

De - feated Death stands sul-len by, The world ex - ult - ing sings.
Not tears, but songs, this joy-ful day Should greet the ris - en King."
Je - sus, De - liv - 'rer, set us free From the dread death of sin.
On earth, in heav'n, to God Most High, For Christ's great vic - to - ry.

CHORUS.

Sing, oh, sing.......... the praise of Je - sus! Sing, oh,
Sing, oh, sing

sing........... the praise of Je - sus! Sing, oh,
Sing, oh, sing

sing....... the praise of Je - sus! He is ris - en from the dead!
Sing, oh, sing

From "Gates of Praise," by permission.

341   All He Has Done.

I. I. Leslie.

S. J. Vail.

Duet or Semi-Chorus.

1. O, come, let us sing of His mercy, His grace which so long we have known;
2. O, let us give praise for sal-va-tion, Sal-va-tion so great and so free;
3. What love! O what love He has shown us! Thro' all the dark, dangerous way;
4. We'll praise Him forev-er and ev-er; We'll praise Him who gave us His Son;

And praise Him for ev-er-y blessing, And all that for us He has done.
For what He has done to re-deem us, E'en dy-ing up-on the curs'd tree.
By day and by night watching o'er us, To keep us from go-ing a-stray.
We'll praise Him who now is our Saviour, For all that for us He has done.

CHORUS.

All He has done, all He has done; And praise Him for

all He has done; .... All He has done,
all He has done,

all He has done, And praise Him for all He has done......
He has done.

342   I'm Nearing the Gates.

Words Arranged by I. I. L.

I. BALTZELL, by per.

Moderato.

1. I'm near - ing the gates of the cit - y, That cit - y
2. I'm near - ing the gates of the cit - y, Where death has
3. That cit - y will come in its glo - ry, Down, down from

so bright and so fair; When Christ, with the an - gels at -
no ter - ror or sting; I soon shall be hap - py for -
the heav - en and God; 'Tis then I shall en - ter its

- tend - ing, Shall come, O then I shall be there.
- ev - er With Je - sus, my Sav - iour and King.
por - tals— 'Twill be my e - ter - nal a - bode.

CHORUS.

I'm near - - - ing the gates, I'm near - - - ing the gates,

I'm nearing the beau-ti - ful gates, I'm nearing the beau-ti - ful gates,

I'm near - - - ing the cit - y,

I'm nearing the gates of the cit - y, The beau-ti - ful cit - y of God!

Copyright. 1878. by I. BALTZELL

Avon. C. M.

AMES MONTGOMERY.

HUGH WILSON.

1. Ac - cording to thy gracious word, In meek hu - mil - i - ty.

This will we do, our dy - ing Lord, We will re - mem - ber thee!

2 Thy body, broken for our sake,
  Our bread from heaven shall be;
Thy testamental cup we take,
  And thus remember thee!

3 Gethsemane can we forget?
  Or there thy conflict see,
Thine agony and bloody sweat,
  And not remember thee?

344

. My song shall always be of Him
  Who gave himself for me;

Who bled, a sinner to redeem,
  And died upon the tree.

2 I never can his look forget,
  Who suffered for my good:
His wounded head, hands, side, and feet,
  Poured forth the sacred flood.

3 Like him on earth I wish to be,
  That, when He doth appear,
I may rejoice his face to see,
  And his blest voice to hear.

—o—

345   Depth of Mercy. 7s.

J. STEPHENSON.

1. { Depth of mer - cy! can there be   Mer - cy   still re - serv'd for me?
   { Can my God his wrath for - bear? Me, the   chief of   sinners, spare? }

CHORUS.   Smoothly.   Repeat pp.

{ God is love; I do be - lieve {
{ He is waiting to forgive, } He is wait-ing, waiting to for - give.

2 I have long withstood his grace;
Long provoked him to his face;
Would not hearken to his calls;
Grieved him by a thousand falls.

3 Now incline me to repent;
Let me now my sins lament;
Now my foul revolt deplore,
Weep, believe, and sin no more.

346 Clinging to the Cross. L. M.

ISAAC WATTS.   Chorus and Music by Rev. G. C. WELLS.

1. When I sur - vey the wondrous cross On which the prince of glo - ry died,
2. For - bid, O God, that I should boast, Save in the death of Christ, my Lord;
3. Were the whole realm of nature mine, It were an off - 'ring far too small;

My rich-est gain I court but loss, And pour con-tempt on all my pride.
All the vain things that charm me most, I sac - ri - fice them for his blood.
Love so a - maz-ing, so di - vine, Demands my soul, my life, my all.

CHORUS.

The cross, the cross, the precious cross, The wondrous cross of Je - sus;
From all our sin, its guilt and pow'r, And ev - 'ry stain it frees   us.

Then I'm cling-ing, cling-ing, clinging, O, I'm clinging to the cross,

Yea, I'm cling-ing, cling-ing, cling-ing, clinging to the cross.

From "The Revivalist," by permission of JOSEPH HILLMAN.

347   I'm Going Home.   L. M.

1. My heav'nly home is bright and fair; Nor pain, nor death can enter there:
Its glitt'ring tow'rs the sun out-shine; That heav'nly mansion shall be mine.

Chorus, by Congregation.

We're go-ing home, we're go-ing home, We're go-ing home to die no more:

To die no more, to die no more, We're going home to die no more.

2 While here, a stranger far from home,
Affliction's waves may round me foam;
And though, like Lazarus, sick and poor,
My heavenly mansion is secure.

3 Then fail this earth, let stars decline,
And sun and moon refuse to shine;
All nature sink and cease to be,
That heavenly mansion stands for me.

348   L. M.

1 We're in the way that leads to God,
The way that all the saints have trod;

We soon shall see that blissful shore,
Where we shall live to die no more.

2 The ways of God are ways of peace,
And all His paths are pleasantness;
Then, weary souls, your sighs give o'er,
We're going home to die no more.

Chorus.

We're going home, we're going home,
We're going home, to die no more;
To die no more, to die no more;
We're going home to die no more.

Arrangement from "The Armor Bearer."

——o——

349   My Soul's Full of Glory.

1. My soul's full of glo-ry, in-spir-ing my tongue,
Could I meet with an-gels, I'd sing them a song; I'd sing of my

Je-sus, and tell of his charms, And beg them to bear me to his loving arms.

2 O, Jesus! O, Jesus! thou lov'd of my soul,
'Twas thou, my dear Jesus, that made my heart whole;
I'll sing of thy glory, and tell of thy charms—
O, angels! come, bear me to his loving arms.

350 What Will the Harvest Be?

Words by J. I. LESLIE, Music by I. BALTZELL, by per.

1. Sowing the seed when the day has be-gun, Sowing the seed in the
2. Sowing the seed by the way-side so dry, Sowing the seed when the
3. Sowing the seed of the heav-en-ly grain, Sowing the seed in sor-
4. Sowing the good seed up-on the good ground, Sowing where tears of con

noon-day sun; Sow-ing the seed till the day is all done,
hard rocks lie, Sow-ing the seed where the thorns grow so high,
- row and pain; What at the judgment will be the gain?
- trition are found; Sow-ing where faith, hope and love will a - bound,

CHORUS.

Sow - - ing in

What will the har - vest be?
What will the har - vest be?
What will the har - vest be?
Souls will the har - vest be.

Sow-ing in time for e -

time........ for e-ter - - - ni - ty,........
- ter - ni - ty, Sowing in time for e - ter - ni - ty,

What...... will the har - - vest be?

What will the harvest be? what will it be? What will the har-vest be?

212

351 **Oriel. L. M.** WM. B. BRADBURY.

1. 'Tis by the faith of joys to come, We walk this desert dark as night;

Slow and gentle.

rit. ad lib:

Till we shall gain our endless home, Faith is our guide, and faith our light.

2 The want of sight she well supplies,
   She makes the pearly gates appear;
   Far into things unseen she pries,
   And brings eternal glories near.

3 Cheerful we tread the desert through,
   While faith inspires a heavenly ray,
   Though lions roar, and tempests blow,
   And rocks and dangers fill the way.

352

1 Blest are the merciful, who prove
   By acts, their sympathy and love;
   From Christ, the Lord, shall they obtain
   Like sympathy and love again.

2 Blest are the pure, whose hearts are clean
   From the defiling power of sin;
   With endless pleasure they shall see
   A God of spotless purity.

3 Blest are the men of peaceful life,
   Who quench the coals of growing strife;
   They shall be called the heirs of bliss,
   The sons of God, the God of peace.

4 Blest are the sufferers, who partake
   Of pain and shame for Jesus' sake!
   Their souls shall triumph in the Lord
   Glory and joy are their reward,

—o—

353 **That Beautiful Land. 9s & 8s.**
WM. B. BRADBURY.

With gentleness.

1. A beautiful land by faith I see, A land of rest, from sorrow free,
   The home of the ransom'd, bright and fair, And

CHORUS.

beautiful angels too are there. Will you go? will you go? Go to that beautiful

land with me? Will you go? will you go? Go to that beautiful land?

2 That beautiful land, the City of Light,
   It ne'er will know the shades of night;
   The glory of God, the light of day
   Will scatter the darkness far away.

3 In vision I see its streets of gold,
   Its beautiful gates I too behold,

   The river of life, the crystal sea,
   The ambrosial fruit of life's fair tree.

4 The heavenly throng arrayed in white,
   In rapture range the plains of light;
   And in one harmonious choir they praise
   Their glorious Saviour's matchless grace.

354 Testify To-Night.

JOHN BARBOUR.

Prof. WM. A. McNEAL, by per.

1. Oh, tes - ti - fy to-night, dear brother, And own your bless-ed Lord,
2. Oh, tes - ti - fy to-night, dear sis - ter, For 'tis your du - ty too:
3. Oh, tes - ti - fy to-night, dear sin - ner, For Je - sus died for you;

It will help you on your jour - ney, And bring you nigh to God;
It will cheer our hearts to lis - ten, We know it will help you.
Seek him now, while he stands wait - ing, The heav'n-ly course pur-sue:

It will strengthen you in weak-ness, And give to you new light:
Grace to grace will them be ad - ded, Your hopes will grow more bright;
He will guide your feet, so err - ing, In paths of glorious light;

The spir - it now is call - ing you, Oh tes - ti - fy to - night.

REFRAIN.

Oh, tes - ti - fy   Oh, tes - ti - fy,   Oh,
Oh, tes - ti - fy,   Oh, tes - ti - fy,

Repeat Chorus pp.

tes-ti-fy to-night, The spir-it now is calling you, Oh, tes-ti-fy to-night.

—o—

355 Alas! and Did My Saviour Bleed?

ISAAC WATTS.   S. J. VAIL.

1. A - las and did my Saviour bleed? And did my Sovereign die?..

Would He de - vote that sa - cred head For such a worm as I?..

CHORUS.

Je - sus died for you, Je - sus died for me, Yes,

Je - sus died for all man-kind, Bless God, sal - va - tion's free.

2 Was it for crimes that I have done?
   He groaned upon the tree?
   Amazing pity! grace unknown!
   And love beyond degree!—*Cho.*

3 Well might the sun in darkness hide,
   And shut his glories in,
   When Christ, the mighty Maker, died
   For man, the creature's sin.—*Cho.*

4 Thus might I hide my blushing face,
   While His dear cross appears;
   Dissolve my heart in thankfulness,
   And melt mine eyes to tears.—*Cho.*

5 But drops of grief can ne'er repay
   The debt of love I owe;
   Here, Lord, I give myself away;
   'Tis all that I can do.—*Cho.*

356 Let Him Come In.

"Behold I stand at the door and knock."—Rev. iii: 20.

B.

1. Be - hold, a stranger at the door, He gently knocks, has knock'd before:
2. Oh! love-ly at - ti-tude—he stands With melting heart and load-ed hands;
3. But will he prove a friend in-deed? He will, the ver - y friend you need;
4. Rise, touch'd with grati-tude di - vine, Turn out his en - e - my and thine—

Has wait - ed long, is wait-ing still: You treat no oth - er friend so ill.
Oh, match-less kind-ness, and he shows This matchless kindness to his foes.
The friend of sin - ners? yes, 'tis he, With garments dy'd on Cal - va - ry!
That soul - de - stroy-ing monster, sin, And let the heav'nly stranger in.

CHORUS.

Let him come in,........ Let him come in,........ Let the dear
Let him come in, Let him come in,

Saviour en - ter in; Linger no more,...... but o - pen the
Linger no more,

door,........ And let the dear Sav - iour en - ter in.
O - pen the door,

From "Gates of Praise," by permission.

216

357   On the Cross.   7s, 6s & 8s.

Andante.

1. Be - hold, behold! the Lamb of God, On the cross, on the cross:
   For you he shed his precious blood, On the cross, on the cross.

Andantino.

Now hear his all - im-por-tant cry, "E - loi la - ma sa - bac-tha - ni."

a tempo.

Draw near, and see your Saviour die, On the cross, on the cross.

2 Behold! his arms extended wide,
   On the cross, on the cross;
Behold! his bleeding hands and side,
   On the cross, on the cross.
The sun withholds its rays of light,
The heav'ns are cloth'd in shades of night,
While Jesus doth with devils fight,
   On the cross, on the cross.

3 Where'er I go, I'll tell the story
   Of the cross, of the cross;
In nothing else my soul shall glory,
   Save the cross, save the cross.
Yes, this my constant theme shall be,
Through time and in eternity,
That Jesus suffered death for me,
   On the cross, on the cross.

—o—

358   Land of Pleasure.   7s & 8s.

1. There is a land of pleasure, Where streams of joy for - ev-er roll;
   'Tis there I have my treasure, And there I hope to - - - - -

rest my soul; Long, darkness dwelt around me, With scarcely once a cheering ray:

But since my Saviour found me, A light has shone a - long my way.

1. We are on our way up Zi-on's ho - ly hill, We will work in faith, and
D.C. We are on our journey seeking for the light, For the blessed land be -
2. 'Tis a glorious tho't while marching on the road, That our rest is sure, as
3. As we journey on, still brighter grows the way, For a-bove the hill we

1. la - bor with a will ; For we know the Lord, our Saviour's with us still,
- yond our earthly sight : Come and go with us to regions fair and bright,
2. promis'd in his word ; "For a rest remains to all who serve the Lord,"
3. see the com-ing day, And we know its light will nev - er pass a - way,

Fine. *CHORUS.*

1. So we'll sing our hap-py song. To the Lord, to the
Come and join our pil - grim throng.
2-3. So we'll sing our hap - py song. To the Lord,

Lord, Let us sing, let us sing Hymns of
to the Lord, Let us sing, let us sing

D.C.

praise,......hymns of praise, As we journey to our home.
Hymns of praise, hymns of praise,

From "The Chorister," by per. of OLIVER DITSON & Co.

360   Roll, Jordan, Roll.

Words Arr. by I. I. L.   Southern Melody.

1. Roll, Jor-dan, roll, Thy foaming bil-lows roll   a-long; The hosts of God once
2. Roll, Jor-dan, roll, Thy judgment bil-lows roll   a-long; We're go-ing o'er to
3. Roll, Jor-dan, roll, Thy judgment bil-lows roll   a-long; Beyond thee lies the
4. Roll, Jor-dan, roll, Thy judgment bil-lows roll   a-long; Thy fearful tide we

thro' thee trod, With trumpet and with song. Amid thy waves, that stood in awe, Tri-
yon-der shore, Although thy waves be strong. The Leader of this mighty host Will
Par - a - dise, Where the redeem'd be-long. Fair Canaan there we now behold, And
shall a - bide. And sing the vic-tor's song. The wilderness is left behind, And

-umphantly they pass'd ; In the great Name with joy they came To Canaan's land at last.
come and thee divide ; And we shall stand upon the land, Beyond thy foaming tide.
waiting here we stand, To all go o'er to yonder shore, When Christ shall give command.
Egypt far away ; To Canaan's shore we shall go o'er, When breaks redemption's day.

CHORUS.

Roll swiftly, thou Jordan, roll, With thy bil-lows dash-ing   on the shore;

Thy rush-ing tide we shall a - bide, And soon be safe-ly o'er.

219

361   Hope.   C. M.

1. O what hath Jesus bought for me! Be - fore my ravished eyes......

And trees of par-a - dise, And trees of par - a - dise;......

Riv - ers of life di - vine I see, And trees of par - a - dise.

Riv - ers of life di - vine I see, And trees of par - a - dise.

2 In hope of that immortal crown
I now the cross sustain;
And gladly wander up and down,
And smile at toil and pain!

3 O, what are all my sufferings here,
If, Lord, thou count me meet

With that enraptured host t' appear,
And worship at thy feet?

4 Give joy or grief, give ease or pain,
Take life or friends away;
But let me find them all again
In that eventful day.

—o—

362   Advent Call.   7s & 6s.

A. T. GORHAM.

Lively.

1. Re - joice, all ye be - liev - ers, And let your lights ap - pear;

The eve - ning is ad - vanc - ing, The midnight now is near.

The Bridegroom is a - ris - ing, And soon he draw - eth nigh,

Advent Call. Concluded.

Up, up, and watch, and wres-tle, At midnight comes the cry.

2 See that your lamps are burning,
  Replenish them with oil,
And wait for your salvation,
  The end of earthly toil.
The watchers on the mountain,
  Proclaim the Bridegroom near;
Go meet him as he cometh,
  With hallelujahs clear.

3 Ye wise and holy virgins,
  Now raise your voices higher,
Till, in the songs of glory,
  They meet the angel choir.
The marriage-feast is waiting,
  The doors wide open stand:
Be ready then to meet him,
  The Bridegroom is at hand.

4 Ye saints, who here in patience
  Your cross and sufferings bore,
Shall live and reign forever,
  When sorrow is no more.
Upon the throne of glory,
  The Lamb ye shall behold;
In triumph cast before him,
  Your diadems of gold!

5 Our hope and expectation,
  O Jesus! now appear;
Arise, thou Sun, so longed for,
  O'er this benighted sphere.
With heart and hands uplifted,
  We plead, O Lord, to see,
The day of earth's redemption,
  That brings us unto thee!

—o—

363 God Speed the Right.

Words by W. E. HICKSON.   Music from the German.
                                            DUET.

1. { Now to heav'n our pray'rs ascending, God speed the right; } [re-
   { In a noble cause contending, God speed the right; } Be our zeal in heav'n

- corded, With success on earth rewarded, God speed the right, God speed the right.

2 Be that prayer again repeated,
  God speed the right;
Ne'er despairing, though defeated,
  God speed the right;
Like the good and great in story,
If we fail, we fail with glory,
  |: God speed the right. :||

3 Patient, firm, and persevering,
  God speed the right;
Ne'er th' event nor danger fearing,
  God speed the right;

Pains, nor toils, nor trials heeding,
And in heav'n's own time succeeding,
  |: God speed the right. :||

4 Still our onward course pursuing,
  God speed the right;
Ev'ry foe at length subduing,
  God speed the right;
Truth our cause, whate'er delay it,
There's no power on earth can stay it,
  |: God speed the right. :||

221

364 Invitation. 8s & 7s.

ANNA-SHIPMAN.   F. A. BLACKMER, by per.

Gently.

1. Come to Je - sus! Are you lone-ly? Sol-ace sweet He will af-ford;

rit.

Lean on Je - sus, Je - sus on-ly! Come and find a lov-ing Lord.

2 He is waiting—will you leave Him,
  Pleading at your heart in vain?
  He is willing—Oh, believe Him;
  He may never call again.

3 Now it is the time to test Him,
  Test Him by His written Word;

Come, for He will ne'er deny it;
  Come to Christ, the risen Lord.

4 By still waters He will lead you,
  In green pastures you shall rest;
  And the pierced hands that freed you,
  Bear you near His tender breast.

——o——

365 Capua. S. M.

J. D. VINTON.

1. Be - hold, what wond - rous grace The Fa-ther has be - stow'd

On sin-ners of a mor-tal race, To call them sons of God!

2 Nor doth it yet appear
  How great we shall be made;
  But when we see our Saviour here,
  We shall be like our Head.

3 A hope so much divine
  Will help us to endure;
  Will purify our souls from sin
  As Christ, the Lord, is pure.

4 Father, if in thy love,
  We share a filial part,
  Send down thy Spirit like a dove,
  To rest on every heart.

366

1 With hearts and lips unfeigned,
  We praise thee for thy word;
  We bless thee for the joyful news
  Of our redeeming Lord.

2 Water thy sacred seed,
  And give it great increase;
  Let neither fowls, nor rocks, nor thorns,
  Hinder the fruits of peace.

3 Then, though we weeping sow,
  And tears our hours employ;
  We know we shall return again,
  And bring our sheaves with joy.

The Old-Fashioned Bible. 11 & 12.

Copied from "The American Vocalist," by   W. H M.

1. How painful-ly pleasing the fond re - col - lection Of youthful emotions and
   When blest with parental ad-vice and af-fection, Surrounded with mercies and

Chorus. The old-fashion'd Bible, the dear blessed Bi - ble, The fam-i - ly Bi-ble that

in-no-cent joy, . .
peace from on high, }   *FINE.*   I still view the chair of my sire and my mother,

lay on the stand

The seats of their offspring arranged on each hand, And that blessed book which ex -

rit.   D.C.

- cels ev'ry other, The fam - i - ly Bi - ble, that lay on the stand.

2 That Bible, the volume of God's inspiration,
    At morn and at evening could yield us delight;
  The prayer of our sire was a sweet invocation,
    For mercy by day, and safety through night:
  Our hymns of devotion in harmony swelling,
    All warm from the heart of a family band,
  Half raised us from earth to that rapturous dwelling
    Described in the Bible that lay on the stand.—*Chorus.*

3 Ye scenes of tranquility, long have we parted;
    My hopes almost gone, and my parents no more,
  In sorrow and sadness I roam broken-hearted,
    And wander alone on a far distant shore:
  Yet how can I doubt a dear Saviour's protection,
    Forgetful of gifts from his bountiful hand?
  Oh! let me with patience receive his correction,
    And think of the Bible that lay on the stand.—*Chorus.*

Trumpet. **10s, 11s & 12s.**

1. Lift your glad voices in triumph on high, For Je - sus hath ris - en, the
D.C. Loud was the chorus of angels on high, The Sav-iour hath ris-en, the
2. Glo-ry to God, in full anthems of joy; Our life in the future Death
D.C. Lift, then, your voices in triumph on high, For Je - sus hath ris-en, the

Fine.

saints shall not die; Vain were the ter - rors that gath-er'd a-round him, And
saints shall not die.
can - not de - stroy: Sad were the life we may part with to - mor-row, If
saints shall not die.

short the do - min-ion of death and the grave; He burst from the fetters of
tears were our birthright, and death were our end; But Jesus hath cheer'd the dark

D.C.

darkness that bound him, Re-splen-dent in glo - ry, to live and to save:
val - ley of sor-row—We'll rise when he comes, and to meet him as - cend:

—o—

369 **Ware.** **L. M.**

Isaac Watts.   Geo. Kingsley.

1. Now to the Lord a no-ble song! A-wake, my soul! a - wake, my tongue!

Ware. Concluded.

Ho - san - na to th' e - ternal Name! And all His boundless love proclaim.

2 See where it shines in Jesus' face,
  The brightest image of his grace:
  God in the person of his Son,
  Hath all his mightiest works outdone.

3 Grace! 'tis a sweet, a charming theme:
  My thoughts rejoice at Jesus' name!

Ye angels! dwell upon the sound!
Ye heavens! reflect it to the ground!
4 Oh may we reach that blissful place,
  Where he unvails his lovely face;
  Where all his beauties we'll behold,
  And sing his name to harps of gold.

———o———

370   What Can I Do For Thee?

Words and Music by F. A. BLACKMER, by per.

1. I hear thy voice, O Lord, It tells me of thy love!

How thou, to save lost man, Didst leave thy home a - bove;

Thy glo - ry thou didst leave for me, What shall I leave for thee?

2 And Thou didst suffer much,
  And shed Thy precious blood
To save me from my sins,
  Thou blessed Lamb of God:
Yes, Thou didst give thy life for me,
What can I do for Thee?

3 'Twas all that I might have
  Salvation, full and free:
Rich are the gifts indeed,
  That Thou hast brought to me,
Yes, Thou hast brought rich gifts to me,
What shall I bring to Thee?

4 I'll bring my heart, dear Lord,
  'Tis all that I can do;
Though vile, I pray that thou
  Wilt cleanse it through and through;
Yes, I'll forsake my sins for Thee--
My Saviour, help Thou me.

5 I know the way is rough,
  And trackless as the sea;
Except Thou guide my feet,
  I soon would stray from Thee;
O, as I strive to follow Thee,
Dear Jesus, lead Thou me.

Awake and Sing.

1. Awake, and sing the song Of Mo-ses and the Lamb! Wake

Wake ev'ry heart and ev'ry tongue To praise the Saviour's name!

2 Sing of his dying love—
Sing of his matchless power—
Sing how he intercedes above
For us, whose sins he bore.

3 Sing, till we feel our heart
Ascending with our tongue;
Sing, till the love of sin depart
And grace inspire our song.

4 Sing on your heavenly way,
Ye ransomed sinners, sing;
Sing on, rejoicing every day,
In Christ th' eternal King.

5 Soon shall each raptured tongue
His endless praise proclaim;
And sweeter voices tune the song
Of Moses and the Lamb'

———0———

372

1 The Lord my Shepherd is,
I shall be well supplied;
Since he is mine, and I am his,
What can I want beside?

2 He leads me to the place
Where heavenly pasture grows;
Where living waters gently pass,
And full salvation flows.

3 If e'er I go astray,
He doth my soul reclaim,
And guides me, in his own right way,
For his most holy name.

4 While he affords his aid,
I cannot yield to fear;   [shade.
Tho' I should walk thro' death's dark
My Shepherd's with me there.

———0———

373

1 Stand up and bless the Lord
Ye people of his choice;
Stand up and bless the Lord your God,
With heart and soul and voice.

2 Though high above all praise,
Above all blessing high,
Who would not fear his holy name,
And laud and magnify?

3 O for the living flame
From his own altar .rought,
To touch our lips, our souls inspire,
And wing to heaven our thought.

4 God is our strength and song,
And his salvation ours;
Then be his love in Christ proclaimed
With all our ransomed powers.

Pardon for All.

"To our God, for he will abundantly pardon."—Isa. lv: 7.

Words Adapted.   I. B.

1. I once was a stranger to grace and to God; I knew not my
dan-ger, and felt not my load; I flew to the cross when I heard Je-sus

REFRAIN.

call, "Come, poor, trembling sinner, there is pardon for all." Par-don for all,
par-don for all; Bless the name of Je-sus, there is par-don for all.

2 Then free grace awoke me by light from on high;
  I cried, "Jesus, save me, O save, or I die!"
  He heard my deep pleading, he answered my call;
  Bless the name of Jesus, there is pardon for all.

3 My terrors all vanished before that sweet name;
  My guilty fears banished, with boldness I came
  To him who had saved from the curse of the fall;
  Bless the name of Jesus, there is pardon for all.

4 Dear Jesus, dear Jesus, my treasure and boast;
  Dear Jesus, dear Jesus, I ne'er can be lost;
  This watchword shall be my last song when I fall;
  Bless the name of Jesus, there is pardon for all.

From "Songs of Grace," by permission.

Anselm. L. M.

Dr. Hayne.

1. Je-sus, thy church, with longing eyes, For thine ex-pect-ed coming waits;

When will the promis'd light a-rise, And glo-ry beam on Zi-on's gates?

2 E'en now when tempests round us fall,
And wintry clouds o'ercast the sky,
Thy words with pleasure we recall,
And deem that our redemption's nigh.

3 O come and reign o'er ev'ry land;
Let Satan from his throne be hurled,
All nations bow to thy command,
And grace revive a dying world.

4 Teach us in watchfulness and prayer,
To wait for thine appointed hour;
And fit us, by thy grace, to share
The triumphs of thy conq'ring power.

376

1 Of him who did salvation bring,
I could forever think and sing;

Arise, ye needy, he'll relieve;
Arise, ye guilty, he'll forgive.

2 To purge our sins he shed in blood,
He closed his eyes to show us God;
Let all the world fall down and know,
That none but God such love can show.

3 'Tis Thee I love, for Thee alone,
I shed my tears and make my moan!
Where'er I am, where'er I move,
I meet the object of my love.

4 Insatiate to this spring I fly;
I drink, and yet am ever dry;
Ah! who against thy charms is proof?
Ah! who that loves can love enough?

377 Gone! 10s & 7s.

Mrs. Agnes Haskell. Geo. E. Lee.

Affetuoso.

1. Gone!—and the word to go on as be-fore? Gone, with a

mp

smile, from the old homestead door, Dear, faith-ful heart, to come

Gone! Concluded.

rit.

back nev - er - more? Oh,.......... sad nev - er-more!

2
Gone! and the seasons still to come and go,
Wreathing her grave in blossom and snow?
Snow on the bosom that sheltered us so,—
    Cruel and pitiless snow!

3
Home is not home, for mother is not there!
Dark is her room,—empty is her chair;
Now will she rest from her labor and care,
    Till that morning so fair.

4
Oft the dear eyes grew dim from sad tears,
Guiding our untried feet through the years;
Planning our future with hopes and with
    Drying our falling tears. [fears—

5
Sleep, mother, sleep, with your hands on
    your breast!
Poor, weary hands! they needed their rest:
Well have we lov'd you, but God lov'd you
    'Tis thy God giveth rest. [best!

—o—

378   Duke Street.   L. M.

Mrs. Voke, 1806.   J. Hatton, 1793.

Bold.

1. Soon may the last glad song a - rise, Thro' all the mil-lions of the skies;

That song of tri-umph which re - cords That all the earth is now the Lord's.

2 Let thrones and powers and kingdoms be
  Obedient, mighty God, to thee!
And over land, and stream, and main,
  Now wave the sceptre of thy reign.

3 O let that glorious anthem swell;
  Let host to host the triumph tell,
That not one rebel heart remains,
  But over all the Saviour reigns.

379

1 The Saviour comes, his advent's nigh,
  He soon will rend the azure sky;

Descending swift to earth again,
  Then God shall dwell indeed with men.

2 O happy day, when wars shall cease,
  And ransomed earth be filled with peace;
When sin and death no more shall reign,
  And Eden bloom on earth again!

3 Saints, lift your heads; the day is near,
  When your Redeemer will appear;
He'll take the kingdom and the crown,
  And make his ransomed bride his own.

380 The Watchers. 7s & 6s.

Words by A. HALE.

Edw. I. White.

1. As Time's last sands seem'd wasting, The world at large was stirr'd!
Man saw his doom was hast'ning, The warn-ing all had heard:

But now the world is sleep-ing In slum-ber most pro-found;

But few the watch are keep-ing, Tho' fast to judgment bound!

2 The few that still are heeding
That awful judgment call,
And, while they wait, are pleading
Like Lot at Sodom's fall:
They seem, like Lot, but mocking,
To all the worldly throng;
Reproach and curses shocking
They now have suffer'd long.

3 They hear the scoffer railing,
In triumph and in pride,
With blasphemies unfailing,
God's promise is denied;
But mercy's long endurance
With that vain infidel
Gives them a strong assurance
By which the day they tell.

4 The Christian steward, slothful,
Puts off the evil day.
Disturbed in scenes unlawful,
He says, "It must delay."

But still, though by his smiting,
The faithful sigh in pain;
While he the truth is spiting,
The Master comes again!

5 The thrones of earth are reeling,
In sad perplexity;
Their retribution sealing
By pride and cruelty.
As ruler, warrior, banker,
Attest their hast'ning doom,
More steadfast is our anchor;
God's kingdom soon will come.

6 But see that remnant humble,
Who hold the faithful word,
So fearful they should stumble,—
While hope is long deferred.
The sons of earth are leaving
Their honor, mirth, and gold;
And these shall end their grieving,
In joys that can't be told.

—o—

381 My Home is Over Jordan.

1. O, when shall I see Jesus, O, when shall I see Je-sus,
O, when shall I see Jesus, (Omit................   [dwell?
And in his presence

Cho. My home is over Jordan, My home is o-ver Jor-dan,
My home is over Jordan, (Omit................   [land.
In Cannan's happy

2. When shall I be deliver'd, When shall I be deliver'd,
When shall I be deliv-er'd (Omit................   [of sin?
From this vain world

230

382 Wells. L. M.

I. Watts. I. Holdroid, 1740.

Slow.

1. From all that dwell be-low the skies, Let the Cre-a-tor's praise a - rise;

Let the Re-deem-er's name be sung Thro' ev-'ry land, by ev - 'ry tongue.

2 Eternal are thy mercies, Lord,
  Eternal truth attends thy word;
Thy praise shall sound from shore to shore
Till suns shall rise and set no more.

3 Your lofty themes, ye mortals, bring,
  In songs of praise divinely sing;
The great salvation loud proclaim,
And shout for joy the Saviour's name.

383

1 High in the heavens, eternal God,
  Thy goodness in full glory shines;
Thy truth shall break thro' every cloud
That veils and darkens thy designs.

2 Forever firm thy justice stands,
  As mountains their foundations keep;
Wise are the wonders of thy hands;
Thy judgments are a mighty deep.

3 Thy providence is kind and large;
  Both man and beast thy bounty share;
The whole creation is thy charge,
But saints are thy peculiar care.

4 My God! how excellent thy grace,
  Whence all our hope and comfort
The sons of Adam in distress [springs;
  Fly to the shadow of thy wings.

——0——

384 Passing Away. L. M.

1. To - day, if you will hear his voice, Now is the time to make your choice;

Say, will you to Mount Zi - on go? Say, will you have this Christ or no?

CHORUS.

We are pass - ing a - way, We're pass - ing a - way,

We are pass - ing a - way To the great Judgment day.

2 Ye wandering souls, who find no rest,
Say, will you be forever blest?
Will you be saved from death and sin,
And crowns of fadeless glory win?

3 Come, you who are to ruin bound,
Obey the Gospel's joyful sound;
Come, go with us, and you shall prove
The joys of Christ's redeeming love.

385 Lonely and Weary. 10s.

A. D. MERRILL.

1. { Lone-ly and wea-ry, by sorrows op-prest, Onward we hasten, with
   Bid-ding a-dieu to the world, with its pride, Longing to dwell by Im-

long-ings for rest; { But 'mid our pil-grim-age, lo, on our eyes, }
-man-u-el's side. { Visions of beauty and glo-ry a-rise; } Visions of

crowns which we hope soon to wear, Visions of heav'n!—O, we long to be there!

2 There is the city in splendor sublime,
   O, how its turrets and battlements shine!
   Pearls are its portals surpassingly bright,
   Jasper its walls, and the Lamb is its light.
   Pathways of gold that fair city adorn,
   Glitt'ring with glory far brighter than morn;
   Angels stand beck'ning us onward to share
   Glory unfading—we long to be there.

3 Rivers are gliding 'mid unfading trees,
   Songs of the blessed are borne on the breeze;
   Glory-gilt mountains resplendent are seen,
   Valleys and hills clad in Eden-like green:
   There shall the glory of God ever be,
   Filling the earth as the waves fill the sea;
   There shall the ransomed, immortal and fair,
   Evermore dwell,—O, we long to be there!

——o——

386 O! the Blood of Jesus. C. M.

1. { There is a fountain fill'd with blood Drawn from Immanuel's veins, }
   { And sin-ners plung'd beneath that flood Lose all their guilty . . } stains.

CHORUS.

O, the blood of Je-sus, The pre-cious blood of Je-sus,

O, the blood of Je-sus, It cleanses from all sin.

387 Crucifixion. P. M.

1. Saw ye my Saviour? Saw ye my Saviour? Saw ye my Saviour, God?

O, he died on Calvary, To a - tone for you and me, And to

purchase our pardon with blood!

2 He was extended, he was extended,
Painfully nailed to the cross;
There he bowed his head and died,
There my Lord was crucified,
To atone for a world that was lost.

3 Jesus hung bleeding, Jesus hung bleeding,
Three dreadful hours in pain:
And the solid rocks were rent,
Through creation's vast extent,
When the Jews crucified the Lamb.

4 Darkness prevailed, darkness prevailed,
Darkness prevailed o'er the land;
And the sun refused to shine,
While his Majesty divine
Was derided, insulted and slain.

5 When it was finish'd, when it was finish'd,
And the atonement was made,
He was taken by the great,
And embalmed in spices sweet
And was in a new sepulchre laid.

6 Hail, mighty Saviour, hail, mighty Sav-
Author and Prince of peace,   [iour,
O! he burst the bars of death,
And triumphant from the earth,
He ascended to mansions of bliss.

——o——

388 Hallelujah to Jesus.

Music and Words by GEO. S. BROWN.

1. { When the last trum-pet's sound shakes the earth all a - round,
{ There to meet him who died for his glo - ri - ous bride,
Cho. { Hal - le - lu - jah to Je - sus, A - men and A - men,
{ To the Lamb that was slain, and who liv - eth a - gain,

And the dead shall a - rise and as - cend to the skies, }
(Omit, second time.)..
We will praise him for - ev - er, a - gain and a - gain;

Repeat tune for Chorus.

And to there be for - ev - er by Im - man - u - el's side.
Hal - le - lu - jah, hal - le - lu - jah, A - men and A - men.

389   I Will Never Leave Thee.

"Lo! I am with you always."

ENGLISH.   I. B. WOODBURY

1. I will nev - er, nev - er leave thee, I will nev - er thee for-sake;

I will guard, and save, and keep thee, For my name and mer-cy's sake:

Fear no e - vil, fear no e - vil, On - ly all my counsel take.

REFRAIN.

For I'll nev-er, nev - er leave thee, I will nev-er thee for-sake.

2
When the storm is raging round thee.
  Call on me in humble prayer,
I will fold my arms about thee,
  Guard thee with the tend'rest care,
In the trial, in the trial,
  I will make thy pathway clear.

3
When the sky above is glowing,
  And around thee all is bright;
Pleasure like a river flowing,
  All things tending to delight,
I'll be with thee, I'll be with thee
  I will guide thy steps aright.

4
When thy soul is dark and clouded,
  Fill'd with doubt, and grief and care;
Thro' the mist by which 'tis shrouded,
  I will make a light appear,
And the banners, and the banners,
  Of my love I will uprear.

5
When life's latest hour is flying,
  And thou comest to death's gloom;
When thy pulse is sinking, dying,
  And the darkness round thee come,
I will never, never leave thee,
  I will bring thee from the tomb.

390   Lyons.   10s & 11s.

FRANCIS JOSEPH HAYDN.

1. Though troubles as - sail, and dan-gers af - fright, Tho' friends should all fail, and foes all u - nite, Yet one thing se - cures us, what- ev - er be-tide, The promise as-sures us, "The Lord will provide."

2 When Satan appears to stop up our path,
And fills us with fears, we triumph by faith;
He cannot take from us, though oft he has tried,
The heart-cheering promise, "The Lord will provide."

3 He tells us we're weak, our hope is in vain;
The good that we seek we ne'er shall obtain:
But when such suggestions our graces have tried,
This answers all questions, "The Lord will provide."

4 No strength of our own, nor goodness we claim;
Our trust is all thrown on Jesus' great name:
In this our strong tower for safety we hide;
The Lord is our power, "The Lord will provide."

391

——o——

1 O worship the King, all glorious above,
And gratefully sing his wonderful love;
Our Shield and Defender, the Ancient of Days,
Pavillioned in splendor, and girded with praise!

2 O, tell of his might, and sing of his grace,
Whose robe is the light, whose canopy, space;
His chariots of wrath the deep thunder-clouds form,
And dark is his path on the wings of the storm!

3 Thy bountiful care what tongue can recite,
It breathes in the air, it shines in the light,
It streams from the hills, it descends to the plain,
And sweetly distils in the dew and the rain.

4 Frail children of dust, and feeble as frail,
In thee do we trust, nor find thee to fail;
Thy mercies, how tender! how firm to the end!
Our Maker, Defender, Redeemer and Friend!

235

392 Ayrtoun. L. M.

1. Triumphant Zi-on, lift thy head From dust, and darkness, and the dead!

Though humbled long, a-wake at length, And gird thee with a Saviour's strength.

2 Put all thy beauteous garments on,
And let thy excellence be known;
Decked in the robes of righteousness,
Thy glories shall the world confess.

3 No more shall foes unclean invade,
And fill thy hallowed courts with dread;
No more shall Satan's mighty host
Their victory and thy sorrows boast.

4 God from on high has heard thy prayer,
His hands thy ruins shall repair;
Nor will thy watchful Monarch cease
To guard thee in eternal peace.

393

1 He reigns, the Lord, the Saviour reigns.
Praise him in evangelic strains;
Let the whole earth in songs rejoice,
And distant islands join their voice.

2 Deep are his counsels and unknown,
But grace and truth support his throne:
Tho' gloomy clouds his way surround,
Justice is their eternal ground.

3 In robes of judgment, lo, he comes!
Shakes the wide earth and cleaves the
Before him burns devouring fire. [tombs;
The mountains melt, the seas retire.

——o——

394 Lake Enon. S. M. I. B. Woodbury.

1. While my Re-deem-er's near, My Shepherd and my Guide,

I bid farewell to ev-'ry fear; My wants are well sup-plied.

2 To ever fragrant meads,
Where rich abundance grows,
His gracious hand indulgent leads,
And guards my sweet repose.

3 Dear Shepherd, if I stray,
My wand'ring feet restore;
And guard me with thy watchful eye,
And let me rove no more.

My Beautiful Home.

Words and Music by A. T. GORHAM.

Moderato.

1. There is sweet rest for me in my beauti-ful home On the banks of the shadowless shore, Where the tempest-rock'd billows of time cease to foam, And the cold blasts of death come no more.

Chorus. *cres.*

Beautiful home! Beautiful home! Soon thy bright scenes I shall roam; There the clear river flows, there the tree of Life glows, And blooms in my beautiful home.

2 There is sweet rest for me with the dear ones of old,
   Who have bow'd 'neath the stroke of the foe;
   I shall meet them at length in the mansions of gold,
   Where their life-crowns forever shall glow.—*Cho.*

3 There is sweet rest for me with my Saviour and King,
   When he comes in his might from above;
   When the hosts of the deathless his triumph shall sing,
   And dwell in the light of his love.—*Cho.*

4 There is sweet rest for me, and I sigh to be there;
   Lord Jesus, O come, quickly come!
   Let thy gathering angels the faithful ones bear
   To the shores of that beautiful home.—*Cho.*

396 Mornington. S. M.

LORD MORNINGTON.

1. Far down the a - ges now, Her jour - ney well-nigh done,

The pilgrim Church pursues her way, In haste to reach the crown.

2 The story of the past
  Comes up before her view;
How well it seems to suit her still;
  Old, and yet ever new.

3 'Tis the same story still,
  Of sin and weariness;
Of grace and love still flowing down,
  To pardon and to bless.

4 No wider is the gate,
  No broader is the way,

No smoother is the ancient path,
  That leads to light and day.

5 No sweeter is the cup,
  Nor less our lot of ill;
'Twas tribulation ages since,
  'Tis tribulation still.

6 'Tis the old sorrow still,
  The briar and the thorn;
And 'tis the same old solace yet,—
  The hope of coming morn.

———0———

397 Home. 8s & 7s.

H. W. JACKMAN.

GEO. E. LEE, by per.

1. Home, when life's rough voyage is o'er; Home, when sor-row comes no more;

Home, beyond death's swelling tide, For - ev - er by the Saviour's side.

2 Home, where trials ne'er can come,
Grief and anguish find no room;
There, with joy, the raptur'd throng,
Swell loud and clear redemption's song.

3 Parted ones shall gather there,
Joy and bliss forever share;

There shall death be known no more,
Nor fear'd at all on that blest shore.

4 Glorious prospect! heav'nly rest,
There with all the pure and blest;
Soon will that blest morning come,
When all the saints shall rest at home.

243

398 Armageddon.

Arranged by A. Ross.

1. Ho-san-na! hark, the mel-o-dy, Strikes sweetly on my ravish'd ear!
The con-stel-la-tions make reply, In echoes from each distant sphere,

Till all the wide ex-pansion rings With "Live for-ev-er, King of kings!"

2

He comes! he comes! the heavens rend;
 Floods, clap your hands; ye mountains,
Forests in glad obeisance bend!
Earth, raise your hallelujahs high,
Let Zion wake the lofty strain—
"Live, King of kings! forever reign."

3

Ripe is the vintage of the earth;
 Its clustering grapes are round and full,
And vengeance, vengeance bursts to birth,
 Sudden and irresistible:
Messiah comes to tread amain
The wine-press of the battle-plain.

4

The cry is up, the strife begun,
 The struggle of the mighty ones,
And Armageddon's day comes on,
 The carnival of Slaughter's sons;
War lifts his helmet to his brow—
O God! protect thy people now.

PART SECOND.

5

The graves are cleaved, the saints arise!
 The resurrection of the just:
And now unto the opening skies

Up leap the tenants of the dust!
They rise to meet their Lord in air,
[Joy] And tune their hallelujahs there.

6

Wake, Zion, wake! put on thy strength;
 Don thy rich garb, Jerusalem;
Rise, shine, thy light is come at length,
 And thou the wicked shalt condemn:
But, hark! the war-cry nearer sounds;
From land to land destruction bounds.

7

Assemble quickly, fowls of air;
 Come to the supper of the Lord;
The great ones of the earth prepare
 To reap the harvest of the sword;
And captains' flesh shall be your food,
And ye shall drink of heroes' blood.

8

The cry is up, the strife begun;
 Destruction spreads from field to field,
And soon shall Slaughter's work be done;
 Soon shall Abaddon's legions yield:
Unnumber'd thousands shall be slain,
And cover all Megiddo's plain.

399 I Own I'm Base. C. M.

1. Father, I stretch my hands to thee, No oth-er help I know:

If thou with-draw thy-self from me, Ah! whith-er shall I go?

Cho. { I own I'm base, I own I'm vile, But mer-cy's all my plea;
Re-mem-ber, Lord, thy dy-ing groans, Re-mem-ber Cal-va-ry!
Re-mem-ber, Lord, thy dy-ing groans, And then re-mem-ber me.

400 Silver Street. S. M.

1. O, Lord, thy work re-vive, In Zi-on's gloom-y hour;
And let our dy-ing gra-ces live By thy re-stor-ing pow'r!

2 O let thy chosen few
  Awake to earnest prayer;
Their sacred vows again renew,
  And walk in fil al fear!

3 Now lend thy gracious ear;
  Now listen to our cry;
O, come, and bring salvation near!
  Our souls on thee rely.

——o——

401 The Sun-Bright Clime.

1. Have you heard, have you heard of that sun-bright clime, Undimm'd by sin, and un-
curs'd by crime: Where Death hath no more the pow'r to reign, And they
live for - ev - er, and know no pain: Have you heard of that sun-bright clime?

2 There's a city fair,—the saints' "sweet home,"
  Which ne'er shall know night's saddening gloom;
With its gates of pearl, and its streets of gold,
  It will shine with the glory of God untold,
    Over there in that sun-bright clime.

3 A river of water floweth there,
  Mid scenes of beauty, strangely fair;
And rich-plumed songsters flit through the bowers
  Of the Tree of Life on the golden shores,
    Over there in that sun-bright clime.

4 Soon the ransomed host, enrobed in white,
  Will range those fields in pure delight,
And pluck rich fruit from the Life-Tree bowers,
  Mid a thousand hues of fadeless flowers,
    Over there in that sun-bright clime.

5 Not far, far away is that sinless clime,
  For now are we nearing the promised time;
When the Lord will come for his bride in white,
  Then we'll bid adieu to these scenes of night,
    And go home to that sun-bright clime.

240

402 Hear the News.

Words Arranged.

J. E. Hall.

Lively.

1. Hear the news, glad news of Je - sus: He is com-ing back a - gain;
2. Hear the news, ye blind ones, hear it, Je - sus comes you sight to give;
3. Hear the news, oh, sad and wea - ry, For his com-ing now is near,
4. Hear the news, ye sick and dy - ing: Je - sus comes his pow'r to show;

O, what blessings he will bring us, When he comes on earth to reign.
All ye deaf and dumb, be - lieve it, And the blessing soon re - ceive.
He will banish all your sor - row, When a - gain he shall ap - pear.
Ask his aid and trust his mer - cy: Per - fect health you then shall know.

CHORUS.

Hear the news, hear the news, He is com-ing back a - gain;
Hear the news, hear the news,

Hear the news, hear the news, He is com-ing soon to reign.
hear the news, hear the news,

From "The International Hymnal" by permission.

403   He Leadeth Me.

"He leadeth me by the still waters."—Ps. xxiii: 2.

Jos. H. Gilmore, 1861.   (Copyright, 1864, by W. B. Bradbury.)   Wm. B. Bradbury.

1. He leadeth me, oh! blessed thought, Oh! words with heav'nly comfort fraught;
2. Sometimes 'mid scenes of deepest gloom, Sometimes where Eden's bowers bloom,
3. Lord, I would clasp Thy hand in mine, Nor ev-er mur-mur nor re-pine—
4. And when He comes to claim His own, And give the vic-t'ry and the crown,

What-e'er I do, where'er I be, Still 'tis God's hand that lead-eth me.

By wa-ters still, o'er troubled sea—Still 'tis His hand that lead-eth me.

Con-tent, whatev-er lot I see, Since 'tis my God that lead-eth me.

To liv-ing fountains clear and free, Then still 'tis He that lead-eth me.

REFRAIN.

He lead-eth me! He lead-eth me! By His own hand He lead-eth me;

His faith-ful follower I would be, For by His hand He lead-eth me.

404   Behold! What Love!

F. A. BLACKMER.   Arranged by F. A. B. by per.

1. Be-hold! what love! what boundless love, The Fa - ther hath be-stow'd
2. Though now in-deed the sons of God, The world knoweth us not;
3. What we shall soon in glo - ry be, It doth not yet ap - pear;
4. And ev - 'ry man that hath this hope, Him-self doth pu - ri - fy;

Up - on His servants, that they should Be call'd the sons of God.
Be - cause it knew not Christ, the Lord, Who hath our son - ship bought.
But this we know, that when He comes, We shall His im - age bear.
E - ven as He, our Lord, is pure, In whom no sin doth lie.

CHORUS.

Be - hold............ what man-ner of love, What manner of love,

Behold what manner of love, what manner of love,................

That we,   that

The Fa - ther hath be-stow'd up - on us, That we should be call'd, that

we should be call'd,

we   should be call'd the sons of God.

Copyright, 1881, by F. A. BLACKMER.
243

405   Watchman, Tell Me.

"*Watchmen, what of the night?*"—Isa xxi: 11.

SIDNEY SMITH BREWER.   (*By Permission.*)   WM. B. BRADBURY.

Fine.

1. { Watchman tell me does the morning Of fair Zi - on's glo - ry dawn; }
   { Have the signs that mark His com-ing, Yet up - on my pathway shone? }
D.C. Spurn the un - be - lief that bound thee, Morning dawns, a - rise, a - rise!

D.C.

Pil-grim, yes, a - rise, look round thee, Light is breaking in the skies;

2 See the glorious light ascending
  Of the grand Sabbatic year,
Hark! the voices loud proclaiming
  The Messiah's kingdom near ;
Watchman! yes; I see just yonder,
  Canaan's glorious heights arise ;
Salem, too, appears in grandeur,
  Towering 'neath her sunlit skies.

3 Pilgrim in that golden city,
  Seated on the jasper throne,
Zion's King, arrayed in beauty.
  Reigns in peace from zone to zone ;

There, on verdant hills and mountains,
  Where the golden sunbeams play,
Purling streams, and crystal fountains,
  Sparkle in th' eternal day.

4 Pilgrim, see! the light is beaming
  Brighter still upon thy way;
Signs thro' all the earth are gleaming,
  Omens of the coming day,
When the last loud trumpet sounding,
  Shall awake from earth and sea
All the saints of God now sleeping,—
  Clad in immortality.

From "Golden Censer," by per. BIGLOW & MAIN.

406   Nothing Unclean.

By Permission of Jno. R. Sweney. Copyright, 1872.

JAMES NICHOLSON.   JNO. R. SWENEY.

1. Nothing un - clean can en - ter in Where Christ will ev - er reign;

His eyes, so pure, can-not en - dure The sight of spot or stain.

Nothing Unclean. Concluded.

Nothing un-clean, my gra - cious Lord, Nothing unclean, nothing un-clean.

2 Nothing unclean must stand between
The Holy Ghost and me;
Saviour from sin, the work begin;
Wash me, till thou canst see.—*Cho.*

3 Nothing unclean can mortals screen
From the All-seeing eye;
Spirit of God, apply the blood,
Until I hear Thee cry,—*Cho.*

4 Nothing unclean; oh, glorious scene!
My heart, washed in the blood,
With rapture thrills, as now it feels
The mighty power of God!—*Cho.*

5 Nothing unclean doth intervene
To dim the Spirit's light;
It shines each day along my way,
Nor fails to shine at night.—*Cho.*

——0——

407   At the Judgment Seat.

1. O, there will be mourning, mourning, mourning, mourning, O, there will be
2. O, there will be mourning, &c.
3. O, there will be mourning, &c.

mourning at the Judgment seat of Christ; Parents and children there will part,
Brothers and sisters, &c.
Friends and neighbors, &c.

Pa-rents and children there will part, Parents and children there will part,
Brothers and sis - ters, &c.
Friends and neighbors, &c.

Will part to meet no more!

4 O, there will be glory, glory, glory, glory,
O, there will be glory at the Judgment
seat of Christ;
|: Saints and angels there will meet, :|
Saints and angels there will meet.
Will meet to part no more.

245

408   Safe Within the Vale.

JNO. M. EVANS,—ARR. by H. P. MAIN.

1. "Land a - head!" Its fruits are waving O'er the hills of fadeless green;
2. Onward, bark! the cape I'm rounding, See! the bless-ed wave their hands;

And the liv - ing wa-ters laving Shores where heav'nly forms are seen.
Hear the harps of God re-sound-ing From the bright, im-mor-tal bands.

CHORUS.

Rocks and storms I'll fear no more, When on that e - ter - nal shore:

Drop the an - chor! Furl the sail! I am safe within the vail!

3 There, let go the anchor, riding
  On this calm and silv'ry bay;
Seaward fast the tide is gliding,
  Shores in sunlight stretch away.
  Chorus.

4 Now we're safe from all temptation,
  All the storms of life are past;
Praise the Rock of our Salvation,
  We are safe at home at last!
  Chorus.

Copyright, 1869, in "*Bright Jewels.*" and used by per. of *Biglow & Main.*

409   Mear. C. M.

1 Jesus, I love thy charming name!
  'Tis music to my ear;
Fain would I sound it out so loud,
  That earth and heaven might hear.

2 Yes, thou art precious to my soul!
  My transport and my trust;
Jewels to thee are gaudy toys,
  And gold is sordid dust.

Fine

1. Sin - ner go, will you go, To the high-lands of heaven?
D.C. And the leaves of the bow'rs In the breez - es are flitting.

Where the storms nev - er blow, And the long summer's giv - en:

D.C.

Where the bright blooming flow'rs Are their o - dors e - mit - ting,

2 Where the rich golden fruit
  In bright clusters are pending,
And the deep-laden boughs
  Of life's fair tree are bending;
And where life's crystal stream
  Is unceasingly flowing,
And the verdure is green,
  And eternally growing.

3 Where the saints, robed in white,
  Cleansed in life's flowing fountain,
Shining beauteous and bright,
  Shall inhabit the mountain.

Where no sin nor dismay,
  Neither trouble nor sorrow
Shall be felt for a day,
  Nor be feared for the morrow.

4 He's prepared thee a home;
  Sinner, canst thou believe it?
And invites thee to come;
  Sinner, wilt thou receive it?
O come, sinner, come,
  For the tide is receding,
And the Saviour will soon,
  And forever cease pleading.

—o—

411 **The Prodigal's Return.**

1. The long-lost son, with streaming eyes, From fol - ly just a - wake,

Re - views his wand'rings with sur-prise: His heart be - gins to break.

2 "I starve," he cries, "nor can I bear
  The famine in this land,
While servants of my Father share
  The bounty of his hand.

3 "With deep repentance I'll return,
  And seek my Father's face—
Unworthy to be called a son,
  I'll ask a servant's place."

4 Far off the Father saw him move—
  In pensive silence mourn—
And quickly ran. with arms of love,
  To welcome his return.

5 Through all the courts the tidings flew,
  And spread the joy around;
The angels tuned their harps anew—
  The long-lost son is found!

412   Will You Go With Me?

T. C. O'KANE, by per.

1. A beau-ti-ful land by faith I see, A land of rest from

sor-row free; The home of the ran-som'd, bright and fair, And

CHORUS.

beau-ti-ful an-gels will be there. Will you go? will you go?

Go to that beau-ti-ful land with me? land with me?

2	3
That beautiful land, where all is light, It ne'er will know the shades of night, The glory of God, the light of day, Hath driven the darkness far away.	The heavenly throng array'd in white, In rapture range the plains of light; In harmony grand and pure they praise Their glorious Saviour's matchless grace.

——o——

413   Woodland.   C. M.

1 Repent! the voice celestial cries;
No longer dare delay!
The soul that scorns the mandate dies,
And meets a fiery day.

2 O sinners, in his presence bow,
And all your guilt confess;

Accept the offered Saviour now,
Nor trifle with his grace!

3 Amazing love, that yet will call,
And still prolong our days!
Our hearts, subdued by goodness, fall,
And weep, and love, and praise.

414 We'll Work till Jesus Comes.

"Thy work shall be rewarded."—Jer. xxxi: 16.

MRS. ELIZABETH MILLS.   *(By Permission.)*   DR. WM. MILLER.

1. O, land of rest, for thee I sigh; When will the mo-ment come,
2. No tran-quil joys on earth I know, No peace-ful, shelt'ring dome;
3. To Je-sus Christ I fled for rest; He bade me cease to roam,
4. I sought at once my Saviour's side; No more my steps shall roam:

When I shall lay my ar-mor by, And dwell in peace at home?
This world's a wil-der-ness of woe, This world is not my home.
And lean for suc-cor on his breast, Till he con-duct me home.
With Him I'll brave life's chilling tide, And reach my heav'nly home.

CHORUS.

We'll work till Je-sus comes, We'll work till Je-sus comes, We'll
We'll work till Je-sus comes, We'll work till Je-sus comes,

work till Je-sus comes, And we'll be gath-er'd home.
We'll work till Je-sus comes,

From "Golden Censer," by per. BIGLOW & MAIN.

249

415 "Almost Persuaded."

*"Almost thou persuadest me to become a Christian."—*Acts xxvi: 28.

I. B.   I. BALTZELL

Gently.

1. "Al - most per-suad - ed" to leave the ways of sin; "Al - most per -
2. "Al - most per-suad - ed!" what is it keeps you back? "Al - most per -
3. "Al - most per-suad - ed!" why not re - pent to - day? "Al - most per -
4. "Al - most per-suad - ed" will not a - vail at last; "Al - most per -

- suad - ed" to let the Saviour in; "Al - most per - suad - ed" to
- suad - ed!" what is it yet you lack? "Al - most per - suad - ed," the
- suad - ed!" Oh, come with-out de - lay! "Al - most per - suad - ed" will
- suad - ed" will bring a bit - ter past; Ful - ly per - suad - ed will

give your wand'rings o'er; "Almost per-suad-ed" to o - pen now the door.
Sav-iour bids you come; "Almost per-suad-ed," yet still in sin you roam.
nev - er give thee rest; "Almost per-suad-ed" can nev - er calm thy breast.
bring you joy and peace; Ful-ly per-suad-ed will bring a sweet re-lease.

From "Songs of Grace," by permission.

416 He Shall Appear.

From "Song Evangel," by per. of Biglow & Main.   Arranged by H. P. MAIN.

1. { "The sec - ond time" "He shall ap-pear"—We'll be gather'd home—
     The "dead in Christ" shall then a - rise—We'll be gather'd home—

To res - cue those to Him so dear; We'll be gather'd home. }
And "with the Lord" meet in the skies, We'll be gather'd home. }

He Shall Appear. Concluded.

CHORUS.

We'll watch till Je-sus comes, We'll pray till Je-sus comes,

We'll watch till Je-sus comes, We'll pray till Je-sus comes,

We'll wait till Je-sus comes, And then be gather'd home.

We'll wait till Je-sus comes, And then be gather'd home.

2 He comes, he comes to save his own—
　We'll be gather'd home—
　He comes upon the great white throne—
　We'll be gather'd home—
　The trump of God the world will hear--
　We'll be gather'd home—
　And at the Judgment seat appear—
　We'll be gather'd home.—*Cho.*

3 Then will the saints in glory sing—
　We'll be gather'd home—
　Then will the heav'ns with praises ring—
　We'll be gather'd home—
　Then will their sufferings all be o'er—
　We'll be gather'd home—
　Then will they live to die no more—
　We'll be gather'd home.—*Cho.*

—o—

417　A Charge to Keep.　S. M.

CHARLES WESLEY.　　　　　　　　　　　　JEREMIAH INGALLS.

1. A charge to keep I have, A God to glo-ri-fy;

And Him who came my soul to save, And who for me did die!

418

2 To serve the present age,
　My calling to fulfil,
　O may it all my powers engage,
　To do my Master's will.

3 Arm me with jealous care,
　As in thy sight to live;
　And O, thy servant, Lord, prepare,
　A strict account to give.

4 Help me to watch and pray,
　And on thyself rely,
　Assured if I my trust betray,
　I shall forever die.

1 And can I yet delay
　My little all to give?
　To tear myself from earth away
　For Jesus to receive?

2 Though late, I all forsake;
　My friends, my all, resign;
　Gracious Redeemer, take, O take,
　And seal me ever thine.

3 My one desire be this,—
　Thy only love to know;
　To seek and taste no other bliss,--
　No other good below.

419   Precious Jesus.

Words Arranged.   *From "Golden Songs," by permission.*

1. Precious Jesus, I am com - ing; Here I come to thee to - day;

I am trusting, I'm be - liev - ing, Take, oh, take my sins a - way.

CHORUS

Precious Jesus, make, O make me whole, Ho - ly Spir - it, all my pow'rs con-trol.

2 Precious Jesus, I am longing,
  All thy peace and joy to know ;
Wilt thou grant me that one blessing,
  All the world can ne'er bestow?

3 Precious Jesus, I am clinging,
  I am clinging fast to thee ;

Help me, Saviour, help me ever.
  Let me thy disciple be.

4 Precious Jesus, I am trusting,
  Trusting in thy cleansing blood ;
Precious Jesus, blessed Saviour,
  Thou hast brought me home to God.

——0——

420   Worthy is the Lamb.

1. Worthy, worthy is the Lamb, Worthy, wor - thy is the Lamb,

CHORUS.

Worthy, worthy is the Lamb That was slain : Glo-ry, Hal - le - lu - jah!

Worthy is the Lamb. Concluded.

Praise him, Halle - lu - jah! Glo-ry, Hal - le - lu - jah To.... the Lamb.

2 Sons of morning, sing his praise,
   In the noblest strains you raise,
   Man's redemption claims your lays,
     Praise the Lamb.

3 See, in sad Gethsemane,
   See, on tragic Calvary,
   Sinner, see his love to thee,
     Praise the Lamb.

4 Penitents, dismiss your fears,
   God will hear believing prayers,
   He forgives you when he hears,
     His dear Lamb.

5 Thus may we each moment feel,
   Love him, serve him, praise him still,
   Till we all on Zion's hill
     See the Lamb.

——o——

421 Ward. L. M.

ISAAC WATTS.   Scotch Tune, Arr. by LOWELL MASON.

1. God is the ref-uge of his saints, When storms of sharp distress in - vade;

Ere we can of-fer our complaints, Be-hold him pre-sent with his aid.

2 Let mountains from their seats be hurled
   Down to the deep, and buried there;
   Convulsions shake the solid world,
   Our faith shall never yield to fear.

3 There is a stream, whose gentle flow
   Supplies the city of our God;
   Life, love, and joy still gliding through,
   And wat'ring our divine abode.

422

1 Saviour of men, thy searching eye
   Doth all mine inmost thoughts descry;
   Doth aught on earth my wishes raise,
   Of the world's pleasures, or its praise?

2 The love of Christ doth me constrain
   To seek the wandering souls of men:

With cries, entreaties, tears, to save,—
To snatch them from the gaping grave.

3 For this let men revile my name;
   No cross I shun, I fear no shame:
   All hail, reproach; and welcome, pain;
   Only thy terrors, Lord, restrain.

4 My life, my blood, I here present,
   If for thy truth they may be spent;
   Fulfil thy sovereign counsel, Lord;
   Thy will be done, thy name adored.

5 Give me thy strength, O God of power;
   Then let winds blow, or thunders roar,
   Thy faithful witness will I be:
   'Tis fixed; I can do all through thee.

JOHANN J. WINKLER. TR. BY J. WESLEY.

Christian Soldiers.

mp

1. { Ye val-iant sol-diers of the cross, Ye hap-py, pray-ing band, }
{ Tho' in this world you suf-fer loss, Press on to Canaan's land; }

CHORUS. *accel.*

Let us nev-er mind the scoffs nor the frowns of the world:

Though we all have the cross to bear, It will on-ly make the crown the

bright - er to shine, When we have the crown to wear.

2 All earthly pleasures we'll forsake
While glory is in view;
In Jesus' strength we'll undertake
To fight our passage through.

3 O, what a glorious scene there'll be
When we arrive at home;
Jesus and all His saints we'll see—
To Zion's mount they'll come.

—o—

The Sweet Call.

1. 'Tis the sweet call of mer-cy, That lin-gers for thee; Oh! sin-ner, re-

-ceive it; To Je-sus now flee! He oft-en has call'd thee, But

thou hast re-fus'd! His of-fer'd sal-va-tion And love are a-bus'd!

2 If thou slightest this warning,
 Now offered at last,
Thine will be the sad mourning—
 "The harvest is past,"
'Salvation I've slighted,'
 The summer is o'er,
And now there is pardon,
 Sweet pardon, no more.'

3 'Tis the sweet call of mercy,
 Oh, steel not thy heart,
The Spirit is striving,
 And soon may depart!

The Bride is now calling—
 "Ye thirsty souls, come!"
Oh, come with the ransom'd,
 In glory there's room!

4 'Tis the sweet call of mercy,
 That lingers for thee!
Break away from thy bondage,
 Oh, sinner, be free!
Be not a sad mourner—
 "The harvest is past,
The summer is ended"—
 And perish at last!

—o—

425   I'm a Pilgrim. P. M.

1. I'm a pil-grim, and I'm a stran-ger; I can

Fine.

tar-ry, I can tar-ry but a night; Do not de-tain me,

D.C.

for I am go-ing To where the fountains are ev-er flow-ing.

2 There's the city to which I journey;
My Redeemer, my Redeemer is its light!
There is no sorrow, nor any sighing
Nor any tears there, nor any dying!
I'm a pilgrim, and I'm a stranger, &c.

3 There the glory is ever shining! there;
O, my longing heart, my longing heart is
Here in this country so dark and dreary,
I long have wandered forlorn and weary.
I'm a pilgrim, and I'm a stranger, &c.

426   Jesus, my Shelter.

E. A. A.

GEO. E. LEE, by per.

1. I fly to Je-sus, whose I am: Re-ceive a torn and wea-ry lamb;

Hide me with-in thy shelt'ring fold, And give me love that grows not cold.

2 Let thy sweet patience tame my heart,
So prone to act the wilful part,
Till to each crossing thing I say,
"Thy will be done," be what it may.

3 Remove each selfish thought I feel,
And give a calmly tempered zeal,

That waits on God, and works, or not—
The same, encouraged or forgot.

4 Let all thy pains, thy prayers, thy cries,
Be set before my tearful eyes,
Till I can suffer like my Lord,
Nor utter a complaining word.

———o———

427   Dedham. C. M.

1. O, what a treasure all di-vine Is hid in Christ, the Lord!

From him what rays of glo-ry shine! What peace his paths af-ford!

2 In him our light and life are found,
Though we were dead before;
And now he makes our joys abound,
Who all our sorrows bore.

3 When sore distressed, he to our aid
On rapid pinions flies,

And to the wounds which sin has made
A healing balm applies.

4 'Tis from his fullness we receive,
And daily, grow in grace;
That to his glory we may live.
And see Him face to face.

428   O, I Do Love Jesus.

Words by CHARLES WESLEY.

1. Je - sus, the name high o - ver all That dwell be - low the sky;

An - gels and men be - fore it fall, And de - mons fear and fly.

CHORUS.

O, I do love Je - sus! O, I do love Je - - sus!
How can I for - get Thee? How can I for - get my Lord?

O, I do love Je - sus! Be - cause He first lov'd me.
How can I for - get Thee? Dear Lord, re - mem - ber me.

2 Jesus, the name to saints so dear,
   The name to sinners given;
It scatters all their doubts and fear;
   It makes the earth a heaven.—*Cho.*

3 O that the world might taste and see
   The riches of His grace;

The arms of love that compass me
   Would all mankind embrace.—*Cho.*

4 His only righteousness I show;
   His saving truth proclaim:
'Tis all my business, here below,
   To cry, Behold the Lamb!—*Cho.*

———o———

429   Windham.   L. M.

1 He lives—the great Redeemer lives!
  What joy the blest assurance gives!
And now, enthroned above the skies,
  He pleads his holy sacrifice.

2 Great Advocate, almighty Friend,
  On thee do all our hopes depend!

Our cause can never, never fail,
  For thou dost plead and must prevail.

3 In every dark, distressing hour,
  When sin and Satan join their power,
Let this blest truth repel each dart,
  That Jesus bears us on his heart.

Resurrection. L. M.

1. I know that my Re-deem-er lives, He lives, and on the earth shall stand;

And tho' to worms my flesh he gives, My dust lies number'd in... his hand.

2 In this reanimated clay
I surely shall behold him near;
Shall see him in the latter day
In all his majesty appear.

3 I know what then shall raise me up;
The quick'ning Spirit dwells in me;

This is my confidence and hope,
That I him face to face shall see.

4 Mine own, and not another's eyes,
The King shall in his beauty view;
I shall from him receive the prize,
The starry crown to victors due.

431 When Shall We Meet? 6s & 5s.

1. When shall we meet a - gain? Meet ne'er to sev - er? When will peace
2. Soon shall we meet a - gain, Meet ne'er to sev - er; Soon shall peace

wreathe her chain Round us for - ev - er? Our hearts will ne'er re - pose, Safe
wreathe her chain Round us for - ev - er: Our hearts will then re - pose Se -

from each blast that blows. In this dark vale of woes, Never—no, never!
- cure from fears or woes; Our songs of praise shall close Never—no, never!

Pray Without Ceasing.

CHESTER E POND, by per.

1. My Lord and my Saviour, Cre - a - tor and King, Thy love and thy
2. If meet-ing with saints for com-munion or prayer, Or sing-ing a
3. If searching the Bi - ble for gems of its truth, Or teach-ing its

glo-ry for-ev - er I'll sing; My soul is in raptures: thou reignest within,
song with melo-di - ous air; If aid - ing the low - ly, the poor, or the weak,
precepts to children or youth; If writ-ing for oth - ers on ho-li-est theme,

CHORUS.

To car - ry my burdens and cleanse me from sin.
Or urg-ing a sin-ner thy mer-cy to seek: { Oh, help me remember, by
Or preaching the gospel their souls to re-deem:

night and by day, To "pray without ceasing," thy word to o-bey! For nothing will

rit.

cherish de-vo-tion in me Like se - cret and constant communion with thee.

433 What a Wonderful Saviour!

"And his name shall be called Wonderful."

E. A. H.   ELISHA A. HOFFMAN by per.

1. He saves the sin - ner from his sins, What a won - der - ful Sav-iour!
2. He par-dons sin - ners here be - low, What a won - der - ful Sav-iour!
3. To him my soul, my all, I vow, What a won - der - ful Sav-iour!

He brings his joy and peace with - in! What a won - der - ful Sav-iour!
And makes the soul as white as snow, What a won - der - ful Sav-iour!
I trust him, and he saves me now, What a won - der - ful Sav-iour!

CHORUS.

What a won - der - ful Sav - iour is.... Je - sus, my Je - sus!

What a won - der - ful Sav - iour Is Je - sus, my Lord!

—o—

434 The Happy Land.

1. There is a happy land, not far a - way, Where saints will joy-ful stand,

The Happy Land. Concluded.

Bright, bright as day. Oh, how they'll sweetly sing, "Worthy is our

Sav - iour King, Loud let his prais-es ring, Praise, praise for aye!"

2 Come to that happy land,
   Come, come away,
Why will ye doubting stand,
   Why still delay?
Oh, we shall happy be,
   When, from sin and sorrow free;
Lord, we shall live with thee,
   Blest, blest for aye.

3 When in that happy land,
   Beams bright each eye;
Led by a Saviour's hand,
   They cannot die.
Oh, then, to glory run;
   Be a crown and kingdom won;
And brighter than the sun,
   We'll shine for aye.

—o—

435   Here is no Rest.   P. M.

1. { Here o'er the earth as a stran-ger I roam, Here is no
{ Here as a pil-grim I wan-der a-lone, Yet I am

D.C. My heart doth leap while I hear Je - sus say—There, there is

Fine.

rest, is no rest; }
blest, I am blest: }
rest, there is rest.

For I look for - ward to that glorious day,
When sin and sor - row will van-ish a-way:

D.C.

2 Here fierce temptations beset me around;
   Here is no rest—is no rest:
Here I am griev'd while my foes me sur-
     round;
   Yet I am blest—I am blest.
Let them revile me and scoff at my name,
Laugh at my weeping—endeavor to
     shame,
I will go forward, for this is my theme,
   There, there is rest—there is rest.

3 Here are afflictions and trials severe:
   Here is no rest—is no rest: [dear;
Here I must part with the friends I hold
   Yet I am blest—I am blest.
Sweet is the promise I read in his word;
   "Blessed are they who have died in the
     Lord;"
They will be called to receive their
     reward:
   There, there is rest—there is rest.

436 Beautiful World. P. M.

1. { We're go - ing home, we've had vis-ions bright, Of that ho - ly land, that
   { Where the long, dark night of time is past, And the morn of eternity

world of light, } Where the weary saint no more shall roam, But dwell in a happy and
dawns at last, } Where the brow with sparkling gems is crown'd, And the waves of
[bliss are flow-

REFRAIN.

peaceful home;
- ing around. O, that beauti-ful World! O, that beau-ti - ful World!

2

We're going home, we soon shall be
Where the sky is clear and all are free,
Where the victor's song floats o'er the plain,
And the seraphs' anthems blend with its
    strain;
Where the sun rolls down its brilliant flood,
And beams on a world that is fair and good,
Where stars, once dimm'd at nature's doom,
Will ever shine o'er the new earth's bloom.

3

Where the tears and sighs which here were
    given,
Are exchanged for the gladsome song of
    heaven;   [shine,
Where the beauteous forms which sing and
Are guarded well by a hand divine;

Where the banner of love and friendship's
    wand
Are waving above that princely band,
And the glory of God, like a boundless sea,
Will cheer that immortal company.

4

'Mid the ransom'd throng, 'mid the sea of
    bliss,
'Mid the holy city's gorgeousness,
'Mid the verdant plains, 'mid angel's cheer,
'Mid the saints that round the throne
    appear;
Where the conqueror's song, as it sounds
    afar,
Is wafted on the ambrosial air:
Through endless years we then shall prove
The depth of a Saviour's matchless love.

—— o ——

437 Hamburg. L. M.

1 With all my pow'rs of heart and tongue,
I'll praise my Maker in my song;
Angels shall hear the notes I raise,
Approve the song, and join the praise.

2 To God I cried when troubles rose,
He heard me, and subdued my foes:
He did my rising fears control,
And strength diffused thro' all my soul

438 Will Jesus Find us Watching?

"Watch therefore; for ye know not what hour your Lord doth come."—Matt. xxiv; 42.

FANNY J. CROSBY.   (Copyright, 1870, by W. H. Doane.)   W. H. DOANE.

1. When Je-sus comes to re-ward His ser-vants, Whether it be
2. If at the dawn of the ear-ly morn-ing, He shall call us
3. Have we been true to the trust He left us? Do we seek to
4. Bless-ed are those whom the Lord finds watching, In His glo-ry

noon or night, Faith-ful to Him will He find us watching,
one by one; When to the Lord we re-store our tal-ents,
do our best? If in our hearts there is naught con-demns us,
they shall share; If He shall come at the dawn or mid-night,

rit.   REFRAIN.

With our lamps all trimm'd and bright? Oh, can we say we are
Will He say to thee—"Well done?"
We shall have a glo-rious rest.
Will He find us watch-ing there?

read-y, broth-er? Read-y for the saints' bright home? Say, will He

find you and me still watching, Waiting, waiting when the Lord shall come?

From "Gospel Hymns Combined," by per. BIGLOW & MAIN.

439   Olivet.   6s & 4s.

RAY PALMER.   LOWELL MASON.

1. My faith looks up to thee, Thou Lamb of Calvary, Saviour divine : Now hear me while I pray, Take all my guilt a-way, O let me from this day Be wholly thine.

2
May thy rich grace impart
Strength to my fainting heart,
  My zeal inspire;
As thou hast died for me,
O may my love to thee
Pure, warm, and changeless be,—
  A living fire.

3
While life's dark maze I tread,
And griefs around me spread
  Be thou my guide;

Bid darkness turn to day,
Wipe sorrow's tears away,
Nor let me ever stray
  From thee aside.

4
When time's eventful years,
With sin and toil and tears,
  Shall cease to be,
Blest Saviour then in love,
Descending from above,
My every ill remove,
  And ransom me.

——o——

440   Ames.   L. M.

JAMES HUTTON.   ARR. by LOWELL MASON.

1. My op'ning eyes with rap-ture see The dawn of thy re-turn-ing day; My thoughts, O God, as-cend to thee, While thus my early vows I pay.

2 O, bid this trifling world retire,
  And drive each carnal thought away;
Nor let me feel one vain desire,
  One sinful thought through all the day.

3 Then to thy courts when I repair,
  My soul shall rise on joyful wing,
The wonders of thy love declare,
  And join the strains which angels sing.

441 More Like Thee.

Words and Music by W. J. KIRKPATRICK, by per.

1. Je - sus, Saviour, great Ex-am-ple, Pat-tern of all pu - ri - ty,
2. Lest I wan-der from Thy pathway, Or my feet move wea-ri - ly,
3. When the tempests fiercely low-er, And my shrinking soul would flee,
4. When amidst the clouds and darkness, And thy beauties few can see;

I would fol-low in Thy footsteps, Dai - ly grow-ing more like Thee.
Sav-iour, take my hand and lead me, Keep me steadfast : more like Thee.
Change each weakness in - to pow-er, Make me strong, and more like Thee.
Let me view Thee in Thy brightness, And be more, be more like Thee.

CHORUS.

More like thee, more like Thee : Saviour, this my constant prayer shall be—
More like Thee, more like Thee !

Day by day, where'er I stray, Make me more and more like Thee.

—o—

442 Exhortation. C. M.

1 Sweet rivers of redeeming love
   I see before me lie ;
   Had I the pinions of a dove,
   I'd to those rivers fly.

2 A few more days, or months, at most,
   My troubles will be o'er ;
   I hope to join the heavenly host
   On Canaan's happy shore.

265

443   Auvern. L. M.

By permission of O. Ditson & Co.

1. Triumphant Zi - on, lift thy head From dust, and darkness, and the dead!
2. Put all thy beauteous garments on, And let thy ex - cel - lence be known;

Tho' humbled long, a - wake at length, And gird thee with a Saviour's strength.
Deck'd in the robes of right-eous-ness, Thy glo-ries shall the world con - fess.

And gird thee with a Saviour's strength.
Thy glories shall the world confess.

3 No more shall foes unclean invade,
   And fill thy hallowed halls with dread :
   No more shall hell's insulting host
|: Their victory and thy sorrows boast. :|

4 God from on high has heard thy prayer,
   His hands thy ruins shall repair ;
   Nor will thy watchful Monarch cease
|: To guard thee in eternal peace. :|

—0—

444   Retreat. L. M.

HUGH STOWELL.   THOMAS HASTINGS.

1. From ev - 'ry stormy wind that blows, From ev - 'ry swelling tide of woes,

There is a calm, a sure retreat: 'Tis found be-neath the mer-cy - seat.

2 There is a place where Jesus sheds
   The oil of gladness on our heads
   A place than all besides more sweet:
   It is the blood-bought mercy-seat.

3 There is a scene where spirits blend,
   Where friend holds fellowship with
        friend :
   Though sundered far, by faith they meet
   Around one common mercy-seat.

4 Ah! whither could we flee for aid,
   When tempted, desolate, dismayed ;
   Or how the hosts of sin defeat,
   Had suffering saints no mercy-seat?

5 There, there on eagle wings we soar,
   And sin and sense molest no more ;
   And heaven comes down our souls to
        greet,
   While glory crowns the mercy-seat.

445 Jesus is Waiting to Save You.

"Behold, now is the accepted time."—2 Cor. vi: 2.

E. A. H.   ELISHA A. HOFFMAN, by per.

1. Brother! while fill'd with con-tri - tion, Low down at his feet you bow,
2. Off'ring the cup of sal - va - tion, Sweet mer-cy up - on his brow,
3. Come to this mer - ci - ful Sav-iour, And pay him your faith-ful vow,
4. Free-ly and ful - ly ac-cept him, While down at his feet you bow;

Je - sus is ready and will-ing, And waiting to save you now.
Bringing a full and free par-don, He's waiting to save you now.
While he is ready and will-ing, And waiting to save you now.
Do not re - fuse and re - ject him, He's waiting to save you now.

CHORUS.

Brother! why don't you be-lieve him? Brother! why don't you re-ceive him?

He's wait-ing, He's wait-ing, He's wait-ing to save you now!

—o—

446 Vernon. S. M.

1 Beyond this gloomy night
   Eternal beauties rise,
 A land of love, a land of light,
   Unseen by mortal eyes.

Cho.—There'll be no sorrow there;
      There'll be no sorrow there·
      When Jesus comes, we'll all go home;
      There'll be no sorrow there.

447 Shall we Meet beyond the River?

"The ransomed of the Lord shall return and come to Zion with songs and everlasting joy upon their heads."—Isa. xxx: 10.

HORACE L. HASTINGS, 1858.   (By Permission.)   ELIHU S. RICE, 1866.

Moderato.

1. Shall we meet beyond the riv-er, Where the sur - ges cease to roll?
2. Shall we meet in that blest harbor, When our stormy voyage's o'er?
3. Shall we meet in yon-der cit-y, Where the tow'rs of crys - tal shine?
4. Shall we meet with Christ, our Saviour, When He comes to claim His own?

Where, in all the bright for - ev-er, Sor - row ne'er shall press the soul?
Shall we meet and cast the anchor By the fair, ce - les - tial shore?
Where the walls are all of jasper, Built by work-man-ship di-vine?—
Shall we know his bless-ed fa-vor, And sit down up - on His throne?

CHORUS.

Shall we meet, shall we meet, Shall we meet be-yond the riv-er?

Shall we meet be-yond the riv - er, Where the sur - ges cease to roll?

From "Gospel Hymns Combined." by per. BIGLOW & MAIN.

448   Henley.   11s & 10s.

DR. L. MASON.

By permission of O. Ditson & Co.

1. Come un - to Me when shadows dark-ly gath - er, When the sad

heart is wea - ry and dis-tress'd, Seek - ing for com - fort from your

heav'nly Fa - ther, "Come un - to Me, and I will give you rest."

2 Ye who have mourned when the spring flow'rs were taken,
When the ripe fruit fell richly to the ground,
When the lov'd slept, but to at length awaken,
Where their pale brows with fadeless wreaths are crown'd.

3 Large are the mansions in thy Father's dwelling;
Glad are the homes that sorrows never dim;
Sweet are the harps in holy music swelling;
Soft are the tones which raise the heavenly hymn.

4 There, like an Eden blossoming in gladness,
Will bloom the flowers the earth too rudely pressed;
"Come unto Me," all ye who droop in sadness,
"Come unto Me, and I will give you rest!"

—o—

449 Woodworth. L. M.

WM. B. BRADBURY.

1. Of all the joys we mortals know, Je - sus, thy love ex-ceeds the rest;

Love, the best blessing here be-low, The highest rapture of the blest.

2 Securely held in thine embrace,
No fickle thought attempts to rove;
Each smile that's seen upon thy face,
Fixes and charms, and fires our love.

3 Oft of thine absence we complain,
And sadly weep, and humbly pray;
Yet there is pleasure in the pain, [stay.
The tears are sweet which mourn thy

450   Geneva. C. M.

JOSEPH ADDISON.   JOHN COLE.

1. When all thy mer - cies, O......my God, My rising soul surveys,
When all thy mercies, O my God.

When all thy mercies, O my God,

Trans-port - ed with the view, I'm lost In won - der, love, and praise.

Transported with

2 O, how can words with equal warmth
  The gratitude declare,
That glows within my ravished heart?—
  But thou canst read it there.

3 To all my weak complaints and cries
  Thy mercy lent an ear,
Ere yet my feeble thoughts had learned
  To form themselves in prayer.

4 Thro' hidden dangers, toils, and deaths,
  It gently cleared my way;
And through the pleasing snares of vice,
  More to be feared than they.

5 Through all eternity to thee
  A grateful song I'll raise;
But, O, eternity's too short
  To utter all thy praise!

—o—

451   Ozrem. S. M.

By permission of O. DITSON & Co.   I. B. WOODBURY.

1. Thou ref - uge of my soul, On thee, when sor - rows rise,

On thee, when waves of trou-ble roll, My faint - ing hope re - lies.

2 To thee I tell my grief,
  For thou alone canst heal;
Thy word can bring a sweet relief
  For every pain I feel.

3 But O, when doubts prevail,
  I fear to call thee mine;

The springs of comfort seem to fail,
  And all my hopes decline.

4 Yet, Lord, where shall I flee?
  Thou art my only trust;
And still my soul would cleave to thee,
  Though prostrate in the dust.

452 See that Pilgrim. 8s & 7s.

Unison.

1. See that pilgrim—low-ly bending; Hear his prayer to heav'n as-cend-ing;

Praise and sighs to-geth-er blend-ing From his lips in mournful strain:

Glowing with sin-cere con-tri-tion, And with child-like, blest submission,

Ev-er ris-eth this pe-ti-tion—"Je-sus, come! oh, come to reign!"

2 List again—the low earth sigheth,
And the blood of martyrs crieth
From its bosom, where there lieth
Millions upon millions slain:
"Lord, how long, ere thy word given,
All the wicked shall be driven
From the earth by bolts of Heaven?
Jesus, come! oh, come to reign!"

3 Kingdoms now are reeling, falling,
Nations lie in woe appalling,
On their sages vainly calling
All these wonders to explain;
While the slain around are lying,
God's own little flock are sighing,
And in secret places crying,
"Jesus, come! oh, come to reign!"

4 Here the wicked live securely,
Of to-morrow boasting surely,
While from those who're walking purely
They extort dishonest gain;
Yea, the meek are burden'd, driven;
Want and care to them are given,
But they lift the cry to Heaven,
"Jesus, come! oh, come to reign!"

5 Christian, *cheer thee*—land is nearing,
Still be hopeful—nothing fearing;
Soon, in majesty appearing,
You'll behold the Lamb once slain.
Oh how joyful then to hear him,
While all nations shall revere him,
Saying to his flock who fear him,
"*I have come, on earth to reign.*"

———o———

453 Homeward Bound.

Out on the ocean all boundless we ride,
We're homeward bound, homeward
bound;
Toss'd on the waves of a rough, restless tide,
We're homeward bound, homeward
bound:

Far from the safe, quiet harbor we've
rode,
Seeking our Father's celestial abode,
Promise of which on us each he bestowed,
We're homeward bound, homeward
bound.

454 Beautiful White Robes.

"What are these which are arrayed in white robes?"—Rev. vii: 13.

I. BALTZELL.

1. Who are these ar-ray'd in white, Brighter than the noon-day sun,
2. These are they who bore the cross, No - bly for the Mas-ter stood,
3. Clad in rai - ment pure and white, Vic-tor palms in ev - 'ry hand,
4. Joy and glad-ness ban-ish sighs, Per-fect love dis-pels all fears;

Fore-most of the sons of light, Near-est the E - ter - nal throne?
Suf - f'rers in the no - ble cause, Foll'wers of E - man-uel God.
Thro' their great Re-deem-er's might, More than con-quer-ors they stand.
And for - ev - er from their eyes God shall wipe a - way their tears.

CHORUS.

They have clean robes, beautiful white robes, Wash'd in Jesus' blood di-vine;

May a clean and beautiful white robe, Wash'd in Jesus' blood, be mine.

From "Gates of Praise," by permission.

———o———

455 Jesus is There. 6s & 4s.

1. Haste, my dull soul, a-rise, Shake off thy care; Press for the promis'd prize,

Jesus is There. Concluded.

Mighty in prayer. Christ, he has gone be-fore, Count all thy

suff'rings o'er: He all thy bur-dens bore—Je-sus is there.

2 Souls for the marriage feast,
  Robe and prepare;—
  Holy must be each guest;
  Jesus is there!
Saints, wear your victory palms,
Chant your celestial psalms:
Bride of the Lamb, thy charms
  Oh! let me wear.

3 That bliss is perfect, pure—
  Jesus is there!
  That bliss is ever sure—
  Art thou its heir?
What makes its joys complete?
  What makes its hymns so sweet?
There we the saints will greet—
  Jesus is there.

—o—

456   Amboy. 7s. Double.

Fine.

1. { Wake the song of Ju - bi - lee! Let it e - cho o'er the sea;
   Now is come the promis'd hour; Je-sus reigns with sov'reign pow'r. }

D.C. Let it sound from shore to shore, "Je-sus reigns for - ev - er - more!"

D.C.

All ye saints re - joice and sing, Praise your Sav-iour, praise your King;

2 Hark! the desert lands rejoice;
And the islands join their voice;
Joy! the whole creation sings—
"Jesus is the King of kings!"
Wake the song of Jubilee;
Let it echo o'er the sea;
Let it sound from shore to shore,
"Jesus reigns forevermore!"

3 Hallelujah! hark! the sound
From the centre to the skies,
Wakes above, beneath, around.
All creation's harmonies.
He shall reign from pole to pole,
With illimitable sway;
He shall reign when like a scroll
Yonder heavens shall pass away.

278

457   Consecration.   7s.

FRANCES RIDLEY HAVERGAL.   W. J. KIRKPATRICK, by per

1. Take my   life, and let it   be   Con - se - cra - ted, Lord, to   thee;
2. Take my   feet, and let them be   Swift and beau - ti - ful   for   thee;
3. Take my   lips, and let them be   Fill'd with mes - sa - ges   from thee;

Take my hands, and let them move   At the im-pulse of thy love.
Take my voice, and let me sing   Al - ways, on - ly for my King.
Take my mo - ments and my days,   Let them flow in ceaseless praise.

CHORUS.

{ Wash me in   the Saviour's precious blood, the precious blood, }
{ Cleanse me in   its pu - ri - fy - ing flood, the heal - ing flood. }

Lord, I give to thee my life and all, to be Thine, henceforth, e - ter - nal-ly.

4 Take my will and make it thine;
   It shall be no longer mine.
   Take my heart—it is Thine own,
   It shall be thy royal throne.

5 Take my love—my Lord I pour
   At thy feet its treasure-store!
   Take myself, and I will be
   Ever, only, all for thee!

458 The Shadow of the Cross.

H. BONAR.

1. Oppress'd with noon-day's scorching heat, To yon-der cross I flee;
2. Be - neath that cross, clear waters burst—A fountain sparkling free;
3. A stran-ger here, I pitch my tent Be-neath this spreading tree;
4. For bur-den'd ones a rest-ing-place, Be-side that cross I see;

Be - neath its shel-ter take my seat: No shade like this for me!
And there I quench my des - ert thirst; No spring like this for me!
Here shall my pil-grim life be spent; No home like this for me!
I here cast off my wea - ri - ness: No rest like this for me!

No shade like this for me, No shade like this for me.
No spring like this for me, &c.
No home like this for me, &c.
No rest like this for me, &c.

No shade like this for me, No shade like this
No spring like this for me, No spring, &c.
No home like this for me, No home, &c.
No rest like this for me, No rest, &c.

Be - neath its shel - ter take my seat: No shade like this for me!
for me,

for me. No shade like this for me!

From "Golden Sunbeams," by permission.

459 The Realm of Delight.

Geo. E. Lee, by per.

1. O! have you not heard of that realm of de - light, To which the blest
2. 'Tis a land of fair beau-ty, a realm of de - light, O'er-flow-ing with
3. Its fountains are pure, and its pleasures un - told; Its ful - ness of
4. 'Tis Je - sus in - vites me, the glo - ry to see; "To reign with him"

Sav-iour doth each one in - vite? 'Tis pre-par'd for the good, and the
glad-ness, re-ful-gent with light! Its.... ver-dure ne'er with - ers, its
joy no tongue can un - fold! How its life-breathing zeph - yrs float
there, in the land of the free! Where the wea-ry saints rest, and the

pure, and the blest, 'Tis o - ver the riv-er, where the weary find rest!
flow - ers ne'er fade, Oh! I long to pass o - ver, and im-mortal be made.
gent - ly a - long, While the ransom'd are singing re-demption's sweet song!
wick-ed ne'er come! Yes, o - ver the riv-er, in the saints' E - den home!

CHORUS.

Oh! I want to cross o - ver, don't you, when he reigns? I want to cross

o - ver to E - den's fair plains; I want to be gathered, in

The Realm of Delight. Concluded.

Canaan's bright land, Yes, o - ver the riv - er, where the ransom'd shall stand.

460 Jesus Spoke Peace to My Soul.

"Therefore did my heart rejoice, and my tongue was glad."—Acts ii: 26.

I. B.   I. BALTZELL.

1. I'll sing of a theme most sub - lime, No sor - row my
2. My Sav - iour re - deem'd me from sin, He saves not in

song can con - trol; I'll sing of the rapt - ur - ous time When
part, but the whole; He writes his sal - va - tion with - in,— For,

CHORUS. Arranged.

Je - sus spoke peace to my soul. O! happy, happy day, When my
oh, he spoke peace to my soul.

sins were wash'd a - way, And Je - sus spoke peace to my soul.

3 Resigned to his pleasure I'll live,
   Till time's latest circle shall roll;
   His utmost salvation receive,
   For, oh, he spoke peace to my soul.

4 He bids us leave all for his sake,
   I'll run till I reach the blessed goal;
   Then me to his arms he will take,
   Oh, there will be peace to my soul.

From "Songs of Grace," by permission.
277

461 Gleams of the Golden Morning.

"They shall see the Son of man coming in the clouds of heaven with power and great glory."—Matt. xxiv: 30.

S. J. G.

S. J. GRAHAM, by per.

1. The gold-en morn-ing is fast approaching; Je - sus soon will come
2. The gos - pel summons will soon be car-ried To the na - tions round;
3. At - tend-ed by all the shin-ing an - gels, Down the flaming sky,
4. There those lov'd ones who have long been parted, Will all meet that day;

To take his faith-ful and hap-py children To their promis'd home.
The Bridegroom then will cease to tar - ry, And the trum-pet sound.
The Judge will come, and will take his peo-ple Where they will not die.
The tears of those who are bro-ken-heart-ed Will be wip'd a - way.

CHORUS.

Oh, we see the gleams of the gold-en morning Piercing thro' this night of gloom!

Oh, we see the gleams of the gold-en morn-ing That will burst the tomb.

———o———

462 Remember, Jesus Leads.

W. J. KIRKPATRICK.

1. { Come, soldier, to the charge go forth, With Je - sus to the war; }
   { Till all the kingdoms of the earth Shall hail his name a - far. }

Remember, Jesus Leads. Concluded.

Go, seek the souls that erring stray; For them a Saviour pleads; And while you keep the

CHORUS.

nar-row way, Re-mem-ber, Je-sus leads. Re-mem-ber, re-

Remember, Je-sus leads, Re-

-mem-ber, re-mem-ber, Je - sus

-mem-ber, Je-sus leads, Re-mem-ber, oh, re-mem-ber, Je-sus

leads; Who trust his word are blest, He leads to perfect rest;

leads, Je-sus leads;

Oh, re-mem-ber, Je - - sus leads, Je-sus leads.

Oh, re-mem-ber, oh, re-mem-ber, Je-sus leads.

His valiant hosts, that always strive
His righteous cause to win;
Shall see their Master's work revive,
His vict'ry over sin.
A fallen world in darkness lies,
Each to the rescue speeds;
Though foes on every side arise,
Remember, Jesus leads.—*Chorus.*

3 Go up against sin's fortress walls,
Go in the strength of grace:
And if a standard bearer falls,
Then you must take his place.
Go, tell his love, that cannot fail,
Make known his glorious deeds,
And tho' you walk thro' death's dark vale,
Remember, Jesus leads.—*Chorus.*

By Permission of E. M. BRUCE. Copyright. 1872.

Edinburg. 11s.

By permission of O. Ditson & Co.

Edw. L. White.

1. Glad tidings! glad tidings! the Kingdom is near, Our glorious Deliv'rer will soon, soon appear; In clouds of bright glory to our rescue he'll come, And Angels will hail us to Heaven, our home. Hal-le-lujah, A-men, Hal-le-lu-jah, Hal-le-lu-jah, Hal-le-lu-jah, A-men!

2. Glad tidings! glad tidings! the Kingdom is near, On the plains of fair Canaan we soon shall appear; With harps tun'd celestial, our voices we'll raise To Je-sus our Saviour, in accents of praise. Hal-le-lu-jah, A-men, Hal-le-lu-jah, Hal-le-lu-jah, Hal-le-lu-jah, A-men!

3 Glad tidings! glad tidings! the Kingdom is near!
'Tis the voice of th' Archangel methinks that I hear,
Arousing the nations, awaking the dead
From their cold dusty pillows, where long they have laid. **Hallelujah, &c.**

4 Glad tidings! glad tidings! the Kingdom is near,
Rejoice then, ye pilgrims, and be of good cheer;
The promised possession we soon shall receive,
And with Jesus in glory eternally live. **Hallelujah, &c.**

464 The Coming King. 8s & 7s.

J. R. MACDUFF.   M. G.

1. Christ is com-ing! let cre - a - tion Bid her groans and travail cease;

Let the glorious pro - cla - ma - tion Hope re-store, and faith increase;

Christ is com-ing! Christ is com - ing! Come, thou blessed Prince of peace!

2 Earth can now but tell the story
Of thy bitter cross and pain;
She shall yet behold thy glory
When thou comest back to reign:
‖: Christ is coming! :‖
Let each heart repeat the strain.

3 Long thy exiles have been pining,
Far from rest, and home, and thee;
But, in heavenly vesture shining,
Soon they shall thy glory see;
‖: Christ is coming! :‖
Haste the joyous jubilee.

4 With that "blessed hope" before us,
Let no harp remain unstrung;
Let the mighty advent chorus
Onward roll from tongue to tongue;
‖: Christ is coming! :‖
Come, Lord Jesus, quickly come!

——0——

465 The Coming One.

M. G.

1. Christ is coming in his glory; Sound it wide, He is coming for his bride.

2. Welcome, welcome, blessed Saviour, Come again; Take thy throne, and on it
[reign.

1. Je - sus is gone a-bove the skies, Where our weak senses reach him not;

Here car-nal objects court our eyes, To thrust our Saviour from our thought.

2 He knows what wand'ring hearts we have,
   Apt to forget his lovely face;
And, to refresh our minds, he gave
   These kind memorials of his grace.

3 Let sinful sweets be all forgot.
   And earth grow less in our esteem;
Christ and his love fill every thought,
   And faith and hope be fixed on him.

4 While he is absent from our sight,
   'Tis to prepare for us a place
That we may dwell in heavenly light,
   And live forever near his face.

467

1 Lord, fill me with a humble fear;
   My utter helplessness reveal;
Satan and sin are always near,
   Thee may I always nearer feel.

2 O, that to thee my constant mind
   Might with an even flame aspire,
Pride in its earliest motions find,
   And mark the risings of desire!

3 O, that my tender soul might fly
   The first abhorred approach of ill,
Quick as the apple of an eye,
   The slightest touch of sin to feel!

4 Till thou anew my soul create,
   Still may I strive, and watch, and pray:
Humbly and confidently wait,
   And long to see the perfect day.
             CHARLES WESLEY.

—o—

468   Sweetly Sleeping.   8s & 7s.

Mrs. SMALL.   GEO. E. LEE, by per.

1. Sis - ter, thou art sweetly sleeping, Free from pain, and toil, and care;

Dear-est sis-ter, how we miss thee! Miss thee in the house of prayer.

2 Thou wilt sleep, but not forever
   Jesus died, and rose again;
Soon he'll come in clouds of glory—
   Thou wilt rise with him to reign.

3 Sister, then we hope to meet thee,
   Then we'll take thee by the hand;
Then we'll twine our arms around thee,
   In that bright and happy land.

469 Is Your Lamp Burning?

Geo. H. Ingalls.

1. Say, is your lamp burning my brother? I pray you look quickly and see,

For if it were burning, then surely Some beams would fall brightly on me.

Straight, straight is the road, but I fal-ter, And oft I fall out by the way;

Then lift your lamp high-er, my brother, Lest I should make fatal de-lay.

2

If once all the lamps they were lighted,
 And steadily blazed in a line,
Then over the land and the ocean,
 The light of the gospel would shine:
See many and many around you,
 Who ever are going astray;
Then trim your lamp brighter, my
 brother,
 And guide them back into the way.

3

We hear that the Bridegroom is coming,
 To meet Him with lamps we must go;
And oil we must take in our vessels,
 That brightly each flame it may glow.
Then trim your lamp brightly, my
 brother,
 And suffer it not to grow dim,
That when He shall come to the marriage,
 You gladly may enter with Him.

Revive Us Again.

"O Lord, revive Thy work."—Hab. iii: 2.

W. P. MACKAY.   English Melody.

1. We praise Thee, O God! for the Son of Thy love: For Je - sus, who

died, and is now gone a - bove. Hal - le - lu - jah! Thine the

CHORUS.

glo - ry, Hal - le - lu - jah! A - men. Hal - le -

- lu - jah! Thine the glo - ry, Re - vive us a - gain.

2 We praise Thee, O God! for Thy Spirit of light,
  That has shown us our Saviour, and scattered our night.—*Cho.*

3 All glory and praise to the Lamb that was slain,
  Who has borne all our sins, and removed every stain.—*Cho.*

4 All glory and praise to the God of all grace,
  Who has sought us, and brought us, and guided our ways.—*Cho.*

471

——o——

1 Rejoice and be glad!
  It is sunshine at last!   [past.
The clouds have departed, the shadows are
Cho.—Sound His praises, tell the Story
  Of Him who was slain;
  Sound His praises, tell with gladness,
  He liveth again.

2 Rejoice and be glad!
  Now the pardon is free!
The Just for the unjust has died on the tree.

3 Rejoice and be glad!
  For the Lamb that was slain
O'er death is triumphant and liveth again.

4 Rejoice and be glad!
  For our King is on high,
He pleadeth for us on His throne in the sky.

5 Rejoice and be glad!
  For He cometh again;
He cometh in glory, the Lamb that was slain.

Cho.—Sound His praises, tell the Story
  Of Him who was slain;
  Sound His praises, tell with gladness,
  He cometh again.

H. BONAR.

472   Love Divine.   8s & 7s.   D.

JOHN ZUNDELL.

1. Love di - vine, all love ex - cel-ling, Joy of heav'n, to earth come down;
2. Breathe, O breathe thy peaceful Spir-it In - to ev - 'ry trou-bled breast;

Fine.

Make with us thy glo - rious dwelling; All thy faith-ful peo - ple crown.
D.S. Vis - it us with thy sal - va-tion: Come, and nev - er - more de - part.

Let us all thy grace in - her - it; Bring us to the prom - is'd rest.
D.S. End the work of thy be - ginning; Bring us to th' e - ter - nal day.

Je - sus, thou art all com-pas-sion; Pure, unbounded love thou art;
Take a - way the love of sin-ning; Take our doubts and fears a - way;

D.S.

473

1 Watchman, on the walls of Zion,
  Let thy warning voice be heard;
Blow the blast; for Judah's Lion
  Soon will draw his vengeful sword.
Watchman, mark the coming danger;
  Blow the trumpet, warn the land;
Wake the slothful, rouse the stranger,
  Lest their blood be on thy hand.

2 Watchman, sound a louder measure,
  For the people do not hear;
As a lovely song of pleasure,
  Fall thy words upon their ear.
Watchman, 'mid that desolation,
  Ask, who then shall dare to stand?
Joyful shout, "From tribulation
  Jesus brings his chosen band!"

——0——

474   Lenox.   H. M.

1 Jesus, at thy command,
  I launch into the deep;
And leave my native land,
  Where sin lulls all asleep;
For thee I fain would all resign,
And thus embark with thee and thine.

2 By faith I see the land,
  The port of endless rest;
Through grace I hope to stand
  And sing among the blest:
O may I reach the heavenly shore,
Where winds and waves distress no more!

Azmon. C. M.

C. WESLEY.

by permission of O. Ditson & Co.

Arr. by LOWELL MASON.

1. Je - sus, the Life, the Truth, the Way, In whom I now be - lieve,

As taught by thee, in faith I pray, Ex - pect-ing to re - ceive.

2 Thy will by me on earth be done,
   As by the hosts above,
   Who always see thee on thy throne,
   And glory in thy love.

3 I ask in confidence the grace,
   That I may do thy will,
   As angels who behold thy face,
   And all thy words fulfil.

476

1 Come, let us join our cheerful songs
   With angels round the throne;
   Ten thousand thousand are their tongues,
   But all their joys are one.

2 "Worthy the Lamb that died," they cry,
   "To be exalted thus!"
   "Worthy the Lamb!" our hearts reply,
   "For he was slain for us."

3 Jesus is worthy to receive
   Honor and power divine;
   And blessings more than we can give,
   Be, Lord, forever thine.

4 The whole creation join in one,
   To bless the sacred name
   Of him that sits upon the throne,
   And to adore the Lamb.   I. WATTS

—o—

477   Mason's Chant. C. M.

1. O God! our help in a - ges past, Our hope for years to come,

Our shel - ter from the stormy blast, And our e - ter - nal home.

2 Beneath the shadow of thy throne
   Thy saints have dwelt secure?
   Sufficient is thine arm alone,
   And our defence is sure.

3 Before the hills in order stood,
   Or earth received her frame;

From everlasting thou art God—
   To endless years the same.

4 All nations rose from earth at first,
   And turn to earth again,
   Thy word commands our flesh to dust—
   "Return, ye sons of men!"

478   Sessions. L. M.

CHARLOTTE ELLIOTT.   L. O. EMERSON.

1. Just as I am, with-out one plea, But that thy blood was shed for me,

And that thou bidd'st me come to thee, O Lamb of God, I come! I come!

479

2 Just as I am, and waiting not
  To rid my soul of one dark blot,
  To thee whose blood can cleanse each spot,
  O Lamb of God, I come! I come!

3 Just as I am, though tossed about
  With many a conflict, many a doubt,
  Fightings within, and fears without,
  O Lamb of God, I come! I come!

4 Just as I am—poor, wretched, blind,
  Sight, riches, healing of the mind,
  Yea, all I need, in thee to find,
  O Lamb of God, I come! I come!

1 Jesus, the sinner's Friend, to thee,
  Lost and undone, for aid I flee,
  Weary of earth, myself, and sin;
  Open thine arms, and take me in.

2 Pity and heal my sin-sick soul;
  'Tis thou alone canst make me whole;
  Dark, till in me thine image shine,
  And lost, I am, till thou art mine.

3 At last I own it cannot be
  That I should fit myself for thee:
  Here, then, to thee I all resign;
  Thine is the work, and only thine.

—0——

CHARLES WESLEY.

480   Wellesley. C. M.

WM. B. BRADBURY.

1. How sweet, how heav'nly is the sight, When those who love the Lord

In one an-oth-er's peace de-light, And so ful-fil his word.

2 O, may we feel each brother's sigh,
  And with him bear a part!
  May sorrows flow from eye to eye,
  And joy from heart to heart!

3 Free us from envy, scorn, and pride;
  Our wishes fix above;

  May each his brother's failings hide,
  And show a brother's love.

4 Let love, in one delightful stream,
  Through every bosom flow,
  And union sweet, and fond esteem,
  In every action glow.

481   Lamb of Calvary.   6s & 4s.

1 My faith looks up to thee, Thou Lamb of Cal - va - ry,
Sav - iour di - vine: Now hear me while I pray, Take all my
guilt a - way, O, let me from this day Be wholly thine.

2
May thy rich grace impart
Strength to my fainting heart,
  My zeal inspire;
As thou hast died for me,
O may my love to thee
Pure, warm, and changeless be,—
  A living fire.

3
While life's dark maze I tread,
And griefs around me spread,
  Be thou my guide;

Bid darkness turn to day,
Wipe sorrow's tears away,
Nor let me ever stray
  From thee aside.

4
When time's eventful years,
With sin and toil and tears,
  Shall cease to be,
Blest Saviour then in love,
Descending from above,
My every ill remove,
  And ransom me.

—— 0 ——

482   I Long to be There.

1. In the midst of temp-ta - tions and sor-rows and strife, And e - vils un -
-number'd, of this weary life, I look for a home that is free from all care,

I Long to be There. Concluded.

The king-dom of Je - sus, and long to be there. Long to be there,

long to be there, The king-dom of Je - sus, and long to be there.

2 When poverty comes, and my foes me surround,
Afflictions oppress me, and trials abound,
I think of those mansions which Christ will prepare
When he comes in his glory, and long to be there.
  Long to be there, long to be there,
  Those mansions of glory—I long to be there.

3 I long to be there, and the thought that He's near,
Gives me joy in my sorrow, and takes away fear:
I know when he comes, with his saints I shall share
In the glory he bringeth—I long to be there.
  Long to be there, long to be there,
  And share in his glory—I long to be there.

—o—

483   Lord's Supper.   C. M.

Not too fast.

1. In mem'ry of the Saviour's love, We keep the sa - cred feast,

Where ev - 'ry hum - ble, con-trite heart Is made a wel - come guest.

2 By faith we take the bread of life,
  With which our souls are fed;
The cup, in token of his blood,
  That was for sinners shed.

3 Under his banner thus we sing
  The wonders of his grace,
And thus anticipate the day
  When we shall see his face.

484
1 According to thy gracious word,
  In meek humility,

This will we do, our dying Lord,
  We will remember thee!

2 Thy body, broken for our sake,
  Our bread from heaven shall be;
Thy testamental cup we take,
  And thus remember thee!

3 Gethsemane can we forget?
  Or there thy conflict see,
Thine agony and bloody sweat,
  And not remember thee?

Remember Me.

Arr. by Chas. C. Barker.

1. O, come with me to Cal - va - ry, Cal - va - ry, Cal - va - ry,

And see the Man who died for thee, Up - on the shameful cross!

CHORUS.

How can I for - get thee? How can I for - get my Lord?

How can I for - get thee? Dear Lord, re - mem - ber me.

2 Oh, see him hang upon the tree,
  On the tree, on the tree;
  'Tis there he dies for you and me,
  The loving Son of God.—*Cho.*

3 Oh, see his bitter agony,
  Agony, agony:

"My God, hast thou forsaken me?"
  Oh, hear him loudly cry.—*Cho.*

4 See how it flows, his precious blood,
  Precious blood, precious blood,
  To bring us rebels back to God—
  My soul! what love is this!—*Cho.*

———o———

486 Near the Cross.

1 Jesus, keep me near the cross,
  There a precious fountain
  Free to all—a healing stream,
  Flows from Calvary's mountain.

Cho.—In the cross, in the cross,
  Be my glory ever;

Till my raptured soul shall find
  Rest beyond the river.

2 Near the cross, a trembling soul,
  Love and mercy found me;
  There the bright and morning star
  Shed its beams around me.—*Cho.*

487   Oh! to be Ready!

Mrs. I. M. Hartsough.   Har. by Miss Alice Hartsough.

1. Oh! to be ready, ready! Ready to la-bor or rest, Just as the Master
2. Oh! to be ready, ready! Ready God's word to obey; Shunning the road of
3. Oh! to be ready, ready! Ready to suf-fer and bear; Patient, never com-

pleases, Just as He knows is the best. Oh! to be ready, ready!
fol-ly, Walking the one nar-row way. Oh! to be ready, ready!
-plaining, Tho' ev-er oppress'd with care. Oh! to be ready, ready!

Ready to go or to stay, Just as the Mas-ter chooses,
Ready to suf-fer His will; Read-y to have Him chasten—
Ready to join in the song That shall be sung when Je-sus

CHORUS.

Just as He o-pens the way. Oh! to be read-y, ready! Read-y and
Always for good, not for ill.
Gathers the numberless throng.

watching with prayer; Ready for Jesus' appearing, Read-y His glo-ry to share.

Millennium. H. M.

1. Re-joice—the Lord is King; Your God and King a - dore; Mor - tals, give thanks and sing, And tri-umph ev - er - more; Lift up the heart, lift up the voice, Re - joice a - loud, ye saints, re - joice.

2 He all his foes shall quell,
Shall all our sins destroy;
And every bosom swell,
With pure seraphic joy;
Lift up the heart, lift up the voice,
Rejoice aloud, ye saints, rejoice.

3 Rejoice in glorious hope,
Jesus, the Judge, shall come—
The pearly gates shall ope
To take the ransomed home.
We soon shall hear th'archangel's voice:
The trump of God shall sound—rejoice!

489

1 Let every creature join
To bless Jehovah's name,
And every power unite
To swell th'exalted theme;
Let nature raise from every tongue
A general song of grateful praise.

2 But, O, from human tongues
Should nobler praises flow,
And every thankful heart
With warm devotion glow!
Your voices raise, ye highly blest;
Above the rest declare his praise.

3 Assist me, gracious God;
My heart, my voice inspire;
Then shall I humbly join
The universal choir;
Thy grace can raise my heart and tongue,
And tune my song to lively praise.

490

1 The day comes on apace;
Soon shall the night be past;
Who trust the Saviour's grace
Shall see his face at last;
The clouds that now obstruct their sight
Shall quickly all be put to flight.

2 Ye saints, lift up your heads,
Salvation draweth nigh;
See where the morning spreads
Its radiance through the sky!
O, let the sight your spirits cheer!
The Lord himself will soon appear.

3 Though men your hope deride,
Nor will in God believe;
Do ye in him confide,
Whose word can ne'er deceive;
When heaven and earth shall pass away,
Then will there be a glorious day.

491 The Good Time Coming.

Sel. by G. R. WENTWORTH.   Arr. by F. A. BLACKMER.

1. { Praise God, the time is com - ing, When Je - sus Christ shall reign;
He'll come to meet His peo - ple, Who've wait-ed long for Him:

When from the realms of glo - ry He will re - turn a - gain : }
Oh! how those eyes will brighten That with watch-ing have grown dim! }

CHORUS.

Yes, in clouds of daz-zling splen-dor He's com-ing by - and - by;

Oh! be read - y, friends, to meet Him! For the time is draw-ing nigh.

2 How blest to be with Jesus,
  That holy Son of God,
And walk with Him those golden streets
  No sinful feet have trod;
We then shall be immortal
  And clothed in purest white,
And wear a crown of glory
  Ever beautiful and bright.—*Cho.*

3 And then with saints and angels,
  Through an eternal day,
We will praise our blessed Saviour
  And his loving voice obey;
There we shall roam forever,
  With loved ones by our side,
And Jesus will go with us,
  And be our constant guide.—*Cho.*

——o——

492 Hallelujah! 'Tis Done!

1 'Tis the promise of God, full salvation to give
  Unto him who on Jesus, his Son, will believe.
  Hallelujah! 'tis done! &c.

2 Though the pathway be lonely, and dangerous too,
  Surely Jesus is able to carry me through.—Hallelujah! &c.

3 There's a part in that chorus for you and for me,
  And the theme of our praises forever will be:—Hallelujah! &c.

293

493   At Home.   L. M.

Words by D. T. TAYLOR.

1. I see them on the fair, green lands That skirt the sands of time's bleak shore;

At home, amid the blood-wash'd bands, To tread these rugged paths no more.

2 No more, 'mid toil and grief to weep;
    No more, 'mid sweat and tears to roam;
    No more to pine in dungeons deep—
    All dangers past, now safely home.

3 From pillows wet with many tears,
    From fields all drenched with human blood,
    Now free from all their toils and fears,
    At home, at last, to be with God.

4 At home, where enemies come not,
    From which no friend shall go away;

At home, where death is all forgot,
    And night is lost in endless day.

5 Soon, soon will come the glorious day,
    When this faith vision shall be known:
    When earthly things are passed away,
    Then shall the sav'd surround the throne.

6 And God will bid them welcome there,
    And Christ shall smile their tears away,
    And angels wait, their bliss to share,
    Throughout the everlasting day.

———0———

494   Mount Zion.   C. M.

1. Oh! how I long to see the day When the redeem'd shall come

To Zi-on's mount in bright ar-ray— Zi-on, their bliss-ful home!

CHORUS.

Oh, car-ry me home, car-ry me home To Mount Zi-on!

Mount Zion. Concluded.

Oh, car-ry me home to that cit-y of light, Where saints and an-gels dwell.

2 I long to hear that song arise
  From the unnumbered throng;
  The anthem that shall fill the skies,
  And help the notes prolong.—*Cho.*

3 Oh! shout! the glorious morn is nigh,
  Which prophets longed to see;

The day when Sin and Death shall die;
  Creation's Jubilee!—*Cho.*

4 Dear Saviour, still we cry, O **come!**
  Creation calls to thee!
  Thy weary people sigh for home
  And immortality.—*Cho.*

——o——

495   O, Sinner, Come.

Sel. by G. R. WENTWORTH.   Arr. by F. A. BLACKMER.

1. O, sin-ner, come, with-out de-lay, And seek a home in glo-ry!

The Lord is call-ing you to-day, He bids you share his glo-ry,

CHORUS.

O glory! O glory! There's room enough in Paradise For all a home in glory.

2 Repent, and give him now your heart;
  He is the Lord of glory;
  Confess his name, secure a part
  When he shall come in glory.—*Cho.*

3 This is your time; no more delay,
  For soon he'll come in glory;
  When, shut without, in vain you'll pray;
  Lost then is hope of glory.—*Cho.*

4 O, do not madly slight his grace,
  And lose the crown of glory;
  But now, before you leave this place,
  Begin the way to glory.—*Cho.*

5 Awake! awake! the Judge is near;
  Prepare, prepare for glory;
  If sleeping when he shall appear,
  You cannot bear his glory.—*Cho.*

496 Brethren, While we Sojourn.

Music by W. G. FISCHER. By permission.

1. Brethren, while we sojourn here, Fight we must, but should not fear; Foes we have, but we've a friend

One that loves us to the end. Forward, then, with courage go; Long we shall not dwell below;

Soon the joy - ful news will come, 'Child,' your Fath - er calls, 'Come home.'

'Come home!' 'Come home!' 'Come home!' 'Come

Chorus.

'Come home, come home, come home, come home,' Thy Father calls, 'Come home, come home, come

home, 'Come home!'

home, come home, come home, come home!' Thy Fath - er calls 'Come home!'

2 In the way, a thousand snares
Lie to take us unawares;
Satan, with malicious art,
Watches each unguarded heart.
But from Satan's malice free,
Saints shall soon delivered be;
Soon the joyful news will come,
'Child,' your Father calls, 'Come home.'

3 But of all the foes we meet,
None so oft mislead our feet,
Nor betray us into sin,
Like the foes that dwell within;
Yet let nothing spoil your peace,
Christ shall also conquer these:
Soon the joyful news will come,
'Child,' your Father calls, 'Come home.'

Woodworth L. M.

JOSEPH GRIGG.   WM. B. BRADBURY.

1. Je - sus, and shall it ev - er be, A mor-tal man asham'd of thee?

Asham'd of thee, whom angels praise, Whose glories shine thro' endless days?

499

2
Ashamed of Jesus! that dear friend
On whom my hopes of life depend!
No; when I blush, be this my shame,
That I no more revere his name.

3
Ashamed of Jesus! yes, I may,
When I've no guilt to wash away,
No tears to wipe, no good to crave,
No fears to quell, no soul to save.

4
Till then, nor is my boasting vain,
Till then, I boast a Saviour slain;
And, oh! may this my glory be,
That Christ is not ashamed of me.

498

1
A little while, and He will come,
    Then we shall wander here no more;
He comes to take us to that home
    Where all our sorrows will be o'er.

2
A little while, he'll come again;
    Let us the precious hours redeem;
Our greatest grief to give him pain,
    Our joy to serve and follow him.

3
A little while, 'twill soon be past,
    Why should we shun the shame and
Oh! let us in his footsteps haste, [cross?
    Counting for him all else as loss.

4
A little while—come, Saviour, come!
    For thee thy church has waited long;
Take thy poor, wearied people home,
    To sing the new, unending song.

1
Lord, grant thy blessing here to-day;
    Oh! give thy people joy and peace;
The tokens of thy love display,
    And favor that shall never cease.

2
We seek the truth which Jesus brought;
    The path of light we joyful tread;
Here be his holy doctrines taught,
    And here their purest influence shed.

3
May faith, and hope, and love, abound;
    Our sins and errors be forgiven;
And we, from day to day, be found
    Children of God and heirs of Heaven.

500

1
My gracious Lord, I own Thy right
    To every service I can pay,
And call it my supreme delight
    To hear thy dictates and obey.

2
What is my being but for Thee—
    Its sure support, its noblest end?
'Tis my delight Thy face to see,
    And serve the cause of such a **Friend**

3
I would not sigh for worldy joy,
    Or to increase my earthly good;
Nor future days nor powers employ
    To spread a sounding name abroad.

4
'Tis to my Saviour I would live—
    To Him who for my ransom died:
Nor could all worldly honor give
    Such bliss as crowns me at His side.

501   China. C. M.

1. And must I be to judgment brought, And an- - - - swer, in that day,
2. Yes, ev-'ry se-cret of.. my heart Shall short- - - ly be made known,

3. How care-ful, then, ough: I.. to live, With what re - li - gious fear,
4. Thou mighty Judge of quick and dead, The watch - ful pow'r be - stow;

For ev - - - 'ry vain and i - dle tho't, And ev-'ry word I say.
And I..... re - ceive my just de - sert For all that I have done.

Who such.... a strict ac - count must give For my be - hav-ior here!
So shall.... I to my ways take heed In all I speak or do.

502

1 How long shall Death the tyrant reign,
  And triumph o'er the just,
While the rich blood of martyrs slain
  Lies mingled with the dust?

2 When shall the tedious night be gone?
  When will our Lord appear?
Our fond desires would pray him down,
  Our love embrace him here.

3 Let faith arise and climb the hills,
  And from afar descry
How distant are his chariot wheels,
  And tell how fast they fly.

4 We hear the voice, "Ye dead, arise!"
  And, lo, the graves obey!
And waking saints, with joyful eyes,
  Salute th' expected day.

——o——

503

1 That awful day will surely come,
  Th' appointed hour makes haste,
When I must stand before my Judge,
  And pass the solemn test.

2 Jesus, thou source of all my joys,
  Thou ruler of my heart,
How could I bear to hear thy voice
  Pronounce the sound, "Depart!"

3 The thunder of that awful word
  Would so torment my ear,
'Twould tear my soul asunder, Lord,
  With most tormenting fear.

4 What! to be banished from my Lord,
  To rocks and mountains cry;
And yet to them must call in vain,
  For who his wrath can fly?

——o——

504

1 Life is a span, a fleeting hour;
  How soon the vapor flies!
Man is a tender, transient flower,
  That e'en in blooming dies.

2 The once loved form, now cold and dead,
  Each mournful thought employs;
And nature weeps her comforts fled,
  And withered all her joys.

3 Hope looks beyond the bounds of time,
  When what we now deplore
Shall rise in full, immortal prime,
  And bloom to fade no more

4 Cease, then, fond nature, cease thy tears;
  Behold the Saviour nigh;
And when in glory he appears,
  Thy joys shall never die.

505 Are You Washed in the Blood?

By Permission.
Words and Music by E. A. HOFFMANN.

1. Have you been to Je-sus for the cleansing pow'r? Are you wash'd in the
2. Are you walk-ing dai-ly by the Saviour's side? Are you wash'd in the
3. When the Bridegroom cometh, will your robes be white, Pure and white in the
4. Lay a-side the garments that are stain'd with sin, And be wash'd in the

blood of the Lamb? Are you ful-ly trusting in His grace this hour?
blood of the Lamb? Do you rest each mo-ment in the Cru-ci-fied?
blood of the Lamb? Will you be all read-y for the mansions bright,
blood of the Lamb; There's a fountain flow-ing for the heart un-clean,

CHORUS.

Are you wash'd in the blood of the Lamb? Are you wash'd in the
Are you wash'd in the blood of the Lamb?
And be wash'd in the blood of the Lamb?
O, be wash'd in the blood of the Lamb! Are you wash'd

blood, In the all cleansing blood of the Lamb? Are your garments
in the blood, of the Lamb?

spotless? Are they white as snow? Are you wash'd in the blood of the Lamb?

506 Evan. C. M.

ISAAC WATTS.

WM. HENRY HAVERGAL.

1. My drowsy pow'rs, why sleep ye so? A-wake, my slug-gish soul!

Noth-ing hath half thy work to do, Yet noth-ing's half so dull.

2 We, for whose sake all nature stands,
  And stars their courses move;
  We, for whose guard the angel bands
  Come flying from above;

3 We, for whom God's own Son came down,
  And labored for our good;
  How careless to secure that crown
  He purchased with his blood!

4 Lord, shall we live so sluggish still,
  And never act our parts?
  Come, holy Dove, from th' heavenly hill,
  And warm our frozen hearts!

5 Give us with active warmth to move,
  With vigorous souls to rise;
  With hands of faith, and wings of love,
  To fly and take the prize.

507

1 O thou! whose tender mercy hears
  Contrition's humble sigh,
  Whose hand, indulgent, wipes the tears
  From sorrow's weeping eye,—

2 See, low before thy throne of grace,
  A wretched wand'rer mourn;
  Hast thou not bid me seek thy face?
  Hast thou not said, "Return?"

3 And shall my guilty fears prevail,
  To drive me from thy feet?
  O! let not this dear refuge fail—
  This only safe retreat.

4 Oh! shine on this benighted heart,
  With beams of mercy shine;
  And let thy healing voice impart
  A taste of joys divine.

508 Howard. C. M.

1. Sal-va-tion! O, the joy-ful sound! What pleasure to our ears!

A sovereign balm for ev-'ry wound, A cor-dial for our fears.

2 Salvation! let the echo fly
  The spacious earth around;
  While all the armies of the sky
  Conspire to raise the sound!

3 Salvation! O thou bleeding Lamb,
  To thee the praise belongs;
  Salvation shall inspire our hearts,
  And dwell upon our tongues.

509 Sing of His Love.

J. CENNICK, 1717.   (By permission.   W. J. KIRKPATRICK.

Copyright, 1874, by Asa Hull.

1. Children of the heav'nly King, As ye journey, sweetly sing; Sing your
2. Lift your eyes, ye sons of light; Zi - on's cit - y is in sight; There our
3. Fear not, brethren, joyful stand On the bor-ders of our land; Je - sus
4. Lord, o - bediently we'll go, Glad-ly leav-ing all be-low; On - ly

CHORUS.

Sav-iour's worthy praise, Glorious in his works and ways. Sing of his
end-less home shall be, There our Lord we soon shall see.
Christ, our Father's Son, Bids us un - dis-may'd go on.
thou our Lead-er be, And we still will fol - low thee.

love, ye an - gels of light, Car - ol his praise, ye
Sing of his love, ye an-gels of light, Carol his praise,

seraphs so bright; Join in the song, ye saints, with de -
ye seraphs so bright, Join in the song, ye

- light, Prais-ing the name, won-der - ful name of Je-sus.
saints, with delight, Prais-ing the

From "Garlands of Praise," by permission.

301

Arlington. C. M.

THOMAS AUGUSTINE ARNE.

1. Come, Ho - ly Spir - it, from a - bove, With thy ce - les - tial fire;

Come, and with flames of zeal and love Our hearts and tongues in - spire.

2 The Spirit, by a heavenly breath,
New life creates within;
It quickens sinners from the death
Of trespasses and sin.

3 The things of Christ the Spirit takes,
And to our hearts reveals;
Our bodies it a temple makes,
And our redemption seals.

511

1 Come, let us all adore the Lord,
Whose judgments yet delay;

Who yet suspends the lifted sword,
And gives us time to pray.

2 Great is our guilt, our fears are great,
But let us not despair;
Still open is the mercy-seat
To penitence and prayer.

3 Kind Intercessor, to thy love
This blessed hope we owe:
O, let thy mercies plead above,
While we implore below.

——o——

512 Happy Zion. 8s & 7s.

Fine.

1. { Glorious things of thee are spoken, Zi - on, cit - y of our God; }
  { He whose word can not be broken, Form'd thee for his own a - bode. }
D.C. With sal - va - tion's walls surrounded, Thou may'st smile at all thy foes.

D.C.

On the Rock of A - ges founded, What can shake thy sure re - pose?

2 See, the streams of living waters,
Springing from eternal love,
Still supply thy sons and daughters,
And all fear of want remove:
Who can faint while such a river
Ever flows our thirst t' assuage?
Grace which, like the Lord, the Giver,
Never fails from age to age.

3 Round each habitation hov'ring,
See the cloud and fire appear!
For a glory and a cov'ring,
Showing that the Lord is near;
He who gives us daily manna,
He who listens when we cry,
Let him hear the loud Hosanna,
Rising to his throne on high.

513   Save Me, Gracious God!

"Hear my cry, O God; attend unto my prayer."—Ps. lvi: 1.

Dr. G. W. WAGONER.   (*By Permission.*)   I. BALTZELL.

1. O, Je - sus, at thy cross I fall! From sin and shame I fly;
2. Speak par - don, Lord! show pit - y now; What yet have I to flee?
3. God of Al - might - y pow'r and love, Say, is there grace for me?
4. Yes, bless the Lord, I now be - lieve Thy blood was shed for me!

And on thy hal - low'd name I call; Save, Je - sus, or I die.
See! at thy feet I hum - bly bow; My life I give to thee.
Oh, let my cry thy pit - y move! Oh, let me fly to thee.
Glo - ry to God! I now re - ceive A par - don full and free.

REFRAIN.

Now, save me, save me, gra - cious God! As now to thee I fly;

Oh, wash me in thy cleansing blood! Oh, wash me, or I die!

From "Songs of Grace," by permission.

514 What A Gath'ring That Will Be.

"Gather my saints together unto me."—Psalm l: 5.

J. H. K.

J. H. KURZENKNABE.

1. At the sounding of the trumpet, when the saints are gather'd home, We will
2. When the angel of the Lord proclaims that time shall be no more, We shall
3. At the great and final judgment, when the hidden comes to light, When the
4. When the golden harps are sounding, and the angel bands proclaim In tri-

greet each oth-er by the crys-tal sea, crystal sea; When the
gath-er, and the sav'd and ran-som'd see, gladly see, Then to
Lord in all his glo-ry we shall see, we shall see, At the
-umph-ant strains the glo-rious ju-bi-lee, ju-bi-lee, Then to

Lord him-self from heaven to his glo-ry bids them come, What a
meet a-gain to-geth-er, on the bright, ce-les-tial shore, What a
bid-ding of our Saviour, "Come, ye bless-ed, to my right," What a
meet and join to sing the song of Mo-ses and the Lamb, What a

CHORUS.

What a gath - - - 'ring,

gath'ring of the faithful that will be! What a gath'ring of the lov'd ones, when we'll

gath - - - 'ring,

meet with one an-oth-er, At the sounding of the glo-rious ju-bi-

From "The Song Treasury," by permission.

What a Gath'ring That Will Be. Concluded.

What a gath - - - - 'ring,

- lee, ju - bi - lee! What a gath'ring, when the friends and all the

gath - - - 'ring,

dear ones meet each other, What a gath'ring of the faith-ful that will be!

515   Eltham 7s. 8 lines.

JAMES MONTGOMERY.   By permission of O. DITSON & Co.   LOWELL MASON.

Fine.

1. { Hark! the song of ju - bi - lee, Loud as mighty thun - ders roar, }
{ Or the full - ness of the sea, When it breaks up - on the shore: }
D.C. Hal - le - lu - jah! let the word Echo round the earth and main.

D.C.

Hal - le - lu - jah! for the Lord God om - ni - po - tent shall reign;

516

2 Hallelujah!—hark! the sound,
  From the center to the skies,
Wakes above, beneath, around,
  All creation's harmonies:
See Jehovah's banner furled,   [done,
  Sheathed his sword: he speaks—'tis
And the kingdoms of this world
  Are the kingdoms of his Son.

3 He shall reign from pole to pole
  With illimitable sway;
He shall reign, when, like a scroll,
  Yonder heavens have passed away:
Then the end;—beneath his rod,
  Man's last enemy shall fall;
Hallelujah! Christ in God,
  God in Christ, is all in all.

1 All the world is God's own field,
  Fruit unto his praise to yield;
Wheat and tares together sown,
  Unto joy or sorrow grown;
First the blade, and then the ear,
  Then the full corn shall appear:
Lord of harvest, grant that we
  Wholesome grain and pure may be.

2 For the Lord our God shall come,
  And shall take his harvest home;
From his field shall in that day
  All offences purge away;
Give his angels charge at last
  In the fire the tares to cast;
But the fruitful ears to store
  In his garner evermore.   H. ALFORD.

517 Saviour Shepherd. 8s & 7s.

DOROTHY THRUPP.   WM. B. BRADBURY.

1. Saviour, like a shep-herd lead us; Much we need thy tend'rest care;
   In thy pleasant pastures feed us; For our use thy folds prepare:

Bless-ed Je - sus, Bless-ed Je - sus, Thou hast bought us, thine we are.

Blessed Je - sus, Bless-ed Je - sus, Thou hast bought us, thine we are.

2 We are thine; do thou befriend us;
  Be the Guardian of our way;
Keep thy flock; from sin defend us;
  Seek us when we go astray;
|: Blessed Jesus, Blessed Jesus,
  Hear, oh, hear us when we pray.:|

3 Thou hast promised to receive us,
  Poor and sinful though we be;
Thou hast mercy to relieve us,

Grace to cleanse, and pow'r to free:
|: Blessed Jesus, Blessed Jesus,
  We will early turn to thee.:|

4 Early let us seek thy favor,
  Early let us do thy will;
Blessed Lord and only Saviour,
  With thy love our bosoms fill:
|: Blessed Jesus, Blessed Jesus,
  Thou hast loved us, love us still.:|

Copyright, 1859, in *"The Oriola."* and used by per. of *Biglow & Main.*

518 What a Friend.

1. What a Friend we have in Je - sus, All our sins and griefs to bear;

What a priv-i-lege to car-ry Ev-'ry thing to God in prayer.

2 Have we trials and temptations?
  Is there trouble anywhere?
We should never be discouraged,
  Take it to the Lord in prayer
Can we find a Friend so faithful,
  Who will all our sorrows share?
Jesus knows our every weakness,
  Take it to the Lord in prayer

3 Are we weak and heavy laden,
  Cumbered with a load of care?
Precious Saviour, still our refuge,—
  Take it to the Lord in prayer.
Do thy friends despise, forsake thee?
  Take it to the Lord in prayer;
In His arms He'll take and shield thee,
  Thou wilt find a solace there.

519   Let Me Go.

Words by I. I. LESLIE.   Music by L. HARTSOUGH, by per.

1. Let me go where they are go-ing, Who will ev - er-more be blest;

Let me go, when Christ, my Saviour, Comes to give his people rest.

I would see the jas - per cit-y, Where the night comes nev-er-more,

I would stand a - mid the glo-ry On that ev - er - shin-ing shore.

2 Let me go, for I am weary,
    And my spirit longs for rest:
Let me go, for earth is dreary;
    I would be where all are blest.
Let me go when He shall gather
    All His people unto him,
Where His glory shines forever,
    And where eyes grow never dim.

3 Let me go where youth and beauty
    Never fade, nor forms grow old;
Where the smile of love shall ever
    Linger, and no look be cold.

Let me go when they are ransomed,
    Who for Jesus gave up all;
Let me go and be immortal
    When he comes, and them shall call.

4 Let me go through pearly portals,
    With the throng that shall be there;
Let me join them in the chorus,
    They will sing in mansions fair.
I would be among the number
    That shall gather near His throne;
I would hear Him speak and tell me
    He had chosen me his own.

520 The New Song.

FLORA L. BEST.   (Words Arranged by I. I. L.)   JNO. R. SWENEY, by per.

Moderato.

1. There are songs of joy that I lov'd to sing, When my heart was as blithe as a
2. There are strains of home that are dear as life, And I list to them oft 'mid the
3. Can my lips be mute, or my heart be sad, When the gracious Master has
4. I will sing, will sing till that cit - y bright, With its fair foundations shall

bird.... in Spring; But the song I now sing is so full of cheer, That the
din..... of strife; But I know of a home that is wondrous fair, And far
made... me glad? When he tells us of mansions that he will bring When he
come... in sight; Then I'll sing that oth-er and sweeter song, As I

CHORUS. *Vivace.*

dawn shines out in the darkness drear. O, the new,   new song,   O, the
sweeter than these will the strains be there.
comes in his glo-ry to be our King?
en-ter there with the raptur'd throng.   O, the new,   new song,

new,   new song,   I will sing   it soon,   With the
O, the new,   new song,   I will sing,   yes, soon With the

The New Song. Concluded.

ran - - - som'd throng:
ransom'd, the ransom'd throng: Pow - er and do - min - ion to

him that shall reign; Glo - ry and praise to the Lamb that was slain.
that shall reign;

521   Deliverance Will Come.

Arranged by I. I. LESLIE.

1. I saw a lone - ly trav'ler, In dust - y gar - ments clad,
His step was slow and hea - vy, His strength was al - most gone;

And toil - ing up a mountain; He look'd both worn and sad.
Yet he shout-ed as he journey'd, "De - liv - er - ance will come."

CHORUS.

Then palms of vic-to-ry, Crown of glo-ry, Palms of vic-to-ry, I shall wear.

2 The summer sun was shining,
   The sweat was on his brow;
He fainter grew and weary,
   His step more weak and slow.
But he kept pressing onward,
   For he was going home,
And singing as he journey'd,
   "Deliverance will come."—*Cho.*

3 I saw him in the evening,
   The heavens were all aglow,
He'd reached the mountain's summit,
   The vales were all below.
His toils and sweat we're ended,
   For he had reached his home;
I heard his "Hallelujah—
   Deliverance has come!"—*Cho.*

309

522 Haven of Rest.

Moderate.

1. On the banks of yon-der stream, Where the rays of glo - ry beam,

There's no night, but end-less day,—There is where I hope to stay.

There's no pain, no sor - row there; There's no part-ing, fare-well tear;

There no clouds or tem-pests come, All is bright and fair at home.

2 There the Eden land is seen;
There the fields are fresh and green;
There the trees immortal grow—
There is where I want to go.
There with all the loved and blest,
In immortal beauty dressed—
There it is I hope to be,
Living on eternally.

3 Soon the curse will pass away;
Soon we'll see th'eternal day;
Soon we'll join the ransomed throng,
Then to sing redemption's song.

Pearly gates will open wide
For the Saviour's spotless Bride;
There my mansion I shall see,
There with angels I shall be.

4 Earthly friends, adieu! adieu!
Earthly hopes, and friendship too;
To them all I bid, Farewell!
In the Eden land to dwell.
Hallelujah! He will come!
Hallelujah! there's my home;
Brethren, let us weep no more,
Soon we'll gain that blissful shore.

——o——

523 Over There.

1. I can see be-yond the riv-er, O-ver Jor-dan's dash-ing tide;
2. O-ver there is no more weeping, O-ver there all pain is o'er;

The Home of the Blest.

Mrs. ELLEN H. GATES. Arranged.

Arranged from PHILIP PHILLIPS.

1. I will sing you a song of that beau-ti-ful land, That fair, E-den home of the blest, Where no storms ever beat on that glittering strand, And the waves are for-ev-er at rest, And the waves are for-ev-er at rest. Where no storms ev-er beat on that glittering strand, And the waves are forever at rest.

2
O, that home of the blest in my visions
and dreams,
Its bright jasper walls I can see,
Till I fancy but thinly the vail intervenes
|: Between the fair city and me; :|
Till I fancy but thinly the vail intervenes
Between the fair city and me.

3
That unchangeable home is for you and for
me,
Where Jesus of Nazareth stands;
The King of all kingdoms forever is He,

|: And he holdeth our crowns in his hands; :|
The King of all kingdoms forever is He,
And He holdeth our crowns in His hands.

4
O, how sweet it will be in that beautiful
land,
So free from all sorrow and pain;
With songs on our lips, and with harps in
our hands,
|: To meet one another again; :|
With songs on our lips, and with harps in
our hands,
To meet one another again.

525   We are Voyagers.

Words by J. ALBERT LIBBY.   Music by B. R. HANBY.

1. We are voy'gers on an ocean, and our des-ti-ny we know, For our chart has been pointing out the way; And our Captain he is cheering us as through the night we go, Saying, "Courage, sailors, soon you'll see the day."

CHORUS.

Then we'll watch and we'll pray, as our ves-sel bears a-way, And we'll nev-er be dishearten'd any more, For the port is getting near-er, and I hear the Mas-ter say, "We shall soon reach the har-bor and the shore."

2 Though the winds are strongly blowing, and though high the billows roll,
It will only make us sigh for land the more;
And our rest will be the sweeter when we reach that heav'nly goal,
There to shout our voyage over on the shore.—*Cho.*

3 We have passed the coast of Babylon, and Medo-Persian piers,
We have left the realm of Grecia far behind;
We've been sailing down the Roman coast for eighteen hundred years,
And our chart declares the port we soon shall find.—*Cho.*

4 Oh! how glorious the moment when our keel shall strike the strand,
And our watching eyes once greet the hills of home!
There our stay will be eternal with the holy, happy band,
And the blissful bow'rs of Eden we may roam.—*Cho.*

526 Yield not to Temptation.

H. R. PALMER.

H. R. PALMER, by per.

1. Yield not to temp-ta - tion, For yield-ing is sin; Each vic-t'ry will

help you Some oth - er to win: Fight man-ful - ly on-ward,

Dark pas-sions sub-due, Look ev-er to Je-sus, He'll car-ry you through.

CHORUS.

Ask the Sav-iour to help you, Comfort, strengthen, and keep you;

He is wil-ling to aid you, He will car-ry you through.

2 Shun evil companions
  Bad language disdain,
God's name hold in rev'rence,
  Nor take it in vain;
Be thoughtful and earnest,
  Kind-hearted and true,
Look ever to Jesus,
  He'll carry you through.

3 To him that o'ercometh,
  God giveth a crown;
Through faith we shall conquer,
  Though often cast down:
He who is our Saviour,
  Our strength will renew;
Look ever to Jesus,
  He'll carry you through.

527   Oh, Think of the Home!

Words Arranged.

By Permission of Philip Phillips.

T. C. O'KANE.

1. Oh, think of the home o - ver there, By the side of the riv - er of
2. Oh, think of the friends who'll be there, Friends we've laid in the cold, silent
3. Oh, think of the joys o - ver there; Of the pleasures that nev-er will
4. We soon shall be safe o - ver there, In the E - den of peace and of

light,   Where the saints, all im - mor - tal and fair, Will be
grave;   Of the songs they will breathe on the air, When they
end;   Of the free - dom from pain and from care, With
love;   We shall soon with the glo - ri - fied share The

o - ver there.

REFRAIN.

rob'd in their garments of white, o - ver there. O-ver there,   o - ver
sing of His pow-er to save, o - ver there.
Je - sus our Saviour and Friend, o - ver there.
king-dom that comes from a - bove, o - ver there.

o - ver there,

there,   Oh, think of the home o - ver there, o - ver there; Over

o - ver there,   o - ver there,

there, o-ver there, o-ver there, o-ver there, Oh, think of the home o - ver there.

Buckfield. L. M.

1. When strangers stand and hear me tell What beauties in my Saviour dwell,

Where he is gone, they fain would know,
Where he is gone, they fain would know,
Where he is gone,
Where he is gone, they fain would know, That they may seek

That they may seek and love him too. Where he
That they may seek and love him too, That they may seek and love
they fain would know, That they may seek and love him too.
and love him too, That they may seek and love him too.

is gone, they fain . . . . . would know, . . . That they may seek and love him too.
him too, Where he is gone, they fain would know, That they may seek and love him too.
Where he is gone, &c.

2 In paradise, within the gates,
A higher entertainment waits;
Fruits new and old laid up in store;
There we shall eat, but want no more.

3 Religion bears our spirits up,
While we expect that blessed hope,

The bright appearance of the Lord,
And faith stands leaning on his word.

4 Come, my beloved, haste away,
Cut short the hours of thy delay;
Fly, like a youthful hart or roe,
Over the hills where spices grow.

529 He Will Save You.

Words by W. H. BURRELL. (By Permission.) Music by J. H. STOCKTON, ART. by WM. G. FISCHER.

1. Come, wand'rer, come, re - trace thy steps, In sin no long-er roam;

Thy Fa - ther calls, with pleading voice, Come home, dear child, come home.

CHORUS.

Come to Je - sus, Come to Je - sus, Come to Je - sus now!

He will save you, He will save you, He will save you now

2 Though grieved and wounded by thy sin,
His mercies o'er thee yearn,
His spirit longs and groans within,
To hail thy safe return.

3 Lo! all these years he's sought in vain
To win thy heart to peace;

Oh, come thou back, from sin refrain,
And let thy wand'ring cease.

4 "The fatted calf" shall then be slain,
And music charm thine ear;
Thy Father's house shall joy again,
And heaven thy welcome cheer.

——o——

530 "None of Self, and All of Thee."

THEO. MONOD. FRANK A. PELTON.

1. Oh! the bit - ter shame and sor - row, That a time could ev - er

"None of Self, and All of Thee." Concluded.

be,.... When I let the Sav - iour's pit - y

Plead in vain, and proudly answer'd "All of self, and none of thee."

2

Yet, he found me; I beheld him
  Bleeding on the accursed tree; [ther!"
Heard him pray: "Forgive them, Fa-
And my wistful heart said faintly,
  "Some of self, and some of thee."

3

Day by day, his tender mercy,
  Healing, helping, full and free,

Sweet and strong, and, oh! so patient,—
Brought me lower, while I whispered,
  "Less of self, and more of thee."

4

Higher than the highest heavens,
  Deeper than the deepest sea,
Lord, thy love at last has conquered;
Grant me now my soul's desire,
  "None of self, and all of thee."

—0—

531 Time's Farewell.

1. { 'Tis near the hour of Time's farewell, And soon with Je-sus we shall dwell;
     { The clos-ing day is quick-ly gone, The work of life will soon be done.

CHORUS.

I'm go - ing, I'm go - ing—I'm on my journey home; I'm travelling
Yes, I'm go - ing, I'm go - ing—I'm on my journey home, I'm travelling

to a cit - y just in sight!
to the new Je - ru - sa - lem.

2 Soon will the sleeping saints arise,
  And meet the Saviour in the skies;
  The martyrs crying, "Lord, how long,"
  Will soon join in redemption's song.

3 The joyful news is spreading wide;
  He comes to take his waiting bride:
  And sinners they may come and be
  Prepared to hail the Jubilee.

532   Glad Tidings of Joy.

Words by Mrs. E. C. ELLSWORTH.

1. Speed thee with the mes-sage, Sent us from a-bove;
2. Light he sends for dark-ness, To the lost, a guide;
3. Par-don for the sin-ner, Free-dom for the slave!

Quick-ly bear the ti-dings Of a Sav-iour's love.
'Mid the storms a shel-ter, Where the wea-ry hide.
Praise the name of Je-sus, Sing his pow'r to save.

CHORUS.

Glad ti-dings, Glad ti-dings, Glad ti-dings of joy, Go

bear to the na-tions these ti-dings of joy: Glad ti-dings of joy.

From "Golden Sunbeams," by permission.

—o—

533   Come, Children, Come.

"Come unto me."—Matt. xi: 28.

I. BALTZELL.

1. To-day the Saviour calls, Come, children, come; O, tender, youthful souls, Why longer [roam?

2 To-day the Saviour calls,
   Oh, listen now!
Within these sacred walls
   To Jesus bow.

3 To-day the Saviour calls,
   For refuge fly
To him who never fails
   To hear our joy.

534   Come, Little Soldiers.

From "Golden Songs," by permission.

Spirited.

1. Come, lit-tle sol-diers, list in the ar-my, March to the king-dom
2. Hark to the voic-es, bid-ding us wel-come Home to the land wher:
3. Soon shall we hear the voice of the Cap-tain Shout-ing a-loud, "The

bright and fair; Fear-less of dan-ger, on-ward we're moving; Je-sus will
all are bless'd; Je-sus, our Captain, bids us go on-ward, Fighting to
war is o'er; Come, lit-tle sol-diers, come to your mansion, Come to your

CHORUS.

lead us safe-ly there. Glo-ry to Je-sus! hear the children sing;
gain e-ter-nal rest.
home on Ca-naan's shore."

Glo-ry to Je-sus! hear the cho-rus ring; Christ is our Cap-tain,

He'll safe-ly lead us On-ward, to Ca-naan's hap-py land.

535 Joy In Heaven.

FANNY CROSBY.   (Words Arranged by I. I. L.)   A. J. ABBEY.

"Joy shall be in heaven over one sinner that repenteth."—Luke. xv: 7.

Bold and Spirited.

1. Joy! joy! joy! Joy joy! joy! Joy at the pearl-y gates of light;
2. Joy! joy! joy! Joy! joy! joy! Joy in the courts of heav'nly song;
3. Joy! joy! joy! Joy! joy! joy! Joy in the heav'n of heav'ns a-bove;

ff

Joy in the heav'n of heav'ns so bright; Louder the cho-ral anthems roll—They
Joy where the ho-ly an-gels throng, Striking their tuneful harps of gold, O -
Joy where they sing of boun-dless love; Higher and higher th'joyful sound; "The

CHORUS.

Glo - ry, glo - ry, Glo - - - ry,

are songs of joy for a new-born soul. Glo-ry to God, Glo-ry to God,
- ver a sin-ner brought to the fold.
dead are a-live, the lost is found."

f

Glo - ry to God, our Re - deem-er and King; Glo-ry to Him that

once was slain, An - oth - er has come to the fountain of life, A

REFRAIN. for last verse.

rit.

sin-ner is born a-gain. Joy! joy! joy! Joy! joy! joy! Joy at the pearly

mf

gates of light, Joy in the heav'n of heav'ns so bright; An-

cres. *rit.*

-oth-er has come to the fountain of life, A sin-ner is born a-gain.

——0——

536 The Lord Will Provide.

Prof. C. S. HARRINGTON, by per. E. TOURJEE.

1. In some way or oth-er the Lord will provide; It may not be *my* way,

It may not be *thy* way, And yet, in His *own* way "The Lord will provide."

2 At some time or other the Lord will
  provide;
  It may not be *my* time,
  It may not be *thy* time,
  And yet, in His *own* time,
  "The Lord will provide."

3 Despond then no longer; the Lord
  will provide;
  And this be the token—

No word he hath spoken
Was ever yet broken,—
"The Lord will provide."

4 March on, then, right boldly; the sea
  shall divide;
  The pathway made glorious,
  With shoutings victorious,
  We'll join in the chorus,
  "The Lord will provide."

537 Blessed are the Faithful Servants.

E. A. WALKER.   (By Permission.)   J. H. TENNEY.

1. Blessed are the faithful ser-vants, Who are watching for the Lord;
2. Blessed are the faithful ser-vants, Who are toil-ing all the day,

They shall have his full ap - prov-al, And re-ceive the great re - ward;
Bear-ing all the heat and bur - den Of the earth-ly pil - grim way;

With their Lord shall en - ter in, Dwell for - ev - er with their King.
They shall en - ter in - to rest, With the Lord be ev - er blest.

CHORUS.

Bless-ed are the faith-ful ser - vants, Bless-ed, bless-ed, bless - ed,

Bless - ed are the faith - ful ser-vants, They shall dwell for - ev - er,

Blessed are the Faithful Servants. Concluded.

They shall dwell for-ev - er, They shall dwell for-ev - er with their King.

——o——

538   Child's Hymn.

"Suffer little children to come unto me."   I. BALTZELL.

1. Precious Sav-iour, gen - tle, mild, Hear, oh hear a fee - ble child,
2. Waves of sor - row o'er me roll; Storms of pas - sion shake my soul;
3. Thron'd in maj - es - ty and might, In the realms of fade - less light,
4. Precious Sav-iour, be my Guide, O'er the rough, tem-pestuous tide,

Who, on life's tem-pestuous sea, Drifts a - lone; oh, suc - cor me.
Dan - gers press on ev - 'ry side; Je - sus, Sav-iour, be my Guide.
Je - sus, Sav-iour, hear my prayer, Prove to me thy lov - ing care.
Till I walk this way no more, But be with thee ev - er - more.

CHORUS.

Guide me, oh, my Sav - iour, guide, O'er the rough, tem-pest-uous tide;

When the storm of life is past, Let me dwell with thee at last.

Words by permission of ASA HULL.

J. H. TENNEY.

1. O'er the hill the sun is setting, And the night is drawing on; Slowly
2. One day near-er, sings the sail-or, As he glides the wa-ters o'er, While the
3. Worn and weary, oft, the pilgrim Hails the set-ting of the sun; For the
4. Nearer home! yes, one day near-er To the peaceful land of rest; To the

comes the gen-tle twi-light, For an-oth-er day is gone. Gone for
light is soft-ly dy-ing On his dis-tant, na-tive shore. Thus the
goal is one day near-er; And his jour-ney near-er done. Thus we
green fields and the fountains, Where we shall meet all the blest. For the

aye, its race is o-ver, Soon the dark-er shades will come; Still 'tis
Christian on life's o-cean, As his light boat cuts the foam, In the
feel, when o'er life's des-ert, Heart and san-dal-worn we roam, As the
heav'ns grow brighter o'er us, And the lamps hang in the dome, And our

CHORUS.

sweet to know at eve-ning We are one day near-er home. Near-er
eve-ning cries with rap-ture, "I am one day near-er home."
twi-light gath-ers o'er us, We are one day near-er home.
tents are pitch'd still clos-er, For we're one day near-er home.

home,   Near-er home,   To the green fields and the fountains;
Near-er home,   Near-er home,

Nearer Home. Concluded.

Near-er home, Near-er home, Where the saints will ev - er rest.

Near-er home, Nearer home,

—o—

540 Watch, for the Time is Short.

Music by A. HULL, by per.

1. Watch, for the time is short; Watch, while 'tis call'd to - day;
2. Chase slum-ber from thine eyes, Chase doubt-ing from thy breast;
3. Take Je - sus for thy trust: Watch, watch for - ev - er - more;

Watch, lest temp-ta - tions o - ver come; Watch, Christian, watch and pray.
Claim now as thine the promis'd prize, And saints' e - ter - nal rest.
Watch, for in death thou soon must sleep, With all who've gone be - fore.

Watch, for the flesh is weak, Watch, for the foe is strong·
Watch, Christian, watch and pray, Thy Sav-iour watch'd for thee;
Now, when thy sun is up,— Now, while 'tis call'd to - day;

Watch, lest the bridegroom knock in vain, Watch, though he tar - ry long.
Till from his brow the blood-sweat pour'd In drops of a - go - ny!
O, now in thine ac - cept-ed time, Watch, Christian, watch and pray.

Copyright, 1871, by ASA HULL.

541   Draw Me Closer to Thee.

"And I will cause him to draw near."—Jer. xxx: 21.

Mrs. E. W. Chapman.   (*By Permission.*)   J. H. Tenney.

1. Clos - er to thee, my Fa - ther, draw me, I long for thine em -
2. Clos - er to thee, my Sav - iour, draw me, Nor let me leave thee
3. Clos - er by thy sweet Spir - it draw me, Till I am all with

- brace; Clos - er with - in thine arms en - fold me, I seek a rest - ing
more; Sigh - ing to feel thine arms a - round me, And all my wand'rings
thee; Quick - en, re - fine, and wash, and cleanse me, Till I am pure and

CHORUS.

place. Clos - - - er with the cords of love,
o'er.
free. Clos - er, clos - er with the cords of love,

Draw me to thy - self a - bove; Clos - - - er
Draw me, draw me to thy - self a - bove; Closer with the cords of love,

draw me To thy - self a - bove.
Draw me to thy - self a - bove, Draw me to thy - self a - bove.

542 Walk in the Light.

Words by Asa Hull.　　　(By Permission.)　　　Music by Geo. C. Hugg.

1. Walk in the light the Lord hath giv'n, To guide thy steps a - right;
2. Walk in the light of gos - pel truth, That shines from God's own word;

His ho - ly Spir - it, sent from heav'n, Can cheer the dark - est night.
A light to guide in ear - ly youth The faith - ful of the Lord.

CHORUS.

Walk..... in the light,............. Walk........ in the
Walk in the light, in the beau-ti-ful light of God, Walk in the light, in the

light,............ ...... Walk........ in the light,.............
beau-ti-ful light of God, Walk in the light, in the beau-ti-ful light of God,

Walk in the light, the light of God.

3 Walk in the light! tho' shadows dark
　Like spectres cross thy way;
　Darkness will flee before the light
　Of God's eternal day.—*Chorus.*

4 Walk in the light! and thou shalt know
　The love of God to thee;
　The fellowship so sweet below,
　In heav'n will sweeter be.—*Chorus.*

543   O, Hail, Happy Day!

Har. by F. A. BLACKMER.

1. O, hail, hap-py day, that speaks our tri - als end - ed, Our
Lord has come to take us home; O, hail, hap - py day!
No more by doubts or fears de - press'd, We now shall gain our
promis'd rest, And be for - ev - er blest! O, hail, hap-py day!

2 Swell high the glad song, our bondage now is over;
  The Jubilee proclaims us free;
    O hail, happy day!
  The day that brings a sweet release,
  That crowns our Lord, the Prince of Peace,
  When all our sorrows cease!
    O hail, happy day!

3 O hail, happy day, that ends our tears and sorrows,
  That brings us joy without alloy,
    O hail, happy day!
  Now peace shall wave her sceptre high,
  And love's fair banner greet the eye,
  Proclaiming victory!
    O hail, happy day!

4 All hail thy bright beams, O morn of Zion's glory!
  Thy blissful light breaks on our sight,
    O hail, happy day!
  Fair Beulah's fields before us rise,
  And sweetly burst upon our eyes
  The scenes of Paradise!
    O hail, happy day!

544 The Golden Shore.

By Permission of Asa Hull. Words and Melody by Rev. R. H. McRay.

1. We shall meet in that beautiful land, On the banks of the bright golden shore,
2. O-ver there, on the bright a-zure plains, Where the riv-er of life sweetly flows;

And with all the redeem'd happy band, There with Je-sus to reign ev-er-more.
Where the Saviour e-ter-nal-ly reigns, And the beautiful gates never close.

CHORUS.

In a bright, happy home, we shall meet, In that beau-ti-ful, beau-ti-ful
we shall meet,

land, In a bright, happy home we shall meet, In that
beautiful land, we shall meet,

beau-ti-ful, beautiful land.
beautiful land.

3
Blessed Jesus has gone to prepare
Us a crown that is brighter than day;
Then forever we'll dwell with Him there,
And His hand shall wipe all tears away.
4
There no sorrow shall e'er taint the air,
Where He dwells, evil never can come;
And no weeping will break on the ear,
In that land, and our beautiful home.

329

545 Jesus Soon Is Coming.

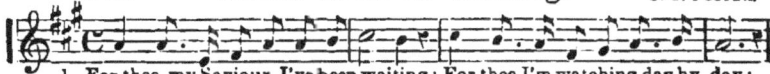

1. For thee, my Saviour, I've been waiting; For thee I'm watching day by day;
Long-ing for that expected meeting, When I shall never from thee stray.

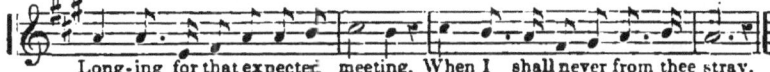

CHORUS.

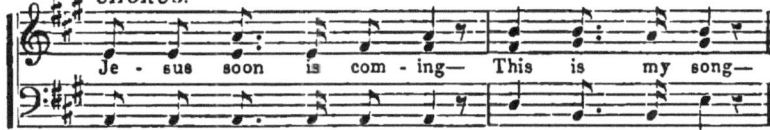

Je-sus soon is com-ing— This is my song— It cheers the heart when joys de-part, And sor-row presses strong.

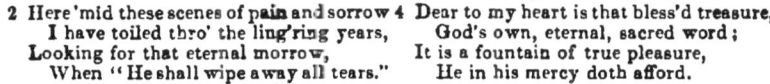

2 Here 'mid these scenes of pain and sorrow
I have toiled thro' the ling'ring years,
Looking for that eternal morrow,
When "He shall wipe away all tears."

3 Ofttimes the tempter comes with power,
And darkness gathers o'er my way;
But when the clouds begin to lower,
'Tis then I trust and watch and pray.

4 Dear to my heart is that bless'd treasure,
God's own, eternal, sacred word;
It is a fountain of true pleasure,
He in his mercy doth afford.

5 It will be but a little longer,
I shall this heavy cross endure;
Shall need His grace to make me stronger,
Or help me trust His promise sure.

—o—

546 Forever With the Lord. S. M.

JAMES MONTGOMERY.   By permission of O. DITSON & Co.   ISAAC B. WOODBURY.

1. "For-ev-er with the Lord," A-men, so let it be; Life for the dead is in that word: 'Tis im-mor-tal-i-ty. Here 'neath the cross I'm bent, And ab-sent from him roam; Yet night-ly pitch my mov-ing tent A

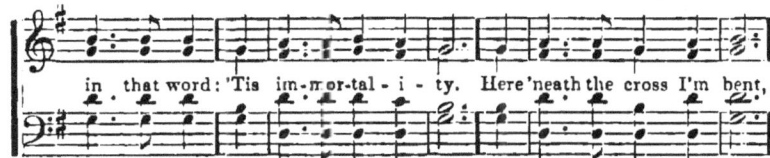

Forever with the Lord. Concluded.

day's march nearer   home, Nearer home, nearer home, A day's march nearer home.

2 My Father's house on high,
   Home of the blest, how near,
   At times, to faith's aspiring eye,
   Thy golden gates appear!
   Ah, then my spirit faints,
   To reach the land I love:
   The bright inheritance of saints,
   The city from above;
   From above, from above, etc.

3 Yet doubts still intervene,
   And oft my comfort flies;
   Like Noah's dove, I flit between
   Rough seas and stormy skies:
   Anon the clouds depart,
   The winds and waters cease,
   While sweetly o'er my gladden'd heart
   Expands the bow of peace,
   Bow of peace, bow of peace, etc.

4 So when that day shall come,
   The vail be rent in twain,
   Through grace I shall escape the tomb,
   And life eternal gain;
   Then knowing, "as I'm known,"
   How shall I love that word,
   And often sing before the throne,
   "Forever with the Lord,"
   With the Lord, with the Lord, etc.

547

1 The Church has waited long
   Her absent Lord to see;
   And still in loneliness she waits,
   A friendless stranger she.
   Age after age has gone,
   Sun after sun has set;
   And still in weeds of widowhood
   She weeps, a mourner yet.
   Mourner yet, mourner yet:
   Come, then, Lord Jesus, come!

2 Saint after saint on earth
   Has lived and loved and died;
   And, as they left us one by one,
   We laid them side by side;
   We laid them down to sleep,
   But not in hope forlorn:
   We laid them but to ripen there,
   Till the last glorious morn.
   Glorious morn, glorious morn:
   Come, then, Lord Jesus, come!

3 We long to hear thy voice,
   To see thee face to face,
   To share thy crown and glory then,
   As now we share thy grace.
   Should not the loving bride
   The absent bridegroom mourn?
   Should she not wear the weeds of grief
   Until her Lord return?
   Lord return, Lord return:
   Come, then, Lord Jesus, come!

4 The whole creation groans,
   And waits to hear that voice
   That shall restore her comeliness,
   And make her wastes rejoice.
   Come, Lord, and wipe away
   The curse, the sin, the stain,
   And make this blighted world of ours
   Thine own fair world again.
   World again, world again:
   Come, then, Lord Jesus, come!
                                    H. Bonar.

548

1 Rest for the toiling hand,
   Rest for the anxious brow,
   Rest for the weary, way-sore feet,
   Rest from all labor now.

2 Rest for the fevered brain,
   Rest for the throbbing eye; [more
   Through these parched lips of thine ne
   Shall pass the moan or sigh.

3 Soon shall the trump of God
   Give out the welcome sound,
   That shakes thy silent chamber-walls,
   And breaks the turf-sealed ground

4 Ye dwellers in the dust,
   Awake, come forth and sing!
   Sharp has your frost of winter been,
   But bright shall be your spring.

5 'Twas sown in weakness here,
   'Twill then be raised in power;
   That which was sown an earthly seed,
   Shall rise a heavenly flower.

6 Then evermore to bloom,
   On the eternal shore,
   Beyond the shadows of the tomb,
   Where death shall come no more.
                                    H. Bonar.

Forever Here My Rest.

1. For - ev - er here my rest shall be, Close to thy bleeding side;

2. Wash me, and make me thus thine own, Wash me, and mine thou art;

'Tis all my hope, and all my plea, For me the Saviour died.

Wash me, but not my feet a - lone—My hands, my head, my heart.

My dy - ing Saviour and my God, Fountain for guilt and sin,

Th' a - tone-ment of thy blood ap - ply, Till faith to sight im - prove;

Sprinkle me ev - er with thy blood, O cleanse and keep me clean.

Till hope in full fru - i - tion die, And all my soul be love.

—o—

550

1 Speak gently,—it is better far
To rule by love than fear;
Speak gently,—let no harsh word mar
The good we may do here.

2 Speak gently to the young,—for they
Will have enough to bear;
Pass through this life as best they may,
'Tis full of anxious care.

3 Speak gently to the aged one,
Grieve not the care-worn heart;
The sands of life are nearly run,
Let them in peace depart.

4 Speak gently to the erring ones;
They must have toiled in vain;
Perchance unkindness made them so;
O, win them back again!

551 What a Friend we have in Jesus.

ANON.

C. C. CONVERSE, by per.

1. What a Friend we have in Je - sus, All our sins and griefs to bear!

What a priv - i - lege' to car - ry Ev - 'ry thing to God in prayer!

O, what peace we oft - en for - feit, O, what need-less pain we bear,

All be-cause we do not car - ry Ev - 'ry thing to God in prayer!

2 Have we trials and temptations?
   Is there trouble anywhere?
We should never be discouraged,
Take it to the Lord in prayer.
Can we find a friend so faithful
Who will all our sorrows share?
Jesus knows our every weakness,
Take it to the Lord in prayer.

3 Are we weak and heavy laden,
   Cumbered with a load of care?—
Precious Saviour, still our refuge,—
Take it to the Lord in prayer.
Do thy friends despise, forsake thee?
Take it to the Lord in prayer;
In his arms he'll take and shield thee,
Thou wilt find a solace there.

——o——

552   Sweet By-and-By.

By permission of O. DITSON & Co.

1. There's a land that is fair - er than day, And by faith we can see it a - far;
2. We shall sing on that beau-ti-ful shore The me - lo-di-ous songs of the blest;
3 To our boun-ti-ful Fa-ther a - bove, We will of-fer our tribute of praise:

553 Showers of Blessing.

Mrs. E. Codner.   (*By Permission.*)   J. H. Tenney.

1. Lord, I hear of show'rs of bless-ing Thou art scat-t'ring full and free;
2. Pass me not, O God, my Fath-er, Sin - ful though my heart may be;
3. Pass me not, O gra-cious Sav-iour! Let me live and cling to thee;
4. Love of God, so pure and changeless; Blood of Christ, so rich, so free;

Show'rs the thirst-y land re-fresh-ing, Let some drops now fall on me.
Thou might'st leave me, but the rath - er, Let thy mer - cy light on me.
I am long-ing for thy fa-vor; Whil'st thou'rt calling, O, call me.
Grace of God—so strong and boundless, Mag-ni - fy them all in me.

CHORUS.

E - ven me,   E - ven me,   Bless me, Saviour, E - ven me.
E - ven me,   E - ven me,

E - ven me,   E - ven me,   Bless me, Sav-iour, E - ven me.
E - ven me,   E-ven me,

554 Rejoice, His Name is Jesus.

L. H.

L. Hartsough, by per.

1. "I bring you ti-dings of great joy," For Je - sus comes to save His own:
2. Just at the door, with lifted hand, He stands and knocks—would enter in;
3. No oth- er friend can bless as He— You've welcom'd others, all the way;

Yes, Je - sus comes, tho' Lord of all, For you He leaves His heav'nly home.
Who welcomes Christ, with heart and soul, Will prove that Jesus saves from sin.
The friends you've had were not like Him; He's e'er true, by night and day.

REFRAIN.

Re-joice, His name is Je - sus, for He saves; Re - joice, His name is
He saves,

Je - sus, for He saves,.... For He saves, For He
He saves, He saves,

saves, For He saves His peo-ple from their sins, from their sins.
He saves,

4
Besetting sins to Christ will yield,
   Through Him all self will find a grave:
And all this deadly strife will cease,
   As Jesus proves his power to save.

5
And Purity is His free gift,
   Thus saving to the uttermost;
And by the Holy Spirit's power,
   He gives to us our Pentecost.

555 God is Love!

J. H. K. "God is love."—1 John iv: 8. J. H. KURZENKNABE.

1. God is love! for us he car - eth, While up - on the earth we move;
2. God is love! and par-don dwelleth Where a soul his grace doth prove;
3. God is love! and as for - ev - er, Years roll by and a - ges move;

Ev - 'ry work of his de - clar-eth The Al - mighty God is love.
Ev - 'ry-where his good-ness tell-eth God is mer - cy, God is love.
On - ly He, He changes nev-er, The un - changing God is love.

CHORUS.

Might - y love, Match-less love, In - fi - nite

Might - y love, Match-less love,

and un - chang - ing love, Ten - der

In - fi - nite and un - chang - ing love, Ten - der

love, Sav-ing love, God is e - ter - - - nal love.

Ten - der love, Sav-ing love, God is e - ter - nal love.

From "The Song Treasury," by permission.

556 When the Angels Come.

"He shall send his angels with a great sound of a trumpet, and they shall gather together his elect."—Matt. xxiv : 31.

Words by I. I. Leslie. Music by E. Manford Clark.

1. When the an-gels come to take All the cho-sen ones a-way; When the
2. When the shin-ing angels come, With the trumpet's mighty sound; Calling
3. Oh! what glo-ry there will be When the heav'nly hosts appear! When the

sleep-ing saints of God a-wake, At the dawning of that day; When the
from the o-pen'd grave and tomb, All the saints the world a-round, As they
countless an-gel forms we see, And their seraph voices hear! When those

sav'd shall gath-er'd be, Will, O will some an-gel come for me?
rise from land and sea, Will, O will some an-gel come for me?
scenes at length I see, May, O may an an-gel come for me?

CHORUS.

Oh, then to be known by the angel band! Oh, to have them then take us by the hand!

Oh! what joy, what joy! Oh! what joy that day, When they carry, carry us away!

From "The Crowning Triumph," by permission of F. A. NORTH & Co

557 Fast Falls the Eventide.

W. H. MONK.

1. A - bide with me! Fast falls the ev - en - tide; The dark-ness deep - ens—Lord, with me a - bide! When oth - er help - ers fail, and com-forts flee, Help of the help - less, O, a - bide with me!

2 Swift to its close ebbs out life's little day;
Earth's joys grow dim, its glories pass away;
Change and decay in all around I see;
O thou, who changest not, abide with me!

3 Not a brief glance I beg, a passing word,
But as thou dwell'st with thy disciples, Lord,
Familiar, condescending, patient, free:
Come, not to sojourn, but abide with me.

4 Thou upon me in early youth didst smile,
And though rebellious and perverse meanwhile,
Thou hast not left me, oft as I left thee:
On to life's close, O, Lord, abide with me.

5 I need thy presence every passing hour;
What but thy grace can foil the tempter's power!
Who, like thyself, my guide and stay can be?
Through cloud and sunshine, Lord, abide with me!

6 I fear no foe, with thee at hand to bless;
Ills have no weight, and tears no bitterness:
Death's sting where then? the grave's proud victory,
When evermore Thou shalt abide with me?

558 Beautiful Zion.

1. Beau-ti-ful Zi - on, built a - bove, Beau-ti-ful cit-y that I love,

Copyright, 1859, in "The Oriola," and used by per. of Biglow & Main.

Beautiful Zion. Concluded.

Beau-ti-ful gates of pearl-y white, Beau-ti-ful tem-ple—God its light;

He, who was slain on Cal-va - ry, Opens those pearly gates to me.

2 Beautiful city, filled with light,
Beautiful angels cloth'd in white,
Beautiful strains that never tire,
Beautiful harps through all the choir;
There shall I join the chorus sweet,
Worshipping at the Saviour's feet.

3 Beautiful crowns on every brow,
Beautiful palms the conquerors show,
Beautiful robes the ransom'd wear,

Beautiful all who enter there;
Thither I press with eager feet,
There shall my rest be long and sweet.

4 Beautiful throne of Christ, our King,
Beautiful songs the saints shall sing,
Beautiful rest, all wand'rings cease,
Beautiful home in perfect peace;
There shall my eyes the Saviour see—
Haste to this heav'nly home with me.

559 Hark! The Blest Tidings.

1. Hark! hark! hear the blest tidings; Rob'd, rob'd in honor and glory,
Soon, soon, Jesus will come,

To gather his ransom'd ones home : Yes, yes, O yes, To gather his ransom'd ones home.

2 Joy, joy, sound it more loudly;
Sing, sing, glory to God:
Soon, soon, Jesus is coming;
Publish the tidings abroad.
Yes, yes, &c.

3 Bright, bright seraphs attending;
Shouts, shouts, filling the air;
Down, down, swiftly from heaven,
Jesus our Lord will appear.
Yes, yes, &c.

4 Now, now, through a glass darkly,
Shine, shine, visions to come;
Soon, soon, we shall behold them,
Cloudless and bright in our home.
Yes, yes, &c.

5 Still, still, rest on the promise;
Cling, cling fast to his word;
Wait, wait, if he should tarry,
We'll patiently wait for the Lord.
Yes, yes, &c.

That Eden Home.

Arr. by AMANDA BAILEY.

1. There's a land that is beam-ing with glad-ness, There's a
2. Oh, the lov'd and the dear ones shall meet us, We shall
3. In our dreams e-ven now it is shin-ing, Yon-der
4. Not a mem-'ry of pain or of sor-row, Shall be

home we are long-ing to see; Though the heart may be heav-y with
walk there with them by our side; And the an-gels all bright there shall
land, that is fair-er that day; And the hearts of the wea-ry are
found in that sweet land of light; Oh, that fair and that joy-ful to-

sad-ness, Yet we know there are bright joys to be.
greet us, In our home by the fair, crys-tal tide.
pin-ing For the mes-sage that calls them a-way.
-mor-row, It will bring nei-ther shad-ows nor night.

CHORUS.

In that home, E-den home,

In that home, E-den home, In that home, E-den home, O, the

In that home, E-den

wea-ry shall sigh nev-er-more, In that home, E-den home, In that

That Eden Home. Concluded.

home, E - den home, We shall meet to be part - ed no more.

———0———

561 The Blood! The Precious Blood!

Words and Music by J. H. STOCKTON, by per.

1. The cross! the cross! the blood-stain'd cross! the hal-low'd cross I see!

Re - mind-ing me of pre - cious blood that once was shed for me.

CHORUS. *Slow and soft.*

Oh! the blood! the pre - cious blood! That Je - sus shed for me

rit.

Up - on the cross, in crim-son flood, Just now by faith I see.

2 The cross! the cross! the heavy cross,
The Saviour bore for me,
Which bowed him to the earth with grief
On sad Mount Calvary.—*Cho.*

3 The crown! the crown! the glorious
The crown of victory! [crown!
The crown of life! it shall be mine
When Jesus I shall see.—*Cho.*

341

562 Saviour, Pilot Me.
Sel. by AMANDA BAILEY.

1. Je - sus, Sav-iour, pi - lot me O - ver life's tem-pest-uous sea;
D.S. Chart and com-pass came from thee: Je - sus, Sav-iour, pi - lot me.

Fine.

Unknown waves be - fore me roll, Hiding rock and treach'rous shoal;

D.C.

2 As a mother stills her child,
Thou canst hush the ocean wild;
Boisterous waves obey thy will,
When thou sayest to them, "Be still."
Wond'rous Sovereign of the sea,
Jesus, Saviour, pilot me.

3 When at last I near the shore,
And the fearful breakers roar
'Twixt me and the peaceful rest,
Then, while leaning on thy breast,
May I hear thee say to me,
"Fear not, I will pilot thee!"

563 *Salem. 8s & 7s.
ITHAMAR CONKEY.

1. In the cross of Christ I glo-ry, Tow'ring o'er the wrecks of time;

All the light of sa - cred sto-ry Gathers round its head sub-lime.

564

2 When the woes of life o'ertake me,
Hopes deceive, and fears annoy,
Never shall the cross forsake me;
Lo! it glows with peace and joy.

3 Bane and blessing, pain and pleasure,
By the cross are sanctified:
Peace is there, that knows no measure,
Joys that through all time abide.

4 In the cross of Christ I glory,
Towering o'er the wrecks of time;
All the light of sacred story
Gathers round its head sublime.

1 Praise the Lord; ye heavens, adore him;
Praise him, angels, in the height;
Sun and moon, rejoice before him;
Praise him, all ye stars of light.

2 Praise the Lord, for he is glorious;
Never shall his promise fail:
God will make his saints victorious;
Sin and death shall not prevail.

3 Praise the God of our salvation;
Hosts on high his power proclaim;
Heaven and earth, and all creation,
Praise and magnify his name.

342

* By permission of O. DITSON & Co.

565 Child, your Father Calls, come Home.

ANNIE M. STOCKTON.　　　(By Permission.)　　　J. H. STOCKTON.

1. Come home, dear sin-ner, while the light Is beaming on your way;
2. Come home, dear sin-ner; by the cross Your Saviour waits for you;
3. Come home, dear sin-ner, while you may, The church is call-ing too;
4. Come home, dear sin-ner, Je-sus' blood Can wash out ev-'ry stain;

The door stands o-pen wide to-night, Re-turn while yet you may.
He'll cleanse a-way your earthly dross, And make you hap-py too.
With ear-nest faith be-gin to pray, And all will wel-come you.
Plunge now in-to the crim-son flood Of Him who once was slain.

CHORUS.

Come home, come home, dear child, come home, Your Father bids you come;

Come home, come home, this night come home, O, wea-ry wand'rer, come.

566. Safely Hide Me.

J. H. K.

From "Silvery Echoes."

J. H. KURZENKNABE, by per.

1. Precious thought with comfort fraught, What-ev - er may be-tide me;
2. Precious love that gives me proof, Though all the world de- ride me;
3. Precious hope that bears me up, When sin and Sa - tan chide me;
4. Precious peace, in my dis-tress, When death's form stands beside me,

Je - sus gave his life to save, And he will safe-ly hide me.
I have heard the pard'ning word, And he will safe-ly hide me.
I shall know the way to go, And he will safe-ly hide me.
From a - bove he'll come in love, To shield and safe-ly hide me.

CHORUS.

Safe - ly hide me, Safe - ly hide me, When the

Safe-ly hide me, Safe-ly hide me,

storms and bil - lows rage,........ He will

When the storms, the storms and bil - lows rage,

guide me, safe - ly guide me Through this earth-ly pil-grim-age.

567   In the Sweet By and By.

"And God shall wipe away all tears from their eyes: and there shall be no more death, nor sorrow, nor crying, neither shall there be any more pain."—Rev. xxi: 4.

E. A. HOFFMAN.   J. H. KURZENKNABE, by per.

1. By and by all this weeping and this sorrow Will be drown'd in a glorious to-
2. By and by all this en-vy and this er-ror, All the darkness of death and its
3. By and by all our anguish and our crying, With this wearisome heartache and

-mor-row, That will dawn when this earth-life shall cease, shall cease, And will
ter-ror, Will be swept in the grave to its doom, its doom, When his
sigh-ing, All shall cease; for no tear-moisten'd eye, dim eye, Will be

CHORUS.

fill ev-'ry heart with its peace. }
glo-ry our souls shall il-lume. }   In the sweet By and
known in the sweet By and by. }

By and by,   In the

by, By and by, We shall rest In the sweet, In the sweet By and by,

sweet By and by,   In the sweet By and by,   By and

In the sweet By and by, By and by, We shall rest in the sweet By and by.

by,   In the sweet By and by,

From "The Song Treasury."
345

The Beautiful Hills.

By permission of O. Ditson & Co.

JAMES G. CLARK.

1. Oh! the beau-ti - ful hills, where the blest shall tread In the
years when the earth's made new ; By .... faith we gaze on the
fields of God, From the vale we are journeying through. We have
seen those hills in their brightness rise, Thro' the tears that burn-ing
flow, And we've felt the thrill of im - mor - tal eyes In the

The Beautiful Hills. Concluded.

CHORUS.

night of our darkest woe. We sing of the beau-ti-ful hills.... That

rise from the ev - er - green shore;...... O! sing of the

rit. *ad lib.*

beau-ti - ful hills.... Where the wea-ry shall toil no more.

2 The cities of yore, that were reared in crime,
   And renowned by the praise of seers,
Went down to the dust in the march of Time,
   To sleep with his gray hair'd years;
But the beautiful hills rise bright and strong,
   Through the smoke of old Time's red wars,
As on that day when the first deep song
   Rolled out from the morning stars.—*Cho.*

3 We dream of rest on the beautiful hills,
   Where the trav'ler shall thirst no more;
And we hear the hum of a thousand rills
   That wander the green glens o'er.
We feel the zeal of the martyred men
   Who have braved a cold world's frown;
We can bear the burden which they did then,
   Nor shrink from their thorny crown.—*Cho.*

4 Our arms are weak, yet we would not fling
   To our feet this load of ours;
The winds of Spring to the valleys sing,
   And the turf replies with flow'rs—
And thus we learn on our weary way,
   How a mightier arm controls;
And we press to enter the gates of day,
   Where the glory to sight unfolds.—*Cho.*

569   Prayer, Silent Prayer.

CHANT.

Selected by AMANDA BAILEY.

CHORUS.

1 When torn is the bosom with sorrow and care,
Be it ever so simple, there's | nothing..like | prayer;
It eases, and softens, subdues, yet sus-| tains,
Gives rigor to hope, and puts | passion..in | chains.

Chorus.—Prayer, prayer, O sweet prayer!
Be it ever so simple there's nothing like prayer.

2 When far from the friends we hold dearest, we part,
What fond recollections still | cling..to the | heart;
Past converse, past scenes, past enjoyments are | there;
How hurtfully pleasing till | hallowed..by | prayer.—*Cho.*

3 When pleasure would woo us from piety's arms,
The siren sings sweetly, or | silent..by | charms;
We listen, look, loiter, are caught in the | snare;
In looking to Jesus we | conquer by | prayer.—*Cho.*

4 While strangers to prayer, we are strangers to bliss,
Heav'n pours its full streams through no | medium but | this!
And till in the seraph's full ecstasy | share,
Our chalice of joy must be | guarded by | prayer.—*Cho.*

——o——

570   The Time Hastens On.

1. Lo! the time hastens on when the bright day will dawn, And the

King in his glo-ry des-cend; We shall soon hear the song of the

glo-ri-fied throng, And the an-them that nev-er shall end.

CHORUS.

O, Saviour, dear Sav-iour! O, Sav-iour, come! 'Tis for thee that we

348

The Time Hastens On. <small>Concluded.</small>

sigh, 'tis to thee that we cry, Come and gath-er the faithful ones home.

2 O, we long to be there, free from sorrow and care,
    In the land of the pure and the blest;
    There where love will abide, and where nought can divide,
    And the weary forever shall rest.—*Cho.*

3 There our friends we shall meet, and our loved ones shall **greet**,
    Who are lying in death's cold embrace;
    From the tomb they will come to their bright **Eden** home,
    Clad in heavenly beauty and grace.—*Cho.*

4 That bright day now is near, and the tidings we hear,
    As they come o'er the land and the sea;
    And our hearts that were sad, are now joyful and glad,
    While we know that we soon shall be free.—*Cho.*

—o—

571   The Great Physician.

WILLIAM HUNTER, 1842.   Arr. by J. H. STOCKTON, by per.

1. { The great Phy-si cian now is near, The sym-pa - thiz-ing Je - sus; }
   { He speaks the drooping heart to cheer, Oh, hear the voice of Je - sus. }

CHORUS.

Sweet-est note in ser-aph song, Sweetest name on mor-tal tongue.

rit.

Sweet-est car - ol ev - er sung, Je - sus, bless-ed Je - sus!

2 All glory to the dying Lamb!
    I now believe in Jesus;
    I love the blessed Saviour's name,
    I love the name of Jesus.—*Cho.*

3 His name dispels my guilt and fear,
    No other name but Jesus;

Oh, how my soul delights to hear
    The precious name of Jesus.—*Cho.*

4 And when He comes to bring the crown,
    The crown of life and glory;
    Then by his side we will sit down,
    And tell redemption's story.—*Cho.*

349

Love and Grace.

Words by I. I. L.

A. T. GORHAM.

1. O, 'twas love that bro't me to Him, And 'tis love that keeps me there;

By His grace it was I knew Him, He, my Saviour, dear and fair.

REFRAIN.

Love and grace—His love and grace I will sing, will sing in ev-'ry place,

cres.

Till I reach that blissful shore, Where I'll praise Him ev-er-more.

2 Dark it was before I found Him,
  And the way I could not see;
Now the light that shines around Him,
  As I follow, falls on me.
  Refrain.—Love and grace, &c.

3 O how blest to walk with Jesus!
  Joy we never knew before;
From our fears His presence frees us,
  While we trust Him more and more.
  Refrain.—Love and grace, &c.

4 Now it is by faith I view Him,
  As I walk this narrow way;
But He soon will call me to Him,
  In that bright, approaching day.
  Refrain.—Love and grace, &c.

5 Then my joy will be forever,
  There no clouds will intervene;
And the darkness comes there never—
  I shall see Him as I'm seen.
  Refrain.—Love and grace, &c.

573 One Sweetly Solemn Thought.

"Now they desire a better country, that is, an heavenly."—Heb. xi: 16

Miss PHŒBE CAREY.　　　　　　　　　　　PHILIP PHILLIPS, by per.

1. One sweet - ly sol - emn thought Comes to me o'er and
2. Near - er my Fa - ther's house, Where ma - ny man-sions
3. Near - er the bound of life, Where bur - dens are laid
4. Be near me when my feet Are slip - ping o'er the

o'er; I'm near - er home to - day, to - day, Than
be; Near - er the great white throne to - day, Near -
down; Near - er to leave the cross to - day, And
brink, For I am near - er home to - day, Per -

CHORUS.

I have been be - fore. Near - er my home, Near - er my home,
- er the crys - tal sea.
near - er to the crown.
- haps, than now I think.

Near-er my home to - day, to - day, Than I have been be - fore.

574 Cross of Christ.

Words by D. T. TAYLOR.   (*By Permission*.)   Music by J. C. STODDARD.

1. Cross of Christ, O sa - cred tree, Hide my sins, and shel-ter me;

Claim or mer - it have I none, I am vile, and all un-done:

I to thee for suc - cor fly; Give me ref - uge, or I die:

Cross of Christ, O, sa - cred tree, All my hopes are hung on thee.

2 Cross of Christ, O, sacred tree,
Let me to thy shadow flee;
Here they mocked the crucified,
Here the royal sufferer died;
Here was shed the atoning blood,
Till it crimsoned all the sod.
Cross of Christ, O, sacred tree,
Can the guilty trust in thee?

3 Cross of Christ, O sacred tree,
Type of love's deep mystery;
'Twas my sins provoked this love,
I this matchless passion moved;

For my soul this love was stored,
On my head the blessing poured.
Cross of Christ, O, sacred tree,
Now I solve love's mystery.

4 Cross of Christ, O, sacred tree,
This my boast shall ever be:
That the blood for me was shed,
That for me he groaned and bled;
Now I catch that gracious eye,
Now I know I shall not die.
Cross of Christ, O, sacred tree,
All my guilt is lost in thee.

575 Happy in the Lord.

J. H. K.

From "The Song Treasury."

J. H. KURZENKNABE, by per.

1. Lit - tle chil - dren come to - day, Hap-py in the Lord;
2. Je - sus loves to hear our praise, Hap-py in the Lord;
3. By the Sav-iour's pard'ning blood, Hap-py in the Lord;
4. Then when done with mor - tal praise, Hap-py in the Lord;

D. C. Lit - tle chil - dren come to - day, Hap-py in the Lord;

We u - nite to sing and pray, Hap-py in the Lord.
He will keep us all our days, Hap-py in the Lord.
We are cleans'd from ev - 'ry spot, Hap-py in the Lord.
We shall wor - ship face to face, Hap-py in the Lord.

We u - nite to sing and pray, Hap-py in the Lord.

CHORUS.

Here with tune - ful voi - ces, All in sweet ac - cord;

D.C.

Ev - 'ry one re - joic - es, Hap-py in the Lord.

"Ask, and ye shall receive, that your joy may be full."—John xvi: 24.

Words by J. C. PROCTOR.

1. To ev-'ry lit-tle, lov-ing child, With-in these sa-cred walls,
2. To ev-'ry lit-tle, lov-ing child, Who longs the Lord to see,
3. To ev-'ry lit-tle, lov-ing child, Who longs to be for-given,

The bless-ed Sav-iour speaks to-day, And gen-tly, sweetly calls:—
The bless-ed Sav-iour calls to-day, "Come, lit-tle child, to Me:
The bless-ed Sav-iour says to-day, "I am the door to heav'n;

"Come, lit-tle one, come, 'Ask' for grace; And 'Ask' for mer-cy too;
Come, lit-tle one, come, 'Seek' for grace; And 'Seek' with earnest mind;
Come, lit-tle one, come 'Knock' for grace; And 'Knock' for mercy too;

To all who 'Ask' the promise is,—It shall be giv-en you.'
To all who 'Seek' the promise is,—'Seek, Seek,' and ye shall find."
To all who 'Knock' the promise is,—It shall be open'd you."

577 My Brighter Home.

Words Arranged.   (*By Permission.*)   J. H. TENNEY.

1. Brighter home! Brighter home! Better home for me! I love to think the
2. Brighter home! Brighter home! There no clouds arise, No tear-drops fall, no
3. Brighter home! Brighter home! Ne'er shall sorrow's gloom, Nor doubts, nor fears [dis-

time will come When I shall rest in thee. I've no a-bid-ing cit-y here, I
dark nights dim Thy ev-er smil-ing skies.This earthly home is fair and bright, Yet
-turb me there, For all is peace at home. I know I ne'er shall worthy be To

seek for one to come; And thro' this pilgrimage so drear, I know there's rest at home.
clouds will often come; And oh, I long to see the light That gilds my brighter home.
dwell 'neath that bright dome, But Christ, my Saviour, died for me, And gives me there [a home.

CHORUS.

Bright-er home!   Bright-er home!   Bet-ter home   for

Bright-er home!   Bright-er home!   Bet-ter home for

me! I love to think the time will come When I shall rest in thee.

578 Close to Thee.

"It is good for me to draw near God."—Psalm lxxiii: 28.

FANNY CROSBY.

S. J. VAIL.

Copyright, 1874, in "Songs of Grace and Glory," and used by per. Biglow & Main.

1. Thou, my ev - er-last-ing portion, More than friend or life to me, All along my

pilgrim journey, Saviour, let me walk with Thee. Close to Thee, close to Thee, Close to

Thee, close to Thee; All along my pilgrim journey, Saviour, let me walk with Thee.

2 Not for ease or worldly pleasure,
Nor for fame my prayer shall be;
Gladly will I toil and suffer,
Only let me walk with Thee.
Close to Thee, close to Thee,
Close to Thee, close to Thee,
Gladly will I toil and suffer,
Only let me walk with Thee.

3 Lead me through the vale of shadows,
Bear me o'er life's fitful sea;
Then the gate of life eternal,
May I enter, Lord, with Thee.
Close to Thee, close to Thee,
Close to Thee, close to Thee,
Then the gate of life eternal,
May I enter, Lord, with Thee.

————o————

579 How Happy Are They.

1. Oh, how hap - py are they Who their Sav-iour o - bey, And have

laid up their treasures a - bove! Tongue can nev - er ex - press The sweet

com - fort and peace Of a soul in its ear - li - est love.

2 That sweet comfort was mine
When the favor divine
I first found in the blood of the Lamb;
When my heart it believed
What a joy I received,
What a heaven in Jesus' dear name!

3 Jesus all the day long
Was my joy and my song:
O that all his salvation might see!

He hath loved me, I cried,
He hath suffered and died,
To redeem even rebels like me.

4 O the rapturous height
Of that holy delight
Which I feel in the life-giving blood!
Of my Saviour possessed,
I am perfectly blest,
As if filled with the fulness of God.

580 Clinging to the Rock.

Words and Music by Prof. C. S. HARRINGTON.

From A. Hull's "S. S. Gem," by permission.

1. When the tem-pest ra-ges high, Sail-ing on life's boist-'rous sea;
2. When 'mid drift-ing wrecks I'm cast, Darkness set-tling thick-ly round;
3. When the conq'ring waves shall close Proudly o'er me as I die;

Storm-y bil-lows I de-fy, If I then may on-ly be
Hope shall lift her light at last, If I then be on-ly found
O-ver these brief vic-tor foes, I shall tri-umph by and by,

REFRAIN.

An-chor'd to the Rock, An-chor'd to the Rock, Shel-ter for me
Cling-ing to the Rock, Cling-ing to the Rock, Shel-ter, &c.
Cling-ing to the Rock, &c.

ev-er, Strength that fail-eth nev-er— When the storms of life

are o'er, Look for me on Canaan's shore, An-chor'd to the Rock.

357

581   Wake the Song of Jubilee.

Music by ASA HULL, by per.

1. Wake the song of ju - bi - lee, Let it ech - o o'er the sea;

Now is come the promis'd hour: Je - sus reigns with sov - - - 'reign pow'r.

REFRAIN. *for each verse.*

mp   *cres.*

Wake the song.   of ju - bi - lee,   Let it
Wake the song, the song of ju - bi - lee,

ech - - - o o'er the sea;   Now is come   the promis'd
Let it ech - o, ech - o o'er the sea;   Now is come, is come the

Wake the Song of Jubilee. Concluded.

hour,   Je - sus reigns   with sov - - 'reign pow'r.

prom-is'd hour,   Je - sus reigns with sov - - 'reign pow'r.

Quartette.

2. All ye na - tions join and sing, Christ of lords and kings, is King!

Full Chorus.   D.S.

Let it sound from shore to shore, Je - sus reigns for - ev - er - more!

Solo.

3. Now the des-ert lands re-joice,   And the is - lands join their voice:

Full Chorus.   D.S.

Yea, the whole cre - a - tion sings, Je - sus is the King of kings!

NOTE.—*Return to Refrain after singing the 2d verse, also after 3d verse.*

359

582 Nuremberg. 7s.

I. I. L.

JOHANN RUDOLF AHLE.

1. Here u-nit-ed let us join In the hymns of love di-vine;
Let our harps be tun'd to praise, Thro' the yet re-main-ing days:

'Tis not long these earthly songs Will be sung by mor-tal tongues.

2 Now a little while and we
Shall be over life's rough sea;
Then a sweeter song we'll sing
Than the ones we here do bring—
Song of our redemption there,
Free from death, and pain and care.

583

1 Come, and let us sweetly join,
Christ to praise in hymns divine;
Give we all, with one accord,
Glory to our common Lord;
Hands, and hearts, and voices raise;
Sing as in the ancient days.

2 Strive we, in affection strive;
Let the purer flame revive,
Such as in the martyrs glowed,
Dying champions for their God:
We like them may live and love;
Called we are their joys to prove.

3 Sing we, then, in Jesus' name,
Now as yesterday the same;
One in every time and place,
Full for all of truth and grace:
We for Christ, our Master, stand,
Lights in a benighted land.

CHARLES WESLEY.

584

1 Christians, brethren, ere we part,
Every voice and every heart
Join, and to our Father raise
One last hymn of grateful praise;
For his mercy and his love,
Sing as angels do above.

2 Though we here should meet no more,
Yet there is a brighter shore;
There, released from toil and pain,
There we all may meet again,
Meet again to part no more;
There our wanderings will be o'er.

H. KIRKE WHITE, ALT.

585

1 Now may He who from the dead
Brought the Shepherd of the sheep,
Jesus Christ, our King and Head,
All our souls in safety keep;
From the grave and death us bring,
And the victory to sing.

2 To that great Redeemer's praise,
Who the covenant sealed with blood,
Let our hearts and voices raise
Loud thanksgivings to our God.
Christ the Son has ris'n that we
Might o'er death have victory.

JOHN NEWTON, ALT.

586

1 Now to Him who gave us breath,
And to Him who saves from death,
Be our praise and sweetest song—
'Tis to Him we each belong:
'Tis his mercy and his grace
Bring us to our heavenly place.

2 While we wait to join the throng
That shall come with sweeter song,
Let us love and sing and pray,
Looking for that brighter day:
Hearts and voices joined to bring
Glory to the Coming King.

I. L. L.

HYMNS.

587 L. M. *Tune*, No. 95.

1 THE perfec' world, by Adam trod,
Was the first temple built by God;
His fiat laid the corner-stone:
He spake, and lo! the work was
done.

2 He hung his starry roof on high,
The broad expanse of azure sky:
He spread its pavement, green and
bright,
And curtained it with morning light.

3 The mountains in their places stood,
The sea, the sky —and all was good;
And when its first pure praises rang,
The morning stars together sang.

4 Lord, 'tis not ours to make the sea,
And earth and sky, a house for thee;
But in thy sight our off'ring stands,
A humble temple built with hands.

---

588 L. M. *Tune*, No. 97.

1 THERE is a God — all nature speaks,
Thro' earth, and air, and seas, and
skies,
See, from the clouds his glory breaks,
When the first beams of morning
rise.

2 The rising sun serenely bright,
O'er the wide world's extended frame,
Inscribes, in characters of light,
His mighty Maker's glorious name.

3 Ye curious minds, who roam abroad,
And trace creation's wonders o'er,
Confess the footsteps of your God,
And bow before him, and adore.

---

589 L. M. *Tune*, No. 106.

1 ALL people that on earth do dwell,
Sing to the Lord with cheerful voice;
Him serve with mirth, his praise
forth tell,
Come ye before him and rejoice.

2 Know that the Lord is God indeed;
Without our aid he did us make;
We are his flock, he doth us feed,
And for his sheep he doth us take.

3 Oh, enter then his gates with praise,
Approach with joy his courts unto;
Praise, laud and bless his name
always,
For it is seemly so to do.

4 For why? the Lord our God is good,
His mercy is forever sure;
His truth at all times firmly stood,
And shall from age to age endure.

---

590 L. M. *Tune*, No. 164.

1 LET all that wait the Coming King,
Now to his name sweet praises bring;
He cometh quickly, sound it high,
Till echoes meet the vocal sky.

2 Earth shall depart, and like a scroll,
The passing heavens together roll;
For Jesus' faithful words shall be
Enduring as eternity.

3 Now let thy kingdom come, O Lord,
As thou hast promised in thy word —
Fill earth with glory like a sea —
Oh, speak the word, and it shall be.

---

591 L. M. *Tune*, No. 140.

1 THE Lord is coming! let this be
The herald note of jubilee;
And when we meet, and when we
part,
The salutation from the heart.

2 The Lord is coming! sound it forth,
From East to West, from South to
North.
Speed on! speed on the tidings glad,
That none who love him may be sad.

3 The Lord is coming! watch and
pray!
Watch ye, and haste unto the day;
So shalt thou then escape the snare,
And Christ's eternal glory share.

361

592 L. M. *Tune, No. 214.*

1 COMMAND thy blessing from above,
O God, on all assembled here!
Behold us with a Father's love,
While we look up with filial fear.

2 Command thy blessing, Jesus, Lord;
May we thy true disciples be;
Speak to each heart the mighty word,
Say to the weakest, "Follow me."

3 O thou, our Maker, Saviour, Guide,
Our gracious God, by us confessed;
May naught in life or death divide
The saints in thy communion
blessed.

4 With thee, and these, forever bound,
May all who here in prayer unite,
With harps and songs thy throne
surround,
Rest in thy love, and reign in
light.

---

593 L. M. *Tune, No. 378.*

1 LORD, when thou didst ascend on
high,
Ten thousand angels filled the sky:
Those heavenly guards around thee
wait,
Like chariots that attend thy state.

2 Not Sinai's mountain could appear
More glorious when the Lord was
there,
While he pronounced his dreadful
law,
And struck the chosen tribes with
awe.

3 Raised by his Father to the throne,
He sent the promised Spirit down,
With gifts and grace for rebel men,
That God might dwell on earth again.

---

594 L. M. *Tune, No. 140.*

1 So let our lips and lives express
The holy gospel we profess;
So let our works and virtues shine
To prove the doctrine all divine.

2 Thus shall we best proclaim abroad
The honors of our Saviour God,
When his salvation reigns within,
And grace subdues the power of sin.

3 Our flesh and sense must be denied,
Passion, and envy, lust and pride;
While justice, mercy, truth and love,
Our inward piety approve.

4 Religion bears our spirits up,
While we expect that blessed hope,
The bright appearance of the Lord;
And faith stands leaning on his word.

---

595 L. M. *Tune, No. 214.*

1 JEHOVAH reigns! he dwells in light,
Girded with majesty and might;
The world, created by his hands,
Still on its first foundation stands.

2 But ere this spacious world was
made,
Or had its first foundation laid,
Thy throne eternal ages stood,
Thyself the ever-living God.

3 Like floods the angry nations rise,
And aim their rage against the skies,
In vain their rage they aim so high!
At thy rebuke the billows die.

4 Forever shall thy throne endure;
Thy promise stands forever sure;
And everlasting holiness
Becomes the dwellings of thy grace.

---

596 L. M. *Tune, No. 54.*

1 THE morning flowers display their
sweets,
And gay their silken leaves unfold,
All careless of the noontide heats,
And fearless of the evening cold.

2 Nipped by the wind's untimely blast,
Parched by the sun's intensest ray,
The momentary glories waste,
The short-lived beauties pass
away.

3 So blooms the human face divine,
When youth its pride of beauty
shows,
Fairer than spring the colors shine,
And sweeter than the blushing
rose.

4 But worn by slowly rolling years
Or broke by sickness in a day,
The fading glory disappears,
The short-lived beauties die away.

362

6 Yet these, new rising from the tomb,
　　With lustre brighter far shall shine;
　Shall have a never-ending bloom,
　　Safe from disease and from decline.

597　L. M.　*Tune, No. 54.*

1 How blest the righteous when he
　　　dies,
　When sinks the weary saint to
　　　rest;
　How mildly beam the closing eyes,
　　How gently heaves the faithful
　　　breast.

2 So fades a summer cloud away;
　　So sinks the gale when storms are
　　　o'er;
　So gently shuts the eye of day;
　　So dies a wave along the shore.

3 But soon shall shine that marble
　　　brow,
　　When slumb'ring saints arise and
　　　sing,
　"O grave, where is thy vict'ry now,
　　And where, O death, is now thy
　　　sting?"

598　L. M.　*Tune, No. 214.*

1 He wills that I should holy be:
　That holiness I long to feel;
　That full, divine conformity
　To all my Saviour's righteous will.

2 See, Lord, the travail of thy soul
　　Accomplished in the change of
　　　mine;
　And plunge' me, every whit made
　　　whole,
　In all the depths of love divine.

3 On thee, O God, my soul is stayed,
　　And waits to prove thine utmost
　　　will;
　The promise, by thy mercy made,
　Thou canst, thou wilt in me fulfill.

4 No more I stagger at thy power,
　　Or doubt thy truth, which cannot
　　　move:
　Hasten the long-expected hour,
　And bless me with thy perfect love.

599　L. M.　*Tune, No. 158.*

1 'Tis finished! the Messiah dies;
　Cut off for sins, but not his own:
　Accomplished is the sacrifice;
　　The great redeeming work is done.

2 'Tis finished! all the debt is paid;
　Justice divine is satisfied;
　The grand and full atonement made;
　Christ for a guilty world hath died.

3 The veil is rent; in him alone
　　The living way to God is seen;
　The middle wall is broken down,
　　And all mankind may enter in.

4 The types and figures are fulfilled;
　Exacted is the legal pain;
　The precious promises are sealed;
　The spotless Lamb of God is slain.

600　L. M.　*Tune, No. 106.*

1 I, Jesus, am ascended high,
　No more to suffer, bleed, and die;
　I live to bless—my name is Love;
　I live with Him who reigns above.

2 Behold, I live forevermore—
　My love's an everlasting store:
　I live to plead the sinner's cause,
　To magnify Jehovah's laws.

3 I live to hear his children's cries;
　I live to wipe their weeping eyes;
　I live to sanctify their woes;
　I live to conquer all their foes.

4 I live to help in each distress;
　I live t' enrich their souls with grace;
　I live to pour my spirit down;
　I live t' insure their heavenly crown.

601　L. M.　*Tune, No. 95.*

1 Sinners exposed to death and woe,
　Arise and to King Jesus go;
　Your guilt confess, his favor seek,
　And wait to hear what God will
　　　speak.

2 Fear not the law; 'tis grace that
　　　reigns;
　Jesus the sinner's cause maintains;
　He ransomed rebels with his blood,
　And now he intercedes with God.

3 To him approach with fervent
　　　prayer,
　And if you perish, perish there,
　Resolved at Jesus' feet to lie,
　Suing for mercy till you die.

4 Thrice happy souls, who thus ad-
　　　dress
　The God of love and boundless
　　　grace!
　Jesus will such completely save,
　And life eternal they shall have.

602 L. M. *Tune*, No. 351.

1 WE have no outward righteousness,
   No merits or good works to plead :
We only can be saved by grace;
   Thy grace, O Lord, is free indeed.

2 Save us by grace, through faith
      alone. —
   A faith thou must thyself impart,
   A faith that would by works be
      shown,
   A faith that purifies the heart, —

3 A faith that doth the mountains
      move,
   A faith that shows our sins forgiven,
   A faith that sweetly works by love,
   And ascertains our claim to
      heaven.

4 This is the faith we humbly seek,
   The faith in thy all-cleansing
      blood ;
   That faith which doth for sinners
      speak,
   O, let it speak us up to God!

603 L. M. *Tune*, No. 378.

1 WHO shall ascend thy heavenly place,
Great God, and dwell before thy face?
The man who minds religion now,
And humbly walks with God below ;

2 Whose hands are pure, whose heart
      is clean :
Whose lips still speak the thing they
      mean :
No slanders dwell upon his tongue ;
He hates to do his neighbor wrong.

3 He loves his enemies, and prays
For those who curse him to his face ;
And does to all men still the same
That he would hope or wish from
      them.

4 Yet when his holiest works are done,
His soul depends on grace alone ;
This is the man thy face shall see,
And dwell forever, Lord, with thee.

604 L. M. *Tune*, No. 227

1 AWAKE, my soul! and with the sun
Thy daily course of duty run ;
Shake off dull sloth, and joyful rise
To pay thy morning sacrifice.

2 Wake, and lift up thyself, my heart !
And with the angels bear thy part,
Who, all night long, unwearied sing
High praises to th' eternal King.

3 Glory to thee, who safe hast kept,
And hast refreshed me while I slept :
Grant, Lord! when I from death
      shall wake,
I may of endless life partake.

4 Lord! I my vows to thee renew ;
Scatter my sins as morning-dew ;
Guard my first springs of thought
      and will,
And with thyself my spirit fill.

605 L. M. *Tune*, No. 214.

1 SERVANTS of God ! in joyful lays,
Sing ye the Lord Jehovah's praise ;
His glorious name let all adore,
From age to age, forevermore.

2 Blest be that name, supremely blest,
From the sun's rising to its rest :
Above the heavens his power is
      known ;
Through all the earth his goodness
      shown.

3 Who is like God? —so great, so high,
He bows himself to view the sky ;
And yet, with condescending grace,
Looks down upon the human race.

4 He hears the uncomplaining moan
Of those who sit and weep alone ;
He lifts the mourner from the dust,
And saves the poor who in him trust.

606 L. M. *Tune*, No. 126.

1 I KNOW that my Redeemer lives ;
What joy the blest assurance gives !
He lives, he lives, who once was
      dead ;
He lives, my everlasting Head.

2 He lives, and grants me daily breath ;
He lives, and I shall conquer death ;
He lives, my mansion to prepare ;
He lives to bring me safely there.

3 He lives, all glory to his name ;
He lives, my Saviour, still the same ;
What joy the blest assurance gives,
I know that my Redeemer lives !

607   S. M.   *Tune, No. 221.*

1 My Maker and my King!
  To thee my all I owe;
  Thy sovereign bounty is the spring
  Whence all my blessings flow.

2 Thou ever good and kind!
  A thousand reasons move,
  A thousand obligations bind
  My heart to grateful love.

3 The creature of thy hand,
  On thee alone I live;
  My God, thy benefits demand
  More praise than I can give.

4 Lord, what can I impart,
  When all is thine before;
  Thy love demands a thankful heart;
  The gift, alas, how poor!

5 Shall I withhold thy due?
  And shall my passions rove?
  Lord, form this wretched heart anew,
  And fill it with thy love.

6 Oh, let thy grace inspire
  My soul with strength divine;
  Let all my powers to thee aspire,
  And all my days be thine.

---

608   S. M.   *Tune, No. 451.*

1 Thou ever-present Aid
  In suffering and distress!
  The mind, which still on thee is
    stayed,
  Is kept in perfect peace.

2 The soul, by faith reclined
  On the Redeemer's breast,
  Mid raging storms, exults to find
  An everlasting rest.

3 Sorrow and fear are gone,
  Whene'er thy face appears;
  It stills the sighing orphan's moan,
  And dries the widow's tears.

4 It hallows every cross,
  It sweetly comforts me;
  It makes me now forget my loss,
  And lose myself in thee.

5 Jesus, to whom I fly,
  Will all my wishes fill;
  What though created streams are
    dry?
  I have the fountain still.

---

609   S. M.   *Tune, No. 417.*

1 Did Christ o'er sinners weep?
  And shall our cheeks be dry?
  Let floods of penitential grief
  Burst forth from every eye.

  The Son of God in tears
  The wondering angels see:
  Be thou astonished, O my soul!
  He shed those tears for thee.

3 He wept, that we might weep;
  Each sin demands a tear:
  In heaven alone no sin is found,
  And there's no weeping there.

---

610   S. M.   *Tune, No. 221.*

1 Through waves, and clouds, and
    storms,
  He gently clears thy way;
  Wait thou his time, so shall this
    night
  Soon end in joyous day.

2 Leave to his sovereign sway
  To choose and to command:
  So shalt thou, wondering, own his
    way,
  How wise, how strong his hand!

3 Far, far above thy thought
  His counsel shall appear,
  When fully he the work hath
    wrought
  That caused thy needless fear.

---

611   S. M.   *Tune, No. 123.*

1 I was a wandering sheep,
  I did not love the fold,
  I did not love my Shepherd's voice,
  I would not be controlled.

2 I was a wayward child,
  I did not love my home,
  I did not love my Father's voice,
  I loved afar to roam.

3 The Shepherd sought his sheep,
  The Father sought his child;
  He followed me o'er vale and hill,
  O'er deserts waste and wild:

4 He found me nigh to death,
  Famished, and faint, and lone,
  He bound me with the bands of love,
  He saved the wandering one.

612 S. M. *Tune, No. 271.*

1 How sweet the cheering words,
  " Whoever will " may come:
  The door of mercy open stands,
  As yet there still is room.
    Cho.— I'm glad salvation's free!
    I'm glad salvation's free!
    Salvation's free for you
      and me,
    I'm glad salvation's free!

2 'Tis the "accepted time,"
  The day of grace and love:
  And God invites " whoever will "
  His faithfulness to prove.

3 The Saviour sits on high,
  The proof that all is done:
  And sinners now God can accept
  Through his beloved Son.

613 S. M. *Tune, No. 234.*

1 Thou Judge of quick and dead,
  Before whose bar severe,
  With holy joy, or guilty dread,
  We all shall soon appear:
  Our cautioned souls prepare
  For that tremendous day,
  And fill us now with watchful care,
  And stir us up to pray:

2 To pray and wait the hour,
  That awful hour unknown,
  When rob'd in majesty and power,
  Thou shalt from heaven come
    down,
  Th' immortal Son of man,
  To judge the human race,
  With all thy Father's dazzling train,
  With all thy glorious grace,

3 O may we thus be found
  Obedient to thy word,
  Attentive to the gospel's sound,
  And looking for our Lord!
  O may we all insure
  A lot among the blest:
  And watch each moment to secure
  An everlasting rest.

614 S. M. *Tune, No. 242.*

1 " All things are ready," come,
  Come to the supper spread;
  Come, rich and poor, come, old and
    young,
  Come, and be richly fed.

2 " All things are ready," come,
  The invitation's given,
  Through Him who now in **glory**
    sits
  At God's right hand in heaven.

3 All things are ready," come,
  The door is open wide;
  O feast upon the love of God,
  For Christ, his Son, has died.

615 S. M. *Tune, No. 191.*

1 The Lord forgives thy sins,
  Prolongs thy feeble breath;
  He healeth thine infirmities,
  And ransoms thee from death.

2 He clothes thee with his love,
  Upholds thee with his truth;
  And like the eagle he renews
  The vigor of thy youth.

3 Then bless his holy name
  Whose grace hath made **thee**
    whole:
  Whose loving-kindness crowns **thy**
    days:
  O bless the Lord, my soul!

616 S. M. *Tune, No. 417.*

1 Down to the sacred wave,
  The Lord of life was led;
  And he who came our souls to **save,**
  In Jordan bowed his head.

2 He taught the solemn way;
  He fixed the holy rite;
  He bade his ransomed ones obey,
  And keep the path of light.

3 Blest Saviour, we will tread
  In thine appointed way;
  Let glory o'er these scenes be **shed,**
  And smile on us to-day.

617 S. M. *Tune, No. 221.*

1 Now is th' accepted time,
  Now is the day of grace;
  Now, sinners come without delay,
  And seek the Saviour's face.

2 Now is th' accepted time,
  The Saviour calls to-day;
  To-morrow it may be too late —
  Then why should you delay?

3 Now is th' accepted time.
The gospel bids you come;
And every promise in his word
Declares there yet is room.

---

618   S. M.   *Tune*, No. 365.

1 AND canst thou, sinner, slight
The call of love divine?
Shall God, with tenderness invite,
And gain no thought of thine?

2 Wilt thou not cease to grieve
The Spirit from thy breast,
Till he thy wretched soul shall leave
With all thy sins oppressed?

3 To-day, a pard'ning God
Will hear the suppliant pray;
To-day, a Saviour's cleansing blood
Will wash thy guilt away.

4 But, grace so dearly bought
If yet thou wilt despise,
Thy fearful doom, with vengeance
fraught,
Will fill thee with surprise.

---

619   S. M.   *Tune*, No. 394.

1 I HEAR thy word with love,
And I would fain obey;
Send thy good Spirit from above
To guide me, lest I stray.

2 Warn me of every sin,
Forgive my secret faults,
And cleanse this guilty soul of mine,
Whose crimes exceed my thoughts.

3 While, with my heart and tongue,
I spread thy praise abroad,
Accept the worship and the song,
My Saviour and my God!

---

620   S. M.   *Tune*, No. 242.

1 JESUS, we look to thee,
Thy promised presence claim;
Thou in the midst of us shalt be,
Assembled in thy name.

2 Thy name salvation is,
Which here we come to prove;
Thy name is life, and health, and
peace.
And everlasting love.

3 Not in the name of pride
Or selfishness we meet;
From nature's paths we turn aside,
And worldly thoughts forget.

---

621   S. M.   *Tune*, No. 191.

1 COME, Lord, and tarry not:
Bring the long-looked-for day;
Oh! why these years of waiting here!
Oh! why this long delay?

2 Come, for creation groans,
Impatient of thy stay,
Worn out by these long years of ill,
These ages of delay.

3 Is not the field now ripe?
Come, with thy sickle, then,
Reap the great harvest of the earth,
Come, gather in the grain.

---

622   S. M.   *Tune*, No. 249.

1 LET every mortal ear attend,
And every heart rejoice;
The trumpet of the gospel sounds
With an inviting voice.

2 Ho! all ye hungry, starving souls,
That feed upon the wind,
And vainly strive, with earthly toys,
To fill an empty mind;

3 Eternal wisdom hath prepared
A soul-reviving feast,
And bids your longing appetites
The rich provision taste.

4 Ho! ye that pant for living streams,
And pine away and die,
Here you may quench your raging
thirst
With springs that never dry.

---

623   C. M.   *Tune*, No. 221.

1 Now let our voices join
To form a sacred song;
Ye pilgrims, in Jehovah's ways,
With music pass along.

2 All honor to his name,
Who marks the shining way!
To him who leads the wanderers on
To realms of endless day!

367

624 C. M. *Tune*, No. 147.

1 I WANT a principle within,
  Of jealous, godly fear;
  A sensibility of sin,
  A pain to feel it near.

2 I want the first approach to feel
  Of pride or fond desire;
  To catch the wand'ring of my will,
  And quench the kindling fire.

3 From thee that I no more may part,
  No more thy goodness grieve,
  The filial awe, the fleshly heart,
  The tender conscience give.

4 Quick as the apple of an eye,
  O God, my conscience make;
  Awake my soul when sin is nigh,
  And keep it still awake.

---

625 C. M. *Tune*, No. 236.

1 COME, Holy Spirit, heavenly Dove,
  With all thy quick'ning powers;
  Kindle a flame of sacred love
  In these cold hearts of ours.

2 Look how we grovel here below,
  Fond of these earthly toys;
  Our souls how heavily they go,
  To reach eternal joys!

3 In vain we tune our formal songs,
  In vain we strive to rise;
  Hosannas languish on our tongues,
  And our devotion dies.

4 Father, and shall we ever live
  At this poor dying rate?
  Our love so faint, so cold to thee,
  And thine to us so great?

5 Come, Holy Spirit, heavenly Dove,
  With all thy quick'ning powers;
  Kindle thy love in all our hearts,
  And that shall kindle ours.

---

626 C. M. *Tune*, No. 28.

1 BURIED beneath the yielding wave,
  The dear Redeemer lies;
  Faith views him in the watery grave,
  And thence beholds him rise.

2 Thus it becomes his saints to-day
  Their ardent zeal t' express,
  And in the Lord's appointed way
  Fulfill all righteousness.

3 With joy we in his footsteps tread,
  And would his cause maintain;
  Like him be numbered with the dead,
  And with him rise again.

---

627 C. M. *Tune*, No. 40.

1 AWAKE, ye saints, and raise your
  eyes,
  And raise your voices high:
  Awake, and praise that sovereign
  love
  That shows salvation nigh.

2 On all the wings of time it flies,
  Each moment brings it near;
  Then welcome each declining day,
  Welcome each closing year.

3 Not many years their rounds shall
  run,
  Nor many mornings rise,
  Ere all its glories stand revealed
  To our admiring eyes.

4 Ye wheels of nature, speed your
  course!
  Ye mortal powers, decay!
  Fast as ye bring the gloomy night,
  Ye bring eternal day.

---

628 C. M. *Tune*, No. 41.

1 I LOVE the Lord: he heard my cries,
  And pitied every groan:
  Long as I live, when troubles rise,
  I'll hasten to his throne.

2 I love the Lord: he bowed his ear,
  And chased my grief away;
  O let my heart no more despair,
  While I have breath to pray.

3 The Lord beheld me sore distressed;
  He bade my pains remove:
  Return, my soul, to God, thy rest,
  For thou hast known his love.

---

629 C. M. *Tune*, No. 64.

1 O GOD, our help in ages past,
  Our hope for years to come,
  Our shelter from the stormy blast,
  And our eternal home!

368

2 Under the shadow of thy throne
Still may we dwell secure;
Sufficient is thine arm alone,
And our defense is sure.

3 A thousand ages, in thy sight,
Are like an evening gone;
Short as the watch that ends the
night,
Before the rising sun.

---

630 C. M.   *Tune*, No. 175.

1 No longer far from rest I roam,
And search in vain for bliss;
My soul is satisfied at home;
The Lord my portion is.

2 His person fixes all my love;
His blood removes my fear;
And, while he pleads for me above,
His arm preserves me here.

3 His word of promise is my food;
His spirit is my guide:
Thus daily is my strength renewed,
And all my wants supplied.

4 For him I count as gain each loss;
Disgrace, for him, renown;
Well may I glory in his cross,
While he prepares my crown.

---

631 C. M.   *Tune*, No. 64.

1 Oh! could I find, from day to day,
A nearness to my God,
Then would my hours glide sweet
away,
While leaning on his word.

2 Lord, I desire with thee to live
Anew from day to day,
In joys the world can never give,
Nor ever take away.

3 Blest Jesus, come and rule my heart,
And make me wholly thine,
That I may never more depart,
Nor grieve thy love divine.

---

632 C. M.   *Tune*, No. 121.

1 Lord, in the morning thou shalt
hear
My voice ascending high;
To thee will I direct my prayer,
To thee lift up mine eye —

2 Up to the hills where Christ is **gone**
To plead for all his saints,
Presenting at his Father's throne
Our songs and our complaints.

3 Oh, may thy Spirit guide my feet
In ways of righteousness!
Make every path of duty straight
And plain before my face.

---

633 C. M.   *Tune*, No. 506.

1 I HEARD the voice of Jesus say,
" Come unto me and rest,
Lay down, thou weary one, lay **down**
Thy head upon My breast."

2 I came to Jesus as I was —
Weary, and worn, and sad;
I found in Him a resting-place,
And He has made me glad.

3 I heard the voice of Jesus say,
" Behold I freely give
The living water — thirsty one
Stoop down, and drink, and live."

4 I came to Jesus, and I drank
Of that life-giving stream;
My thirst was quench'd, my **soul**
revived,
And now I live in Him.

5 I heard the voice of Jesus say,
" I am this dark world's light,
Look unto Me, thy morn shall **rise**,
And all thy day be bright."

6 I look'd to Jesus, and I found
In Him my Star, my Sun;
And in that light of life I'll walk
Till trav'ling days are done.

---

634 C. M.   *Tune*, No. 26.

1 My soul shall praise thee, O my **God**,
Through all my mortal days,
And in eternity prolong
Thy vast, thy boundless **praise**.

2 When anxious grief and gloomy care
Afflict my throbbing breast,
My tongue shall learn to speak thy
praise,
And lull each pain to rest.

3 Nor shall my tongue alone proclaim
The honors of my God;
My life with all its active powers,
Shall spread thy praise abroad

635 C. M. *Tune, No. 506.*

1 Now from the altar of our hearts
Let warmest thanks arise:
Assist us, Lord, to offer up
Our evening sacrifice.

2 This day God was our sun and shield,
Our keeper and our guide;
His care was on our weakness shown,
His mercies multiplied.

3 Minutes and mercies multiplied,
Have made up all this day;
Minutes came quick, but mercies were
More swift and free than they.

4 New time, new favors, and new joys,
Do a new song require:
Till we shall praise thee as we would,
Accept our hearts' desire.

---

636 C. M. *Tune, No. 28.*

1 Jesus, my Lord, how rich thy grace,
Thy bounties how complete!
How shall I count the matchless sum,
How pay the mighty debt?

2 High on a throne of radiant light
Dost thou exalted shine:
What can my poverty bestow,
When all the worlds are thine?

3 But thou hast brethren here below,
The partners of thy grace,
And wilt confess their humble names
Before thy Father's face.

4 In them thou mayst be clothed and fed,
And visited and cheered;
And in their accents of distress
My Saviour's voice is heard.

---

637 C. M. *Tune, No. 32.*

1 She loved her Saviour, and to him
Her costliest present brought;
To crown his head, or grace his name,
No gift too rare she thought.

2 So let the Saviour be adored,
And not the poor despised;
Give to the hungry from your hoard,
But all, give all to Christ.

3 Go, clothe the naked, lead the blind,
Give to the weary rest;
For sorrow's children comfort find,
And help for all distressed:

4 But give to Christ alone thy heart,
Thy faith, thy love supreme;
Then for his sake thine alms impart,
And so give all to him.

---

638 C. M. *Tune, No. 32.*

1 Lord, lead the way the Saviour went,
By lane and cell obscure,
And let love's treasures still be spent
Like his, upon the poor.

2 Like him, through scenes of deep distress,
Who bore the world's sad weight,
We, in their crowded loneliness,
Would seek the desolate.

3 For thou hast placed us side by side
In this wide world of ill;
And that thy followers may be tried,
The poor are with us still.

4 Mean are all offerings we can make;
Yet thou hast taught us, Lord,
If given for the Saviour's sake,
They lose not their reward.

---

639 C. M. *Tune, No. 121.*

1 Grant me within thy courts a place,
Among thy saints a seat,
Forever to behold thy face,
And worship at thy feet;—

2 In thy pavilion to abide,
When storms of trouble blow,
And in thy tabernacle hide,
Secure from every foe.

3 "Seek ye my face!" Without delay,
When thus I hear thee speak,
My heart would leap for joy, and say,
"Thy face, Lord, will I seek."

4 Then leave me not when griefs assail,
And earthly comforts flee;
When father, mother, kindred fall,
My God, remember me!

640 C. M. *Tune*, No. 64.

1 WORKMAN of God! O lose not heart,
But learn what God is like;
And in the darkest battle-field
Thou shalt know where to strike.

2 Thrice blest is he to whom is given
The instinct that can tell
That God is on the field, when he
Is most invisible.

3 Blest too is he who can divine
Where real right doth lie,
And dares to take the side that seems
Wrong to man's blindfold eye.

4 Then learn to scorn the praise of
men,
And learn to lose with God;
For Jesus won the world through
shame,
And beckons thee his road.

641 C. M. *Tune*, No. 32.

1 THE Saviour! O what endless charms
Dwell in that blissful sound!
Its influence every fear disarms,
And spreads delight around.

2 Here pardon, life, and joy divine
In rich effusion flow,
For guilty rebels, lost in sin,
Who to destruction go.

3 The almighty Former of the skies
Stoops to our vile abode;
While angels view with wondering
eyes,
And hail the incarnate God.

4 How rich the depths of love divine,
Of bliss a boundless store!
Redeemer, let me call thee mine,
Thy fullness I implore.

642 C. M. *Tune*, No. 176.

1 I LOVE to meet where Christians do,
Who meet for prayer and praise,
To speak of God's rich grace to them,
And of his works and ways.

2 I love to hear the Christian tell
Of hope beyond the grave;
And, too, to hear him oft express
His faith in Christ to save.

3 I love to hear the voice of praise
Ascending to His throne,
And fervent prayer in faith go up; —
It brings the blessing down.

643 C. M. *Tune*, No. 64.

1 'TIS faith that purifies the heart;
'Tis faith that works by love;
It bids all sinful joys depart,
And lifts the thoughts above.

2 This faith shall every fear control
By its celestial power;
With holy triumph fill the soul,
In death's approaching hour.

3 By faith, where'er His hand shall
lead,
The darkest path we'll tread;
In faith we'll leave these living
scenes,
And mingle with the dead.

644 C. M. *Tune*, No. 40.

1 O LET triumphant faith dispel
Our fear and guilt and woe;
If God be for us, God the Lord,
Who, who shall be our foe?

2 He who his only Son gave up
To death, that we might live;
Shall he not all things freely grant
That boundless love can give?

3 Who now his people shall accuse?
'Tis God hath justified;
Who now his people shall condemn?
The Lamb of God hath died.

4 And he who died hath ris'n again,
Triumphant from the grave;
At God's right hand for us he pleads,
Omnipotent to save.

645 C. M. *Tune*, No. 121.

1 O 'TIS delight without alloy,
Jesus, to hear thy name:
My spirit leaps with inward joy;
I feel the sacred flame.

2 My passions hold a pleasing reign,
When love inspires my breast, —
Love, the divinest of the train,
The sovereign of the rest.

646 11s & 8s.

Tune. " WAITING AND WATCHING FOR ME."

1 O JESUS, we're longing thy face to
    behold,
  To see thee descend from above;
  To walk that fair city with streets of
    pure gold,
  And enter the Eden of love.
  Though trouble and trials encompass
    us here,
  We soon from all these shall be
    free :
  ‖Dear Jesus, our Saviour, O quickly
    appear,
  We're waiting and watching for
    thee :‖
      We're waiting, etc.

2 Here pilgrims and strangers we tread
    the lone way,
  And sigh for that long-looked-for
    home ;
  When in those blest mansions, there
    ever we'll stay,
  And nevermore, nevermore roam.
  And then with the ransomed and
    glorified there,
  The face of our Lord we shall see :
  ‖Dear Jesus, our Saviour, O quickly
    appear,
  We're waiting and watching for
    thee :‖
      We're waiting, etc.

3 O Jesus, thy people are weary and
    sad
  That thou should'st so long be
    away ;
  O hasten, dear Saviour, and make
    our hearts glad ;
  We long for the dawn of that day !
  And many are sleeping in death's
    cold embrace,
  And waiting thy glory to see ;
  ‖Dear Jesus, our Saviour, O quickly
    appear,
  We're waiting and watching for
    thee :‖
      We're waiting, etc.
          J. E. Hudson.

---

647 7s & 6s. *Tune, No.* 253.

1 STAND up ! stand up for Jesus !
  Ye soldiers of the cross ;
  Lift high his royal banner,
  It must not suffer loss ;

From victory unto victory
  His army shall be led,
Till every foe is vanquished,
  And Christ is Lord indeed.

2 Stand up ! stand up for Jesus,
  The trumpet-call obey :
Forth to the mighty conflict,
  In this his glorious day ;
Ye that are men ! now serve him,
  Against unnumbered foes ;
Your courage rise with danger,
  And strength to strength oppose.

3 Stand up ! stand up for Jesus !
  Stand in his strength alone ;
The arm of flesh will fail you —
  Ye dare not trust your own.
Put on the gospel armor,
  And, watching unto prayer,
Where duty calls or danger,
  Be never wanting there.

4 Stand up ! stand up for Jesus !
  The strife will not be long ;
This day the noise of battle,
  The next the victor's song ;
To him that overcometh,
  A crown of life shall be ;
He, with the King of glory,
  Shall reign eternally.

---

648 7s. *Tune, No.* 274.

1 MAKE us of one heart and mind,
Courteous, pitiful, and kind,
Lowly, meek in thought and word,
Altogether like our Lord.

2 Let us for each other care,
Each the other's burden bear ;
To thy Church the pattern give,
Show how true believers live.

3 Free from anger and from pride,
Let us thus in God abide ;
All the depths of love express,
All the heights of holiness.

---

649 8s. *Tune, No.* 244.

1 THE church in her militant state
  Is weary, and cannot forbear ;
The saints with desire still wait,
  To see him again in the air.
The Spirit invites, in the bride,
  Her heavenly Lord to descend ;
And place her, enthroned at his side,
  In glory that never shall end.

2 The news of his coming I hear,
  And gladly I join in the cry;
  O Jesus, in triumph appear!
  Appear in the clouds of the sky.
  Come. Lord, to the bride of thy love,
  In fulness of majesty come;
  And bring me the mansion above,
  Prepared for my heavenly home.

650 7s. *Tune, No. 196.*

1 COMING Saviour, now in faith,
  We remember still thy death;
  Thou wast broken — thou hast died;
  For us thou wast crucified.

2 While in faith we drink the wine,
  Of thy blood we see the sign;
  Wash us pure from every stain,
  Thou that comest soon to reign.

3 Lord, we thus remember thee,
  But we long thy face to see —
  Long to reach our heavenly home;
  Come. Lord Jesus, quickly come!

4 Quickly. thou thyself wilt come;
  Thou wilt raise us to thy throne,
  And thy glories here display
  Through a never-ending day.

651 8s & 7s. *Tune, No. 102.*

1 FAR from mortal cares retreating,
  Sordid hopes and vain desires,
  Here, our willing footsteps meeting,
  Every heart to Heaven aspires.
  From the fount of glory beaming,
  Light celestial cheers our eyes,
  Mercy from above proclaiming
  Peace and pardon from the skies.

2 Who may share this great salvation?
  Every pure and humble mind,
  Every kindred. tongue, and nation,
  From the stains of guilt refined.
  Blessings all around bestowing,
  God withholds his care from none,
  Grace and mercy ever flowing
  From the fountain of his throne,

652 7s. *Tune, No. 101.*

1 HEARTS of stone, relent, relent,
  Break, by Jesus' cross subdued;
  See his body, mangled, rent,
  Cover'd with a gore of blood;
  Sinful soul, what hast thou done?
  Murdered God's beloved Son.

2 Yes, our sins have done the deed,
  Drove the nails that fix'd him there;
  Crown'd with thorns his sacred head,
  Pierced him with a soldier's spear;
  Made his soul a sacrifice,—
  For a sinful world he dies.

3 Will you let him die in vain?
  Still to death pursue your Lord?
  Open tear his wounds again,
  Trample on his precious blood?
  No! with all my sins I'll part,
  Saviour, take my broken heart.

653 7s & 8s. *Tune, No. 101.*

1 WHEN this passing world is done,
  When has sunk you glaring sun,
  When we stand with Christ at last,
  Looking o'er life's journey past,
  Then, Lord, shall I fully know,
  Not till then, how much I owe.

2 When I stand before the throne,
  Dressed in beauty not my own;
  When I see thee as thou art,
  Love thee with un-sinning heart;
  Then, Lord, shall I fully know,
  Not till then, how much I owe.

3 When the praise of heaven I hear,
  Loud as thunders to the ear,
  Loud as many waters' noise,
  Sweet as harp's melodious voice;
  Then, Lord, shall I fully know,
  Not till then, how much I owe.

654 7s. *Tune, No. 177.*

1 HOLY Bible, Book divine;
  Precious treasure! thou art mine:
  Mine to tell me whence I came;
  Mine to teach me what I am:

2 Mine to chide me when I rove;
  Mine to show a Saviour's love:
  Mine art thou to guide my feet;
  Mine to judge, condemn, acquit:

3 Mine to comfort in distress,
  If the Holy Spirit bless:
  Mine to show, by living faith,
  Man can triumph over death!

373

655 6s & 4s. *Tune, No. 113.*

1 Trusting, my God, in Thee,
  Trusting in Thee,
  From every stain of sin,
  Thou cleansest me —
  Glory! my soul is free!
  Trusting, my God, in Thee,
  From every stain of sin,
  Thou cleansest me.

2 Resting, my God, in Thee,
  Resting in Thee,
  From every doubt and fear,
  Thou keepest me —
  Glory! my soul is free!
  Resting, my God, in Thee,
  From every doubt and fear,
  Thou keepest me.

3 Dwelling, my God, in Thee,
  Dwelling in Thee,
  From foes without, within,
  Thou guardest me.
  Glory! my soul is free!
  Dwelling, my God, in Thee,
  From foes without, within,
  Thou guardest me.

4 Rising, my God, in Thee,
  Rising in Thee,
  From scenes that grieve me now,
  Thou takest me —
  Glory! my soul is free!
  Rising, my God, in Thee,
  From scenes that grieve me now,
  Thou takest me.

656 8s & 7s. *Tune, No. 106.*

1 Thou hast said, exalted Jesus,
  " Take thy cross and follow me; "
  And I'll take it, I will take it
  And rejoicing, follow thee.
  I will follow, I will follow,
  Yes, my Lord, I'll follow thee.

2 While this liquid tomb surveying,
  Emblem of my Saviour's grave,
  Shall I shun its brink, betraying
  Feelings worthy of a slave?
  No! I'll enter; no, I'll enter,
  Jesus entered Jordan's wave.

3 Blest the sign which thus reminds me,
  Saviour, of thy love for me;
  But more blest the love that binds me
  In its deathless bonds to thee;
  O what pleasure, O what pleasure,
  Buried with my Lord to be!

4 Should it rend some fond connection,
  Should I suffer shame or loss,
  Yet the fragrant, blest reflection,
  I have been where Jesus was,
  Will revive me, will revive me,
  When I faint beneath the cross.

5 Fellowship with him possessing,
  Let me die to earth and sin;
  Let me rise t' enjoy the blessing
  Which the faithful soul shall win,
  May I ever, may I ever,
  Follow where my Lord has been.

657 7s. *Tune, No. 308.*

1 Never further than Thy cross:
  Never higher than thy feet:
  Here earth's precious things seem
    dross:
  Here earth's bitter things grow
    sweet.

2 Here we learn to serve and give,
  And, rejoicing, self deny;
  Here we gather love to live,
  Here we gather faith to die.

3 Till amid the hosts of light,
  We in thee redeemed, complete,
  Through thy cross made pure and
    white,
  Cast our crowns before thy feet.

658 7s. *Tune, No. 219.*

1 Watchman, tell us of the night,
  What its signs of promise are.
  Traveler, o'er yon mountain height,
  See that glory-beaming star!
  Watchman, does its beauteous ray,
  Aught of hope or joy foretell?
  Traveler, yes; it brings the day,
  Promised day of Israel.

2 Watchman, tell us of the night:
  Higher yet that star ascends.
  Traveler, blessedness and light,
  Peace and truth, its course por-
    tends!
  Watchman, will its beams alone
  Gild the spot that gave them birth?
  Traveler, ages are its own,
  See, it bursts o'er all the earth!

3 Watchman, tell us of the night,
  For the morning seems to dawn.
  Traveler, darkness takes its flight;
  Doubt and terror are withdrawn.

Watchman, let thy wandering cease;
Hie thee to thy quiet home!
Traveler, lo! the Prince of peace,
Lo! the Son of God is come!

---

659   7s & 8s.

1 WHAT subdued and conquered me?
"Nothing but the blood of Jesus;"
What first set my spirit free?
"Nothing but the blood of Jesus."

CHORUS: —
"O precious is the flow
That makes me white as snow;
No other fount I know,
Nothing but the blood of Jesus."

2 What now sanctifies my soul?
"Nothing but the blood of Jesus;"
What now makes my spirit whole?
"Nothing but the blood of Jesus."

3 What now saves me from all sin?
"Nothing but the blood of Jesus;"
What now keeps me pure within?
"Nothing but the blood of Jesus."

4 What gives vict'ry day by day?
"Nothing but the blood of Jesus;"
What gives joy throughout life's way?
"Nothing but the blood of Jesus."

5 What takes me through every snare?
"Nothing but the blood of Jesus;"
What takes out the sting of care?
"Nothing but the blood of Jesus."

6 What brings help in daily toil?
"Nothing but the blood of Jesus;"
What brings peace in life's turmoil?
"Nothing but the blood of Jesus."

---

660   7s.

1 HERE we meet, and here we part;
This we're doing all the way:
Hand to hand, and heart with heart,
And the few words that we say;
Then we go, and tears must come,
Tears we hardly wipe away,
Wand'ring to a distant home,
Or as pilgrims still to stray.

2 By and by this will be o'er,
When immortal there we stand,
Tears and partings nevermore.
When we reach that better land.

There the beautiful will be;
It will be a sinless band;
It is Jesus we shall see;
There with Jesus we shall stand.

3 Love of Jesus! O how strong!
How it binds our hearts in one,
As we join in prayer and song,
Telling what the Lord has done —
And the joy it bringeth here!
Joy which only they can know
Who to Jesus come so near,
And with Jesus onward go.

---

661   8s & 7s.

1 "CALL them in," — the poor, the wretched,
Sin-stained wand'rers from the fold;
Peace and pardon freely offer;
Can you weigh their worth with gold?
"Call them in" — the weak, the weary,
Laden with the doom of sin;
Bid them come and rest in Jesus;
He is waiting — "call them in."

2 "Call them in" — the Jew, the Gentile;
Bid the stranger to the feast;
"Call them in" — the rich, the noble,
From the highest to the least;
Forth the Father runs to meet them,
He hath all their sorrows seen;
Robe, and ring, and royal sandals
Wait the lost ones — "call them in."

3 "Call them in" — the mere professors,
Slumbering, sleeping on death's brink:
Nought of life are they possessors,
Yet of safety vainly think;
Bring them in — the careless scoffers,
Pleasure-seekers of the earth;
Tell of God's most gracious offers,
And of Jesus' priceless worth.

4 "Call them in" — the broken-hearted,
Cowering 'neath the brand of shame;
Speak Love's message, low and tender,
'Twas for sinners Jesus came:
See, the shadows lengthen round us,
Soon the day-dawn will begin;
Can you leave them lost and lonely?
Christ is coming — "call them in."

662   7s & 8s.

1 KNOCKING, knocking, who is there?
   Waiting, waiting, oh, how fair!
   'Tis a pilgrim, strange and kingly,
   Never such was seen before.
   Ah! my soul, for such a wonder,
   Wilt thou not undo the door?

2 Knocking, knocking, still He's there,
   Waiting, waiting, wondrous fair;
   But the door is hard to open,
   For the weeds and ivy-vine,
   With their dark and clinging tendrils,
   Ever round the hinges twine.

3 Knocking, knocking — what, still
      there?
   Waiting, waiting, grand and fair;
   Yes, the pierced hand still knocketh,
   And beneath the crowned hair
   Beam the patient eyes, so tender,
   Of thy Saviour, waiting there.

---

663   7s.

1 SIMPLY trusting every day,
   Trusting through a stormy way;
   Even when my faith is small,
   Trusting Jesus, that is all.

   CHORUS : —
      Trusting as the moments fly,
      Trusting as the days go by,
      Trusting Him whate'er befall,
      Trusting Jesus, that is all.

2 Brightly doth His Spirit shine
   Into this poor heart of mine;
   While He leads I cannot fall,
   Trusting Jesus, that is all.

3 Singing, if my way is clear;
   Praying, if the path is drear;
   If in danger, for Him call;
   Trusting Jesus, that is all.

4 Trusting Him while life shall last,
   Trusting Him till earth is past;
   Till within the jasper wall,
   Trusting Jesus, that is all.

---

664   7s & 8s.

1 On, to be nothing, nothing:
   Only to lie at His feet
   An empty and earthen vessel,
   For the Master's use made meet.

Empty that He might fill me
   As forth to His service I go;
Earthen, that all the glory
   To Him alone might flow.

   CHORUS : —
      Oh, to be nothing, nothing;
      Only to lie at His feet,
      An empty and earthen vessel,
      For the Master's use made
         meet.

2 Oh, to be nothing, nothing,
   Only as led by His hand;
   A messenger at His gateway,
   But waiting for His command;
   Only an instrument ready
   His praises to sound at His will,
   Willing, should He not require me,
   In silence to wait on Him still.

3 Oh, to be nothing, nothing;
   Painful the humbling may be;
   Yet low in the dust I'd lay me
   That the world might my Saviour
      see,
   Rather be nothing, nothing, —
   To Him let their voices be raised:
   He is the fountain of blessing,
   He only is most to be praised.

---

665   6s & 5s.

1 Go bury thy sorrow,
   The world has its share;
   Go bury it deeply,
   Go hide it with care;
   Go think of it calmly,
   When curtained by night,
   Go tell it to Jesus,
   And all will be right.

2 Go tell it to Jesus,
   He knoweth thy grief;
   Go tell it to Jesus,
   He'll send thee relief;
   Go gather the sunshine
   He sheds on the way;
   He'll lighten thy burden,
   Go, weary one, pray.

3 Hearts growing a-weary
   With heavier woe,
   Now droop 'mid the darkness —
   Go comfort them, go:
   Go bury thy sorrows,
   Let others be blest;
   Go give them the sunshine —
   Tell Jesus the rest.

666
11s.

1 To the hall of the feast came the
  sinful and fair;
She heard in the city that Jesus was
  there;
Unheeding the splendor that blazed
  on the board,
‖ : She silently knelt at the feet of the
  Lord. : ‖

2 The frown and the murmur went
  round through them all,
That one so unhallowed should tread
  in that hall;
And some said the poor would be
  objects more meet,
‖ : As the wealth of her perfume she
  shower'd on His feet. : ‖

3 She heard but the Saviour, she spoke
  but with sighs;
She dare not look up to the heaven
  of His eyes;
And the hot tears gushed forth at
  each heave of her breast,
‖ : As her lips to His sandals were
  throbbingly pressed. . ‖

4 In the sky, after tempest, as shineth
  the bow, —
In the glance of the sunbeam, as
  melteth the snow,
He looked on that lost one : "her
  sins were forgiven."
‖ : And the sinner went forth in the
  beauty of heaven. : ‖

667
8s & 7s.

1 THERE is a gate stands open wide,
  And through its portals gleaming
A radiance from the crimson tide
  That from the cross is streaming.

REF.—Oh, depth of mercy! can it be
  That gate was opened wide for me?
  For me, for me?
  Was opened wide for me?

2 That gate stands open wide for all
  Who seek through it salvation;
The rich and poor, the great and
  small,
  Of every tribe and nation.

3 Press onward, then, though foes may
  frown,
  While mercy's gate is open;
Accept the cross, and win the crown,
  Love's everlasting token.

4 Beyond the cross of Calvary,
  Beyond the one we're bearing,
There is the crown for you and me,
  His love and mercy sharing.

668
C. P. M.   *Tune*, No. 124.

1 LET all on earth their voices raise,
To sing the great Jehovah's praise,
  And bless his holy name:
His glory let the heathen know,
His wonders to the nations show,
  His saving grace proclaim.

2 He framed the globe; He built the
  sky;
He made the shining worlds on high,
  And reigns in glory there:
His beams are majesty and light;
His beauties, how divinely bright!
  His dwelling-place, how fair!

3 Come the great day, the glorious
  hour,
When earth shall feel His mighty
  power,
  All nations fear His name:
Then shall the race of men confess
His justice and His holiness;
  His saints His grace proclaim.

669
P. M.   *Tune*, No. 244.

1 AWAY with our sorrow and fear,
  We soon shall recover our home;
The city of saints shall appear,
  The day of eternity come.
From earth we shall quickly remove,
  And mount to our happy abode,
The city that comes from above,
  The palace of angels and God.

2 By faith we already behold
  That lovely Jerusalem here:
Her walls are of jasper and gold,
  As crystal her buildings are clear;
Immovably founded in grace,
  She stands as she ever hath stood,
And brightly her Builder displays,
  And flames with the glory of God.

3 No need of the sun in that day
  Which never is followed by night,
Where Jesus' mild beauties display
  A pure and a permanent light:
The Lamb is their light and their sun,
  And lo! by reflection they shine;
With Jesus ineffably one,
  And bright in effulgence divine.

670   7s.   *Tune*, No. 515.

1 "TILL *He come!*"—Oh, let the words
  Linger on the trembling chords
  Let the "little while" between
  In their golden light be seen;
  Let us think, how rest and home
  Lie beyond that " *Till He come.*"

2 When the weary ones we love
  To the silent grave remove,
  When their words of love and cheer
  Fall no longer on our ear,
  Hush! be every murmur dumb,
  It is only " *Till He come!*"

3 Clouds and darkness round us press;
  Would we have one sorrow less?
  All the sharpness of the cross,
  All that tells the world is loss,
  Death, and darkness, and the tomb,
  Pain us only " *Till He come!*"

4 See the feast of love is spread;
  Drink the wine, and eat the bread;
  Sweet memorials, till the Lord
  Call us round His heavenly board,
  Scattered now, and far from home,
  Severed only " *Till He come!*"

671   9s & 6s.   *Tune*, No. 289.

1 By faith I view my Saviour dying,
    On the tree, On the tree;
  To every nation He is crying,
    Look to me, Look to me;
  He bids the guilty now draw near,
  Repent, believe, dismiss their fear;
  Hark, hark, what precious words I
    hear,
      Mercy's free, Mercy's free.

2 Did Christ, when I was sin pursuing,
    Pity me, Pity me?
  And did He snatch my soul from ruin?
    Can it be, Can it be?
  Oh, yes! He did salvation bring;
  He is my Prophet, Priest and King;
  And now my happy soul can sing,
      Mercy's free, Mercy's free.

3 Jesus my weary soul refreshes;
    Mercy's free, Mercy's free.
  And every moment Christ is precious
    Unto me, Unto me.
  None can describe the bliss I prove,
  While through this wilderness I rove;
  All may enjoy the Saviour's love,
      Mercy's free, Mercy's free.

4 Long as I live, I'll still be crying,
    Mercy's free, Mercy's free.
  And this shall be my theme when
    dying,
    Mercy's free, Mercy's free.
  And when the vale of death I've
    passed,
  When I'm beyond the stormy blast,
  I'll sing, while endless ages last,
      Mercy's free, Mercy's free.

672   9s.
By permission of O. DITSON & Co.

1 THERE'S a land that is fairer than day,
    And no sorrow or death will be
      there;
  And the Father who loveth, they say,
    Will prepare us a home over there.

CHORUS :—
  In the sweet by-and-by,
  We shall meet on that beautiful shore,
  In the sweet by-and-by,
  We shall meet on that beautiful shore.

2 We shall sing on that beautiful shore,
    The melodious songs of the blest;
  We shall labor and sorrow no more,
    Nor again seek the blessing of rest.

3 To our bountiful Father above
    We will offer our tribute of praise,
  For the glorious gift of His love,
    And the blessings that hallow our
      days.

673   8s & 7s.

1 SWEET and precious is the promise,
    God has giv'n each passer by,
  On the way to rest and glory,
    " I will guide thee with mine eye."

REFRAIN :—
    I will guide thee, I will guide thee,
    I will guide thee with mine eye;
    On the way to rest and glory,
    I will guide, thee with mine eye.

2 In thy trouble, care and sorrow,
    And when hope is near to die;
  Let this promise keep thee steadfast,
    " I will guide thee with mine eye."
      Ref. — I will guide thee, &c.

3 When the tempter comes to 'lure thee
    From the way, and foes are nigh,
  Let this promise then assure thee,
    " I will guide thee with mine eye."
      Ref. — I will guide thee, &c.

4 When thy last fond hope is numbered,
  And thy present comforts fly,
  Let this promise be remembered,
  "I will guide thee with mine eye."
    Ref.—I will guide thee, &c.

5 When through deeper shades and
    darkness,
  Onward still thy path may lie,
  Hear Him say, "I will be with thee,"
  "I will guide thee with mine eye."
    Ref.—I will guide thee, &c.

674   8s.

1 My hope is built on nothing less,
  Than Jesus' blood and righteousness;
  I dare not trust the sweetest frame,
  But wholly lean on Jesus' name.

    CHORUS:—
      On Christ, the solid rock, I stand:
      All other ground is sinking sand,
      All other ground is sinking sand.

2 When darkness veils His lovely face,
  I rest on His unchanging grace;
  In every high and stormy gale,
  My anchor holds within the vail.

3 His oath, His covenant, His blood,
  Support me in the whelming flood:
  When all around my soul gives way,
  He then is all my hope and stay.

4 When He shall come with trumpet
    sound,
  O, may I then in Him be found:
  Drest in His righteousness alone,
  Faultless to stand before the throne!

675   8s & 7s.

1 Shall we gather at the river
    Where bright angel feet have trod?
  With its crystal tide forever
  Flowing by the throne of God?

    CHORUS.—
      Yes, we'll gather at the river,
      The beautiful, the beautiful river;
      Gather with the saints at the river
      That flows by the throne of God.

2 On the margin of the river,
    Washing up its silver spray,
  We will walk and worship ever,
  All the happy, golden day,

3 Ere we reach the shining river,
    Lay we every burden down:
  Grace our humble hearts deliver,
  And provide a robe and crown.

4 At the smiling of the river,
    Mirror of the Saviour's face,
  Saints, whom death will never sever,
  Lift their songs of saving grace.

5 Soon we'll reach the silver river,
    Soon our pilgrimage will cease,
  Soon our happy hearts will quiver
  With the melody of peace.

676   P. M.

1 Christian, the morn breaks sweetly
    o'er thee,
  And all the midnight shadows flee,
  Tinged are the distant skies with
    glory,
  A beacon light hangs out for thee.
  Arise, arise, the light breaks o'er
    thee,
  Thy name is graven on the throne,
  Thy home is in that world of glory
  Where thy Redeemer reigns alone.

2 Tossed on time's rude, relentless
    surges,
    Calmly composed and dauntless
    stand;
  For lo, beyond these scenes emerges
    The heights that bound the prom-
    ised land.
  Christian, behold, the land is near-
    ing,
    Where the wild sea-storm's rage is
    o'er:
  Hark, how the heavenly hosts are
    cheering!
    See in what throngs they range
    the shore.

3 Cheer up, cheer up, the day breaks
    o'er thee,
    Bright as the summer's noon-tide
    ray;
  The star-gemmed crowns and realms
    of glory
  Invite thy happy soul away.
  Away, away, leave all for glory,
  Thy name is graven on the throne;
  Thy home is in that world of glory
  Where thy Redeemer reigns alone.
    Rev. JOSEPH RUSLING, 1832.

677   10s.

1 I am so glad that our Father in heaven
  Tells of his love in the Book he has
    given.
  Wonderful things in the Bible I see:
  This is the dearest that Jesus loves
    me.

CHORUS : —
I am so glad that Jesus loves me,
Jesus loves me, Jesus loves me,
I am so glad that Jesus loves me,
Jesus loves even me.

2 Though I forget Him, and wander away,
Then he doth seek me wherever I stray;
Back to his dear loving arms would I flee,
When I remember that Jesus loves me.

3 Oh, if there's only one song I can sing,
When in His beauty I see the great King.
This shall my song in eternity be,
"Oh, what a wonder that Jesus loved me."

---

678   11s & 10s.

1 DARK is the night, and fierce the winds are blowing,
Nearer and nearer comes the breaker's roar:
Where shall I go, or whither fly for refuge?
Hide me, my Saviour, till the storm is o'er.

CHORUS : —
With his loving hand to guide, let the clouds above me roll,
And the billows in their fury dash around me;
I can brave the wildest storm, with his glory in my soul,
I can sing amid the tempest —
Praise the Lord!

2 Dark is the night, but cheering is the promise;
He will go with me o'er the troubled wave:
Safe he will lead me through the pathless waters.
Jesus, the mighty One, and strong to save.

3 Dark is the night, but lo! the day is breaking.
Onward my bark, unfurl thy every sail;
Now at the helm I see my Father standing,
Soon will my anchor drop within the vail.

---

679   7s.

1 TRUSTING Jesus, day by day,
Trusting Him through all the way;
Even though my faith be small,
Trusting Jesus, All-in-All.

CHO. — Trusting as the moments fly,
Trusting as the days go by;
Trusting Him whate'er befall,
Trusting Jesus, All-in-All.

2 Brightly doth the Spirit shine
Into this poor heart of mine;
While He leads I cannot fall,
Trusting Jesus, All-in-All.

3 Singing if my way be clear;
Praying if the path be drear;
If in danger, for Him call:
Trusting Jesus, All-in-All.

4 Trusting Him until that day,
Trusting Him till He shall say,
" Come within the jasper wall " —
Trusting Jesus, All-in-All.

---

680   P. M.

1 THE Lord and Saviour will appear;
He now is near. He now is near;
O sinner list! the warning hear —
What will you do in that day?
CHO. — Turn, turn sinner,
O turn, sinner;
Turn, turn sinner,
What will you do in that day?

2 No longer now go on in sin —
The day of God will soon begin;
When all the saved shall enter in:
What will you do in that day?

3 When you shall see the Judge's face,
O where will be your hiding place?
Without his pard'ning love and grace,
What will you do in that day?

4 When the great trumpet's voice is heard,
When all the world is by it stirred,
And there is then no pardoning word,
What will you do in that day?

5 And when before the throne you stand,
When you shall hear that last command,
Spoken to you, on the left hand,
What will you do in that day?

INDEX TO HYMNS AND TUNES.

The TUNES *in this Index are indicated by a star.*

381

No. of Hymn.		No. of Hymn.	
I'm a lonely traveler here	139, 267	Jesus my Lord how rich	636
I'm a Traveler*	267	Jesus My Shelter*	426
I'm a Pilgrim*	425	Jesus our hope our life our heaven	19
I'm going Home*	347	Jesus our strength and	18
I'm Nearing the Gates*	342	Jesus Paid It All*	4
I'm not ashamed to own my Lord	55	Jesus refuge of my soul	177, 219
I'm Redeemed by His Blood*	257	Jesus Saves Me All the Time*	181
In every trying hour	222, 292	Jesus saves me every day	181
In expectation sweet	12	Jesus Saviour pilot me	562
In God We Trust*	144	Jesus Saviour great Example	441
In memory of the Saviour's love	483	Jesus Soon Is Coming*	545
I often heard a pleading voice	262	Jesus sought me	306
I once was a stranger to grace	374	Jesus Spoke Peace to My Soul*	460
I Own I'm Base*	399	Jesus the name high over all	428
In some way or other	536	Jesus thy blood and righteousness	16
In that beautiful home over there	86	Jesus thy church with longing	375
In the Christian's home in glory	94	Jesus the Life the Truth the Way	475
In the cross of Christ I glory	563	Jesus the sinner's friend	479
In the dark and gloomy day	270	Jesus thy blood	166
In the midst of temptations and	482	Jesus thy church	159, 375
In the Strength of Grace*	254	Jesus was the Lamb of God	248
In the Sweet By and By*	567	Jesus we look to thee	620
Into thy store-house O Lord	211	Jesus while our hearts are	301
Invitation*	364	Joy and Rest*	235
I saw a lonely traveler	521	Joy In Heaven*	525
I see the land of corn and wine	23	Just as I am without one	126, 478
I see them on the fair green	493		
I Shall Be Satisfied*	69	KEEP your lamps burning	312
I Shall Meet Thee*	30	Kings and thrones to God belong	129
Is Your Lamp Burning*	469	Knocking at the Door*	330
It is I, Be Not Afraid*	266	Knocking, knocking	662
I've Been Redeemed*	207		
I've found the pearl of greatest	29	LABAN*	221
I want a principle within	624	Lake Enon*	394
I was a wandering sheep	611	Lamb of Calvary	481
I Will Arise*	213	Land ahead its fruits are waving	408
I Will Believe*	41	Land of Pleasure*	358
I Will Guide Thee With Mine Eye*	307	Land of Rest*	223
I Will Never Leave Thee*	389	Lenox*	8
I will sing for Jesus	174	Let all on earth	668
I will sing you a song of that	524	Let all that wait the coming King	590
I will watch and wait for the	278	Let every creature join	489
I would toil in the field	220	Let every mortal ear attend	622
		Let Her Rest*	78
JEHOVAH reigns exalted high	227	Let Him Come In*	356
Jehovah reigns he dwells	595	Let Me Go*	519
Jerusalem our heavenly home	297	Let Us Praise Him*	272
Jesus and shall it ever be	497	Let us rejoice In Christ the Lord	62
Jesus at thy command	474	Life's Harvest*	77
Jesus died on Calvary's mountain	180	Life is a span a fleeting hour	504
Jesus Is Coming Again*	162	Lift the voice and sound the	329
Jesus I hear thee knocking	246	Lift your glad voices in	85, 368
Jesus I my cross have taken	136	Lift up the trumpet O loud let it	162
Jesus I love thy charming name	409	Lift up your heads Emmanuel's	286
Jesus is gone above the skies	466	Linger Not*	231
Jesus Is Mine*	198	Little children, come	575
Jesus Is There*	455	Lonely and Weary*	385
Jesus is Waiting to Save You*	445	Long Time Ago*	180
Jesus keep me near the cross	486	Look to Jesus*	212

INDEX TO SUBJECTS.

ADDENDA.

INDEX TO METERS.

INDEX TO METERS.

THE END.

SUPPLEMENT.

1   **Chant.**   TALLIS.

1. Our Father, who art in heaven, hallowed | be | thy | name:
2. Give us this day our .... | dai - - ly | bread;
3. Lead us not into temptation, But de - - | liver us from | evil;

Thy kingdom come, thy will be done on .. | earth, as it | is | in | heaven.
And forgive us our trespasses, as we forgive | those who | trespass a- | gainst us.
For thine is the kingdom, And the power, }
and the .... } glory .. for- | ever .. and | ever.   *A-men.*

---

2   UXBRIDGE. L. M.   (214.)

1 With one consent let all the earth
     To God their cheerful voices raise;
     Glad homage pay, with hallowed mirth,
     And sing before him songs of praise;

2 Assured that he is God alone,
     From whom both we and all proceed;
     We, whom he chooses for his own,
     The flock which he delights to feed.

3 O! enter, then, his temple gate;
     Thence to his courts devoutly press;
     And still your grateful hymns repeat,
     And still his name with praises bless.

4 For he's the Lord, supremely good;
     His mercy is forever sure;
     His truth, which always firmly stood,
     To endless ages shall endure.
                TATE AND BRADY.

---

3   BRIDGEWATER. L. M.   (164.)

1 Praise waits in Zion, Lord, for thee;
     Thy saints adore thy holy name;
     Thy creatures bend th' obedient knee,
     And humbly thy protection claim.

2 Thy hand has raised us from the dust;
     The breath of life thy spirit gave;
     Where, but in thee, can mortals trust?
     Who, but our God, has power to save?

3 Eternal source of truth and light,
     To thee we look, on thee we call;
     Lord, we are nothing in thy sight,
     But thou to us art all in all.

4 Still may thy children in thy word
     Their common trust and refuge see;
     Oh, bind us to each other, Lord,
     By one great tie — the love of thee.
                SIR J. E. SMITH, 1814.

---

4   SESSIONS. L. M.   (473.)

1 O come, loud anthems let us sing,
     Loud thanks to our Almighty King;
     For we our voices high should raise,
     When our salvation's Rock we praise.

2 O let us to his courts repair,
     And bow with adoration there;
     Down on our knees devoutly all
     Before the Lord our Maker fall.
                TATE AND BRADY.

---

5   ST. MARTIN'S. C. M.   (40.)

1 To our Redeemer's glorious name,
     Awake the sacred song.
     O may his love — immortal flame!
     Tune every heart and tongue.

2 His love, what mortal thought can reach,
     What mortal tongue display!
     Imagination's utmost stretch
     In wonder dies away.

3 Dear Lord, while we adoring pay
     Our humble thanks to thee,
     May every heart with rapture say:
     "The Saviour died for me."

4 O may the sweet, the blissful theme,
     Fill every heart and tongue,
     Till strangers love thy charming name,
     And join the sacred song.
                ANNE STEELE, 1760.

6 **Mendon. L. M.**

1. He reigns, the Lord, the Saviour reigns, Praise him in e - van - gel - ic strains;
2. Deep are his counsels and unknown, But grace and truth support his throne;
3. In robes of judgment, lo, he comes! Shakes the wide earth and cleaves the tombs;
4. His en - e - mies, with sore dismay, Fly from the sight, and shun the day;

Let the whole earth in songs re-joice, And distant islands join their voice.
Tho' gloomy clouds his way surround, Jus-tice is their e - ter - nal ground.
Be - fore him burns de-vouring fire, The mountains melt, the seas re - tire.
Then lift your heads, ye saints, on high, And sing, for your redemption's nigh.

WATTS.

7 **DUKE STREET. L. M.** (378.)

1 Awake, my soul, awake, my tongue;
My God demands the grateful song;
Let all my inmost powers record
The wondrous mercy of the Lord.

2 Divinely free his mercy flows,
Forgives my sins, allays my woes,
And bids approaching death remove,
And crowns me with indulgent love.

3 His mercy, with unchanging rays,
Forever shines, while time decays;
And children's children shall record
The truth and goodness of the Lord.

4 While all his works his praise proclaim,
And men and angels bless his name,
Oh, let my heart, my life, my tongue
Attend, and join the blissful song.

ANNE STEELE.

8 **HENDON. 7s.** (308.)

1 Songs of praise the angels sang,
Heaven with hallelujahs rang,
When Jehovah's work begun,
When he spake, and it was done.

2 Songs of praise awoke the morn,
When the Prince of Peace was born:
Songs of praise arose, when he
Captive led captivity.

3 Heaven and earth must pass away;
Songs of praise shall crown that day:
God will make new heavens and earth;
Songs of praise shall hail their birth.

4 And shall man alone be dumb,
Till that glorious kingdom come?
No! the church is called to raise
Psalms and hymns of grateful praise.

(MONTGOMERY.)

9 **AMBOY. 7s.** (456.)

1 Praise to God, immortal praise,
For the love that crowns our days!
Bounteous source of every joy,
Let thy praise our tongues employ!
For the blessings of the field,
For the stores the gardens yield,
For the joy which harvests bring,
Grateful praises now we sing.

2 Flocks that whiten all the plain,
Yellow sheaves of ripened grain;
Clouds that drop their fattening dews,
Suns that temperate warmth diffuse:
All that Spring, with bounteous hand,
Scatters o'er the smiling land,
All that liberal Autumn pours
From her overflowing stores: —

3 These, to that dear Source we owe,
Whence our sweetest comforts flow;
These, through all my happy days,
Claim my cheerful songs of praise.
Lord, to thee my soul should raise
Grateful, never-ending praise;
And, when every blessing's flown,
Love thee for thyself alone.

MRS. ANNA L. BARBAULD, 1773.

10 Bava. L. M.

WATTS.

From the "German Psalter," 1562.

1. My God, ac-cept my ear-ly vows, Like morning incense in thy house;
2. Watch o'er my lips, and guard them, Lord, From ev'ry rash and heedless word;
3. O may the righteous, when I stray, Smite and reprove my wand'ring way!
4. When I behold them press'd with grief, I'll cry to heav'n for their re-lief;

And let my nightly worship rise, Sweet as the evening sac-ri-fice.
Nor let my feet in-cline to tread The guilty path where sin-ners lead.
Their gen-tle words, like ointment shed, Shall never bruise, but cheer my head.
And by my warm pe-ti-tions prove How much I prize their grate-ful love.

11 BAVA. L. M.

1 Saviour of all, to thee we bow,
  And own thee faithful to thy word;
We hear thy voice, and open now
  Our hearts to entertain our Lord.

2 Come in, come in, thou heavenly Guest,
  Delight in what thyself hast given;
On thy own gifts and graces feast,
  And make the contrite heart thy heav'n.

3 Smell the sweet odour of our prayers,
  Our sacrifice of praise approve;
And treasure up our gracious tears,
  Who rest in thy redeeming love.

4 Beneath thy shadow let us sit,
  Call us thy friends, and love, and bride;
And bid us freely drink and eat
  Thy dainties, and be satisfied.
WESLEY.

12 OLD HUNDRED. L. M. (106.)

1 Let all that wait the Coming King,
  Now to his name sweet praises bring;
He cometh quickly! sound it high,
  Till echoes meet the vocal sky.

2 Earth shall depart, and, like a scroll,
  The passing heavens together roll;
For Jesus' faithful words shall be
  Enduring as eternity.

3 Now let thy kingdom come, O Lord,
  As thou hast promised in thy word—
Fill earth with glory like a sea—
  Oh! speak the word, and it shall be.
EMILY C. PEARSON.

13 HAPPY ZION. 8s & 7s. (512.)

Praise the God of all creation,
  Praise the Father's boundless love;
Praise the Lamb, our expiation,
  Priest and King enthroned above.
Praise the Fountain of salvation,
  Him by whom our spirits live;
Undivided adoration
  To the one Jehovah give.
JOSIAH CONDER.

14 TAKE MY HEART. 8s & 7s. (10.)

May the grace of Christ, the Saviour,
  And the Father's boundless love,
With the Holy Spirit's favor,
  Rest upon us from above.
Thus may we abide in union
  With each other and the Lord,
And possess, in sweet communion,
  Joys which earth cannot afford.
JOHN NEWTON.

15 PLEYEL's HYMN. 7s. (196.)

1 Now may he, who from the dead
    Brought the Shepherd of the sheep,
Jesus Christ, our King and Head,
    All our souls in safety keep.

2 May he teach us to fulfil
    What is pleasing in his sight;
Perfect us in all his will,
    And preserve us day and night.
NEWTON.

3

16 MISSIONARY CHANT. L.M. (140.)

1 When, as returns this solemn day,
Man comes to meet his Maker. God,
What rights, what honor shall we pay?
How spread his sovereign name
abroad?

2 From marble domes and gilded spires
Shall curling clouds of incense rise;
And gems, and gold, and garlands deck
The costly pomp of sacrifice?

3 Vain, sinful man! creation's Lord
Thy golden offerings well may spare;
But give thy heart, and thou shalt find
Here dwells a God who heareth
prayer.

4 Oh, grant us in this solemn hour,
From earth and sin's allurements
free,
To feel thy love, to own thy power,
And raise each raptured thought to
thee.   ANNA L. BARBAULD.

17 MIGDOL. L. M. (158.)

1 Again the Lord's own day is here,
The day to Christian people dear,
As, week by week, it bids them tell
How Jesus rose from death and hell.

2 For by his flock their Lord declared
His resurrection should be shared;
And they who trust in him to save
In him are risen from the grave.

3 We, one and all, of him possest
Are with exceeding treasures blest;
Though absent yet his grace we share;
Our every need is yet his care.

4 And therefore unto thee we sing,
O Lord of Peace, Eternal King;
Thy love we praise, thy name adore,
Both on this day and evermore.

18 BROWN. C. M. (176.)

1 This is the day the Lord hath made,
He calls the hours his own;
Let heaven rejoice, let earth be glad,
And praise surround the throne.

2 To-day he rose and left the dead,
And Satan's empire fell;
To-day the saints his triumph spread,
And all his wonders tell.

3 Hosanna to th' anointed King,
To David's holy Son;
Help us, O Lord—descend and bring
Salvation from thy throne.

4 Hosanna in the highest strains
The church on earth can raise;
But in the kingdom, when he reigns
He shall have nobler praise.   WATTS.

19 PETERBORO. C. M. (27.)

1 Again the Lord of life and light
Awakes the kindling ray,
Dispels the darkness of the night,
And pours increasing day.

2 O what a night was that which wrapt
The heathen world in gloom!
O what a sun which broke this day
Triumphant from the tomb!

3 Exalted high at God's right hand,
The Lord of all below;
Thro' him is pardoning love dispensed
And boundless blessings flow.

4 This day be grateful homage paid,
And loud hosannas sung;
Let gladness dwell in every heart,
And praise on every tongue.
          MRS. BARBAULD.

20 DUNDEE. C. M. (175.)

1 And now another week begins,
This day we call the Lord's;
This day he rose, who bore our sins—
For so his word records.

2 Hark, how the angels sweetly sing!—
Their voices fill the sky;
They hail their great victorious King,
And welcome him on high.

3 We 'll catch the note of lofty praise;
May we their rapture feel;
Our thankful songs with their's we 'll
raise
And emulate their zeal.

4 Come, then, ye saints! and grateful sing
Of Christ, our risen Lord—
Of Christ, the everlasting King—
Of Christ, th' incarnate word.
               KELLY.

21 SHIRLAND. S. M. (242.)

1 The work, O Lord, is thine,
And wondrous in our eyes;
This day proclaims it all divine—
This day did Jesus rise.

2 We hail the glorious day
With thankful heart and voice,
Which chased each painful doubt away,
And bade the church rejoice.

3 Since he hath left the grave,
His promises are true;
And each exalted hope he gave,
Confirmed of God we view.

4 That we possess thy word,
Which all this grace displays;
Accept, thou Father of our Lord,
Our sacrifice of praise.   WATTS.

4

GOD.

22 WARD. L. M. (421)

1 Praise, everlasting praise, be paid
To him who earth's foundation laid;
Praise to the God whose strong decrees
Sway the creation as he please.

2 Firm are the words his prophets give,
Sweet words on which his children live;
Each of them is the voice of God,
Who spoke and spread the skies abroad.

3 Oh, for a strong, a lasting faith,
To credit what th' Almighty saith;
T' embrace the message of his Son,
And call the joys of heaven our own.

4 Then should the earth's old pillars
shake,
And all the wheels of nature break;
Our steady souls shall fear no more
Than solid rocks when billows roar.
WATTS.

23 WOODWORTH. L. M. (49.)

1 O Lord, how full of sweet content
Our years of pilgrimage are spent!
Where'er we dwell, we dwell with thee,
In heaven, in earth, or on the sea.

2 To us remains nor place nor time;
Our country is in every clime;
We can be calm and free from care
On any shore, since God is there.

3 While place we seek, or place we shun,
The soul finds happiness in none;
But with our God to guide our way,
'Tis equal joy to go or stay.

4 Could we be cast where thou art not,
That were indeed a dreadful lot;
But regions none remote we call,
Secure of finding God in all.
MADAME GUYON.

24 OLD HUNDRED. L. M. (106.)

1 Before Jehovah's awful throne,
Ye nations bow, with sacred joy;
Know that the Lord is God alone;
He can create, and he destroy.

2 His sovereign power, without our aid,
Made us of clay, and formed us men;
And when, like wandering sheep, we
strayed,
He brought us to his fold again.

3 We'll crowd thy gates, with thankful
songs,
High as the heaven our voices raise;
And earth, with her ten thousand
tongues,
Shall fill thy courts with sounding
praise.

4 Wide as the world, is thy command;
Vast as eternity thy love;
Firm as a rock thy truth shall stand,
When rolling years shall cease to
move. WATTS.

25 UXBRIDGE. L. M. (214)

1 Eternal source of every joy,
Thy praise may well our lips employ,
While in thy temple we appear,
Whose goodness crowns the circling
year.

2 Wide as the wheels of nature roll,
Thy hand supports and guides the
whole;
The sun is taught by thee to rise,
And darkness when to veil the skies.

3 The flow'ry spring, at thy command,
Perfumes the air and paints the land;
The summer rays with vigor shine,
To raise the corn and cheer the vine.

4 Thy hand in autumn richly pours
Thro' all our coasts abundant stores;
And winters, softened by thy care,
No more a dreary aspect wear.

5 Still be the cheerful homage paid
With morning light and evening shade,
Seasons and months, and weeks and
days,
Demand successive songs of praise.
RIPPON'S COLL.

26 HEBRON. L. M. (5.)

1 My God! how endless is thy love!
Thy gifts are every evening new;
And morning mercies from above,
Gently distill, like early dew.

2 Thou spread'st the curtains of the
night,
Great Guardian of my sleeping
hours!
Thy sovereign word restores the light,
And quickens all my drowsy powers.

3 I yield my powers to thy command;
To thee I consecrate my days;
Perpetual blessings from thy hand
Demand perpetual songs of praise.
WATTS.

27 MIGDOL. L. M. (158.)

1 Great God, we sing that mighty hand,
By which supported still we stand!
The opening year thy mercy shows;
Let mercy crown it till it close.

2 By day, by night, at home, abroad,
Still we are guarded by our God;
By his incessant bounty fed,
By his unerring counsel led.

3 With grateful hearts the past we own;
The future—all to us unknown,
We to thy guardian care commit,
And peaceful leave before thy feet.

4 When death shall interrupt our songs,
And seal in silence mortal tongues,
Our helper, God, in whom we trust,
Shall keep our souls and guard our dust.
RIPPON'S COLL.

5

28 Lanesboro'. C. M.

1. Early, my God, with-out de-lay, I haste to seek thy face; My thirsty spir-it
2. So pilgrims on the scorching sand, Beneath a burning sky, Long for a cooling
3. I've seen thy glory and thy pow'r Thro' all thy temple shine : My God, repeat that
4. Not life it-self, with all its joys, Can my best passions move, Or raise so high my
5. Thus, till my last, ex-piring day, I'll bless my God and King ; Thus will I lift my

faints a - way, My thirsty spirit faints a - way, Without thy cheering grace.
stream at hand, Long for a cooling stream at hand, And they must drink or die.
heavenly hour, My God, re-peat that heavenly hour, That vis-ion so di - vine.
cheer-ful voice, Or raise so high my cheer-ful voice, As thy for - giv-ing love.
hands to pray, Thus will I lift my hands to pray, And tune my lips to sing.

29 EMMONS. C. M. (61.)

1 God is our refuge and our strength,
When trouble's hour is near
A very present help is he;
Therefore we will not fear.

2 Although the pillars of the earth
Shall clean removed be,
The very mountains carried forth,
And cast into the sea:

3 Although the waters rage and swell,
So that the earth shall shake,
Yea, and the solid mountain roots
Shall with the tempest quake: —

4 There is a river that makes glad
The city of our God,—
The tabernacle's holy place
Of the Most High's abode.

5 The Lord is in the midst of her;
Removed she shall not be,
Because the Lord our God himself
Shall help us speedily.
ALFORD.

30 LANESBORO'. C. M.

Rejoice, ye righteous, in the Lord ;
This work belongs to you:
Sing of his name, his ways, his word,
How holy, just and true !

2 By his creative word of might,
The heavenly arch was reared,
And all the beauteous hosts of light
At his command appeared.

3 He bade the mighty waters flow
To their appointed deep ;
The swelling seas their limits know,
And their own stations keep.

4 His works of nature and of grace,
Reveal his wondrous name ;
His mercy and his righteousness,
Let heaven and earth proclaim.
WATTS.

31 SILOAM. C. M. (32.)

1 Thy goodness, Lord, our souls confess,
Thy goodness we adore :
A spring, whose blessings never fail,
A sea without a shore !

2 Sun, moon and stars, thy love attest,
In every golden ray;
Love draws the curtains of the night,
And love brings back the day.

3 But chiefly thy compassion, Lord,
Is in the gospel seen :
There, like a sun, thy mercy shines,
Without a cloud between.
GIBBONS.

32 OLMUTZ. S. M. (Sup. 52.)

1 Oh, bless the Lord, my soul!
  His grace to thee proclaim;
  And all that is within me join
  To bless his holy name.

2 He will not always chide;
  He will with patience wait;
  His wrath is ever slow to rise,
  And ready to abate.

3 He pardons all thy sins,
  Prolongs thy feeble breath;
  He healeth thy infirmities,
  And ransoms thee from death.

4 He clothes thee with his love,
  Upholds thee with his truth;
  Then, like the eagle, he renews
  The vigor of thy youth.

5 Then bless his holy name,
  Whose grace hath made thee whole;
  Whose loving kindness crowns thy
      days:
  Oh, bless the Lord, my soul!
                    MONTGOMERY.

33 HAPPY ZION. 8s & 7s. (512.)

1 Call the Lord thy sure salvation,
  Rest beneath th' Almighty's shade;
  In his secret habitation
  Dwell, and never be dismayed!
  There no tumult can alarm thee,
  Thou shalt dread no hidden snare,
  Guile nor violence can harm thee,
  In eternal safeguard there.

2 From the sword, at noonday wasting,
  From the noisome pestilence,
  In the depth of midnight blasting,
  God shall be thy sure defense:
  Fear not thou the deadly quiver,
  When a thousand feel the blow;
  Mercy shall thy soul deliver,
  Though ten thousand be laid low.

3 Since, with pure and firm affection,
  Thou on God hast set thy love;
  With the wings of his protection
  He will shield thee from above;
  Thou shalt call on him in trouble,
  He will hearken, he will save;
  Here, for grief, reward thee double,
  Crown with life beyond the grave.
                    MONTGOMERY.

34 AMERICA. 6s & 4s.

1 Praise ye Jehovah's name;
  Praise through his courts proclaim;
      Rise and adore;
  High o'er the heavens above,
  Sound his great acts of love,
  While his rich grace we prove,
      Vast as his power.

2 Now let your voices raise
  Triumphant sounds of praise,
      Wide as his fame;
  Have you the Saviour found?
  Then let your joys abound;
  Loud your glad songs resound,
      Filled with his praise.

3 While his high praise ye sing,
  Shake every sounding string;
      Sweet the accord!
  He vital breath bestows;
  Let every breath that flows,
  His noblest fame disclose:
      Praise ye the Lord.   (W. GOODE.)

35 MY BELOVED. 11s & 8s. (225.)

1 In songs of sublime adoration and
      praise,
  Ye pilgrims for Zion who press,
  Break forth and extol the great Ancient
      of days,
  His rich and distinguishing grace.

2 His love from eternity fixed upon you,
  Broke forth and discovered its flame,
  When each with the cords of his kind-
      ness he drew,
  And brought you to love his great
      name.

3 O, had not he pitied the state you
      were in,
  Your bosoms his love had ne'er felt;
  You all would have lived, would have
      died, too, in sin,
  And sunk with the load of your guilt.

4 What was there in you that could merit
      esteem,
  Or give the Creator delight?
  'Twas "Even so, Father," you ever
      must sing,
  "Because it seemed good in thy
      sight."

5 Then give all the glory to his holy
      name,
  To him all the glory belongs;
  Be yours the high joy still to sound
      his great fame,
  And crown him in each of your
      songs.

36 **Warwick. C. M.**

1. Mor-tals, a - wake, with an-gels join, And chant the sol - emn lay;
2. Wrapt in the si - lence of the night, Lay all the east - ern world,
3. Hark! the che - ru-bic ar-mies shout, And glo-ry leads the song;
4. With joy the cho-rus we'll re - peat, Glo-ry to God on high!
5. Hail! Prince of life, for - ev - er hail! Re-deem-er, broth-er, friend:

Joy, love and grat - - - tude com-bine To hail th' auspicious day.
When, bursting, glo-rious, heavenly light, The wondrous scene unfurled.
Good-will and peace are heard throughout Th' harmonious heav'nly throng
Good-will and peace are now com-plete, Je - sus was born to die!
Tho' earth, and time, and life should fail, Thy praise shall nev-er end.

S. MEDLEY.

37 ANTIOCH. C. M. (Sup, 164.)

1 Hark, the glad sound! the Saviour comes,
  The Saviour promised long!
Let every heart prepare a throne,
  And every voice a song.

2 He comes, the prisoners to release,
  In Satan's bondage held;
The gates of brass before him burst,
  The iron fetters yield.

3 He comes, from thickest films of vice,
  To clear the mental ray,
And on the eye-balls of the blind
  To pour celestial day.

4 He comes, the broken heart to bind,
  The bleeding soul to cure;
And with the treasures of his grace
  To enrich the humble poor.

DODDRIDGE.

38 SILOAM. C. M. (32.)

1 Calm on the listening ear of night,
  Come heaven's melodious strains,
Where wild Judeah stretches far
  Her silver-mantle plains.

2 Celestial choirs, from courts above,
  Shed sacred glories there,
And angels, with their sparkling lyres,
  Make music on the air.

3 "Glory to God!" the sounding skies
Loud with their anthems ring —
"Peace to the earth, good-will to men,
  From heaven's eternal King!"

E. H. SEARS.

39 LAMB OF CALVARY. 6s & 4s. (481.)

1 Come, all ye saints of God;
  Wide through the earth abroad
    Spread Jesus' fame;
Tell what his love has done;
Trust in his name alone;
Shout to his lofty throne,
  "Worthy the Lamb!"

2 Hark! how angelic lays
Filled with the Saviour's praise,
    Dwell on his name;
Soon like them we'll be found,
Whene'er the trump shall sound,
While all the heavens resound —
  "Worthy the Lamb!"

3 To him our hearts we raise,
None else shall have our praise;
    Praise ye his name!
We who have felt his blood,
Sealing our peace with God,
Spread his dear fame abroad,
  "Worthy the Lamb!"

40 HAIL TO THE BRIGHTNESS. (268.)
11s & 10s.

1 Hail, thou blest morn, when the great
   Mediator
   Down from the mansion of heaven
      did descend!
   Shepherds, go worship the babe in the
      manger;
   Lo! for his guard the bright angels
      attend.

2 Low at his feet, we, in humble pros-
      tration,
   Lose all our sorrow, and trouble, and
      strife;
   There we receive his divine consola-
      tion,
   Flowing afresh from the fountain of
      life.

3 Star of the morning! thy brightness
      increases;
   Soon from the mansion of heaven
      shall descend,
   Glorious in light, he whose love never
      ceases;
   Shepherds, and all men, the warning
      attend!   HEBER.

41   No. 10.   ROYAL SONGS.

1 I am redeemed, O wonderful love!
   'Twas love that brought my pardon;
   By him who came the sinner to save,
   Who suffered in the garden.
            CHORUS.
   O, it was love, 'twas wonderful love;
   He who purchased my pardon;
   Praying in sorrow, shedding his blood,
   Jesus alone in the garden.

2 Laden with anguish, smitten with grief,
   He entered in the garden;
   Praying in sorrow, shedding his blood,
   The blood that seals our pardon.

3 I am redeemed, I'm no more my own;
   But his who sealed my pardon;
   Life is the boon, through Jesus alone,
   Who suffered in the garden.
            G. W. SEDERQUIST.

42   No. 12. ROYAL SONGS. C. M.

1 Behold the Saviour of mankind
   Nailed to the shameful tree!
   How great the love that him inclined
   To bleed and die for me!
            CHORUS.
   At the cross, at the cross, where I first
      saw the light,
   And the burden of my heart rolled
      away,
   It was there, by faith I received my sight,
   And now I am happy all the day.

2 "My God!" he cries, all nature shakes
   And earth's strong pillars bend!
   The temple's vail in sunder breaks,
   The solid marbles rend.

3 'Tis finished! now the ransom's paid,
   "Receive my soul!" he cries:
   Behold, he bows his sacred head!
   He bows his head and dies!

4 But soon he'll break death's captive
      chain,
   And in full glory shine;
   O Lamb of God! was ever pain—
   Was ever love like thine?
            (S. WESLEY.)

43   No. 13.   ROYAL SONGS.

1 'Twas early in the morning, at the
      breaking of the day,
   That Mary came with spices to the
      place where Jesus lay;
   She met her friends in sorrow as she
      journeyed from her home,
   And they said to one another, who
      shall roll away the stone?
            CHORUS.
   Bright angels, bright angels, at the break-
      ing of the day;
   Bright angels, bright angels, they rolled
      the stone away.

2 They saw two shining angels, clad in
      garments pure and white;
   They saw the linen grave cloths, and
      they trembled at the sight;
   But Christ, their Lord and Master, was
      not found within the tomb,
   For he conquered death when angels
      came and rolled away the stone.

3 But Mary wept in anguish, for her
      heart was torn with grief;
   She said, Where have you laid him?
      then the angels brought relief:
   He is not here, but risen, as he said
      to you before;
   Go to Galilee and see him; he's alive
      forevermore.

4 He burst death's bars asunder, and he
      triumphed o'er the grave;
   He holds the keys of *hades*, the al-
      mighty one to save;
   Behold my hands, said *Jesus*, I'm your
      living Lord and King;
   From the grave I will redeem you, all
      my jewels I will bring.
            G. W. SEDERQUIST.

44 "Welcome, Happy Morning!" 6s & 5s.

Har. by F. S. STANTON.   W. A. BURCK.

1. { "Welcome, hap - py morn - ing!" Age to age shall say:
   { Lo, the dead is liv - ing, God for - ev - er - more!

Hell to - day is van - quished, Heav'n is won to - day.
Him, their true Cre - a - tor, All his works a - dore.

REFRAIN.

" Wel - come, hap - py morn - ing!" Age to age shall say.

2 Months in due succession,
  Days of lengthening light,
Hours and passing moments,
  Praise thee in their flight;
Brightness of the morning,
  Sky, and fields, and sea,
Vanquisher of darkness,
  Bring their praise to thee.
    " Welcome, happy morning!"
    Age to age shall say.

3 Thou of life the Author,
  Death didst undergo,
Tread the path of darkness,
  Saving strength to show;
Come, then, true and faithful,
  Now fulfil thy word;
'Tis thine own third morning;
  Rise, O buried Lord!
    " Welcome, happy morning!"
    Age to age shall say.

4 Loose the souls long prisoned,
  Bound with Satan's chain;
All that now is fallen,
  Raise to life again:
Show thy face in brightness,
  Bid the nations see;
Bring again our daylight;
  Day returns with thee!
    " Welcome, happy morning!"
    Age to age shall say.

Latin of VENATIUS FORTUNATUS
(Sung by Jerome of Prague at the stake.)

5 " Welcome, happy morning!"
  Age to age has said;
Wait we now another
  Resurrection of the dead.
Soon our Lord returning,
  Easter light once more,
Saints shall hear his summons
  To earth's farthest shore.
    Come, then, "happy morning!"
    Age to age has said.
          Arr.—W. A. B.

10

45 Arnheim. L. M.

1. Our Lord is ris-en from the dead, Our Je-sus is gone up on high;
2. There his tri-umphal chariot waits, And an-gels chant the sol-emn lay;
3. Loose all your bars of mass-y light, And wide un-fold th' e-the-real scene;
4. Who is the King of glo-ry? who? The Lord, that all our foes o'ercame;

The pow'rs of hell are cap-tive led—Dragg'd to the por-tals of the sky.
Lift up your heads, ye heav'nly gates, Ye ev-er-last-ing doors give way!
He claims these mansions as his right, Re-ceive the King of glo-ry in!
The world, sin, death and hell o'er-threw, And Je-sus is the Conq'ror's name!

46 UXBRIDGE. L. M. (214.)

1 When I the holy grave survey,
  Where once my Saviour deigned to lie,
  I see fulfilled what prophets say,
  And all the power of death defy.

2 This empty tomb shall now proclaim
  How weak the bands of conquered death:
  Sweet pledge, that all who trust his name
  Shall rise, and draw immortal breath.

3 Jesus, once numbered with the dead,
  Unseals his eyes to sleep no more;
  And ever lives their cause to plead,
  For whom the pains of death he bore.

4 Thy risen Lord, my soul! behold;
  See the rich diadem he wears!
  Thou, too, shalt bear a harp of gold—
  A crown of joy, when he appears.

5 Though in the dust I lay my head,
  Yet, gracious God! thou wilt not leave
  My flesh forever with the dead,
  Nor lose thy children in the grave.
  WALLIN.

47 HAMBURG. L. M. (126.)

1 The Saviour lives, no more to die;
  He lives our Head, enthroned on high;
  He lives triumphant o'er the grave;
  He lives eternally to save.

2 He lives to still his people's fears;
  He lives to wipe away their tears;

He lives their mansions to prepare;
He lives to bring them safely there.

3 Then let our souls in him rejoice,
  And sing his praise with cheerful voice;
  Our doubts and fears forever gone,
  For Christ is on the Father's throne.

4 The chief of sinners he receives;
  His saints he loves, and never leaves;
  He'll guard us safe from every ill,
  And all his promises fulfil.

48 HENDON. 7s. (308.)

1 Angels, roll the rock away!
  Death, yield up the mighty prey!
  See, the Saviour quits the tomb,
  Glowing with immortal bloom!

2 Shout, ye seraphs! Gabriel, raise
  Fame's eternal trump of praise!
  Let the earth's remotest bound
  Echo to the joyful sound.

3 Now, ye saints, lift up your eyes;
  See the Conqueror mount the skies;
  When he comes, ye conquer too;
  He has triumphed thus for you.

4 Heaven unfolds her portals wide;
  Glorious Hero, through them ride;
  King of glory, mount thy throne!
  Boundless empire is thy own.
  GIBBONS.

11

49   Who is He in yonder Stall?

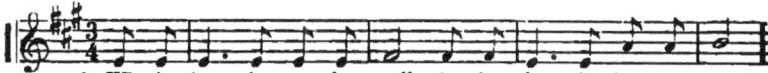

1. Who is he in yon-der stall, At whose feet the shep-herds fall?

'Tis the Lord! O wondrous sto-ry! 'Tis the Lord! the King of glory!

rit.

At his feet we hum-bly fall,—Crown him! crown him Lord of all!

2 Who is he in deep distress,
Fasting in the wilderness?

3 Who is he to whom they bring
All the sick and sorrowing?

4 Who is he who stands and weeps
At the grave where Lazarus sleeps?

5 Lo! at midnight, who is he
Prays in dark Gethsemane?

6 Who is he on yonder tree
Dies in grief and agony?

7 Who is he who from the grave
Comes to succor, help, and save?

8 Who is he who soon shall come
Robed in light, to take us home?

50   P. M

1 'Tis the very same Jesus, 'tis the very
same Jesus,
'Tis the very same Jesus, the Jews cru-
cified.
But he rose, he rose, he rose,
And went to heaven in a cloud.

2 |: The grave, it could not hold him, :|
For he was the Son of God.
And he rose, &c.

3 |: Poor Mary came a weeping, :|
And looking for her Lord. But he'd, &c.

4 |: Two men, in shining raiment, :|
They sat within the tomb. Said he, &c.

5 |: Go preach to every nation, :|
And tell to dying men, that he rose, &c.

6 |: But, O! he said he'd come again, :|
And take his people home. [rise,
Then we'll rise, we'll rise, we'll
And go to meet him in the clouds.

51   TRURO. L. M.   (Sup. 56.)

1 Where high the heavenly temple stands,
The house of God not made with hands,
A great High Priest our nature wears,—
The Guardian of mankind appears.

2 Though now ascended up on high,
He bends on earth a brother's eye;
Partaker of the human name,
He knows the frailty of our frame.

3 Our Fellow-sufferer yet retains
A fellow-feeling of our pains;
And still remembers, in the skies,
His tears his agonies, and cries.

4 With boldness, therefore, at the throne,
Let us make all our sorrows known;
And ask the aid of heavenly power,
To help us in the evil hour.   LOGAN.

52   BALERMA. C. M.   (147.)

1 We may not climb the heavenly steeps,
To bring the Lord Christ down;
In vain we search the lowest deeps,
For him no depths can drown.

2 But warm, sweet, tender, even yet,
A present help is he;
And faith has yet its Olivet,
And love its Galilee.

3 The healing of the seamless dress
Is by our beds of pain;
We touch him in life's throng and press,
And we are whole again.

4 O Lord and Master of us all,
Whate'er our name or sign,
We own thy sway, we hear thy call,
We test our lives by thine.
J. G. WHITTIER.

13

53   Olmutz.   S. M.

1. Lord God, our Fa - ther, hear, In this ac - cept - ed hour;
2. We meet with one ac - cord, In our ap - point - ed place,
3. Like might-y rush - ing wind, Up - on the waves be - neath,

As on the day of Pen - te - cost, Grant us the Spir - it's power.
And wait the prom - ise of our Lord,—The Spir-it of all grace.
Move with one im - pulse ev - 'ry mind; One soul, one feel - ing breathe.

4 The young, the old, inspire
With wisdom from above;
And give us hearts and tongues of fire,
To pray, and praise, and love.

5 On us thy Spirit pour,
And chase our gloom away,
With lustre shining more and more
Unto the perfect day.

54   ARLINGTON. C. M.   (20.)

1 Our blest Redeemer, ere he breathed
His tender, last farewell,
A Guide, a Comforter bequeathed
With us on earth to dwell.

2 He comes, his graces to impart,
A gracious, willing guest,
While he can find one humble heart
Wherein to fix his rest.

3 He breathes that gentle voice we hear,
Soft as the breath of even,   [fear,
That checks each fault, that calms each
And speaks to us of heaven.

4 And all the good that we possess,
His gift to us we own;
Yea. every thought of holiness
Is his, and his alone.

55   MARTYN. 7s.   (177.)

1 Saviour, at thy feet we bow;
O, vouchsafe to meet us now!
At thy people's earnest cry,
Bring thy loving mercies nigh.

2 Thou hast said, where two or three
In thy worship shall agree,
That thou wilt be present there,
Answering their faithful prayer.

3 Lord, we plead thy promise here;
Let thy presence now appear;
On our souls thy spirit pour;
Light, and life, and peace restore:

4 Raise our thoughts from things below;
Faith's discerning eye bestow;
Let our hearts, from sin made free,
Hold sweet intercourse with thee.

56   MENDON. L. M.   (Sup. 6.)

1 Professed followers of the Lamb,
Hark to his word and bless his name;
Your bodies, if in him you trust,
Are temples of the Holy Ghost.

2 Let this important, solemn truth,
Dwell on your minds in age and youth;
Be this your honor and your boast,
You're temples of the Holy Ghost.

3 Let gravity and holiness,
A modest, plain, and decent dress,
And Christ's bright robes adorn you
most,
As temples of the Holy Ghost.

4 Set his example in your view;
Be this the pattern you pursue;
Think as his body so yours must
Be temples of the Holy Ghost.

57 **Truro. L. M.**

Bold.

1. God, in the Gos-pel of his Son, Makes his e - ter - nal counsels known;
2. Wis-dom, its dic-tates here im-parts, To form our minds, to cheer our hearts;
3. Our raging pas-sions it con-trols, And comfort yields to contrite souls;
4. May this blest vol-ume ev - er lie Close to my heart, and near my eye,

'Tis here his rich - est mer - cy shines, And truth is drawn in fair - est lines.
Its influence makes the sin-ner live; It bids the droop-ing saint re-vive.
It brings a bet - ter world in view, And guides us all our journey through.
Till life's last hour my soul en-gage, And be my cho-sen her - it-age.

(BEDDOME.)

58 UXBRIDGE. L. M. (214.)

1 The heavens declare thy glory, Lord,
In every star thy wisdom shines;
But when our eyes behold thy word,
We read thy name in fairer lines.

2 The rolling sun, the changing light,
And night, and day, thy power con-
But the best volume thou hast writ, [fess;
Reveals thy justice and thy grace.

3 Sun, moon and stars convey thy praise
'Round all the earth, and never stand·
So when thy truth began its race,
It touched and glanced on every land.

4 Nor shall thy spreading gospel rest,
Till thro' the world thy truth has run;
Till Christ has all the nations blest,
Which see the light, or feel the sun.

5 Great Sun of Righteousness, arise!
O bless the world with heavenly light!
Thy gospel makes the simple wise;
Thy laws are pure, thy judgments
right. WATTS.

59 TRURO. L. M. (Sup. 56.)

1 Thy presence, gracious God, afford;
Prepare us to receive thy word;
Now let thy voice engage our ear,
And faith be mixed with what we hear.

2 Distracting thoughts and cares remove,
And fix our hearts on things above;
With food divine may we be fed,
And satisfied with living bread.

3 To each thy sacred word apply,
With sov'reign power and energy;
And may we, in thy faith and fear,
Reduce to practice what we hear.

4 Father, in us thy Son reveal;
Teach us to know and do thy will;
Thy saving power and love display,
And guide us to the realms of day.

60 WARWICK. C. M. (Sup. 36.)

1 Before thy mercy-seat, O Lord,
Behold thy servants stand,
To ask the knowledge of thy word,
The guidance of thy hand.

2 Let thy eternal truths, we pray,
Dwell richly in each heart;
That from the safe and narrow way
We never may depart.

3 Lord, from thy word remove the seal,
Unfold its hidden store;
And teach us, as we read, to feel
Its value more and more.

4 Help us to see the Saviour's love
Beaming from every page;
And may these lessons from above
Our inmost souls engage.

5 Thus, while thy word our weakness
Shall we be truly blest; [guides,
And safe arrive where love provides
An everlasting rest.

(WM. H. BATHURST.)

61   Creation.   L. M.   HAYDN.

Bold.

1. With glo - ry clad, with strength ar - - rayed, The Lord that o'er all na - ture reigns; The world's foun-da-tion strongly laid, And the vast fab - ric still sus - tains.

2. How sure - ly 'stab - lished is thy throne, Which shall no change or pe - riod see; For thou, O Lord, and thou a - lone, Art God from all e - ter - ni - ty.

3. The floods, O Lord, lift up their voice, And toss the troub - led waves on high; But God a - lone can still their noise, And make the an - gry sea com - ply.

4. Thy prom - ise, Lord, is ev - - er sure, And they that in thy house would dwell, That hap - py sta - tion to se - cure, Must still in ho - li - ness ex - cel.

---

62   EXHORTATION. C. M.   (45.)

1 Thine oath, and promise, mighty God,
   Recorded in thy word,
Become our hope's foundation broad,
   And confidence afford.

2 Like Abraham, the friend of God,
   Thy faithfulness we prove;
We tread in paths the fathers trod,
   Blest with thy light and love.

3 Largely our consolation flows,
   While we expect the day   [woes,
That ends our griefs, and pains, and
   And drives our fears away.

4 Let nature all convulse and shake,
   And angry nations rage;
Thy name, our hiding-place we make;
   To save thou dost engage.
              EDWIN BURNHAM, 1843.

63   SILOAM. C. M.   (32.)

1 What glory gilds the sacred page!
   Majestic, like the sun,
It gives a light to every age:
   It gives, but borrows none.

2 The hand that gave it still supplies
   The gracious light and heat;

His truths upon the nation rise:
   They rise, but never set.

3 Let everlasting thanks be thine,
   For such a bright display,
As makes a world of darkness shine
   With beams of heavenly day!

4 My soul rejoices to pursue
   The steps of him I love,
Till glory breaks upon my view,—
   The city from above.   (COWPER.)

64   C. M

1 How precious is the book divine,
   By inspiration given!
Bright as a lamp its doctrines shine,
   The light of God from heaven.

2 It shows to man his wandering ways,
   And where his feet have trod;
And brings to view the matchless grace
   Of a forgiving God.

3 It sweetly cheers our fainting hearts,
   In this dark vale of tears;
Life, light, and comfort it imparts,
   And calms our anxious fears.
              JOHN FAWCETT.

15

65   LANESBORO. C. M. (Sup. 28.)

1 Lord, I have made thy word my choice,
    My lasting heritage;
    There shall my noblest powers rejoice,
    My warmest thoughts engage.

2 I'll read the histories of thy love,
    And keep thy laws in sight,
    While through the promises I rove
    With ever fresh delight.

3 'Tis a broad land—of wealth unknown,
    Where springs of life arise,—
    Seeds of immortal bliss are sown,
    And hidden glory lies.

4 The best relief that mourners have;
    It makes our sorrows blest,
    Our fairest hope beyond the grave,
    And our eternal rest.   WATTS.

66   EMMONS. C. M. (61.)

1 Jesus, my Saviour and my Lord,
    To thee I lift mine eyes;
    Teach and instruct me by thy word,
    And make me truly wise.

2 Make me to know and understand
    Thy whole revealed will;
    Fain would I learn to comprehend
    Thy love more clearly still.

3 Help me to read the Bible o'er
    With ever new delight;
    Help me to love its Author more;
    To seek thee day and night

4 O, let it purify my heart,
    And guide me all my days;
    Its wonders, Lord, to me impart,
    And thou shalt have the praise.

67   ZERAH. C. M. (184.)

1 Hail, sacred truth! whose piercing rays
    Dispel the shades of night;
    Diffusing o'er the mental world
    The healing beams of light.

2 Thy word, O Lord, with friendly aid,
    Restores our wand'ring feet;
    Converts the sorrows of the mind
    To joys divinely sweet.

3 O, send thy light and truth abroad
    In all their radiant blaze,
    And bid th' admiring world adore
    The glories of thy grace.

68   MARLOW. C. M. (63.)

1 Thou art my portion, O my God!
    Soon as I know thy way,
    My heart makes haste t' obey thy word,
    And suffers no delay.

2 I choose the path of heavenly truth,
    And glory in my choice;
    Not all the riches of the earth
    Could make me so rejoice.

3 The testimonies of thy grace
    I set before mine eyes;
    Thence I derive my daily strength,
    And there my comfort lies.

4 Now I am thine—forever thine—
    Oh, save thy servant, Lord!
    Thou art my shield, my hiding-place;
    My hope is in thy word.   WATTS

69 1 My Bible leads to glory, &c.
       2 Religion makes me happy, &c.
3 We're fighting for a kingdom, &c.
4 I love this pure religion, &c.
5 We'll have a shout in glory, &c.

70   WATCHMAN. 8s & 7s. (405.)

1 Blessed Bible, how I love it!
    How it doth my bosom cheer!
    What hath earth like this to covet?
    O, what stores of wealth are here!
    Man was lost and doomed to sorrow,
    Not one ray of light or bliss
    Could he from earth's treasures borrow,
    Till his way was cheered by this!

2 Yes, I'll to my bosom press thee,
    Precious word! I'll hide thee here!
    Sure my very heart will bless thee,
    For thou ever say'st, "Good cheer!"
    Speak, my heart, and tell thy pon-
        d'rings;
    Tell how far thy rovings led,
    When this book brought back thy
        wand'rings,
    Speaking life as from the dead.
              PHOEBE PALMER.

71   SICILY. 8s & 7s. (298.)

1 Praise to him, by whose kind favor
    Heavenly truth has reached our ears!
    May its sweet, reviving savor
    Fill our hearts and calm our fears.

2 Truth! how sacred is the treasure!
    Teach us, Lord, its worth to know;
    Vain the hope, and short the pleasure,
    Which from other sources flow.

3 What of truth we have been hearing,
    Fix, O Lord, in every heart;
    In the day of thy appearing
    May we share thy people's part.

16

72 BAVA. L.M. (Sup. 10.)

1 Hark! from the cross a voice of peace
Bids Sinai's awful thunder cease!
Sinner, that voice of love obey,
From Christ, the true, the living way.

2 How else his presence wilt thou bear,
When he in judgment shall appear;
When slighted love to wrath shall turn,
And all the earth like Sinai burn?

3 The trumpet's voice that then did sound,
How soon shall thro' the earth resound;
The Lord will come in vast array;
How will you, sinner, meet that day?

4 His voice at Sinai shook the earth,
But at the new creation's birth,
How vast an earthquake shall dismay
The guilty, found in error's way?

73 ROCKINGHAM. L.M. (95.)

1 Not to condemn the sons of men
Did Christ, the Son of God, appear;
No weapons in his hands are seen,
No flaming sword nor thunder there.

2 Such was the pity of our God—
He loved the race of man so well—
He sent his Son to bear our load
Of sins and save our souls from hell.

3. Sinners, believe the Saviour's word;
Trust in his mighty name and live;
A thousand joys his lips afford,
His hands a thousand blessings give.
WATTS.

74 WINDHAM. L.M. (54.)

1 O for a glance of heavenly day,
To take this stubborn heart away,
And thaw, with beams of love divine,
This heart, this frozen heart of mine!

2 The rocks can rend; the earth can
quake;
The seas can roar; the mountains
shake;
Of feeling, all things show some sign,
But this unfeeling heart of mine.

3 To hear the sorrows thou hast felt,
O Lord, an adamant would melt;
But I can read each moving line,
And nothing moves this heart of mine.

4 But Power Divine can do the deed;
And, Lord, that power I greatly need;
Thy Spirit can from dross refine,
And melt and change this heart of
mine. HART.

75 MISSIONARY CHANT. L.M.(140.)

1 Waste not thy being: back to him
Who freely gave it, freely give;
Else is that being but a dream,
'Tis but to *be*, and not to *live*.

2 Be what thou seemest; live thy creed;
Hold up to earth the torch divine;
Be what thou prayest to be made;
Let the great Master's steps be thine.

3 Sow truth if thou the true wouldst reap;
Who sows the false shall reap the
vain;
Erect and sound thy conscience keep,
From hollow words and creeds re-
frain.

4 Sow love, and taste its fruitage pure;
Sow peace, and reap its harvest
bright;
Sow sunbeams on the rock and moor,
And find a harvest-home of light.

76 MELMORE. L.M. (190.)

1 Say, sinner! hath a voice within
Oft whispered to thy secret soul,
Urged thee to leave the ways of sin,
And yield thy heart to God's control?

2 Hath something met thee in the path
Of worldliness and vanity,
And pointed to the coming wrath,
And warned thee from that wrath to
flee?

3 Sinner! it was a heavenly voice,—
It was the Spirit's gracious call;
It bade thee make the better choice,
And haste to seek in Christ thine all.

4 God's spirit will not always strive
With hardened, self-destroying man;
Ye who persist his love to grieve
May never hear his voice again.

5 Sinner! perhaps, this very day,
Thy last accepted time may be:
Oh! should'st thou grieve him now
away,
Then hope may never beam on thee.
HYDE.

77 LAND OF REST. C.M. (223.)

1 What heavenly music do I hear?
Salvation sounding free!
Ye souls in bondage, lend an ear;
This is the Jubilee.

2 How sweetly do the tidings roll
All round from sea to sea,
From land to land, from pole to pole,
This is the Jubilee.

3 Jesus is on the mercy-seat;
Before him bend the knee;
Let heaven and earth his praise repeat;
This is the Jubilee.

78   St. Ann. C. M.

1. Sin-ners, the voice of God re-gard; 'Tis mer-cy speaks to-day;
2. Your way is dark, and leads to death: Why will you per-se-vere?
3. But he that turns to God shall live, Thro' his a-bound-ing grace;
4. Bow to the scep-tre of his word, Re-nouncing ev-'ry sin;

He calls you by his sa-cred word From sin's de-structive way.
O flee from swift ap-proach-ing wrath, From dark-ness and de-spair.
His mer-cy will the guilt for-give Of those that seek his face.
Sub-mit to him, your sovereign Lord, And learn his will di-vine.

---

79   MERIBAH. C. P. M.   (98.)

1 O God, my inmost soul convert,
And deeply on my thoughtful heart
  Eternal things impress:
Give me to feel their solemn weight,
And tremble on the brink of fate,
  And wake to righteousness!

2 Before me place in dread array
The pomp of that tremendous day,
  When thou with clouds shalt come
To judge the nations at thy bar;
And tell me, Lord, shall I be there,
  To meet a joyful doom?

3 Be this my one great business here,
With serious industry and fear,
  Eternal bliss to insure:
Thine utmost counsel to fulfil,
And suffer all thy righteous will,
  And to the end endure.
             WESLEY.

---

80   OLMUTZ. S. M.   (Sup. 52.)

1 The Spirit, in our hearts,
  Is whisp'ring, "Sinner, come;"
The Bride, the Church of Christ, pro-
    claims
  To all his children, "Come!"

2 Let him that heareth say
  To all about him, "Come;"
Let him that thirsts for righteousness,
  To Christ, the Fountain, come!

(98.) 3 Yes, whosoever will,
  Oh, let him freely come,
And freely drink the stream of life;
  'Tis Jesus bids him come.

4 Lo! Jesus, who invites,
  Declares, "I quickly come;"
Lord, even so; we wait thine hour;
  O, blest Redeemer, come!
           H. U. ONDERDONK.

---

81   SAVIOUR SHEPHERD. 8s & 7s. (517.)

1 Sinners! will you scorn the message,
  Coming from the courts above?
Mercy speaks in every passage;
  Every line is full of love;
  ‖:Oh! believe it, Oh! believe it,—
  Every line is full of love.:‖

2 Now the heralds of salvation,
  Joyful news from heaven proclaim:—
Sinners freed from condemnation,
  Through the all-atoning Lamb!
  ‖: Life receiving, Life receiving,—
  Through the all-atoning Lamb!:‖

3 Who hath their report believed?
  Who received the joyful word?
Who embraced the news of pardon
  Freely offered by the Lord?
  ‖: Life immortal, Life immortal,—
  Freely offered by the Lord.:‖
          ALLEN

82 "One Thing Thou Lackest."

Har. by F. S. STANTON.   Words and Melody by G. W. SÖDERQUIST.

With Expression.

1. A.. ruler once came to Je-sus and said, As low at his feet he did bow,

"From my youth the commands of God I've kept, Is there anything lacking now?"

But the Saviour lov'd him, and tenderly said, "Go sell what thou hast, and give to the [poor:

There is one thing thou lackest, if thou wilt be free, Go take up thy cross, and come fol- [low me."

2 But he turned from the Master, grieved and sad,
  With heart unrepentant and cold:
  He was rich, and the heavenly voice he spurned,
  For he worshiped his store of gold.

3 He came in his strength, his wealth and **pride**;
  None purer nor fairer we're told:
  But his heart was not right in Jesus' sight,
  For he worshiped his glitt'ring gold.

4 There are many, alas! the same as he,
  For self they are living each day,
  Who have gained from the world their store of **gold**,
  But have nothing ro give away.

5 If thou wilt be perfect, pure and clean,
  And enter the heavenly fold,
  Thou must take up the cross and go thy **way**,
  And give up thy store of gold.

83 Fountain. 11s.

1. A fountain in Jesus, which runs always free, For washing and cleansing such sinners as we! Our sins, tho' like crimson, made white as the wool, No lack in the fountain, but always is full.

2 All things now are ready, he invites us to come,
The supper is made by the Father and Son;
Rich bounties, rich dainties, here we may receive,
A home in the kingdom, if we but believe.

3 The guests who were bidden, refused the call;
For they were not ready, nor willing at all [store,
To be stripped of their honor, and part with their
For a feast that was given and made for the poor.

4 If they are not ready, and wish to delay,
My house shall be filled, the Father doth say;
The highways and hedges, tho' halt and the blind,
Shall come and be welcome, the supper is mine.

84

1 We're bound for the land of the pure
and the holy,
The home of the happy, the kingdom
of love;
Ye wanderers from God, in the broad
road of folly,
O say, will you go to the Eden of love?
Cho.—Will you go, &c.

2 In that blessed land, neither sighing nor
anguish
Can breathe in the fields where the
glorified rove;
Ye heart-burdened ones, who in misery
languish,
O say, will you go to the Eden of love?
Cho.—Will you go, &c.

3 No poverty there—no, the saints are all
wealthy,
The heirs of his glory whose nature
is love;
Nor sickness can reach them, that coun-
try is healthy;
O say, will you go to the Eden of love?
Cho.—Will you go, &c.

85 (Tune, "Come, ye Disconsolate."
11s & 10s.

1 Come, ye disconsolate, where'er ye languish;
Come, at the mercy-seat fervently
kneel;
Here bring your wounded hearts, here
tell your anguish;
Earth has no sorrows that heaven
cannot heal.

2 Joy of the comfortless, light of the
straying,
Hope, when all others die, fadeless
and pure;
Here speaks the Comforter, in mercy
saying,
Earth has no sorrows that heaven
cannot cure.

3 Here see the tree of life—see water
flowing
Forth from the throne of God, pure
from above;
Come to the mercy-seat—come, ever
knowing
Earth has no sorrows but heaven can
remove.

20

86 When I was down in Egypt's Land.

1. When I was down in Egypt's land, When I was down in Egypt's land,

CHO.—The grace of God, it is so sweet, The grace of God, it is so sweet,

When I was down in E-gypt's land, I heard there was a promis'd land.

The grace of God, it is so sweet, The grace, the grace, the grace of God!

2 I sought my Saviour's pardoning love,
I sought my Saviour's pardoning, &c.
He sent his Spirit from above.

3 I know my sins have been forgiven, &c.
I'm waiting his return from heaven.

4 Come along, sinner, don't be lost, &c.
Salvation is free, O don't be lost!

87 Tune, "OUT IN THE COLD."

1 Into the tent where a Gypsy boy lay
Dying alone, at the close of the day,
News of salvation was carried; said he,
"Nobody ever has told it to me."

CHORUS.

Tell it again, tell it again;
Salvation's story repeat o'er and o'er,
Till none can say, of the children of
men,
"Nobody ever has told me before."

2 "Did he so love me, a poor little boy?
Send unto me the good tidings of joy;
Need I not perish, my hands will he
hold?
Nobody ever the story has told."

3 Bending, we caught the last words of
his breath,
Just as he entered the valley of death:
"God sent his Son, 'whosover,' said
he;
Nobody ever has told it to me."

4 Smiling, he said as his last sigh was
spent:
"I am so glad that for me he was sent."
Whispered, whilst low sunk the sun in
the west,
"Lord, I believe; tell it now to the
rest."

88

Tune, "I'M THE CHILD OF A KING."

1 When the last gospel message is told in
your ears,
And the last faithful warning is given
you in tears,
When hope shall escape from its place
in thy breast,
Oh! where will your poor weary soul
find its rest.

CHO.—Then beware lest you die,
Beware, lest you die
With sins unforgiven,
Oh! beware lest you die.

2 When the darkness of death shall com-
pass you round,
When friends that you love are all
standing around,
Unable to brighten your way to the
tomb,
Unable to alter your terrible doom.

3 When before the white throne of his
judgment you stand,
"What have you to answer?" the
Judge will demand.
Oh! terrible moment, to stand all
alone,
When mercy forever and ever is gone.

4 Now rest on the promise—get under
the blood
That flowed from the side of the dear
Son of God:
No time for your doubting—the moment
is near,
Decide it forever, he soon shall appear!

89   Hursley. L. M.

Francis J. Haydn.
Arr. W. H. Monk.

1. Sun of my soul, thou Saviour dear, It is not night if thou be near;
2. When soft the dews of kind-ly sleep My wearied eye-lids gent-ly steep,
3. A - bide with me from morn till eve, For without thee I can-not live;

Oh, may no earth-born cloud a-rise, To hide thee from thy ser-vant's eyes.
Be my last thought,—how sweet to rest Forever on my Saviour's breast!
A-bide with me, when night is nigh, For without thee I dare not die.

90   L. M.

1 Jesus, thou everlasting King!
Accept the tribute which we bring;
Accept the well-deserved renown,
And wear our praises as thy crown.

2 Let every act of worship be
Like our espousals, Lord, to thee:
Like the dear hour, when from above
We first received thy pledge of love.

3 The gladness of that happy day!
Our hearts would wish it long to stay;
Nor let our faith forsake its hold,
Nor comfort sink, nor love grow cold.

4 Each following minute, as it flies,
Increase thy praise, improve our joys,
Till we are raised to sing thy name,
At the great supper of the Lamb.
WATTS.

91   WARD. L. M.   (421.)

1 How blest were they who walked in love
With Christ, while yet he dwelt above;
A righteous band, sustained by grace,
The fathers of the faithful race.

2 Strangers and pilgrims here below,
They deemed the world an empty show:
To purer joys their hearts were given,
While waiting Christ's return from heav'n.

3 The soul that truly cleaves to God,
Still longs to gain that blest abode:
O Christ, forbid our souls to roam,
And fix them on our own true home.

92   L. M.

1 O, Holy Father, 'mid the calm
And stillness of this evening hour,
We lift to thee our solemn psalm,
To praise thy goodness and thy pow'r.

2 Kept by thy goodness through the day,
Thanksgiving to thy name we pour;
Night o'er us, with its stars,—we pray
Thy love to guard us evermore.

3 In grief console, in gladness bless,
In darkness guide, in sickness cheer;
Till, perfected in righteousness,
Before thy throne we shall appear.
W. H. BURLEIGH.

93   MENDON. L. M.   (Sup. 6.)

1 New, every morning, is the love
Our wakening and uprising prove:
Thro' sleep and darkness safely brought,
Restored to life, and power, and thought.

2 New mercies, each returning day,
Hover around us while we pray;
New perils past, new sins forgiven,
New tho'ts of God, new hopes of heaven.

3 If on our daily course our mind
Be set to hallow all we find,
New treasures still, of countless price,
God will provide for sacrifice.

4 The trivial round, the common task,
Will furnish all we ought to ask,
Room to deny ourselves, a road
To bring us daily nearer God.

94 Sessions. L. M. (478.)

1 Hail, sov'reign love, that first began
The scheme to rescue fallen man!
Hail, matchless, free, eternal grace,
That gave my soul a hiding place.

2 Against the God that rules the sky,
I fought with hands uplifted high;
Despised the offers of his grace,
Too proud to seek a hiding place.

3 Enwrapped in thick Egyptian night,
And fond of darkness more than light,
Madly I ran the sinful race,
Secure without a hiding place.

4 But thus the eternal counsel ran:
"Almighty love! arrest the man;"
I felt the arrows of distress,
And found I had no hiding place.

5 Vindictive justice stood in view;
To Sinai's fiery mount I flew;
But justice cried with frowning face;
" This mountain is no hiding place."

6 But lo! a heavenly voice I heard—
And mercy's angel soon appear'd;
Who led me on a pleasing pace,
To Jesus Christ, my hiding place.
JEHOIDA BREWER, 1752-1817.

95 Woodworth. L. M. (497.)

1 My God, my Father, while I stray
Far from my home on life's rough way,
Oh! teach me from my heart to say,
Thy will be done!

2 Though dark my path, and sad my lot,
Let me be still, and murmur not,
But breathe the prayer divinely taught,
Thy will be done!

3 What though in lonely grief I sigh
For friends beloved, no longer nigh?
Submissive still would I reply,
Thy will be done!

4 Then when earth's trials shall be o'er,
The prayer oft mixed with tears before
I'll sing upon a happier shore:
Thy will be done!
CHARLOTTE ELLIOTT.

96 Duane St.

1 Jesus, my all, to heaven is gone,
He whom I fix my hopes upon;
His track I see, and I'll pursue
The narrow way till him I view.
The way the holy prophets went,
The road that leads from banishment,
The King's highway of holiness,
I'll go, for all his paths are peace.

2 Lo, glad I come; and thou, blest Lamb,
Wilt take me to thee as I am;
Nothing but sin have I to give,
Nothing but love shall I receive.
Then will I tell to sinners round
What a dear Saviour I have found;
I'll point to thy redeeming blood,
And say, "Behold the way to God."
GENNICK.

97 Star of Bethlehem. L. M.

1 When marshaled on the nightly plain,
The glittering host bestud the sky,
One star alone, of all the train,
Can fix the sinner's wandering eye.
Hark! hark! to God the chorus breaks,
From every host, from every gem;
But one alone the Saviour speaks—
It is the Star of Bethlehem.

2 Once on the raging seas I rode; [dark;
The storm was loud, the night was
The ocean yawned—and rudely blowed
The wind that tossed my foundering
bark.
Deep horror then my vitals froze;
Death-struck, I ceased the tide to
stem—
When suddenly a star arose—
It was the Star of Bethlehem.

3 It was my guide, my light, my all;
It bade my dark forebodings cease;
And through the storm and danger's
thrall,
It led me to the port of peace.
Now safely moored—my perils o'er—
I'll sing, first in night's diadem,
Forever and forever more,
The Star—the Star of Bethlehem!
HENRY KIRK WHITE, 1806.

98 Missionary Chant. L.M. (140.)

1 Go, labor on; spend and be spent,—
Thy joy to do the Father's will:
It is the way the Master went;
Should not the servant tread it still?

2 Go, labor on; your hands are weak,
Your knees are faint, your soul cast
down;
Yet falter not; the prize you seek
Is near,—a kingdom and a crown!

3 Toil on,—faint not,—keep watch and
pray!
Be wise the erring soul to win;
Go forth into the world's highway;
Compel the wanderer to come in.

4 Toil on, and in thy toil rejoice;
For toil comes rest, for exile home;
Soon shalt thou hear the Bridegroom's
voice,
The midnight peal: "Behold, I
come!" BONAR.

23

99 Narrow Way. C. M.

1. What poor de - spi - sed com - pa - ny Of trav-el - lers are these,
2. Ah, these are of a roy - al line, All children of a King;
3. Why do they then ap - pear so mean? And why so much de - spised?
4. But some of them seem poor, distress'd, And lacking dai - ly bread.

Who walk in yon - der nar-row way, A - long the rug - ged maze?
Heirs of im - mor - tal crowns di - vine, And lo, for joy they sing!
Be - cause of their rich robes, un - seen, The world is not ap - prized.
Ah, they're of bound-less wealth possess'd, With hid-den man - na fed.

5 But why keep they that narrow road,
  That rugged, thorny maze?
Why, that's the way their Leader trod:
  They love and keep his ways.

6 I'd rather be the least of them,
  That are the Lord's alone,
Than wear a royal diadem,
  And sit upon a throne.

100 WOODLAND. C. M. (64.)

1 I love to steal awhile away
  From every cumbering care,
And spend the hours of setting day
  In humble, grateful prayer.

2 I love in solitude to shed
  The penitential tear,
And all his promises to plead,
  Where none but God can hear.

3 I love to think on mercies past,
  And future good implore,
And all my cares and sorrows cast
  On him whom I adore.

4 Thus, when life's toilsome day is o'er,
  May its departing ray
Be calm as this impressive hour,
  And lead to endless day.
            Mrs. BROWNE.

101 ST. MARTIN's. C. M. (40.)

1 While thee I seek, protecting Power,
  Be my vain wishes still'd;
And may this consecrated hour
  With better hopes be fill'd.

2 Thy love the pow'rs of thought bestow'd!
  To thee my thoughts would soar;
Thy mercy o'er my life has flowed;
  That mercy I adore.

3 In each event of life, how clear
  Thy ruling hand I see!
Each blessing to my soul more dear,
  Because conferred by thee.

4 In every joy that crowns my days,
  In every pain I bear,
My heart shall find delight in praise,
  Or seek relief in prayer.
      Mrs. H. M. WILLIAMS, 1786.

102 AVON. C. M. (343.)

1 O for a heart to praise my God,
  A heart from sin set free,
A heart that always feels thy blood,
  So freely spilt for me;

2 A heart resigned, submissive, meek,
  My great Redeemer's throne;
Where only Christ is heard to speak,
  Where Jesus reigns alone;

3 A humble, lowly, contrite heart,
  Believing, true, and clean,
Which neither life nor death can part
  From him that dwells within;

4 A heart in every thought renewed,
  And full of love divine;
Perfect, and right, and pure, and good,
  A copy, Lord, of thine.
           WESLEY.

103 I Do Believe. C. M. (41.)

1 How sweet the name of Jesus sounds
In a believer's ear!   [wounds,
It soothes his sorrows, heals his
And drives away his fear.

2 It makes the wounded spirit whole,
And calms the troubled breast;
'Tis manna to the hungry soul,
And to the weary, rest.

3 Jesus! my shepherd, guardian, friend,
My prophet, priest, and king;
My Lord, my life. my way, my end,
Accept the praise I bring.

4 Weak is the effort of my heart,
And cold my warmest thought;
But when I see thee as thou art,
I'll praise thee as I ought. NEWTON.

104 MEAR. C. M. (121.)

1 With joy we meditate the grace
Of our High Priest above;
His heart o'erflows with tenderness,
And yearns with faithful love.

2 Touched with a sympathy within,
He knows our feeble frame;
He knows what sore temptations mean,
For he has felt the same.

3 He, in the days of feeble flesh,
Poured out his cries and tears,
And still, in glory, feels afresh,
What every member bears.

4 Then let our humble faith address
His mercy and his power;
We shall obtain delivering grace
In each distressing hour. (WATTS.)

105 AZMON. C. M. (475.)

1 Thou boundless source of every good,
Our best desires fulfil;
We would adore thy wondrous grace,
And mark thy sovereign will.

2 In all thy mercies may our souls
Thy bounteous goodness see;
Nor let the gifts thy hand imparts
Estrange our hearts from thee.

3 In every changing scene of life,
Whate'er that scene may be,
Give us a meek and humble mind,
A mind at peace with thee.

4 Do thou direct our steps aright;
Help us thy name to fear;
And give us grace to watch and pray,
And strength to persevere.

106 ORTONVILLE. C. M. (28.)

1 The Saviour bids us watch and pray
Through time's brief, fleeting hour,
And gives the Spirit's quickening ray
To those who seek its power.

2 The Saviour bids us watch and pray,
Maintain a warrior's strife;
Help, Lord, to hear thy voice to-day;
Obedience is our life.

3 The Saviour bids us watch and pray,
For quickly he will come,
To call us from our toils away
To our eternal home.

4 The Saviour bids us watch and pray,
For lo! the Judge is near;
Oh, may we joyfully obey,
And watch till he appear.
THOMAS HASTINGS

107 AVON. C. M. (343.)

1 Faith adds new charms to earthly bliss,
And saves us from its snares;
Its aid in every duty brings,
And softens all our cares.

2 The wounded conscience knows its
power
The healing balm to give;
That balm the saddest heart can cheer,
And make the dying live.

3 It shows the precious promise sealed
With the Redeemer's blood,
And helps our feeble hope to rest
Upon a faithful God. (TURNER.)

108 (No. 30. GOSPEL IN SONG.) C. M.

1 The Crucified of Calvary
Has taken all my load of sin;
Has cleansed my heart from every
stain,
And brought the glorious fulness in.

CHORUS:
The Crucified of Calvary,
I'm sweetly resting in the Crucified;
He saves me now, and all the time,
I'm sweetly resting in the Crucified.

2 Weary and sad I wandered long,
Oppressed with burdens hard to bear,
But when the Crucified I sought,
I found sweet rest and solace there.

3 Oh, what a resting place is this,
And refuge for the weary soul!
Where sin's wild ocean cannot drown,
Though near its threat'ning billows
roll.

4 Secure from every foe am I,
While resting in the Crucified;
Here is a calm and safe retreat,
And here I ever would abide.
(By permission.)   F. A. BLACKMER

25

109 (E. M. A.) White as Snow. E. M. Andrews.

1. Plung'd beneath the cleansing fountain, We may full sal - va - tion know;
2. Weak and wea - ry, Lord. re - ceive me, Let thy mer - cy to me flow;
3. Trusting Je - sus in temp-ta-tion, When we're tried to him we'll go;
4. When he comes to call his cho - sen, When the saints to meet him go,

Con - se - cra - ted to his service, Cleans'd and made as white as snow.
Plung'd beneath the waves of cleansing, Make me white as driv - en snow.
He will shield us from all dan - ger, And will keep us white as snow.
He will bring us to his presence, If we're found as white as snow.

CHORUS.

White as snow, white as snow: Christ can make as white as snow.

110 Tune, "My Maryland."

1 I hear my dying Saviour say,
  "Follow me, come, follow me;"
His voice is calling all the day,
  "Follow me, come, follow me: —
For thee I tread the bitter way,
For thee I give my life away,
And drink the gall thy debt to pay,
  Follow me, come, follow me.
2 "Come, cast upon me all thy cares,
  Follow me, come, follow me;
Thy heavy load my arm upbears,
  Follow me, come, follow me:
Lean on my breast, dismiss thy fears,
And trust me through the future years,
My hand shall wipe away thy tears,
  Follow me, come, follow me."
3 Dear Lord, I yield to all thy will,
  I'll follow thee, yes, follow thee;
O, bid my struggling soul be still,
  I'll follow thee, yes, follow thee.
Come cleanse, and with thy Spirit fill,
And keep me safe from every ill,
And all thy word in me fulfil.
  I'll follow thee, yes, follow thee.
(By permission.) G. D. Watson, D. D. 26

111 8s & 7s.

1 I will follow thee, my Saviour,
  Wheresoe'er my lot may be;
Where thou goest, I will follow,
  Yes, my Lord, I'll follow thee.
Cho.—I will follow thee, my Saviour,
  Thou didst shed thy blood, &c.
2 Though the road be rough and thorny,
  Trackless as the foaming sea;
Thou hast trod this way before me,
  And I gladly follow thee.
3 Though 'tis lone, and dark, and dreary,
  Cheerless though my path may be;
If thy voice I hear before me,
  Fearlessly I'll follow thee.
4 Though to Jordan's rolling billows,
  Cold and deep, thou leadest me,
Thou hast crossed the waves before me,
  And I still will follow thee.

112 ——

Grace! 'tis a charming sound;
  Harmonious to the ear;
Heaven with the echo shall resound,
  And all the earth shall hear.
Cho.—I'm glad salvation's free! &c.

113 NAOMI. C. M. (135.)

1 Father, I know that all my life
  Is portioned out to me;
The changes that will surely come
  I do not fear to see;

2 I ask thee for a thoughtful love,
  Through constant watching wise,
To meet the glad with joyful smiles,
  And wipe the weeping eyes;

3 I ask thee for the daily strength,
  To none that ask denied,
A mind to blend with outward life,
  While keeping at thy side;

4 I'd have my spirit filled the more
  With grateful love to thee;
More careful—not to serve thee much,
  But please thee perfectly.
                          ANNA WARING

114 ROCKINGHAM. L. M. (95.)

1 O deem not they are blest alone
  Whose lives a peaceful tenor keep,
For God, who pities man, has shown
  A blessing for the eyes that weep.

2 The light of smiles shall fill again
  The lids that overflow with tears;
And weary hours of woe and pain
  Are promises of happier years.

3 There is a day of sunny rest
  For every dark and troubled night;
And grief may bide an evening guest,
  But joy shall come with early light.
                          BRYANT.

115 LABAN. S. M. (221.)

1 Thou very present aid
  In suffering and distress;
The mind which still on thee is stayed,
  Is kept in perfect peace.

2 Sorrow and fear are gone,
  Whene'er thy face appears;
It stills the sighing orphan's moan,
  And dries the widow's tears.

3 It hallows every cross;
  It sweetly comforts me;
Makes me forget my every loss,
  And find my all in thee.

4 Jesus, to whom I fly,
  Doth all my wishes fill;
What though created streams are dry?
  I have the fountain still.   WESLEY.

116 BOYLSTON. S. M. (12.)

1 Not all the blood of beasts,
  On Jewish altars slain,
Could give the guilty conscience peace,
  Or wash away the stain.

2 But Christ, the heavenly Lamb,
  Takes all our sins away;
A sacrifice of nobler name,
  And richer blood than they.

3 My faith would lay her hand
  On that dear head of thine,
While like a penitent I stand,
  And there confess my sin.

4 My soul looks back, to see
  The burden thou didst bear,
When hanging on the cursed tree,
  And know her guilt was there.

117 DENNIS. (191.)

1 Not what these hands have done
  Can save this guilty soul;
Not what this toiling flesh has borne
  Can make my spirit whole.

2 Thy work alone, O Christ,
  Can ease this weight of sin;
Thy blood alone, O Lamb of God,
  Can give me peace within.

3 I bless the Christ of God;
  I rest on love divine;
And with unfaltering lips and heart,
  I call this Saviour mine.

4 His cross dispels each doubt;
  I bury in his tomb
Each thought of unbelief and fear,
  Each lingering shade of gloom.

5 My life with him is hid,
  My death has passed away,
My clouds have melted into light,
  My midnight into day.   BONAR.

118 SHIRLAND. (242.)

1 Jesus, who knows full well
  The heart of every saint,
Invites us all our griefs to tell,
  To pray and never faint.

2 He bows his gracious ear—
  We never plead in vain;
Then let us wait till he appear,
  And pray, and pray again.

3 Jesus, the Lord will hear
  His chosen when they cry;
Yes, though he may awhile forbear,
  He'll help them from on high.

4 Then let us earnest cry,
  And never faint in prayer;
He sees, he hears, and from on high,
  Will make our cause his care.
                  JOHN NEWTON, 1779

27

119 HENDON. 7s. (308.)

1 They who seek the throne of grace,
  Find that throne in every place;
  If we live a life of prayer,
  God is present everywhere.

2 In our sickness or our health,
  In our want, or in our wealth,
  If we look to God in prayer,
  God is present everywhere.

3 When our earthly comforts fail,
  When the foes of life prevail,
  'Tis the time for earnest prayer;—
  God is present everywhere.

4 Then, my soul, in every strait,
  To thy Father come and wait;
  He will answer every prayer;
  God is present everywhere.
                    (OLIVER HOLDEN.)

120 8s & 6s.

1 My heart is fixed, eternal God,
  Fixed on thee, fixed on thee;
  And my immortal choice is made,
  Christ for me, Christ for me.
  He is my Prophet, Priest, and King,
  Who did for me salvation bring;
  And while I've breath, I mean to sing,
  Christ for me, Christ for me

2 Let others boast of heaps of gold,
  Christ for me, Christ for me.
  My riches never can be told,
  Christ for me, Christ for me.
  Their gold will waste and wear away,
  Their honor perish in a day,
  My portion never can decay,
  Christ for me, Christ for me.

3 In pining sickness, or in health,
  Christ for me, Christ for me.
  In deepest poverty or wealth,
  Christ for me, Christ for me.
  And in that awful judgment day,
  When I his summons must obey,
  And heaven and earth shall pass away,
  Christ for me, Christ for me.

121

1 I've found a friend in Jesus, he's every-
    thing to me,
  He's the fairest of ten thousand to my
    soul;
  The Lily of the Valley in him alone I see,
  All I need to cleanse and make me
    fully whole:
  In sorrow he's my comfort, in trouble
    he's my stay,
  He tells me every care on him to roll:

He's the Lily of the Valley, the bright
    and Morning Star,
  He's the fairest of ten thousand to my
    soul.
CHO.—In sorrow he's my comfort, &c.

2 He all my griefs has taken, and all my
    sorrows borne;
  In temptation he's my strong and
    mighty tower;
  I've all for him forsaken, I've all my
    idols torn
  From my heart, and now he keeps me
    by his pow'r:
  Tho' all the world forsake me, and Satan
    tempts me sore,
  Thro' Jesus I shall safely reach the
    goal.
  He's the Lily of the Valley, &c.

3 He'll never, never leave me, nor yet for-
    sake me here,
  While I live by faith and do his
    blessed will;
  A wall of fire about me, I've nothing
    now to fear;
  With his manna he my hungry soul
    shall fill;
  Then sweeping on to glory we'll see his
    blessed face,
  Where rivers of delight shall ever flow.
  He's the Lily of the Valley, &c.

122 Tune, THE GREAT PHYSICIAN
          8s & 7s.

1 How lost was my condition,
    Till Jesus made me whole;
  There is but one Physician
    Can cure the sin-sick soul:
  Next door to death he found me,
    And snatched me from the grave,
  To tell to all around me
    His wondrous power to save.

2 The worst of all diseases
    Is light, compared with sin;
  On every part it seizes,
    But rages most within:
  'Tis palsy, plague, and fever,
    And madness, all combined;
  And none but a believer
    The least relief can find.

3 At length this great Physician,
    (How matchless is his grace!)
  Accepted my petition,
    And undertook my case:
  First, gave me sight to view him,
    For sin my eyes had sealed;
  Then bade me look unto him,
    I looked, and I was healed!
                    NEWTON.

123 No. 53. GOSPEL IN SONG.

1 Once I thought I walked with Jesus,
Yet such changeful feelings had;
Sometimes trusting, sometimes doubt-
ing,
Sometimes joyful, sometimes sad.

CHORUS:

O the peace the Saviour gives!
Peace I never knew before;
And my way has brighter grown,
Since I've learned to trust him more

2 But he called me closer to him,
Bade my doubting, fearing cease;
And when I had fully yielded,
Filled my soul with perfect peace.

3 Now I'm trusting every moment,
Nothing less can be enough;
And the Saviour bears me gently
O'er those places once so rough.

[By permission.]   F. A. BLACKMER.

124 No. 17. ROYAL SONGS.

1 The Saviour is coming; he calleth for
thee;
Awake and the message receive;
His blood is the ransom, thy pardon is
If thou wilt repent and believe. [free,

CHORUS:

Earnestly labor, patiently labor;
Labor for Jesus till he shall come;
Earnestly labor, patiently labor.
Till he appears and welcomes you home.

2 The Saviour is coming, he calleth thee
now;
Oh! enter his vineyard to-day,
To labor and toil, with the sweat on
thy brow,
And whate'er is right he will pay.

3 The Saviour is coming; a crown he
will give
To all who are faithful and tried;
The just and the pure shall eternally
In Zion forever abide. [live,

4 The Saviour will call from the heav-
ens above:
The angels obey his command,
And gather his saints to the Eden of
love,
To dwell in that beautiful land.

G. W. SEDERQUIST.

125 8s&7s. COME THOU FOUNT. (60.)

1 Hark! the voice of Jesus crying,—
"Who will go and work to-day?
Fields are white and harvest waiting;
Who will bear the sheaves away?"
Loud and strong the Master calleth,
Rich reward he offers thee:
Who will answer, gladly saying,
"Here am I; send me, send me!"

2 If you cannot cross the ocean,
And the heathen lands explore,
You can find the heathen nearer,
You can help them at your door.
If you cannot give your thousands,
You can give the widow's mite;
And the least you do for Jesus,
Will be precious in his sight.

3 If you cannot speak like angels,
If you cannot preach like Paul,
You can tell the love of Jesus,
You can say he died for all.
If you cannot rouse the wicked
With the judgment's dread alarms,
You can lead the little children
To the Saviour's waiting arms.

4 Let none hear you idly saying,
"There is nothing I can do,"
While the souls of men are dying,
And the Master calls for you.
Take the task he gives you gladly,
Let his work your pleasure be;
Answer quickly when he calleth,
"Here am I; send me, send me."

REV. DAN'L MARCH, 1869

126 No. 14. ROYAL SONGS.

1 Many souls on life's dark ocean,
Without helm, or sail, or oar,
Struggling with the wave's commotion,
Seek a quiet rest on shore.
Christian brother, join to labor,
By the light of love divine;
Help to save thy drowning neighbor;
Trim thy lamp and let it shine.

CHORUS:

Haste! to the rescue; fear not wind or
wave;
God's grace will aid you, sinking ones
to save.

2 Hold the light for one another;
'Tis thy loving Lord's command;
Seize the shipwrecked, drowning
brother,
With a manly, loving hand.
Rouse him up to life and action;
Quick apply the means to save;
And by love's divine attraction,
Lift him, lift him from the wave.

3 Lift the light up higher, higher!
Thousands, thousands need your aid;
Throw its flashes nigher, nigher;
Plead and urge, constrain, persuade.
Borrow torches from the altar,
Blazing like the noonday sun;
Hold them up, nor flag, nor falter,
Till thou hear the words, "Well
done."   G. W. S.

127 TUNE—"*America.*" 6s & 4s.

1 Come, thou almighty king,
Help us thy name to sing,
Help us to praise!
Father all glorious,
O'er all victorious,
Come and reign over us,
Ancient of days.

2 Jesus, our Lord, descend;
From all our foes defend,
Nor let us fall;
Let thine almighty aid
Our sure defense be made,
Our souls on thee be stayed;
Lord, hear our call. MADAN.

128 BOYLSTON. S. M. (12.)

1 Come to the house of prayer!
O thou afflicted, come;
The God of peace shall meet thee
there;
He makes that house his home.

Come to the house of praise!
Ye who are happy now,
In sweet accord your voices raise,
In kindred homage bow.

3 Ye aged, hither come!
For ye have felt his love;
Soon shall your trembling tongues be
dumb—
Your lips forget to move.

4 Ye young! before his throne,
Come, bow; your voices raise;
Let not your hearts his praise disown,
Who gives the power to praise.
E. TAYLOR.

129 AVON. C. M. (343.)

1 How did my heart rejoice to hear
My friends devoutly say,
"In Zion let us all appear,
And keep the solemn day."

2 I love her gates, I love the road;
The Church, adorned with grace,
Stands like a palace, built for God,
To show his milder face.

3 Up to her courts, with joys unknown,
The holy tribes repair;
The Son of David holds his throne,
And sits in judgment there.

4 He hears our praises and complaints;
And while his awful voice
Divides the sinners from the saints,
We tremble and rejoice.

5 Peace be within this sacred place,
And joy a constant guest!
With holy gifts and heavenly grace
Be her attendants blest! WATTS

130 DENNIS. S. M. (191.)

1 I love thy Church, O God!
Her walls before thee stand,
Dear as the apple of thine eye,
And graven on thy hand.

2 For her my tears shall fall,
For her my prayers ascend;
To her my cares and toils be given,
Till toils and cares shall end.

3 Beyond my highest joy
I prize her heavenly ways,
Her sweet communion, solemn vows,
Her hymns of love and praise.

4 Jesus, thou friend divine,
Our Saviour, and our King,
Thy hand from every snare and foe,
Shall great deliverance bring.

5 Sure as thy truth shall last,
To Zion shall be given,
The brightest glories earth can yield,
When Jesus comes from heaven.
(DWIGHT.)

131 AZMON. C. M. (475.)

1 A little flock! so calls he thee,
Who bought thee with his blood;
A little flock—disowned of men,
But owned and loved of God.

2 Not many rich or noble called,
Not many great or wise;
They whom God makes his kings and
priests,
Are poor in human eyes.

3 But the chief Shepherd comes at
length,
Her feeble days are o'er;
No more a handful in the earth,
A little flock no more.

4 No more a lily among thorns,
Weary, and faint, and few;
But countless as the stars of heaven,
Or as the early dew.

5 Then entering the eternal halls,
In robes of victory,
That mighty multitude shall keep
The joyous jubilee.

132   ARLINGTON.   C. M.   (20.)

1 Buried with Christ! yes, thus we lie
    Immers'd beneath the wave;
So he, the Saviour from on high,
    Found on this earth his grave.

2 We rise with him! to live anew
    A holy life of faith;
Believing what this brings to view,
    And what the scripture saith.

3 The glorious resurrection morn!
    When Jesus from the skies
Descending, whence he now has gone,
    Shall bid the sleeping rise.

4 Eternal life we then receive
    From him our blessed Lord;
Help us, O Father, to believe,
    And trust thy holy word.

133   BALERMA.   C. M.   (147.)

1 Saviour, we seek the watery tomb,
    Illumed by love divine;
Far from the deep, tremendous gloom
    Of that which once was thine.

2 Down to the hallowed grave we go,
    Obedient to thy word;
'Tis thus the world around shall know
    We're buried with the Lord.

3 'Tis thus we bid its pomps adieu,
    And boldly venture in:
Oh, may we rise to live anew,
    And only die to sin!
           MARIA G. SAFFERY.

134   HAPPY ZION.   8s & 7s.

1 Humble souls, who seek salvation
    Through the Lamb's redeeming
Hear the voice of revelation; [blood,
    Tread the path that Jesus trod.

2 Plainly here his footsteps tracing
    Follow him without delay,
Gladly his command embracing;
    Lo, your Captain leads the way.

3 View the rite with understanding;
    Jesus' grave before you lies;
Be interred at his commanding,
    After his example rise.
           FAWCETT.

135   C. M.

1 Proclaim, saith Christ, my wondrous
        grace,
    To all the sons of men:
He that believes and is baptised,
    Salvation shall obtain.

2 Let plenteous grace descend on those,
    Who, hoping in thy word,
This day have solemnly declared
    That Jesus is their Lord.

3 With cheerful feet may they advance.
    And run the Christian race,
And, through the troubles of the way,
    Find all-sufficient grace.

136   DENNIS.   7s.   (191.)

1 Jesus invites his saints,
    To meet around his board,
And sup in memory of the death
    And sufferings of their Lord.

2 We take the bread and wine,
    As emblems of thy death,
Lord, raise our souls above the sign,
    To feast on thee by faith.

3 Soon shall the night be gone,
    Our Lord will come again;
The Marriage Supper of the Lamb
    Will usher in his reign.

137   ROCK OF AGES.   7s.   (101.)

1 Meeting in the Saviour's name,
    Breaking bread by his command,
To the world we thus proclaim,
    On what ground we hope to stand,
When the Lord shall come with clouds,
Joined by heaven's exulting crowds.

2 Sing we then of him who died;
    Sing of him who rose again;
By him we are justified,
    And with him we hope to reign;
Soon we hope to see our Lord,
And to share his bright reward.
           ADVENT HARP.

138   MARTYN.   7s.   (177.)

1 Many centuries have fled
    Since our Saviour broke the bread,
And this sacred feast ordain'd,
Ever by his church retain'd:
Those his body who discern,
Thus shall meet till his return.

2 Through the church's long eclipse,
When, from priest or pastor's lips,
Truth divine was never heard—
'Mid the famine of the word,
Still these symbols witness gave
To his love who died to save.

3 All who bear the Saviour's name,
Here their common faith proclaim;
Though diverse in tongue or rite,
Here, one body to unite;
Breaking thus one mystic bread,
Till he comes to raise the dead.
           (CONDER.)

139 GLORIOUS DAYS. 7s & 6s. (253.)

1 From Greenland's icy mountains,
From India's coral strand,
Where Afric's sunny fountains
Roll down their golden sand;
From many an ancient river,
From many a palmy plain,
They call us to deliver
Their land from error's chain.

2 Shall we, whose souls are lighted
With wisdom from on high,
Shall we to men benighted
The lamp of life deny?
Salvation, O salvation!
The joyful sound proclaim,
Till each remotest nation
Has learned Messiah's name.

3 Waft, waft, ye winds, his story,
And you, ye waters, roll,
Till, like a sea of glory,
It spreads from pole to pole;
Till o'er our ransomed nature
The Lamb for sinners slain,
Redeemer, King, Creator,
In bliss returns to reign.   HEBER.

140 TUNE—"*Richmond.*" 11s.

1 Daughter of Zion! awake from thy
sadness!
Awake! for thy foes shall oppress
thee no more;
Bright o'er thy hills dawns the day-
star of gladness,
Arise! for the night of thy sorrow
is o'er. Daughter of Zion! &c.

2 Strong were thy foes, but the arm that
subdued them,
And scattered their legions, was
mightier far;
They fled like the chaff from the
scourge that pursued them:
Vain were their steeds and their
chariots of war.

3 Daughter of Zion! the power that
hath saved thee,
Extoll'd with the harp and the tim-
brel should be,
Shout! for the foe is destroyed that
enslaved thee,
Th' oppressor is vanquished, and
Zion is free. FITZGERALD COLL.

141 OLD HUNDRED. L. M. (106.)

1 When here, O Lord, we seek thy face,
And dying sinners pray to live,
Hear thou, in heaven, thy dwelling-
place,
And when thou hearest, Lord, for-
give.

2 When here thy messengers proclaim
The blessed gospel of thy Son,
Still by the power of his great name
Be mighty signs and wonders done.

3 When children's voices raise the song,
Hosanna! to their heavenly King—
Let heaven with earth the strain pro-
long;
Hosanna! let their angels sing.

4 But will, indeed, Jehovah deign
Here to abide, no transient guest?
Here will our great Redeemer reign,
And here the Holy Spirit rest?
MONTGOMERY.

142 ST. MARTINS. C. M. (40.)

1 O thou, whose own vast temple stands,
Built over earth and sea,
Accept the walls that human hands
Have raised to worship thee!

2 Lord, from thine inmost glory send,
Within these courts to bide,
The peace that dwelleth without end,
Serenely by thy side!

3 May erring minds that worship here
Be taught the better way;
And they who mourn, and they who
fear,
Be strengthened as they pray.

4 May faith grow firm, and love grow
warm,
And pure devotion rise,
While round these hallowed walls the
storm
Of earth-born passion dies.
BRYANT.

143 *Welcome to a Pastor.*
BRIDGEWATER. L. M. (164.)

1 We bid thee welcome in the name
Of Jesus, our exalted head;
Come as a servant: so he came,
And we receive thee in his stead.

2 Come as a shepherd; guard and keep
This fold from hell, and earth, and
sin;
Nourish the lambs, and feed the sheep,
The wounded heal, the lost bring in.

3 Come as a teacher, sent from God,
Charged his whole council to de-
clare;
Lift o'er our ranks the prophet's rod,
While we uphold thy hands with
prayer.

4 Come as a messenger of peace,
Filled with the Spirit, fired with love,
Live to behold our large increase,
And welcome Jesus from above.
(MONTGOMERY.)

144 HEBRON. L. M. (5.)

1 Life is the time to serve the Lord,
The time t' insure the great reward;
And while the lamp holds out to burn,
The vilest sinner may return.

2 The living know that they must die;
But all the dead forgotten lie;
Their mem'ry and their sense are gone,
Alike unknowing and unknown.

3 Their hatred and their love is lost,
Their envy buried in the dust;
They have no share in all that's done
Beneath the circuit of the sun.

4 Then what my thoughts design to do,
My hands, with all your might, pursue,
Since no device nor work is found,
Nor faith, nor hope, beneath the
ground.   WATTS.

145 ORTONVILLE. C. M. (28.)

1 Death's not the "gate of paradise,"
Nor "opening key" to heaven;
Nor a bright "angel from the skies,"
Or boon in mercy given.

2 Death, to the saint, is not the hour
When Christ his Lord hath come,
In all the glory of his power,
To waft him to his home.

3 Nature will mourn departing friends,
And shake at death's alarms;
'Tis not "the voice that Jesus sends
To call them to his arms."

4 No! 'tis a dark and cruel foe,
Which has invaded earth;
And to distress, and fear, and woe
Intense hath given birth.

5 But death, and he who hath its power,
Shall be at last destroyed,
And saints no more, O joyful hour!
Will be by them annoyed.

146 PASSING AWAY. L. M. (384.)

1 Sweet is the memory of the dead,
While sleeping in their dusty bed,
They safely rest in silence where
No glimmering sun can enter there.

2 But soon the trump of God will sound,
And wake the sleeping in the ground;
Then robed in light and beauty rare,
They'll meet their Saviour in the air.

3 When all the sleeping saints come
forth,
Who lie entombed in sea and earth,
No more will death the tyrant reign,
Nor longer hold the righteous slain.

4 Then Daniel in his lot shall stand,
When Christ shall beautify the land;
And all the saints from Abel down,
Received with Abraham their crown.

5 In that bright world no tears are shed,
No badges worn to mourn the dead;
But youth shall bloom on every brow,
And there our lov'd ones we shall
know.   S. G. HOOPER.

147 AMAZING GRACE. C. M. (132.)

1 My faith shall triumph o'er the grave,
And trample on the tomb,
My Jesus, my Redeemer, lives,
And on the clouds shall come.
Ere long I know he shall appear,
In power and glory great,
And death, the last of all his foes,
Lie vanquished at his feet.

2 Then, though the worms my flesh de-
vour,
And make my form their prey,
I know I shall arise with power,
On the last judgment day.
When God shall stand upon the earth,
Him there mine eyes shall see,
My flesh shall feel a second birth,
And ever with him be.

3 Then shall he wipe all tears away,
And hush the rising groan;
And pains, and sighs, and griefs, and
fears,
Shall ever be unknown.
How long, dear Saviour, O how long
Shall this bright hour delay?
O hasten thy appearance, Lord,
And bring the welcome day.

148 CROSS & CROWN. C. M. (204.)

1 When the last trumpet's awful voice
This rending earth shall shake;
When op'ning graves shall yield their
charge,
And dust to life awake,—

2 Those bodies that corrupted fell
Shall incorrupt arise,
And mortal forms shall spring to life
Immortal in the skies.

3 Behold, what heavenly prophets sung,
Is now at last fulfilled;
And death yields up his ancient reign
And, vanquished, quits the field.

4 Let faith exalt her joyful voice,
And now in triumph sing :—
O grave, where is thy victory?
And where, O death, thy sting?
WM. CAMERON.

149   **Stockwell. 8s & 7s.**

(CHRISTOPHER C. COX.)   D. E. JONES.

Slowly, gently.

1. Si - lent - ly the shades of eve-ning Gath-er round my low - ly door;
2. O! the lost, the un - for - got - ten, Tho' the world be oft for - got;
3. Sleep-ing in their grave so si - lent, Whither mor - tal foot-steps tend,
4. How such ho - ly mem'ries clus-ter, Like the stars, when storms are past;
5. Soon the trumpet, loud re-sound-ing, Shall a - wake the sleep-ing dead;

rit.

Si - lent - ly they bring be - fore me Fa - ces I now see no more.
O! the shrouded and the lone-ly—In our hearts they per - ish not.
They are freed from earth-ly trouble; We, still hop-ing for its end.
Point-ing on to Je - sus' com-ing, When we hope to meet at last.
O, what joy to greet our lov'd ones, Ris-ing from earth's dust - y bed.

150   (110.)
"CHRISTIAN HYMNS AND SONGS."

1 Sleep on, beloved, sleep, and take thy rest;
Lay down thine head upon the Saviour's breast;
We loved thee well, but Jesus loved thee best:
Good night, good night.

2 Calm is thy slumber, as an infant's sleep,
But thou shalt wake, and no more toil nor weep;
Thine is a perfect rest, secure and deep:
Good night, good night.

3 Until the Easter glory lights the skies;
Until the dead in Jesus shall arise,
And he shall come, but not in lowly guise,
Good night, good night.

4 Until made beautiful by pow'r divine,
And in the likeness of thy Lord shalt shine,
And he shall bring that golden crown of thine,
Good night, good night.

(By permission.)

151   BAVA. L. M. (Sup. 101.)

1 Shall man, O God of light and life,
Forever moulder in the grave?
Canst thou forget thy glorious work,
Thy promise, and thy power to save?

2 In those dark, silent realms of night,
Shall peace and hope no more arise?
No future morning light the tomb,
Nor day-star gild the darksome skies?

3 Cease, cease, ye vain, desponding fears:
When Christ, our Lord, from dark-ness sprang,
Death, the last foe, was captive led,
And heav'n with praise and wonder rang.

4 Faith sees the bright, eternal doors
Unfold, to make his children way;
They shall be clothed with endless life,
And shine in everlasting day.

5 The trump shall sound, the dust awake,
From the cold tomb the slumb'rers spring:
Thro' heav'n with joy their myriads rise,
And hail their Saviour and their King.

DWIGHT.

152 REST. L. M. (103.)

1 The saints, who now in Jesus sleep,
His own almighty pow'r shall keep,
Till dawns the bright illustrious day,
When death itself shall die away.

2 How loud shall our glad voices sing,
When Christ his risen saints shall bring
From beds of dust, and sleeping clay,
To realms of everlasting day!

3 When Jesus we in glory meet,
Our utmost joys shall be complete;
When landed on that heav'nly shore,
Death and the curse shall be no more.

4 Our sleeping ones till then we trust
To him who numbers every dust;
Our Saviour faithfully will keep
His own—their death is but a sleep.

153 DUNDEE. C. M. (175.)

1 The time draws nigh, when from the clouds
Christ shall with shouts descend,
And the last trumpet's awful voice
The heavens and earth shall rend.

2 Then they who live shall changed be,
And they who sleep shall wake;
The graves shall yield their ancient charge;
While earth's foundation's shake.

3 The saints of God, from death set free,
With joy shall mount on high:
The heavenly hosts, with praises loud,
Shall meet them in the sky.

4 A few short years of exile past,
We reach the happy shore,
Where death-divided friends at last
Shall meet to part no more.
Scotch Paraphrase.

154 ONLY WAITING. 8s & 7s. (326.)

1 If we enter into glory,
At the resurrection light,
And in triumph sing the story
Of the love that banished night,
Shall we murmur at the sleeping
Till that great resplendent day?
Will it be a cause for weeping,
When our tears are wiped away?

2 When we see the saints all beaming
In their crowns and robes of white,
And our loved ones in the gleaming,
With their forms so pure and bright,
When we meet beyond the sighing,
In the home beyond the gloom,
Shall we grieve because of lying
In the dark and silent tomb?

3 If we see the harvest glowing
In the grand eternal rays,
And then gladly reap from sowing
In these tears through sorrow's days,
Shall we then be heard repining,
Though the seed in earth remain?
In that morning's splendid shining,
It will wave in golden grain.

4 Let us wait for Christ from heaven,
As the church in days of old;
Then to us will crowns be given,
We will walk the streets of gold.
It will be no cause of sadness
That we parted when we died,
We shall be in perfect gladness,
With the Psalmist satisfied.

CHO.—(If sung to Music by F. O. Wellcome.)
Let us wait for Christ from heaven, &c.
Till the Resurrection Morn.
G. R. KRAMER.

155 Tune, "YOUR MISSION." 8s & 7s.

1 Sweetly sing, ye winds, the brightness
That remaineth for the dead,
Who, in robes of stainless whiteness,
Soon shall leave the dusty bed.
Darkness reigns where they are lying,
But they only wait the day
When shall cease the mourner's sighing,
As the death-gloom flees away.

2 Summer winds be softly singing
All around their blessed graves;
Flowers sweet, be fragrance flinging,
As the verdure o'er them waves.
Nevermore shall they know sorrow,
Nevermore shall sadly weep,
For there comes a glad to-morrow,
When they rise from sacred sleep.

3 They shall leave the dust, all beaming,
Like the plumage of the dove,
Gay with gold and silver gleaming,
As it sings its song of love.
Christ shall raise them in his glory,
They shall in his image shine,
And the blaze of song and story
Shall be dimmed by light divine.

4 Sweetly sing ye birds their brightness,
When, through all the summer day,
Ye may leap with wings of lightness,
When the frosts have passed away.
Even now the silver lining
Is around the gloom we dread,
Glowing with an endless shining,
Which shall robe the blessed dead.
G. R. KRAMER.

156 TUNE — "*Hold the Fort.*"

1 Look, my brethren, see the tokens
  O'er the earth abroad,
All that holy seers have spoken
  In the Word of God.

CHORUS.

Hold the faith, the Lord is coming!
  Joy, the Kingdom's near!   [ing,
Let your lamps be trimmed and burn-
  Christ will soon appear!

2 Swift the sands of time are running,
  Day of doom draws near;
Soon with all his angels coming,
  Throne and Judge appear.

3 Long 'mid scoffs and jeers we've waited,
  Mingling joy with tears;
For the truth despised and hated,
  Soon the crown we'll wear.

4 Then redemption's wondrous story
  Is forever told,
In God's Kingdom filled with glory,
  On its streets of gold.
                   S. S. BREWER.

157   CROSS OF CHRIST. 7s. (574.)

1 When from scatter'd lands afar,
Spreads the voice of rumor'd war,
Nations in tumultuous pride
Heave like ocean's roaring tide,
When the solar splendors fail,
When the crescent waxeth pale;
World! do thou the signal dread,
We exalt the drooping head;

2 When the pow'rs that star-like reign
Sink dishonor'd to the plain,
We uplift th' expectant eye,—
Our redemption draweth nigh,
When the fig-tree shoots appear,
Men behold their summer near;
When the hearts of rebels fail,
We the coming Conqueror hail:

3 Bridegroom of thy weeping spouse,
Listen to her longing vows,
Listen to her widowed moan,
Listen to creation's groan;
Bid, O bid thy trumpet sound,
Gather thine elect around:
Call them from the cheerless gloom,
Call them from the marble tomb.

4 From the grass-grown village grave,
From the deep dissolving wave,
From the whirlwind and the flame,
Mighty Head, thy members claim.

Where thy cross in anguish stood,
Where thy life distilled in blood,
Where they mocked thy dying groan,
King of nations, plant thy throne.
          CHARLOTTE ELIZABETH

158   JESUS SOON IS COMING. (545.)

1 Borne on the breeze from distant na-
    tions,
Distress and sad perplexity;
Deep throes of anguish heave creation,
  While loudly roar the waves and sea.

CHORUS.

Haste and get ready; list to the cry!
Loud it swells — it is the knell —
The close of gospel day.

2 All things foretold by holy prophets,
  In grand review are passing by;
God spake that man by these may profit
  And quick to Christ for shelter fly.

3 See how the men of might are waking!
  Weak nations now becoming strong!
All things bespeak their final shaking;
  Soon God will speed the war-cry on.

4 Now hasten famine, death and mourn-
    ing,
  God's wrath upon the harlot power;
The smoke is rising; see her burning;
  Down, down she sinks, to rise no
    more.

159 WATCHMAN, TELL ME, &c. (405.)
            8s 7s.

1 Watchman, has the tribulation
  Of the cruel Man of Sin
Ceased his bloody persecution?
  Will it not return again?
Pilgrim, no, his times have ended;
  Never shall the monster reign;
Tekel on his brow is written —
  Soon he will consume in flame.

2 Watchman, were there signs attending
  At the ending of the time?
With the closing moments pending,
  Did the sun refuse to shine?
Pilgrim, yes; the sun was shrouded
  In a veil of gloom that day;
Nature was in darkness clouded
  On that nineteenth day of May,
              (1780.)

3 Watchman, see! the land is nearing,
  With its vernal fruits and flowers!
On! just yonder, oh, how cheering,
  Bloom forever Eden's bowers.
Hark the choral strains there ringing,
  Wafted on the balmy air!
See the millions! hear them singing!
  Soon the pilgrims will be there!
             S. S. BREWER.

160   Zerah. C. M.   (184.)

1 The Lord our Saviour will appear;
    His day is nigh at hand;
    The signs bespeak his coming near,
    And all may understand.

2 Behold, he comes! he comes to reign
    On earth with all his saints;
    Jesus, the Lamb of God, once slain,
    Will end our long complaints.

3 The prince of darkness he'll destroy;
    The hosts of sin o'erthrow;
    Satan shall then no more annoy,
    But Christ shall reign below;

4 Then those who suffered in his name,
    And did obey his word,
    Shall rise in glory and proclaim
    The goodness of their Lord.

161   The Watchers. 7s & 6s. (380.)

1 The sands of time are sinking,
    The dawn of heaven breaks,
    The summer months we've sighed for,
    The fair, sweet morn awakes.
    Dark, dark has been the midnight,
    But day-spring is at hand;
    And glory, glory dwelleth
    In fair Immanuel's land.

2 The signs in heaven thicken,
    The nations are distressed,
    Men's hearts for fear are failing—
    The ocean cannot rest;
    But amid the foaming billows,
    And wrecks upon the strand,
    We hail the glory dawning
    In fair Immanuel's land.

3 Old Babylon has fallen,
    With Medo-Persia's throne;
    The Grecian horn is broken,
    And Rome is almost gone.
    But another King is coming,
    With his bright angelic band,
    To take the throne of David
    In fair Immanuel's land.

162   Millenial Dawn. 7s & 6s. (36.)

1 The clouds at length are breaking;
    The dawn will soon appear,
    And "signs" there's no mistaking,
    Proclaim Messiah near.
    Awake, awake from sleeping,
    Attend the "midnight cry;"
    Ye saints refrain from weeping,
    Your Great Deliverer's nigh.

2 Ye mortals, take the warning,
    Ten thousand calls invite;
    Should you neglect the morning,
    Then comes the awful night.
    Now mercy's hand extended,
    The vilest wretch would save;
    But oh! if this be ended,
    You're lost beyond the grave.

163   11s.

1 The Bridegroom is coming, O hark,
    hear the cry!
    He's coming in glory—his Kingdom is
    nigh;
    Myriads of angels await his command,
    To gather the faithful from every
    land.

Chorus.—O Pilgrim, haste! the day
    rolls on,
    Quickly will the night of thy sorrow
    be gone,
    O Pilgrim, haste! awake and arise,
    To go and meet your Saviour in the
    skies.

2 The storm-cloud of vengeance is
    gathering fast,
    The harvest is ripening and soon will
    be past;
    Then gird on thine armor, O Christian,
    with care;
    The time of great peril prevails every-
    where.

3 O hail the glad morning when Jesus
    shall reign!
    No more of our loved ones by Death
    will be slain;
    He'll awake all his people who sleep
    in the tomb,
    And make them immortal, forever to
    bloom.

4 The earth robed in beauty will soon
    be our home—
    The pure golden city with high tow-
    'ring dome;
    The songs of the ransomed will roll
    o'er the plain,
    In glory unending with Jesus we'll
    reign!

164   Antioch.   C. M.

1. Joy to the world! the Lord will come! Let earth re-ceive her King!

Let ev-'ry heart pre-pare him room, And heav'n and nature sing, And
And heav'n and nature

heav'n and na-ture sing, And heav'n, And heav'n and na-ture sing.
sing, And heav'n and nature sing,

sing, And heav'n and nature sing,

1 Joy to the world! the Lord shall reign!
  Let men their songs employ; [plains,
  While fields and floods, rocks, hills, and
  Repeat the sounding joy.

3 He'll rule the world with truth and grace,
  And make the nations prove
  The glories of his righteousness,
  And wonders of his love.

165 THE WATCHERS. 7s & 6s. (380.)

1 The angels soon are coming,
    To gather all the just,
  Who are in death reposing,
    Unconscious in the dust:
  They hear the trumpet sounding —
    It penetrates the graves;
  Now into life they're bounding,
    No more to death are slaves.

2 The resurrection morning,
    With all its dazzling light,
  Is now upon us dawning
    In rays of glory bright:
  The saints are made immortal —
    The living and the dead;
  Their bodies are celestial,
    Like Christ their living head.

3 A city, too, in splendor,
    Shall to the earth descend;
  Earth's kingdoms shall surrender,
    And wickedness shall end:
  Messiah's kingdom holy
    Upon the earth shall bloom, —
  There all the meek and lowly
    Will find an endless home.

166 ON THE CROSS. P. M. (387.)

1 Soon shall we see the glorious morning!
    Saints, arise! saints, arise!
  Sinners, attend the notes of warning!
    Saints, arise! saints, arise!
  The resurrection day draws near,
  The King of saints shall soon appear,
  And high his royal standard rear!
    Saints, arise! saints, arise!

2 Hear ye the trump of God resounding,
    Saints, arise! saints, arise! [bounding,
  Through death's dark vaults its notes re-
    Saints, arise! saints, arise!
  To meet the Bridegroom, haste! prepare!
  Put on your bridal garments fair,
  And hail your Saviour in the air!
    Saints, arise! saints, arise!

3 Fast by the throne of God behold them,
    Crowned at last! crowned at last!
  See in his arms the Saviour fold them,
    Crowned at last! crowned at last!
  With wreaths of glory round their head,
  No tears of sorrow now are shed,
  To joy's full fountain all are led,
    Crowned at last! crowned at last!

167 PETERBORO. C. M. (27.)

1 My soul is happy when I hear
The Saviour is so nigh;
I long to see his sign appear
Upon the opening sky.

2 I love to wait, and watch, and pray,
And trust his living word,
And feel the coming of that day
No longer is deferred.

3 I do rejoice that life was given
In these last days to me,
That deathless I may rise to heaven,
And my Redeemer see.

4 Then, waiting brethren, let us sing;
He will not tarry long;
And fill with love the hours that bring
The glory of our song.

168 (TUNE No. 39. GOSPEL IN SONG.)

1 I'm waiting for thee, Lord,
Thy beauty to see, Lord,
I'm waiting for thee,
For thy coming again.
Thou 'rt gone over there, Lord,
A place to prepare, Lord,
Thy home I shall share
At thy coming again.

2 'Mid danger and fear, Lord,
I'm often weary here, Lord,
The day must be near
Of thy coming again.
'Tis all sunshine there, Lord,
No sighing nor care, Lord,
But glory so fair
At thy coming again.

3 Whilst thou art away, Lord,
I stumble and stray, Lord;
Oh, hasten the day
Of thy coming again.
This is not my rest, Lord,
A pilgrim confest, Lord,
I wait to be blest
At thy coming again.

4 Our loved ones before, Lord,
Their troubles are o'er, Lord,
I'll meet them once more
At thy coming again.
The blood was the sign, Lord,
That marked them as thine, Lord,
And brightly they'll shine
At thy coming again.

5 E'en now let my ways, Lord,
Be bright with thy praise, Lord,
For brief are the days
Ere thy coming again.
I'm waiting for thee, Lord,
Thy beauty to see, Lord,
No triumph for me
Like thy coming again!

169 HENDON. 7s. (308.)

1 Come, desire of nations, come!
Hasten, Lord, the general doom!
Hear the spirit and the bride;
Come and take us to thy side.

2 Thou, who hast our place prepared,
Make us meet for our reward;
Then with all thy saints descend;
Then our earthly trials end.

3 Plant thy heavenly kingdom here;
Glorious in thy saints appear;
Speak the sacred number sealed;
Speak the mystery revealed.

4 Take to thee thy royal power;
Reign! when sin shall be no more;
Reign! when death no more shall be;
Reign to all eternity!   WESLEY.

170 O HAIL, HAPPY DAY. (543.)

1 O come, come away! for time's career
is closing;
Let worldly care henceforth forbear,
O come, come away!
Come, come! our holy joys renew,
Where love and heavenly friendship
grew;
The Spirit welcomes you! O come,
come away!

2 Awake ye! wake! no time now for
reposing;
"The Lord is near!" breaks on the
ear,
O come, come away!
Come, come, where Jesus' love will be,
Who says, "I meet with two or
three:"
Sweet promise made to thee! O come,
come away!

3 O come, come away, my Saviour, in
thy glory!
"Thy kingdom come, thy will be
done,"
O come, come away!
O, come, my Lord, thy right maintain,
And take thy throne and on it reign;
Then earth shall bloom again! O come
come away!

171   Lift up your Heads.

1. Lift up your heads, desponding pilgrims, Give to the winds your needless fears;

Cho.—Thro' endless years earth's coming glo-ry—'Tis the glad day so long foretold:

He who hath said redemption's nearing, Soon is to reign thro' endless years.

'Tis the bright morn of Zi-on's glo-ry, Prophets foresaw in times of old.

2 What if the clouds do for a moment
  Hide the blue sky, where morn appears;
Soon the glad sun, of promise given,
  Rises to shine through endless years.

3 Tell the whole world these blessed tidings,
  Speak of the time of bliss that nears;

Tell the oppressed of every nation,
  Jubilee lasts through endless years.

4 Haste thee along, ages of glory,
  Haste the glad time when Christ appears—
Oh, for the faith of ancient worthies;
  Oh, for that reign thro' endless years.

172 Tune, "Old Churchyard."

1 We shall see the Saviour coming,
On the resurrection morning,
While the saints of God are watching
  And waiting for the Lord.
|: Are your lamps well burning, :|
And your vessel filled with oil?

2 We have felt the Advent glory,
While the vision seemed to tarry,
When we've comforted each other
With the words of holy writ.
|: Are your garments pure, :|
And unspotted from the world?

3 In the midst of opposition,
Daniel keeps the same position,
And is waiting for the promise
  At the ending of the days.
|: Every one shall have deliverance, :|
Who is written in the Book.

4 O, ye saints of God, take courage,
You will soon be freed from bondage,
For Jesus leads the army,
  And he's sure to win the day.
|: When we've gained the victory, :|
We shall lay our armor down.

173 Only Waiting. 8s & 7s. (326.)

1 "Coming! Oh, the bliss and gladness
  bound up in that blessed word.
Coming! and our eyes shall see him—
  him our own beloved Lord.

Coming! how our hearts leap upward,
  with a joy no words can say!
Coming! so we watch and wonder, hour
  by hour, and day by day.

2 Coming! then shall his dominion reach
  from distant sea to sea:
From the river to earth's ending shall
  his glorious kingdom be;
Then the foes of Christ be vanquished,
  truth and righteousness shall reign
Over all the earth triumphant; joy shall
  follow in his train.

3 Coming! but to those that scorn him,
  those that now dispute his right,
What shall be their awful portion when
  he cometh in his might?
Fire and sword, and flaming vengeance,
  showering on them from above,
Oh, while yet that time remaineth, seek
  his face and plead his love.

4 He is lingering yet a moment, that
  before it be too late
You may find his pardoning mercy, ere
  forever sealed your fate.
Coming! yes, it *still* is 'coming,' but
  how soon it may be '*come!*'
Then the shout of 'Christ triumphant!'
  then the glorious 'Welcome home'!"

Mrs. C. M. Pym.

174 Zion. 8s 7s & 4.

WESLEY.　　　　　　　　　　　　　　　　TH HASTINGS.

1. { Lo, he comes, with clouds descending, Once for favored sinners slain! }
{ Thousand, thousand saints attending, Swell the triumph of his train. } Hal - le - lu - jah!

Je-sus comes on earth to reign! Hal-le - lu - jah! Je-sus comes on earth to reign!

2 Every eye shall now behold him,
　Robed in dreadful majesty;
Those who set at naught and sold him,
　Pierc'd and nailed him to the tree,
　‖: Deeply wailing,
　Shall the true Messiah see. :‖

3 Now redemption long expected,
　See in solemn pomp appear,
All his saints, by man rejected,
　Rise to meet him in the air:
　‖: Hallelujah!
　See the day of God appear ! :‖

4 Answer thine own Bride and Spirit;
　Hasten, Lord, the general doom;
The new heaven and earth t' inherit,
　Take thy pining exiles home;
　‖: All creation,
　Travails, groans, and bids thee come ! :‖

5 Yea, amen: let all adore thee,
　High on thine eternal throne!
Saviour, take the power and glory,
　Make thy righteous sentence known,
　‖: O, come quickly!
　Claim the kingdom for thine own ! :‖

175 8s 7s & 4.

1 Day of Judgment, day of wonders!
　Hark! the trumpet's awful sound,
Louder than a thousand thunders,
　Shakes the vast creation round!
　How the summons
　Will the sinner's heart confound!

2 At his call the dead awaken,
　Rise to life from earth and sea;
All the powers of nature, shaken,
　From his face prepare to flee:
　Careless sinner,
　What will then become of thee?

3 But to those who have confessed,
　Loved and served the Lord below,
He will say, "Come near, ye blessed,
　See the kingdom I bestow!
　You, forever,
　Shall my love and glory know."

NEWTON.

176 THE BEAUTEOUS DAY. (111.)
8s & 7s.
1 That great day of wrath and terror,
　That last day of woe and doom,

Like a thief at darkest midnight,
　On the sons of men shall come.

2 When the pride and pomp of ages
　All shall utterly have past,
And they stand in anguish, owning
　That the end is nere at last:

3 Let thy loins be strictly girded,
　Life be pure, and heart be right,
That, whene'er the Bridegroom cometh,
　Full thy lamp may shine, and bright.

Hymn of the 7th Century.

177 WINDHAM. L. M. (54.)

1 That day of wrath! that dreadful day,
　When heaven and earth shall pass away!
What power shall be the sinner's stay?
　How shall he meet that dreadful day?

2 O, on that day, that dreadful day,
　When man to judgment wakes from clay,
Be thou, O God, the sinner's stay,
　Tho' heaven and earth shall pass away.

SIR WALTER SCOTT.

41

RESTITUTION.

Resting By-and-By.

(By Permission.)

GEO. E. LEE.

1. { When faint and weary toiling, The sweat drops on my brow, }
   { I   long to rest from la-bor, To drop the burden now: } There comes a gen-   [tle

D.C. Work while the day is shining, There's resting by-and-by.

2. { This   life to toil is giv-en, And he improves it best, }
   { Who   seeks by patient la-bor, To en-ter in-to rest: } Then, pilgrim, worn   [and

D.C. The prize is straight before thee, There's resting by-and-by.

D.C *CHORUS.*

chiding, To quell each mourning sigh, Resting by-and-by, There's resting by-and-by;

wea-ry, Press on, the goal is nigh;

We shall not always labor, We shall not always cry; The end is drawing nearer,

The end for which we sigh; We'll lay our heavy burdens down, There's resting by-and-   [by.

3 Nor ask, when overburdened,
    You long for friendly aid,—
  "Why idle stands my brother,
    No yoke upon him laid?"
  The Master bids him tarry,
    And dare you ask him why!
  "Go, labor in my vineyard."— *Cho.*
    There's resting by-and-by."

4 Wan reaper in the harvest,
    Let this thy strength sustain,—
  Each sheaf that fills the garner
    Brings you eternal gain.
  Then bear the cross with patience,
    To fields of duty hie:
  'Tis sweet to work for Jesus,—
    There's resting by-and-by.— *Cho.*

179 RESTING BY AND BY. 7s & 6s.

1 The world is very evil,
  The times are waxing late:
Be sober and keep vigil,
  The Judge is at the gate;
The Judge that comes in mercy,
  The Judge that comes with might,
To terminate the evil,
  To diadem the right.

2 Brief life is here our portion,
  Brief sorrow, short-lived care;
The life that knows no ending,
  The tearless life is there.
The morning shall awaken,
  The shadows pass away,
And each true-hearted servant
  Shall shine as doth the day.

3 Jerusalem, the golden!
  With milk and honey blest,
Beneath thy contemplation
  Sink heart and voice opprest.
And though just now I may not
  My spirit seeks thee fain,
The resurrection morning
  When Jesus comes again.

4 Oh, home of fadeless splendor,
  Of flowers that fear no thorn,
Where they shall dwell as children,
  Who here as exiles mourn!
Strive, man, to win that glory;
  Toil, man, to gain that light;
Send hope before to grasp it,
  Till hope be lost in sight.

180 I LOVE THEE. P. M. (15.)

1 I'm weary of straying—O when shall
    I rest
  In that promised land of the good
    and the blest,
Where sin shall no longer her bland-
    ishments spread,
And tears and temptations forever are
    fled.

2 I'm weary of sighing o'er sorrows of
    earth,
  O'er joys' glowing visions that fade at
    their birth;
O'er the pangs of the loved that we
    cannot assuage,
O'er the blightings of youth, and the
    weakness of age.

3 I'm weary of hoping, where hope is
    untrue,
  As fair but as fleeting as morning's
    bright dew;
I long for that land whose blest
    promise alone,
Is changeless, and sure as eternity's
    throne.

4 I'm weary of loving, where all pass
    away,
  The brightest and fairest, alas! can-
    not stay;
I long for that land where these part-
    ings are o'er,
Where death and the tomb can divide
    us no more!

————

181

1 O I love to tell the story,
  To me it has a charm,
That we'll soon move into glory,
  To the Abrahamic farm.

CHORUS:

  Christ is coming, Christ is coming;
    He is coming in his kingdom;
  He will take the throne of David,
    And reign forevermore.

2 Paul writing to Galatians,
  Makes mention of the deed,
And by him it is asserted
  That Jesus is the seed.

3 And joint heirs too with Jesus,
  Are all that do believe,
The meek of all the ages,
  The new earth shall receive.

4 Soon Christ will come in glory,
  Build up this ruined earth,
Restore our faded paradise,
  Creation's second birth.

————

182 COME THOU FOUNT. 8s, 7s. (60.)

1 Come thou long expected Jesus,
  Born to set thy people free;
Now from fears and sin thou savest,
  Free from sorrow we would be.

2 Israel's strength and consolation,
  Hope of all the saints thou art;
Dear desire of every nation,
  Joy of every longing heart.

3 Born, thy people to deliver;
  Born a child—and yet a King,
Born to reign on earth forever,
  Now thy promised kingdom bring.

4 Bring ere long the glorious city;
  Stablish on the earth thy throne;
Thine the power and the glory,
  Claim the kingdoms for thine own!

183 A Home for the Weary.

(By Permission.) Geo. E. Lee.

1. There's a home for all the blest, When my Saviour comes; Where the weary
2. Signs are seen on ev-'ry hand, Je-sus soon will come; Signs in heav'n, on
3. All that sleep beneath the sod, When my Saviour comes, Will a-wake to
4. Then with all the ransom'd throng, When my Saviour comes, We will sing re-

ones shall rest, When my Saviour comes. In that land of glory bright. Saints shall
sea and land, Je-sus soon will come. Nations angry now appear, Men's hearts
meet their God, When my Saviour comes. All our friends we then shall meet, All the
demption's song, When my Saviour comes. Glo-ry be to Je-sus' name, Glo-ry

walk with him in white, Faith shall then be turn'd to sight, When my Saviour comes.
fail - ing them for fear, For the things they see and hear, Je-sus soon will come.
faith - ful ones we'll greet, At the low-ly Je-sus' feet, When my Saviour comes.
to the Lamb once slain! He has come on earth to reign, Glo-ry to the Lamb!

CHORUS.

Je-sus, come; come and reign; O, my Saviour, quickly come, Come on earth to
[reign.

184 Dennis. S. M. (191.)

1 'Tis but a little while,
And he shall come again,
Who died that we might live, who lives
That we with him may reign.

2 A few more storms shall beat
On this wild, rocky shore:
And we shall be where tempests cease,
And surges swell no more.

3 A few more struggles here,
A few more partings o'er,
A few more toils, a few more tears,
And we shall weep no more.

4 A few more Sabbaths here,
Shall cheer us on our way,
And we shall reach the endless rest
Th'eternal Sabbath day.

H. Bonar.

185 Tune—"*The Old Granite State.*"

1 This earth with its flowers is not the
rest for me,
Death lurks in its bowers, and sweeps
the sparkling sea;
There is no spot so sunny, so peaceful
or so fair,
Where love twines its tendrils, but
death is brooding there.
Soon his requiem I'll be singing in
the new Eden Home.

2 There are suffering millions in this
dark vale of tears,
Who believe not the Gospel but die
in their fears;
But the church breathes a prayer with
each sorrowing breath,
Buoyed up by a love that is stronger
far than death—
Ever looking for a kingdom, in the
new Eden Home.

3 There no rose will be tinted with the
blood of the slain,
Or the spotless lily bend or the fou.
crimson stain;
The air will not be burdened with
grief's softest sigh,
Or the tear ever sparkle in the immortal eye.
Blessed Kingdom, bright its glory,
in the new Eden Home.

4 Thus I walk through the shadows with
the cross as my rest,
While earth's bloody sun is setting
low in the crimson west,
And the misty vail is parting, and
through its azure fold
I see the crystal river and the streets
of gold.
Harps are ringing, crowns are given,
in the new Eden Home.

186 Gideon's Band.
Tune—"*Battle Cry of Freedom.*"

1 Say, brethren and sisters,
How fare you in the way,
Fighting in the army, hallelujah!
Are your heads still uplifted.
Have you strength enough to say,
Jesus is coming, hallelujah!

Chorus:
Jesus is coming, awake ye, awake!
The saints will be ready the kingdom
to take,
At the shout and voice of the trum-
pet,
All sleeping ones will wake,
And give us the kingdom, hallelu-
jah!

2 The feaful and faint-hearted
Have permission to go back,
Leaving the army, hallelujah!
Our Captain only wants such men
As will march and water lap,
Fighting in the army, hallelujah!

3 We've been down to the Midian camp,
And we've heard them tell the
dream—
The cake of barley, hallelujah!
And they fear the sword of Gideon,
Though small his numbers seem,
The victory is ours, hallelujah!

4 And what is best of all,
Is the evidence so clear—
Jesus is coming, hallelujah!
In harmony with prophecy,
His coming's very near,
Coming in his kingdom, hallelujah!

187 Lenox. 6s & 8s. (8.)

1 O the amazing change!
A world created new!
My thoughts with transport range,
The lovely scene to view;
Thee, Lord, divine, in all I trace;
The work is thine—thine be the praise

2 Where pointed brambles grew,
Entwined with horrid thorn,
Gay flowers, forever new,
The painted fields adorn;
The lily there, and blushing rose,
The union fair, their sweets disclose.

3 Where the bleak mountain stood,
All bare and disarrayed,
See the wide branching wood
Diffuse its grateful shade;
Tall oaks, and pines, and cedars nod,
And elms and vines confess their God.

4 The tyrants of the plain
Their savage chase give o'er;
No more they rend the slain,
They thirst for blood no more;
But infants' hands fierce tigers lead,
And lions with the oxen feed.

5 O when, Almighty Lord,
Shall these glad scenes arise,
To verify thy word,
And bless our wondering eyes?
That earth, with all her tongues may
United songs of ardent praise. [raise

45

188   "All Things New."

1. There's shadow on earth's fairest light, Of human guilt and human tears;

She gropes her way thro' realms of night, That once sung with the spheres,
D.S. She waits a full deliverance When God makes (OMIT) .... all things new,

But now the sport of blinded chance, The heav'nly record standeth true;

2 The world is old with centuries,
  But not for these she bows her head;
Close to her heart the sorrow lies —
  She holds so many dead;
Sad discords mingle in her song,
  Tears fall upon her with the dew,
The whole creation groans—How long
  Ere all shall be made new?

3 No place shall be in that new earth
  For all that blights this universe;
No evil taint the second birth —
  "There shall be no more curse."
Ye broken-hearted, cease your moan;
  The day of promise dawns for you,
For he who sits upon the throne
  Says, "I make all things new."

4 We mourn the dead, but they shall wake!
  The lost, but they shall be restored!
Oh, well our human hearts might break
  Without that sacred word!
Dim eyes, look up, and hearts rejoice,
  Seeing God's bow of promise through,
At sound of that prophetic voice —
  "I will make all things new."

5 How long? The ages falter, dumb,
  As on the threshold of new birth:
The nations pray, "Thy kingdom come"–
  "The new heavens and new earth."
Earth turning, turning, nears that day,
  When all the angel-choirs anew
Shall sing, "Old things are pass'd away;"
  God hath made "All things new."
H. BONAR.

189   I'M GOING HOME.   (347.)

1 Six thousand years are nearly past,
Since Adam from thy sight was cast,
And ever since his fallen race,
From age to age are void of grace.

CHORUS.
Thy kingdom come, thy will be done
Upon the earth as 'tis in heaven;
With glory filled, from shore to shore,
When sin and death shall be no more.

2 When will the happy trump proclaim
The judgment of the martyred Lamb?
When shall the captive troops be free,
And keep the eternal jubilee?

3 Till then, we will not let thee rest;
Thou still shalt hear our strong request:
And this our daily prayer shall be —
Lord, sound the trump of jubilee.
JOHN CENNICK.

190   JESUS SOON IS COMING.   (545.)
9s & 8s.

1 I murmur not that now a stranger,
  I pass along the smiling earth;
I know the snares, I dread the danger,
  I hate the haunts, I shun the mirth.

2 Earth, what a sorrow lies before thee!
  None like it in the shadowy past; —
The sharpest throe that ever tore thee,
  E'en though the briefest and the last.

3 I see the fair moon veil her lustre,
  I see the sackcloth of the sun;
The shrouding of each starry cluster,
  The threefold woe of earth begun.

4 There comes the moaning and the sighing,
  There comes the hot tear's heavy fall,
The thousand agonies of dying; —
  But I shall be beyond them all.
H. BONAR.

191 FOUNTAIN. (8s.)

1 On the high cliffs of Jordan with pleasure I stand,
  And view in perspective the fair promised land;
  The land where the ransomed with singing shall come,
  And enter the kingdom prepared as their home.

2 All over those peaceful, delectable plains,
  The Lord our Redeemer in righteousness reigns.
  His sceptre of empire he now doth assume,
  And kindly doth welcome his followers home.

3 How blest are those regions, the realms of repose,
  Where with fruit, oh, how grateful, the " tree of life " grows;
  The regions ambrosial, forever in bloom,
  God's own habitation, the saint's happy home!

4 Those pleasures of glory, oh, when shall I share,
  And crowns of celestial felicity wear;
  And range o'er those landscapes exempt from a sigh:
  The home of our fathers, now specially nigh?

192 Tune.—"IN THE SWEET BY AND BY." 8s.

1 We speak of the realms of the blest;
  Of that country so bright and so fair;
  And oft are its glories confest;
  But what must it be to be there?
  CHORUS.
  In the sweet by-and-by, etc.

2 We speak of its pathways of gold;
  Of its walls decked with jewels so rare;
  Of its wonders and pleasures untold:
  But what must it be to be there?

3 We speak of its freedom from sin,
  From sorrow, temptation and care,
  From trials, without and within;
  But what must it be to be there?

4 May we, then, midst pleasure or woe,
  For that kingdom our hearts now prepare;
  And shortly we also shall know,
  And feel what it is to be there.

193 Tune.—"DISMAL SWAMP." P.M.

1 The groaning earth is too dark and drear
  For the saints' eternal home;
  But the city from heaven will soon be here;
  We know that the moment is drawing near
  When she in her glory shall come.
  Her gates of pearl we soon shall see,
  And her music we soon shall hear;
  Joyous and bright our home shall be,
  And we'll walk in the shadow of life's fair tree,
  With our Saviour forever near.

2 We'll gladly exchange a world like this
  Where death triumphant reigns,
  For a beautiful home in that land of bliss
  Where all is happiness, joy and peace,
  And nothing can enter that pains.
  There is no more sorrow and no more night,
  For the darkness shall pass away,
  The crucified Lamb is its glorious light
  And the saints shall walk with him in white
  In that happy, eternal day.

3 Oh, there the loved of earth shall meet,
  Whom death has sundered here;
  The prophets and patriarchs there we'll greet,
  And all shall worship at Jesus' feet,
  No more separation to fear.
  Though trials and griefs await us here,
  The conflict will soon be o'er;
  This glorious hope our hearts doth cheer,
  For we know that the Saviour will soon appear,
  And then we shall grieve no more.

194 (Tune.—JOHN BROWN.)

1 The Saviour who suffered,
  The Lamb that was slain,
  Shall come in his glory
  Forever to reign.
  The earth when renewed
  Shall be beauteous again,
  And freed from death and pain.
  CHORUS.
  Glory, glory, etc.........Jesus comes to reign.

195 "Waiting."

(By Permission.)

S. C. HANCOCK.

Andante.

1. I am wait-ing, ev - er waiting, For a bright-er, bet-ter day,
2. All the prophets of past a - ges, Saw its brightness from a - far,
3. Now the world is full of suffering, Sounds of woe fall on my ears,
4. I am wait-ing, hoping, praying, For Mes - si - ah's glo-rious reign,

Just be-yond the clouds and shadows That surround my lone-ly way;
And in words sub-lime have spoken Of the peace and glo - ry there.
Sights of wretch-ed-ness and sorrow Fill my eyes with pitying tears.
For I know he'll rule in jus-tice, Right and truth will triumph then.

For a day of light and gladness, Such as earth has nev - er known,
Now they sleep in those green valleys, Which in wea - ri - ness they trod,
'Tis the earth's dark night of weeping, Wrong and e - vil tri-umph now,
Worldly pleasures cannot win me, While I wait for that bright day,

When in e - qui-ty and jus-tice, Christ shall reign on David's throne.
Soon they'll come with songs of triumph, To the ho - ly mount of God.
I can wait, for just be - fore me Beams the morn-ing's ro-seate glow.
Worldly splendor can-not charm me, While its light beams on my way.

196 Tune, No. 2, ROYAL SONGS.

1 Long we've been waiting for Christ to
      come,
  Long we have watched for the morning;
  Still for that happy, eternal home,
  The pilgrims are earnestly longing.

CHORUS.

  Come, come, dear Saviour, come
    Comfort thy saints who are weeping;
  Come, come, dear Saviour, come
    Waken thy dear ones who are sleeping.

2 Then in the kingdom forevermore,
  Chanting redemption's glad story,
  Safely at home, where the storms are o'er,
  We'll dwell in the mansions of glory.

197

1 When the great jubilee shall come,
    Then we'll sing the New Song,
  And Christ shall take his ransomed
      home,
    Then we'll sing the New Song.

CHO.—Wait a little while, Then we'll sing
      the New Song, &c.

2 When the glad shout shall rend the sky,
    Then we'll sing the New Song.
  "O grave, where is thy victory?"
    Then we'll sing the New Song.

3 When sorrow, pain and death are o'er,
    Then we'll sing the New Song,
  And sighs and tears shall be no more,
    Then we'll sing the New Song.

4 Where all will be immortal, fair,
    There we'll sing the New Song,
  When blood-washed robes are ours to
      wear,
    Then we'll sing the New Song.

(By permission.)   H POLLARD.

198 Tune 43, GOSPEL IN SONG.

1 When we enter the portals of glory,
    And the great host of ransom'd we see,
  As the numberless sands of the sea-shore,
    What a wonderful sight that will be.

CHORUS.

  Numberless as the sands of the sea-shore,
  Numberless as the sands of the shore;
  Oh, what a sight 'twill be,
  When the ransom'd hosts we see,
  As numberless as the sands of the shore.

2 When we see all the sav'd of the ages,
    Who from cruel death-partings are
      free,
  Greeting there with a heavenly greeting.
    What a wonderful sight that will be.

3 When we look on the form that re-
      deem'd us,
  And his glory and majesty see,
  While as King of the saints he is reign-
      ing,
  What a wonderful sight that will be.

(By permission.)   F. A. BLACKMER.

199 Tune No. 26, ROYAL SONGS.

1 Lift the head, O weary pilgrim! let the
      heart exultant spring,
  As you gladly journey onward to the
      palace of your King;
  On the steadfast, flaming beacon of his
      truth still keep your eye,
  And you soon shall share his glory, for
      he's coming by-and-by!

REFRAIN.

  He is coming by-and-by,
  He is coming by-and-by,
  On the wings of faith triumphant we
      shall meet him in the sky,
  And the sorrow and the sighing shall
      depart forevermore,
  Lost in swelling songs of rapture on the
      fair and fadeless shore.

2 We shall hear the trumpet sounding
      just before the break of day;
  We shall see the somber shadows of the
      ages roll away;
  We shall hail the saints' uprising, clad
      in glory, ne'er to die,
  When he gathers home his jewels,—
      when he cometh by-and-by!

                      A. T. GORHAM.

200 Tune 47, GOSPEL IN SONG.

1 Hark! a voice from Eden stealing,
    Such as but to angels known,
  Hope its song of cheer is singing,
    ‖: It is better farther on. :‖

2 Hope is singing, still is singing,
    Softly, in an under tone;
  Singing as if God had taught it,
    ‖: It is better farther on. :‖

3 On the grave it sits and sings it,
    Sings it when the heart would groan;
  Sings it when the shadows darken,
    ‖: It is better farther on. :‖

4 Farther on! Oh! how much farther?
    Count the mile-stones one by one:
  No! no counting, only trusting,
    ‖: It is better farther on. :‖

49

RESTITUTION.

201 The Life-Boat.

Rev. J. J. Denver.

Miles H. Aborn.

1. We're floating down the stream of Time, We hav'nt got long to stay;
Chorus.—Then cheer, my brothers, cheer, ... Our trials will soon be o'er,

These stormy clouds of dark-ness Will turn to brighter day.
Our lov'd ones we shall meet, shall meet, Up-on that gold-en shore.

Then let us all take cour-age, For we're not left a-lone;
We're pilgrims and we're strangers here, We seek a City to come;

Chorus. D.C.

The Life-Boat soon is com-ing, To gather the jew-els home.
The Life-Boat soon is com-ing, To gather the jew-els home.

2 Sometimes we feel discouraged,
  And think 'tis all in vain
For us to live a Christian life,
  And walk in Jesus' name:
But then we hear the Master's Voice,—
  "I'll lend a helping hand,
And, if you'll only trust me,
  I'll guide you to that land."
                              Chorus.

3 The Life-Boat soon is coming,
  By the eye of faith I see,
As she sweeps through the waters
  To rescue you and me,
And land us safely in the Port,
  With friends we love so dear:
"Get Ready," cries the Captain,—
  O, look! he's almost here!
                              Chorus.

By permission of J. J. Denver.
50

INDEX TO SUPPLEMENT.

NOTE. — This Supplement has been compiled to meet the expressed desire of many for a larger collection of the hymns of the fathers, and while our limits have not permitted the introduction of many new pieces, we trust that it will be found a serviceable addition to our present collection.

We tender our thanks to F. A. Blackmer, G. W. Sederquist, McDonald and Gill, publishers of "Hymns of the Advent," and others, who have kindly permitted us the use of their hymns and music.

The figures in parenthesis at the commencement of the hymns give the numbers of the tunes in the New Jubilee Harp.

When the author's name is in parenthesis, it signifies that the hymn has been altered since first written.

W. A. BURCH.
E. M. ANDREWS.
F. BURR.

INDEX TO SUPPLEMENT.

INDEX TO SUPPLEMENT.